Systematic
Family Therapy

Systematic Family Therapy

Luciano L'Abate, Ph.D.

BRUNNER/MAZEL, *Publishers* • New York

Library of Congress Cataloging-in-Publication Data

L'Abate, Luciano, 1928-
    Systematic family therapy.

    Bibliography: p.
    Includes index.
    1. Family psychotherapy. I. Title.
RC488.5.A23 1986   616.89'156   85-28009
ISBN 0-87630-404-8

Published by
BRUNNER/MAZEL, INC.
19 Union Square West
New York, New York 10003

MANUFACTURED IN THE UNITED STATES OF AMERICA

Humans are too variable to ever have one theory for all people.

C. Gilbert Wrenn
Guidepost, 1982, *25*, 7

The answer lies not in restricting human endeavors, but in evolving new alternatives, new possibilities, new dimensions, new options, and new avenues for creative uses of human beings based on the recognition of the multiple and unusual talents so manifest in the diversity of the human race.

E. R. Hall
Beyond Culture, 1976, p. 3

Foreword

Whatever happened to the boy who pointed out that the emperor had no clothes? If we were told, I don't remember. I hope he fared well. I hope this book fares well. L'Abate deserves our thanks even more than the boy with the courage of his perceptions deserved the gratitude of his fellow citizens. The boy was unwitting in his courage, while L'Abate is witting in his. And the boy didn't try, after his revelation, to provide the emperor with a more complete wardrobe, as L'Abate strives to do in this book for the field of family therapy.

Such courage cum conscientiousness and caring in the service of family therapy are but a few of the many positive qualities that make *Systematic Family Therapy* a book that should be read by every family therapist. An example of the courage:

> The field [of family therapy] is characterized by gurus who have produced "schools" based on little or no empirical evidence! We would not accept the same criteria . . . in the treatment of our pet [as we do] in the treatment of families. . . . War stories, magic episodes with supposedly positive outcomes, are recounted as evidence of the gurus' sensitivity, ingenuity, and cunning. It seems irrelevant whether external criteria were used to assess whether the gurus' impressions were valid or not!

L'Abate's conscientiousness shows through in the way he provides a balanced perspective on the issues facing family therapists (e.g., to balance the above charge of anti-empiricism, L'Abate also warns against the dangers of "super-scientism, irrelevant pseudoscience, or dehumanizing pragmatism"). It shows through also in his effort to provide a comprehensive theoretical perspective to guide the hand of the practitioner.

L'Abate's caring shows itself in his concern for the clients of family therapists. This caring is what lies behind his attempt to devise theoretical structures and treatment models that will not only allow therapists to become more helpful to their clients but also to reach more of the many families who presently cannot bring themselves to ask for help or to benefit from it, and to provide that help at the lowest possible cost.

Those who stand up for their convictions, and care deeply, sometimes are zealots or narrow in their focus; so it is important to point out that the opposite is true here. I know of no other family therapy model-builder who seems more open to the incorporation of diverse viewpoints than L'Abate, as exemplified in this book. His approach to theory building is an eclectic one, but eclectic in a particular manner: "systematic eclecticism," which seeks to *integrate* a variety of contemporary theories of family therapy and to derive specific models of family therapy from this integration. As L'Abate points out, such models should be replicable and empirically verifiable. They should serve to link not only theory with practice, but the training of therapists to such practice.

Not the least of the many satisfactions readers will derive from this work stems from L'Abate's openness and breadth of vision. It is true that L'Abate never hesitates to take a clear-cut stance even where others might see things differently or be ambivalent (e.g., ". . . The hope that changes in awareness bring about changes in behavior is an illusion. If we were to [wait for families to change] on the basis of changes in awareness, we could wait forever. . . . Better introduce or instigate changes in behavior and let awareness take care of itself!"). It is equally true, however, that consistent with advocating "paradoxical positivism" in conducting therapy, L'Abate also welcomes diversity and the challenge of reconciling apparent opposites in his theory and model building.

Consistent with such openness and an acute awareness of the diversity of the human condition, L'Abate incorporates a vast array of conceptual and empirical investigations by others in his theorizing and model building. In the writings of some other family therapists it sometimes seems as though they believe family therapy exists in a world unto itself: that there is no legitimate overlap in issues and answers between say, individual therapy and family therapy, or personality theory and family therapy, or empirical research on the family and family therapy. One of the great strengths of this book is that it shows the relevance of psychological theory, and psychological and family research in general, to family therapy in particular. It may hurt one's pride to be less than unique, but family therapists and theorists are not really like lonesome mariners adrift. There are useful signs, tools, concepts, even, I daresay, some navigational charts available from nonfamily theorists and therapists.

All theorists and practitioners who have struggled with the question of how to change another's behavior are fellow mariners. Perhaps therapists who work with individuals sail where the weather is more predictable, and perhaps family researchers encounter less tricky currents, but there is no reason to believe that what such fellow sailors have learned about the weather and the currents is useless to us as family therapists. We are not entirely alone. L'Abate's comprehensive view of individuals, families, the process of change, his understanding and respect for pertinent research wherever it may be found, all impart the advantage of closely connecting us to our fellow mariners, even as he never allows us to lose sight of the special problems and solutions necessary to navigate our own particular waters.

As a family therapist you, as I did, likely will find some ideas you disagree with in *Systematic Family Therapy*. That is to be expected in a work aimed at creating major conceptual and practical changes in the field. But, much more important, I am confident you will find many new ideas and methods with which to help the families depending on you.

Bernard G. Guerney, Jr., Ph.D.
Professor of Human Development and
Head, Individual and Family
Consultation Center of
The Pennsylvania State University
University Park, PA

Acknowledgments

First and foremost I want to acknowledge my debt of appreciation to Dr. Carl Whitaker who, in reviewing a summary paper of the present work submitted for publication to a therapy journal, described it as "grandiose," "paranoid," and, worst, "boring"! I do not mind the first two attributions, but I do mind the third. That kind of name calling without substantiating criticism from such a renowned therapist motivated me to finish this manuscript. Thank you, Dr. Whitaker!

I am indebted to my students for supporting me in this often lonely endeavor. Particularly, I want to thank Michael Levis for his rewriting of the Depression Program (Appendix A), John Lutz not only for rewriting the Negotiation Program (Appendix B) but also for testing it for his Master's thesis, and Colleen Chauvin for rewriting the Intimacy Program (Appendix C). Without their help the job would have been more difficult, and without their moral support, hard to complete. I am sure there are others I have overlooked. In that case I apologize to them, whomever they may be!

I also want to thank the Cross Keys Counseling Center, and particularly Dr. Doris Hewitt, Gregory Samples, Dan Laird, and Tere Canzonieri, for trying out these programs and taking a chance at applying them to clinical couples and families. Without their affirmation it would have been hard to validate consensually what remains a strictly private experience; that is, I have used these programs in my private practice of marriage and family therapy with very satisfactory results. However, someone else rather than me or my students needs to validate this approach. In this regard, I also want to thank Dr. Peggy Baggett for her application of these programs to clinical couples with her usual and inimitable care and feedback. Her understanding, support, and friendship have meant a great deal to me over the last few years. Thank you, Dr. Baggett!

I am particularly indebted to Lisa Reddy, my research assistant, for working on the references and hunting down lost references that seemed to be untraceable. Marie Morgan, who edited selected chapters, and Marti Hagan, typist, were ultimately the ones who corrected my typos and poorly worded sentences and produced a final manuscript. This manuscript, of course, would not have seen the light of day without the concrete support of Bernard Mazel, who made it easy for me to acquire a McIntosh computer that allowed me to join the ranks of new writers who may have forgotten how to use a pen or a pencil!

Contents

Preface

The purpose of this book is to present an approach to family therapy that will be (a) systematically eclectic, (b) systematically empirical, and (c) systematically sequential. By systematic, therefore, is meant a rationale based on classifiable, ordered plans and methods. The concept of classification will apply directly to eclecticism (Chapter 2). The concept of method will apply especially to empiricism (Chapter 3). The concept of ordered plans will refer specifically to the sequence of therapy (Chapter 4). Ordered sequences of family therapy replicate themselves in a variety of theoretical and therapeutic viewpoints. An eclectic approach implies that these various viewpoints can be put together and integrated into a classifiable order, whereas an empirical approach implies testability and replicability.

Consequently, the process of family therapy can be divided into four different stages (Chapter 4). The first stage may require the use of circular (or paradoxical) techniques that need to be tailor-made for each specific family, making it very difficult to subsume this stage within an empirical approach (Section II). This first stage can be considered comfortably (at least up to the present time) under a dialectic paradigm. The next three stages (Sections III, IV, and V), on the other hand, can be subsumed under an empirical paradigm through the use of testable interpersonal and relational models. These models have produced systematic homework assignments (SHWAs) to be administered to couples and families in an ordered, sequential fashion (Appendices). Thus, the theory underlying these models is tested in its application of systematic homework assignments (SHWAs). Hence, this book is an elaboration of a variety of methodological concepts (eclecticism, empiricism, sequential stages of therapy) and theoretical models (depression, negotiation, and intimacy). If these systematic homework assignments produce changes in couples and families, then they become a new way of testing the validity of the models underlying them and of the theory underlying the models.

Systematic Family Therapy

SECTION I

Introduction to a Systematic Framework

Chapter 1

The Two Faces of Family Therapy

If one is allowed to pontificate, the field of family therapy is filled with false dichotomies, that is, dichotomies that do not portray or fit into an observable reality (if there is one!). Often, our tendency to dichotomize may reflect a necessity to simplify complex situations. Sometimes, in fact, the present writer will fall prey to this tendency to separate and dissect issues in a manageable fashion. Examples of such dichotomies can be found in the following: content versus process, individual versus family system, rational versus irrational, etc. Thus, most dichotomies, especially when dealing with human behavior, are convenient fictions used (and abused) for expository purposes.

One of the most important and relevant dichotomies in the field of family therapy, which has received a great deal of attention recently, has been the aesthetic versus the pragmatic distinction (Keeney & Sprenkle, 1982). The former term emphasizes the stylistic, personal, and intuitive quality of the therapist's personality as well as his/her interventions, whereas the latter term emphasizes the quantitatively methodological and technical contribution of the therapist to the therapeutic process and outcome, regardless of personality and style. Even though, as will be expanded later in this chapter, the original proponents of this dichotomy failed to cite relevant and similar distinctions made in the past, this distinction in its many aspects cuts across a variety of therapeutic viewpoints, theoretical differences, or methodological biases (Hansen & L'Abate, 1982).

Rather than a dichotomy, this distinction, as in many dichotomies, could be best understood and appreciated as a continuum defined by polarities similar or equivalent to the aesthetic-pragmatic ones. This continuum, which was presented by Keeney and Sprenkle (1982) as new and original, is actually neither. It has existed in different forms in many other writings going back to the scientific-artistic or the empirical-impressionistic or hard-headed versus soft-hearted variations on the same theme (Kimble, 1984; Royce, 1982). Reichenbach (1969) actually considered this distinction in terms of the two different contexts of "discovery" and "justification." Rychlack (1968), instead, considered the whole history of thought and ideas as being characterized by two different perspectives, i.e., the demonstrative (scientific) and the dialectical (artistic). The distinction between these two faces of family therapy and their correlates can be found in Table 1–1.

Arguments in favor of the aesthetic position can be found mainly in the humanistic schools of therapy, which in the family therapy field have been represented by Keeney (1983), Kempler (1981), Satir (1972), and Whitaker (Neill & Kniskern, 1982). As will be considered in greater detail in Chapter 10, these schools tend to emphasize the importance of subjective, phenomenological experience and the supremacy of emotions in the functionality or dysfunctionality of family life.

Table 1–1
THE TWO FACES OF EPISTEMOLOGY IN FAMILY THERAPY

Demonstrative	Dialectical
Quantitative	Qualitative
Empirical	Experiential
Objective	Subjective
Logical	Intuitive
Scientific	Humanistic
Lawfulness	Indeterminism
Observation	Impression
Nomothetic (normative)	Ideographic (individual)
Reductionistic	Holistic
Justification	Discovery
Pragmatic	Artistic (aesthetic)
Operational	Existential
Method	Style
Linear	Circular
Structuring skills	Relationship skills
Laboratory	Clinic (office)

Arguments in favor of a pragmatic position consist mainly of questioning the nonrepeatable value and validity of the therapist's personality and the importance of an objective methodology and substantive expertise to obtain chanes in clinical families. This position has been represented, among others, by Alexander and Parsons (1982), Epstein and Bishop (1981), and Minuchin (1974). In its extremes, this position would seriously question whether most of what goes on in the name of family therapy is indeed useful and relevant. If an approach is not testable and is untested, it should not be used.

The validity of this dichotomy is not only sustantiated by a variety of studies (Kimble, 1984), but is also supported by studies in the process and outcome of family therapy as being determined mainly by two distinct and somewhat unrelated variables (Alexander & Barton, 1976). The first variable, which has been called *relationship skills*, appears to be responsible for approximately 45% of the therapy outcome. This variable includes such therapist characteristics as affect, warmth, humor, and another factor called "behavioral integration." The second variable, called *structuring skills*, was responsible for about 36% of the therapy outcome. It consisted of such attributes as directiveness, self-confidence, and technical expertise. These findings were also supported by additional studies of psychoanalytically oriented individual therapy sessions, whose videotaped segments were rated by expert therapists. Again, these studies (Mintz & Luborsky, 1971; Mintz, Luborsky, & Auerbach, 1971) supported the conclusion that two separate and distinct variables determine a great deal of the therapy outcome, i.e., "optimal empathic relationship" and "directiveness." *Both* variables were found to be necessary to the satisfactory outcome of therapy.

These two major variables can be reinterpreted in terms of the two faces of family therapy: *style*, that is, the aesthetic, human quality of the therapist's personality and techniques, which, as a whole, are nonrepeatable events, and *method*, that is, the pragmatic quality of the therapist's professional preparation and competence, which include repeatable types of interventions. These interventions remain the same from one therapist to another, provided, of course, they have received the same training. Hence, up to now, we can conclude that the family therapy process and outcome is the result of two different aspects or faces of the therapist's makeup. *Both* faces are necessary. Neither can operate without the other. Eventually, the reader will learn where the present writer's bias lies.

Before this discovery, however, it is important to elaborate in greater detail about both faces. Murphy and Leeds (1975), for instance, put the demonstrative-dialectic distinction within the context of self-deception:

> Basically we have two ways of ordering reality: the way of science and the way of personal desire. We need experience and skill in order to find objective relevance in most of distant events of a drastic

world before we succomb to seeing them in terms of our personal needs. For the most part, one chooses a good blend of the two, including, as a kind of middle ground, perceptions in terms of the needs of other members of the community. (p. 8)

Polanyi (Schwartz, 1974) emphasized the dual nature of knowing. One is the detached traditional definition of scientific empiricism. The other is personal knowing based on our individual (and idiosyncratic!) awareness, beliefs, and convictions. Again and again, Polanyi pointed out that fundamental concepts of science are drawn from everyday experience in which measurement plays no part.

THE DIALECTIC FACE IN FAMILY THERAPY: DISCOVERY

As a whole, and most generalizations of this kind have exceptions, the field of family therapy, perhaps necessarily like most therapies, can currently be described as being dominated by a dialectic perspective. In this section, some of the most recent developments, the pros and the cons, of this dialectic perspective and its implications for family therapy will be reviewed.

The most important characteristics of a dialectic perspective (Wozniak, 1975) are (a) an emphasis on the unity and struggle of opposites; (b) transformation from quantitative to qualitative change; and (c) negation of past arguments with the replacement of new arguments and even newer arguments (negation of negation). Since behavior carries within itself the quality of contradiction, it also carries within itself the potential for newer interpretations, hopefully producing change. Personal styles in encountering and in escaping reality make up much of the world of history, literature, biography, arts, and politics.

Change as a Dialectical Process

Change, whether at the individual or multirelational systems, as will be discussed in greater detail in Chapter 5, relates to confrontation of contradictions. If contradiction represents the reconciliation of opposites (i.e., synthesis of thesis and antithesis), then change must be considered directly under a dialectical perspective that encompasses at least three major emphases: (a) emphasis on conflict, (b) emphasis on context, and (c) emphasis on circularity.

Emphasis on Conflict: This aspect of dialectics seems left out from Rychlack's otherwise excellent review (1968). In this perspective, conflict is an ever-present aspect of human nature, and as such makes it pivotal for an understanding of family blowups, uproars, and mutinies. Conflict is acknowledged and recognized as an intrinsic part of behavior that is not considered or usually encompassed by a demonstrative perspective. Emphasis on conflict is relevant not only to an understanding of family functionality/dysfunctionality but also to an understanding of the field of family therapy.

The dialectic perspective has been summarized best by Murphy and Leeds (1975): "Life involves a more or less continuous battle, a struggle toward reality and a struggle against it." They foresaw one of the truisms of a dialectic stance that is relevant to variability; i.e., "We all need the strength of our weaknesses and the weakness of our strengths" (p. 160). Riegel (1975a) included the concept of crisis as one aspect of conflict:

> If we look at the history of sciences as a continuous accumulative growth process, crises are offensive disturbances; if we look at the history of sciences as a progression through discrete leaps, crises are necessary steps in the advancement of knowledge. (pp. 152–153)

Crises, struggles, revolutions, reactions, and counterreactions—all these terms signify the importance of conflict as a confrontation of opposing, often antagonistic viewpoints within families and within the field of family therapy! The conciliation of oppositions, both familially and therapeutically, brings about change, hopefully for the better!

Emphasis on Context: The importance of contextual, i.e., family, factors is taken for granted in the field of family therapy. However, we have as yet to distinguish among various types of contexts, i.e., immediate versus transcendental, internal versus external, spatial versus temporal, concrete versus abstract, material versus symbolic, etc. This topic will be dealt with in greater detail in Chapter 11.

Emphasis on Circularity: As shown in Table 1–1, a dialectic perspective involves a nonlinear irregularity that can border on chaos and confusion. Whereas a demonstrative perspective subsumes linearity, precision, and predictability, a dialectic perspective implies complexity, unpredictability, and irregularity. This is the very characteristic of emotions and emotionality, a topic that will be discussed in Chapter 10. Hence, this perspective raises the question of whether behavior can be ultimately controlled. Complexity demands originality, creativity, and innovation. It challenges change. But change often requires a loss, i.e., giving up of old habits and traditional ways of doing things. Change is especially difficult when we do not know how to replace what we need to give up. The devil we have may be better than the devil we may get. Change is difficult not only for families but also for professions, and family therapy is no exception!

Theory as a Dialectical Process

As shown in Table 1–1, the term "scientific" is usually equated with the demonstrative perspective. From this equation it would follow that any approach or perspective that is nondemonstrative, i.e., dialectical, is considered "unscientific." Of course, such an equation and dichotomy is unfortunate and misleading. It leads one to equate "scientific" with the quantitative. Science has been so equated with methodology and quantification that any other approach or perspective not using these tools is put down as being "armchair philosophy" and outside the realm of scientific respectability! This unfortunate equation not only leads to many professional schisms and rivalries, as in the case of experimental versus clinical psychology, but it detracts from appreciation of many descriptive sciences like anthropology, botany, zoology, and so-called "soft" social sciences approaches.

Advances in science are mostly dialectic and nonquantitative (Kuhn, 1962). Demonstrativeness is usually evolutionary, whereas dialectics is mostly revolutionary. Paradigmatic change takes place within a dialectic process and seldom within a demonstrative perspective. By the same token, theoretical advances are based on contextual and conceptual interpretations of empirical evidence. But interpretation is a dialectical process. As Campbell (1975) reminded us of epistemological humility:

> All scientific knowing is indirect, presumptive, obliquely and incompletely corroborated at best. The language of science is subjective, provincial, approximative, and metaphoric, never the language of reality itself. (p. 1120)

Dewey and Bentley (1949) emphasized this point clearly:

> Science does not require that we study man and society in a detached manner. On the contrary, the part played by personal knowledge [as in Polanyi, cited previously] in science suggests that the science of man should rely on greatly extended uses of personal knowing. . . .
> A personal knowledge of man may consist in putting ourselves in the place of persons we are studying and in trying to solve their problems as they see them or as we see them. (p. 52)

If both Polanyi and Dewey and Bentley are in any way correct, then the main source of knowledge (i.e., discovery) about ourselves and our families derives from therapy and not laboratory experiments. Yet, as emphasized at the beginning of this chapter, *both* are necessary because *both* are complementary.

Experimentation as a Dialectical Process

A quantitative, demonstrative approach isolated from the qualitative is virtually impossible. One cannot survive without the other. Experimentation per se is not enough, just as qualification by itself is insufficient to settle epistemological arguments. As Riegel (1975a) reminded us in this regard, "Facts are merely theories to which we become sufficiently accustomed." No matter how demonstrative an investigator wants to be, one cannot escape the dialectical perspective. An interpretation of empirical results depends on the theoretical and metatheoretical biases of the investigator. As long as interpretation is a matter of controversy, and controversy is vital to the growth of scientific research, it is part and parcel of the dialectic; i.e., experimental results need qualitative interpretations that consider externally contextual factors not usually considered in controlled experimentation. Thus, each perspective serves as a corrective context for the other. Each enhances the other, and *both should be mastered*! Both are metatheoretical; that is, they both transcend or go beyond a specific theory. To think of one without the other would be tantamount to dealing with half the realities surrounding us. We need both for our survival and the survival of the families we serve.

THE DANGERS OF A DIALECTICAL PERSPECTIVE

Unfortunately, the field of family therapy is so imbued with a dialectical perspective that it has forgotten, bypassed, and practically ignored the demonstrative perspective. Emphasis on one has taken place at the expense of the other. This emphasis has led to excessive imbalances that would ultimately retard the progress of the field. As a result, family therapy can be characterized as being (a) antireductionistic with a parallel overemphasis on constructivism; (b) overparticularistic and exaggeratedly antieclectic; and (c) strongly antiempirical and, instead, strongly impressionistic. The field favors single, one-sided approaches and viewpoints and discourages eclectic views, belittling many possibilities of objective empirical verification. If such a conclusion sounds too brutally harsh and rhetorically extreme, let us consider more specific arguments to support this conclusion.

One of the major dangers in the extreme aesthetic position can be found in the cult of personality and omnipotence of the therapist as found especially in the blind admiration of gurus, without any checks or balances that would allow a blending of personality (i.e., style) and professionalism (i.e., method). The danger here is one of style versus substance. Can a therapeutic approach survive on style, that is, the exquisitely unique qualities of the individual therapist that are not repeatable from one therapist to the other? In addition, within this position, one person's claims are as acceptable as another's. How can the public and the profession discriminate the charlatan from the competent professional? How much should a profession rely on personal charm and charisma rather than effectiveness and demonstrable and demonstrated competence? The guru then becomes akin to the clown with a great deal of patina to cover the real self, a concurrent avoidance of any kind of evaluation, a strong antiempirical stance, and a rejection of technology and of method.

By the same token, extremes in the scientific position will lead to a view of science as "superscience" and "scientism" blind to possible errors and ignorant of critical feedback stemming from a dialectical perspective! When method then is exalted at the expense of style (as seen especially in the behavioral school), one realizes that the extreme of cultism has been reached, just as in the extreme of a dialectical perspective!

Since the extreme aesthetic position is now so ingrained in family therapy at the expense of the pragmatic position, it may be relevant here to highlight the latter in greater detail to discuss critically the emphasis on personality that culminates in guru adoration and exaltation. The guru is usually recognized by a cult, a group of followers who obediently and uncritically accept the guru's precepts unquestioningly. Under these conditions such precepts become dogma and are accepted as given truths, becoming a way of life or a system by which the follower lives and which overshadows any other system. Reviews of the family therapy field (Hansen & L'Abate, 1982; Levant, 1984; Nichols, 1984) readily reveal that the field is characterized by gurus who have produced "schools" based on little or no empirical evidence! We would not accept the same kind of criteria to be used in the treatment of our pet, but we accept them in the treatment of families! What makes gurus so popular and considered as being more important than method? It may be important for the reader to consider the following characteristics of the successful guru so that they can be identified and critically considered in their dangers:

First, the guru is a very seductive person, charming beyond belief! What s/he says appears very plausible, making intuitive good sense, appealing to the side of the brain many of us do not exercise enough, the right side! There is a sense of immediacy and caring that appeals instantly to any of us. Usually gurus are brilliant human beings who attract us with their humaneness and warmth. After all, is not style what they peddle the most? Very often gurus obtain their following from personal contacts in workshops and conferences. Whatever publications they may have would add to their credibility and plausibility. It does not matter if their publications suggest absolutely no evidence that the style produces reliable changes over time in families. When one combines popularity, authority, credibility, plausibility, and warm human caring, how can anyone resist? The guru knows how to solve all the problems presented to him/her and performs feats of magic either on tape or in front of an eager audience. It is completely irrelevant whether any short-term or long-term change does or does not take place! War stories, magic episodes with a supposedly positive outcome, are recounted as evidence of the guru's sensitivity, ingenuity, and cunning. It seems irrelevant whether external criteria were used to assess if the guru's impressions were valid or not!

Second, the guru has high entertainment value. Consequently, his/her presentation is interesting, exciting, and usually rather original. Given all these characteristics, how could anybody resist the guru? Usually, the guru is not only charming and original, but also has a good sense of humor, an ability to laugh, and a strong sense of self and of positive vitality. S/he is witty, articulate, and seemingly knowledgeable, at least experientially. How could a cold, probably boring pragmatist compare and compete with all these qualities?

Third, while all the above qualities make the guru rather seductive and hard to resist, one also needs to ask what the guru is not. It is very easy to find out that usually the guru is not interested in evaluating the validity and reliability of his/her notions or, worse, in assessing the effectiveness of his/her therapeutic interventions and claimed successes. A critical viewer would immediately find a strong antiempirical stance, belittling or downgrading research and evidence, maximizing and rhapsodizing instead the value and importance of the immediate and subjective personal experience. S/he will stress the subjective personal experience as well as the importance of sensitivity, intuition, and warmth, that is, all the factors that fall within the category of relationship skills. Nonreplicable events, such as style, personal feelings, and sudden insights, will be preferred to replicable methods. Given all the positive characteristics, it is difficult to compete with gurus in the marketplace of family therapy! They are hard to beat, especially when one does not possess the same skills!

ANTIREDUCTIONISM AND OVERCONSTRUCTIVISM

The term "reductionism" is used here to mean two separate but related processes: (a) to break down complex behavior into smaller and supposedly more manageable parts or components, which is essentially the analytic approach, and (b) to explain complex processes in terms of an underlying concept, such as, explaining resistance in terms of fear or anxiety. In terms of the first meaning, current family therapy practices could be characterized as being *antireductionistic* and *overly holistic*, that is, avoiding breakdown into component parts and emphasizing unduly wholes and molar variables without attempting to look at whatever parts make up the whole. For instance, among some family therapists there is an almost rigid avoidance of individual personalities and emphasis, relying instead on relationships among family members without looking at individual needs, wants, and aspirations of the separate members, that is, looking at families through relationships rather than individual personalities. Consequently, the field of personality development in the family is totally overlooked (L'Abate, 1976).

The field of family therapy is full of untested and untestable therapeutic approaches (Hansen & L'Abate, 1982) that have no way of being reduced or reducible to testable formats and propositions. The issue, then, becomes: if a therapeutic approach is not testable, how good can it be? How can we, the consumers of this approach, know which approach is better (more valid, more effective, more successful) than another, competing approach?

The opposite side of the medal of antireductionism is emergence and constructivism, that is, making things more complex than they may be, with an emphasis on the circular, i.e., paradoxical, as being superior to more straightforward, step-by-step, and linear approaches. Circular is "good"; linear is "bad." If it is complex it is "good"; if it is simple it is "bad." This extreme was well illustrated by a workshop participant who criticized this author for not making things more "complex"! Apparently the field is not interested in asking questions about the validity of each therapeutic approach and its comparative effectiveness with other approaches. This state of affairs could be compared to the claims of the traveling "doctors" who peddled magical ointments that would cure anything from calluses to gallbladder. (And if you did not have a disease it would give it to you!)

The dangers of unbridled dialectics are found in showmanship, guru worship, and downright charlatanry, where simple rules of evidence and success based on objective evidence rather than subjective claims have not only been thrown out, but derisively condemned as irrelevant and unnecessary (Keeney, 1983). Emphasis on discovery is so great that no empirical evidence, i.e., the context of justification, is needed. Subjective impression is confused with evidence! The outcome of this state of affairs is evident: claims and counterclaims (Allman, 1982a; Coyne, Denner, & Ransom, 1982; Watzlawick, 1982; Whitaker, 1982; Wilder, 1982), faddish proliferation of elegant and seductive shibboleths and personal preferences, with an outcome that is tantamount to chaos in the field (Bowen, 1985).

The role of research in the practice of family therapy has been the topic of recent and extended controversy (Gurman, 1983; Kniskern, 1983; Rohrbaugh, 1983; Schwartz & Breunlin, 1983; Tomm, 1983). Most of the writers involved in this ongoing controversy concur about the existence of two different world views, one represented by the research-investigator-empiricist-pragmatist and the other by the artist-dialectician-impressionist. Although most therapists would agree that research is necessary, most of them would also admit that they would do very well without it (and researchers!). Most researchers in family therapy may be destined to become an isolated cliché of individuals talking only to themselves. Research does not have the status or prestige it would like to receive, because it is not viewed as being necessary or even relevant to the whole therapeutic enterprise. How can one perform therapy and research that is relevant at the same time? One of the purposes of this book is to show that both activities can be performed in parallel with each other, neither detracting from the other!

The Dangers of Scientism

By the same token, a "scientific" attitude can be exaggerated to its extreme, just as a dialectic can be. As Gardner (1983) observed in this regard:

> Even though the scientist's self-image nowadays highlights rigor, systematicity, and objectivity, it seems that in the final analysis science itself is a religion, a set of beliefs that scientists embrace with a zealot's conviction. Scientists not only believe in their methods and themes from the depth of their being, but many are also convinced it is their mission to use these tools to explain as much of reality as falls within their power. (p. 150)

Stierlin (1983) added to these dangers by noting that

> Modern science, particularly in the nexus with modern technology, has shown itself in many ways to be the force that often intends to do good (or at least claims to intend this) while at the same time almost inevitably creating evil. (p. 414)

Stierlin did not specify what the nature of this "evil" is, but he seems to imply that one of these "evils" may be specialization.

> One consequence of this specialization among the scientists and the proliferation of therapy and training models is the increasing tendency of more and more workers in a given field to encapsulate themselves in their own area and their own system of notions to the extent that they become completely blinded to everything else. (p. 415)

Among the many issues considered by Stierlin, the most relevant one, which will be considered directly or indirectly in this book, is the one of "reducing complexity without at the same time denying it" (p. 419). Stierlin exhorts us to continue in the name of curiosity (i.e., discovery) rather than in the name of power and control issues (i.e., justification), which will also be considered later on in this book.

Once the need for both aspects, like two sides of the same coin, is acknowledged, one needs to become more aware of possible dangers deriving from extremes in both positions, that is, elevating one at the expense of the other. The extremes of the aesthetic position are just as dangerous as extremes of the pragmatic position. Unfortunately, extollers of the aesthetic position (Keeney, 1983) seem so wrapped up in the glory of aesthetics that they completely ignore a pragmatic position. Hopefully, both sides will be given equal attention here.

The major danger of a pragmatic position is mechanization and dehumanization, looking at and working with families as machines or pieces of machinery. Whereas the dialectical position is seductively romantic, scientifically naive, overidealized, and neglectful of demonstrativeness, by the same token the demonstrative position may ignore simplistically the fact that there are other ways of getting to the "truth" and that demonstrativeness in itself is insufficient to reach the goal of improved effectiveness with families. One needs to be mindful that professionals are not scientists to the extent that they do not practice science and are not active in research activities. However, to the extent that a professional uses a selective blend of both demonstrative and dialectical approaches, a greater degree of competence and, hopefully, effectiveness will result. An effective professional is able to mix both aspects without unduly practicing one at the expense of the other. One would find it as difficult to practice "science" in a clinic as it would be to practice "art" in the laboratory! The pragmatic position in its extreme may become rigid superscientism, irrelevant pseudoscience, or dehumanizing pragmatism. The style of the "superscientist" would be as questionable as the style of the guru!

CONCLUSION: THE FACES BEHIND THE MASKS

The two faces described here represent the two masks of family therapy. Underneath them are the real faces! What has been described thus far may be valid at a superficial level of analysis, a level that will be accepted provided one also accepts the position that these two faces may lead us into witch hunts, irrelevant detours, and distracting pseudoissues. What is more relevant from the viewpoint of the greatest benefit for the least cost are the families we serve. How are we to serve them? How sensitive are we to the costs and cost-effectiveness of our therapies? Should we serve families in dire need or should we also extend our services to families who, down the road, will need our services? How expensive are our services, and how can we cut down on the expense and increase the effectiveness of our interventions? One would estimate that for every family that asks for help and gets it, there may be six to ten families which hurt just as much, but which, for whatever reason, cannot bring themselves to ask for help or to benefit by help. These are questions that, hopefully, directly or indirectly, will be answered in the remainder of this book.

Chapter 2

In Defense of Eclecticism

The word *eclecticism* in family therapy is very much like the proverbial weather. Everybody talks about it and most follow it, but few are doing anything about using it systematically. Instead of participating in territorial disputes or to support (seemingly) mutually antagonistic positions, an eclectic position in family therapy makes sense for those therapists who do not have a theoretical ax to grind and who do not need to profess allegiance to any specific theoretical or therapeutic approach. Most of us do the best we can with all the information and training available to us. We exclude very little and include as much as we need and that makes sense to us, filtering and selecting what fits into our personal and professional values and excluding what we feel uncomfortable with.

Before we discuss and defend the role of eclecticism in family therapy, which is the purpose of this chapter, the role of theory in family therapy will need to be introduced.

THE ROLE OF THEORY IN FAMILY THERAPY

The role of theory is very important in the formulation of a systematically eclectic approach. Its value has been considered repeatedly (L'Abate, 1964, 1976, 1983d). Consequently, different requirements will be considered here that may not have been sufficiently stressed in the past. A theory should fulfill at least four requirements (among others). First, a theory should be *economical*; that is, it should encompass the widest range of behaviors with a minimum of assumptions (L'Abate, 1976, 1983d). Second, a theory should help in the *direction* of clinical practice; that is, if a theory is related to reality and this relationship is valid, then interventions should ideally be derived from the theory as much as is humanly possible. Third, a theory should be connected with clinical practice; that is, ideally, there should be a certain degree of *coherence* between theory and practice. Fourth, a theory should be *testable*; that is, it should be formulated to allow for empirical validation and verification. This requirement will be considered in greater detail in the next chapter.

EXPANSION FROM PARTICULARISM TO ECLECTICISM

Most run-of-the-mill grass-roots therapists are eclectic (Norcross & Prochaska, 1982). Most gurus, by the same token, are particularists; that is, they have the goal of propounding their own theory and/or therapeutic approach.

In addition to being characterized by inordinate and uncritical overuse of the constructivist bias, the field of family therapy is inundated by particularism, the emphasis on specific schools or viewpoints (Hansen & L'Abate, 1982) at the expense of eclecticism. In fact, Liddle (1982) has severely criticized any possible attempt at theorizing that may smack of grandiose eclecticism! Single viewpoints with their attendant charismatic gurus seem to be the order of the day. Particularism would be welcome if it allowed us to test one school or viewpoint against other competing and comparable viewpoints. Unfortunately, comparative testing is not taking place, because *testability* is not considered a desirable or needed criterion. Hence, each particular viewpoint can flourish and extravagant claims can be made *without evidence*! Invidious comparisons are made, but no substantive, empirical demonstration is taking place.

Why is eclecticism necessary? Because comparative testing of competing viewpoints is nonexistent and tremendously difficult and expensive. Most single-minded therapists seem uncritically convinced of the inherent validity of their approach and, with exceptions, are not interested in testing it. In addition, most of these viewpoints are not set in a way that allows testing them easily and inexpensively. If they are not testable, how good are they? It goes without saying that an empirical approach would be on the side of objectivity over impressionism.

One of the worst dangers of particularism is *cultism*, one step short from orthodoxy. It is possible that many theoretical and therapeutic approaches may become substitutes for absolute and unshakeable beliefs. On this point, Pittman (1983) commented:

> Often partisans of one school don't talk with partisans of other schools, or read what they write or learn from those who think differently. Orthodoxy has a stifling effect, met by producing conflict, but by preventing interaction and doubt. Religious power simplifies, stifles and bypasses substance in favor of ritual. The cults

seem more dangerous to the field than the flying circus ever was. Superstars now are not trapeze artists but cult leaders. (p. 29)

The major danger of particularism is emphasis on the *person* of the therapist rather than on the *method* of the therapist. The therapist is a nonrepeatable event. As such, it cannot be supplanted. However, this distinction is very important because it brings us back to the debate over pragmatism versus aestheticism (Keeney & Sprenkle, 1982). The person of the therapist and his style are particular events that are too specific to be the major variable in therapy. In this regard, one needs to remember that aesthetics views therapy as an art and as behavior that is impossible to study scientifically.

One has only to read most of the family journals to become aware that the level of dialogue is extremely dialectical, impressionistic, and completely devoid of empirical evidence! Claims and counterclaims are made without the possibility of either conciliation or integration. In the extreme, empiricism is considered irrelevant or at least unnecessary (Keeney, 1983).

Without externally objective criteria, theories, dogmas, fads, and shibboleths in the form of techniques, gimmicks, and sleights of hand can proliferate unchecked and undisturbed. Personal satisfaction becomes the criterion of success, and therapists can indulge in orgies of mutual-admiration clichés that reinforce each other's viewpoint unhampered by any kind of external evidence.

The expansion from theory to practice and from the particularism of a theory to an eclectic approach has been made here through the use of models. As in previous formulations (L'Abate, 1976, 1983d), the role of models in theory building and theory testing is crucial to the present formulation. Consequently, models will need to be considered in greater detail here within the context of an eclectic approach.

The Role of Models in Theory Building and Testing

As Stogdill (1970) described it:

> The model-builder is concerned with the description and explanation of events in the real world (p. 5). . . . Although a system of events can be conceptualized in different ways, not all are equally effective in yielding insight and understanding (p. 6). . . . The term *model* may be reported as an unpretentious name for theory.

On the contrary, in the present formulation the theory (Table 2–1) is clearly distinguished from its applications, whereas the models are derivations from the theory as visual summaries of the theory. They help reduce complex, abstract theoretical ideas to very applicable and practical ways of dealing with behavior, symptomatic or otherwise.

Linkage Between Theory and Practice. Models thus serve as the connection between theory and practice, between abstractions and applications. They represent the reduction of theory to a level that makes it concretely testable in the laboratory as well as in the clinic.

Diagnostic Functions—Classification. Because of the assumed concreteness and clarity, models serve also as diagnostic (i.e., evaluative but not pigeonholing) of behavior. The models represent classification of behaviors divided into categories that are easily identifiable and observable. The typological function allows one to evaluate the level of functionality or dysfunctionality of a family's relationships.

Therapeutic Functions. If a therapist is clear about patterns of behavior unfolding in front of him/her, so much more clearly and directly should the therapist be able to intervene. The clearer the therapist's ideas, the clearer and more directly specific should be the interventions.

Propedeutic Functions. Concrete and specific models are easy to teach. Students need concepts that they can carry into the office and that will allow them to meet families with clear ideas, which in turn will allow them to intervene effectively.

Research Functions. To the extent that models are testable, they become vehicles of evaluation for process and progress in therapy. Models are verifiable, but most abstract, theoretical notions are not. Models, therefore, not only link theory with practice, they also link theory and practice with research, as discussed in greater detail in the next chapter.

Table 2–1
SCHEMATIC SUMMARY OF AN ECLECTIC APPROACH TO FAMILY THERAPY

Theory		Models	Applications
Assumptions (L'Abate, 1964, 1976, 1983d, 1985)	Postulates		Systematic homework assignments (SHWAs)
		Depression (Chapter 7)	Appendix A
		Negotiation (Chapter 8)	Appendix B
		Styles (Chapter 9)	
Space		Competence (Chapters 10 & 11)	
	Negotiation	Priorities (Chapter 12)	
Time	Differentiation	Intimacy (Chapter 13)	Appendix C

With all these functions, it is small wonder that models have been given a key position in theory building and testing (L'Abate, 1976).

According to Stogdill, any model builder must be mindful of the following questions:

- Why were the variables selected for the model?
- Why were other possible relevant variables omitted?
- Why was the specific set of relationships between variables postulated for the model?
- What other relationships might have been hypothesized?
- Are variables assumed to be complex or unitary?

If some of the variables are complex in structure, is it assumed that the components interact to produce an averaging-out effect? To what extent does the model appear to describe the set of events in the real world that it was designed to explain?

As noted in the previous chapter, if one were to characterize the field of family therapy within Reichenbach's distinction (1969) between the context of discovery and the context of justification, one would conclude that the field is discovering a great deal and justifying very little. Models can be useful to the process of justification. They are used in the context of justification to provide *testable* models.

Ashby (1970) proposed that models be used for their convenience (p. 94). He also emphasized the multiplicity of models possible: ". . . complex systems are capable of models, with no one able to claim absolute priority" (p. 97). In addition to the convenience and usefulness, Ashby considers relevance as another characteristic of models.

Beavers and Voeller (1983), on the basis of the comparison of their model with Olson's circumplex model (L'Abate, 1985), concluded on the functions of models:

> Models are important. Their usefulness is directly related to their logical force, their close adherence to clinical data, and their assistance in the comprehension and treatment of family difficulty. (p. 96)

As Hall (1976) commented on the role of models:

> Scientists use theoretical models, often mathematical in nature. These are used to symbolically express certain qualities, quantities, and relationships encountered in life. . . . Many different models exist. . . . All theoretical models are incomplete. By definition, they are abstractions and themselves leave things out. . . . Para-

doxically, studying the models that men create to explain nature tells you more about the men than about the part of nature being studied. (pp. 13–14)

A variety of models will be used (Table 2–1). As models were developed, they suggested homework assignments (SHWAs) that would be applied for the families to practice *to a criterion of mastery at home*. These SHWAs were directly derived from the models, and therefore, they directly *test* the models themselves and, consequently, the theory. A schematic summary of this approach is found in Table 2–1.

These models are in one way or another derived from a theory of personality development in the family (L'Abate, 1976, 1983d, 1985), a theory that will not be considered here.

THE MEANING OF ECLECTICISM

There are three types of eclecticism (Norcross & Prochaska, 1982): (1) atheoretical, having no preferred theoretical preference; (2) synthetic, integrating a diversity of contemporary theories; and (3) technical, using a variety of techniques within a preferred theory. As will be demonstrated, it is possible to integrate synthetically and systematically a variety of contemporary theories of family therapy and, at the same time, link this integration to the variety of models derived from this integration.

There are many trends indicating that eclecticism is the norm for most practicing therapists (Palmer, 1980). As Garfield and Kurtz (1976) reported in this survey, 55 percent of clinical psychologists described themselves as eclectic. As shown in the recent survey of Norcross and Prochaska (1982), eclecticism is still the norm for the theoretical orientation of most clinical psychologists (31%). When one adds to this orientation a systems orientation (45%), it appears that at least one third of most clinical psychologists avoid being pinned down to one specific theoretical preference.

The same respondents to this survey ($n = 479$) believed that one's theoretical orientation influences therapeutic practice. As will be shown in the course of this book, each theoretical orientation uses diagnostic and interventional techniques and methods that derive specifically from the theory and that are not shared by other theories. Hence, systematic eclecticism allows the use of most ethically acceptable and interventionally useful models and techniques, provided, of course, that they are applied responsibly. One interesting result of this survey pertains to the relationship between theoretical orientation and experience level. Eclecticism increased slightly with years of clinical experience (from 28.4% to 32%).

Why is eclecticism the norm in therapy? One possibility lies in human individuality. As long as a therapist picks and chooses, s/he can and does retain individuality. In pledging allegiance to one specific orientation—whatever it may be—a therapist may be giving up a bit of his/her self, losing a certain degree of self-determination and originality that is possible with eclecticism.

In a survey of individual psychotherapists from clinical and counseling psychology, Smith (1982) came to grips with the many issues of eclecticism:

> Counselors and therapists who consider single theory orientations to be provincial in both theoretical concepts and methodological options tend to seek an eclectic alternative. Eclecticism promises the possibility for a comprehensive psychotherapy that is based on a unified and well-organized body of knowledge and strategies. . . . Although the eclectic model allows for openness and flexibility, it also encourages an indiscriminate selection of bits and pieces from diverse sources that results in a hodgepodge of inconsistent concepts and techniques. Thus, rejecting a single-theory approach and adopting an eclectic stance does not always improve the therapist's *modus operandi.* (p. 802)

Quoting from previous surveys of clinical psychologists (already cited), who indicated a majority preference for therapeutic eclecticism, Smith qualified this conclusion:

> At the same time, there seems to be a growing dissatisfaction with the label "eclecticism," which suggests laziness, undisciplined subjectivity, and poor systematization. Current literature [on individual counseling and psychotherapy] indicates a trend in the direction of creative synthesis, masterful integration, and systematic eclecticism. (p. 802)

Smith went on to support his conclusion about systematic eclecticism in individual psychotherapy by citing a variety of sources. From his own survey, Smith concluded that most psychotherapy-oriented psychologists tend to follow an eclectic or open-system orientation. Among the various types of eclecticism that Smith considered are (a) simple, (b) technical, (c) emerging, (d) multimodel, and (e) creative, integrative, or systematic eclecticism. The last is the focus of this work.

Allport (1968) was one of the major proponents of theoretical eclecticism, starting from the proposition that "we are still a science without fine postulates, without a commonly accepted comprehensive theory of man" (p. 30). He defined eclecticism as follows:

> A system that seeks the solution of fundamental problems by selecting and choosing what it regards as true in the several specialized approaches to psychological sciences. As of today, it is clearly not

possible to synthesize all plausible theories. The task is beyond the limits of present intelligence. Yet eclecticism in this ambitious sense is still an ideal and a challenge. As such, it merits serious thought. (p. 32)

Allport, aware that one of the weaknesses of eclecticism "is the difficulty of finding guiding principles for uniting fragments" (quoting from E. G. Boring, 1930), believed that an eclectic must, above all, be historically oriented—keenly aware of and charmed by the work of his predecessors. As Allport saw it, "What is required of an eclectic is that he theorize in such a way that his chosen superordinate principles never exclude valid evidence concerning human nature drawn from whatever source" (p. 36).

To function as an eclectic, one needs to accept the pluralistic nature of causation (multicausality; i.e., different causes may produce the same outcome) and equipotentiality (i.e., the same cause can produce different outcomes). After attacking the opposite of eclecticism (i.e., particularism), Allport submitted an attempt at systematic eclecticism by admonishing theorists that they must not forget what they have decided to neglect and that they must theorize in such a way that whatever can be considered valid can be subjected to further validation.

ECLECTICISM IN FAMILY THERAPY AND TRAINING

Brodkin (1980) argued that the family therapy movement has undergone three phases: (a) saving the individual, family style; (b) fighting for the embattled family; and (c) an era of ambiguity in which the movement is still evolving. It is at this stage that eclecticism is relevant. Wathney and Balbridge (1980) have summarized the issue of eclecticism in family therapy as follows:

> Among the numerous approaches to psychotherapy, some emphasize the importance of feelings, others focus on observable behavior, and still others center on intellectual insight. If we accept that psychotherapy in general is beneficial, we should also realize from the evidence that no single approach is measurably more effective than another. Therefore, it seems reasonable to suspect that beneath the theoretical and methodological differences, there are basic similarities in the aspects of therapy that actually effect change in clients. This conclusion is consistent with the observation that experienced and successful therapists, even those from widely divergent schools of thought, operate in many similar ways. (p. 676)

Ellis (982) expressed some pessimism about the possibility of rating different schools of therapy because of the overlap among many of them:

It is doubtful whether any of the "separate" terms, emotion, cognition and behavior, can be properly defined in their own exclusive
right, since each contains salient and essential elements of the other
two. . . . *The whole field of counseling and psychotherapy seems to be
developing a more comprehensive and more eclectic outlook* [emphasis mine].
(p. 7)

Perhaps Alexander and Parsons (1982) have condensed that position in
maintaining that "family therapy cannot simply follow a specific set of procedures nor can it utilize only one set of techniques" (p. 105).

An Eclectic's Position—The Coward's Way Out?

At least two meanings of *eclecticism* need to be clarified before the presentation
of the three meanings of eclecticism as used in this work. Eclecticism can be
seen as a combination of seemingly mutually antagonistic viewpoints and
practices. This is seen, for instance, in cognitive behavior modification, an
example of a combination of what, years ago, would have seemed mutually
antagonistic practices. The second meaning of eclecticism comprises elective
choices from a variety of viewpoints, perhaps in the work of Bell (1975),
Skinner (1976), and other family therapy eclectics. The third meaning of
eclecticism that is affirmed here is essentially the combination of and selective
choices from a variety of pragmatic viewpoints: If any technique works in our
practice, we keep it; if it doesn't work, we don't keep it. To the pragmatic
position will be added an existential one. The viewpoint we want to establish
is basically a pragmatic-existential-eclectic one that we would like to follow
in practice and training.

The Dangers of Eclecticism

Clearly, eclecticism can be an excuse for many outside observers as well as
for those therapists who use it in their work. Eclectics have been denounced
as vague, and therapists *can* be indecisive. There is no question that eclectics
can be accused of trying to please everybody and, in this process (as we in
family therapy well know), pleasing nobody. The third danger of eclecticism
is the difficulty in testing and evaluating an eclectic position. The real point
here is whether or not eclecticism offers sufficient rewards to justify our
practice of it.

Lunde (1974) considered some of the perennial criticism leveled against
eclecticism: (a) opportunistic selectivity, (b) fragmentary and piecemeal approach, (c) glossing over irreconcilable differences among mutually exclusive
viewpoints, (d) inclusion of contradictory positions within one framework.
"A true eclectic tries to maintain an open mind in order to perceive the
element of truth in any theory, whether old or new, and also to maintain a

proper amount of skepticism in matters that are not yet resolved" (p. 382).

Robertson (1979) listed some of the factors that may be responsible for therapeutic eclecticism. Among others, he noted the following: (a) lack of pressures in graduate school or later in one's professional environment that bend one to a doctrinaire position, (b) length of therapeutic experience (i.e., the longer the experience, the less doctrinaire the approach), and (c) making a living, which forces one to have a flexible and wide-ranging armamentarium. Robertson identified at least four varieties of eclecticism: (a) theoretical, (b) technical, (c) existential, and (d) radical, involving sequential applications from a wide range of available techniques.

Liddle's (1979) position was fundamentally critical of eclecticism and supportive of a unilateral viewpoint in therapy and practice as well as training. Liddle's position needs to be opposed by some principles of eclecticism kept in our training program (L'Abate, Berger, Wright, & O'Shea, 1979) and in our practice.

Liddle (1979) criticized eclecticism in family therapy training as follows:

> While drawing techniques from conflicting frames of reference, eclectic therapy-training can itself be conflicting. An unmeasured eclectic model can be an excuse for failing to develop a sound rationale for systematically adhering to certain concepts and procedures which are the extension of these concepts. The training issue becomes whether eclecticists can exist as an orderly combination of different systems' compatible features, rather than a conglomerate of incompatible models, each with incongruous theories of normality, dysfunction, and change. . . . How to teach students to think and act according to an interactional reality is no simple, trivial matter. Indeed, it is in need of considerable attention. (p. 3)

More recently, Liddle (1982) has put it this way:

> Today's clinician is faced with the question To which school of therapy should I profess my allegiance? In response to this pressurized query, many therapists opt out of the dilemma altogether and declare themselves "eclectics." Indeed, in a study conducted on this topic, when asked to describe their theoretical orientation, a majority of therapists labelled themselves eclectic. (p. 243)

He added further support to the notion that most "students of family therapy face a bewildering array of competing approaches in defining and conducting family treatment" (p. 243).

Comparing the various schools of therapy, Liddle commented on the lack of any supporting evidence for one approach over others. Allegiances are made more on the basis of the charismatic influence of a founding guru than on the basis of supporting evidence. In terms of a unitary, integrative perspective, Liddle added that "all of our current theories of therapy are interconnected; it is just that we do not yet have the lenses, or perspective (a metatheory), that could allow the interconnection to be experienced as such" (p. 246). Deciding to develop such a metatheory, according to Liddle, is to fall prey to the sin of "Idolatry of Theoretical Comprehensiveness"; he added, as follows:

> Systematic eclecticism, or the orderly application of theory and technique from differing but compatible schools of thought, cannot be taken as a single task. . . . Systematic integration of complementary models is a complex and difficult endeavor and has only necessarily begun in our field. (p. 246)

In addition to the sin of idolatry of theoretical comprehensiveness, Liddle warned of the growth myth syndrome—bigger is better. Thus, the present attempt is guilty on the counts of *both*: idolatry and bigness. What is the penalty for both counts? What are the costs of systematic eclecticism? Is it better to have a supertheory rather than many small theorettes? Is bigger better than smaller? The reader, upon finishing this work, should be able to answer these and many other questions.

The Safeties of Eclecticism

An eclectic position can be justified on a variety of grounds. Clearly, eclecticism represents a form of synthesis and avoids the thesis-antithesis dialectic brought about by mutually antagonistic viewpoints. In addition to being an integration of various viewpoints, eclecticism can also be characterized by flexibility and openness to viewpoints and avoidance of dogmatic, one-sided positions. Eclecticism also represents safety in numbers; that is, the wider the range of technqiues and methods that we as therapists have in our armamentaria, the better we should be able to meet the needs of the various families we see. Of course, these points need to be demonstrated.

However, the kind of viewpoint that we wish to initiate here is the difference between diffused eclecticism and systematic eclecticism. Many of the criticisms made in the preceding section on the dangers of eclecticism speak to what would be diffused eclecticism, a rather vague, unspecific melange of techniques and viewpoints. We, on the other hand, subscribe to what we might call systematic eclecticism; that is, instead of a wide range of behavior, we shall use *specific* models that will be elaborated in the rest of this monograph.

Gottsegen and Gottsegen (1979) criticized single-approach therapists who justify their ineffectiveness in terms of patients' inadequacies. Single-treatment approaches set up taboos against competing or interfering theoretical view-points, diminishing the therapist's therapeutic effectiveness.

> Therapists who insist on knowing nothing but what their training has told them is God's only truth refuse to apply new techniques from other areas to their work, refuse to recognize the limitations of their interventions, force interpretations on patients, put down other schools, methods, and research that would cause them to reevaluate what they do. They possess either the deadening effect of yesterday's newspaper or the smugness of an Ehrlichman. They have scorn and contempt for other workers, demean the obvious results of the new methods. They write and talk to each other in the foreign language of their particular method. They mis-hear the messages of other groups. (p. 59)

Naar (1979) illustrated through a detailed and prolonged (eight years!) case study how divergent modalities of treatment were used with the same patient at different times, within different theoretical frameworks, indicating that, when one's concern is people in need, there are no mutually exclusive positions.

Theories or Methods?

The issue of one versus many theories (i.e., eclecticism) is further compounded by the use of methods. How many methods should one learn how to apply? Can a behaviorist apply existential methods? By the same token, can a humanist feel good (no pun intended) using behavioral approaches? In view of assumed variability and in an attempt to avoid easy pigeonholes and false stereotypes, it may be helpful to suggest that the relationship between theories and methods in actual practice (i.e., what therapists really do rather than what they say they do) may be very tenuous.

CONCLUSION

Can eclecticism be systematic instead of sloppy, haphazard, and random? The belief underlying this work is that eclecticism does not need to be sloppy, haphazard, or random. Indeed, systematic eclecticism suggests that one can be both systematic and eclectic, valuing each theory for what it can contribute and limiting its impact to what it can do realistically.

How is the goal to be reached? An attempt will be made to obtain a modicum of systematization through models whose role in theory building and testing has been considered in this chapter. In this formulation, models achieve the position of linking theory with practice and hopefully practice with training.

Chapter 3

In Defense of Empiricism

The two major issues (both necessary and sufficient) among many (Hansen & L'Abate, 1982) facing the field of family therapy are (1) generalization and (2) testability. It is the purpose of this chapter to elaborate on the significance of both issues for family therapy and to suggest some ways to resolve them. An empirical approach uses both scientific and professional guidelines, prerequisites, and criteria (Table 3–1). Generalizability is a professional guideline. Testability is a scientific guideline.

GENERALIZATION

How can we ensure or work for change where it should take place (i.e., in the kitchen, the bedroom, the dining room, and the rest of the house)? Most of us assume that whatever changes take place in the therapist's office will generalize outside it. Yet, there is no evidence that this generalization does take place on a systematic basis. When it does, it varies from family to family and is therefore a chancy process that may or may not occur.

To ensure that more generalization occurs in the home, as discussed in the next chapter, one should produce changes right there, not just in the office. Consequently, it is important, if not imperative, that the therapist assign and prescribe homework that will increase the chances for generalization effects from the office to the home. To maximize this effect, then, the therapist should have available tools that the family can use at its own level of functioning and understanding.

Hence, among the prescriptions that can be assigned to families, a set of graduated, sequential SHWAs for practice at home has been found useful. The appendices include the SHWAs (of an eclectic nature) that have been assigned, on a once-a-week basis, to families, who do them until each lesson is mastered and incorporated into the practices of family members. In the author's private practice, couples and families must agree to spend one hour at home to complete or to work on assignments that have been given to them for every hour of therapy.

How can we maximize chances (we cannot guarantee, but we certainly can try to increase them) that the behavior(s) families need to change will transfer from the office to the home? Even if we can transfer such behavior(s), how can we maximize the chances (again, no guarantee!) so that whatever is changed will last? Generalization, then, includes at least two additional concepts—transfer and duration of behavior. The first is strictly a logistical, spatial problem—from the office to the home. The other is a temporal problem—how will changes produced (if any) last over time?

Issues of Generalization

There are at least four different steps in the process of generalization from the office to the home: (a) transfer from the therapist to the family; (b) transfer from the office to the home; (c) transfer from the home back to the office; and finally (d) transfer from the family to the therapist. What is implied in these four steps is a circular process, whereby the therapist needs to influence the family enough not only to come back after the first visit; in addition, the therapist's intervention via his/her personality and style or via his/her method motivates the family to start the process of change, taking with them whatever the therapist may have said or done back to the home. Once at home the

Table 3–1
SCHEMATIC SUMMARY OF AN EMPIRICAL APPROACH TO FAMILY THERAPY

Guidelines	Prerequisites	Criteria
Generalization (professional)	Transfer	Carryover to behaviors at home
		Spread to other positive behaviors
	Duration	Practice to mastery
		Lasting effects
Testability (scientific)	Verifiability	Fragmentation into parts
		Evaluation of processual components
	Accountability	Pre-post-therapy evaluation
		Follow-up evaluation

therapist's influence, in whatever way it may be done, needs to be powerful enough to make a difference on how the family is going to conduct their business. Will they continue business as usual, behaving in ways that have gotten them into trouble, or will they behave in different and positive ways? In other words, is the therapist's intervention, either by deeds or words or both, effective enough to produce change? How is this change to be obtained? If change is achieved at home, will the family come back to the therapist's office showing that something is indeed changed? Will this change be visible to the therapist?

In addition to the process of change, will the family show a spread of effects to other positive behaviors? That is, once the critical reason for referral has been taken care of, will the family show the spiral of positive change which many therapists claim takes place but which few have ever demonstrated? Once the reason for referral has been taken care of, has the family sufficiently changed to show that it has also changed in other respects? All the foregoing questions point to the need to define and deal with what is meant by change, an area that needs to be considered in any systematic formulation.

Issues of Change: What Will It Take?

Change for the better involves at least three processes: (a) doing something positively, (b) doing something differently (new) than it was done in the past, and (c) doing it with sufficient intensity and frequency that it will continue over time, as discussed earlier. Although a great many therapists are satisfied with changing the reason for referral, usually a symptom, change over time implies more than just changing the symptom, as will be discussed in the next chapter. Change also implies a process that will last for the long haul. Hence, it is important to give families experiential, conceptual, and action tools for maintaining change that will last. This issue will be dealt in part through tailor-made prescription during the first phase of therapy, but also through SHWAs, as will be considered in the next chapter.

Once change is obtained, what will it take to demonstrate it in valid and reliable ways? The issue, then, becomes one of testability and accountability, words that seem anathema to most family therapists and, actually, most mental health clinicians!

TESTABILITY

How can a therapeutic approach be tested? The difficulties in testing most therapeutic approaches are insurmountable (i.e., expense, feasibility, comparable groups, etc.). Nevertheless, it is important that a theory be testable.

Why Should a Theory Be Testable?

As noted in Chapter 1, the field of family therapy is replete with theories, theorettes, and theorylike approaches to such an extent that some observers have used the word "chaos" to describe such a state of affairs. The issue then becomes: which theory is better than another theory and by what criteria? In the long run, the theory that lends itself to direct empirical verification should, by all standards of scientific operationalism, prevail. But, as noted in Chapter 1, the field of family therapy does not seem to recognize objective criteria of verification as being as important as criteria of popularity, immediacy, and short-term payoff. Consequently, the search for a more effective theory will be retarded by emphasis on dialectical aspects at the expenses of demonstrative aspects. Be that as it may, it is important, within the context of a systematic empirical approach, to ask why a theory should be testable.

It should for the following reasons. First, its comparative validity should be checked in regard to other theories; i.e., how does it fare vis-à-vis other theories in its therapeutic effectiveness? How far will the theory go in helping families? For instance, a theory may be useful for families of schizophrenic patients but it may bomb with families of juveniles. It will be practically impossible to have a theory so encompassing that it will cover all possible contingencies of human existence. The issue here is one of therapeutic specificity.

Second, a testable theory will allow discrimination between faddish and fashionable clinical practices with questionable outcome and solidly grounded practices based on verified criteria of therapeutic effectiveness. Third, for progress to take place, the field of family therapy will need to rely on replicable, testable methods rather than on nonreplicable individuals. Methods are replicable even from setting to setting, from country to country, and from individual to individual. Unfortunately, individual therapists are not replicable events, and therefore, they are not testable.

The same point was made by Lewis (1984) in perhaps different words:

> There is one topic relevant to family therapy that is often curiously absent from presentations of various techniques and theories. Amidst the claims of clinical superiority by different approaches, epistemological debates, and descriptions of specific strategies for change, the question of the "effectiveness" of therapy is often overlooked. Therapy outcome seems to be frequently excluded from many workshop presentations by some of the most renowned names in the field. Articles reporting intervention strategies often substantiate the effectiveness of the techniques with only one or two case studies, if any supporting evidence at all is included. Hallway chatter during conferences and symposiums [sic] usually included some therapist proclaiming great success using a certain strategy or procedure. But

a simple question regarding the outcome evidence upon which he/she makes the proclamation often brings either a puzzled or annoyed look. Family therapists are also frequently heard to bemoan the lack of well controlled experimental studies investigating the comparative effects of different approaches with various populations and problems. What may be an even more alarming trend, however, is the apparent failure of many family therapists to collect any sort of evidence regarding the outcome of their work. . . . [They] may perceive the informal gathering of outcome evidence as unscientific, irrelevant, or just a complete waste of time. . . . This is obviously an attitude that will result in a great deal of ineffective family therapy being offered to the unsuspecting public and very little advancement in the development of creative interventions. . . . Therefore, outcome must be carefully assessed by all family therapists. (p. 8)*

Reduction to Testability

To be testable an approach needs to fulfill at least two independent guidelines: verifiability and accountability. The former deals with the process of therapy whereas the latter deals with its outcome. Each step of the approach needs to be checked as to whether it makes a difference in the process of therapy (verifiability), and the approach as a whole needs to be checked as to whether it produces the desired outcome (accountability). An approach could be verifiable but produce a poor outcome, whereas an unverifiable approach could produce remarkable results.

Verifiability also includes the concept of reductionism to the extent that each step in the process needs to be looked at and analyzed. Thus, verifiabilty is much more difficult to satisfy or fulfill than accountability. We have a variety of ways to measure outcome but we find it difficult (and expensive) to measure process. For instance, it is estimated that it takes 28 hours of raters' time to evaluate one hour of videotape of marital therapy! Costs, then, are important. The prerequisite of verifiability in turn implies two additional criteria: (a) fragmentation into component parts each of which can be (b) evaluated in its own rights in regard to making a significant difference to the process of change.

The SHWAs provided in the appendices make it relatively easy to test the present formulation. If, indeed, SHWAs derive from the theoretical models underlying them, their applications—to individuals, couples, and families —should bring about significant changes in them as compared with com-

---

*Published with the personal permission of the author and of the editor of *The Underground Railroad*, Steve De Shazer.

parable samples of clients who do not receive similar homework assignments. Of course, testing a theory is not as easy as the preceding seems to make it. Nevertheless, the question that can be verified is whether SHWAs produce significant changes in families who use them as compared with a control group or contrast groups who receive other, non-theory-derived HWAs. This will be an exciting development for the future.

Furthermore, to render valid any idea, concept, or notion, one must be able to subject it to scrutiny by individuals other than those who claim the validity of the concept under consideration. In other words, to be *verifiable*, a concept needs to be testable, or reducible to such a level of operationalization that it is *replicable* by someone other than the original claimant. It would be an understatement to say that the field of family therapy is replete with untestable ideas, concepts, and notions. Aside from the exemplary empirical contributions of Minuchin and his colleagues (Minuchin, Rosman, & Baker, 1978), Patterson and the Oregon Social Learning Project (Hansen & L'Abate, 1982), Alexander and his associates (Barton & Alexander, 1981), the McMaster project (Epstein & Bishop, 1981), and Stanton and his associates (Stanton, Todd, & associates, 1982) with families of drug addicts, very little research is being conducted on the testing of family therapy notions. Furthermore, most of the research cited deals with testing the global *outcome* of a particular theory or therapeutic approach.

We need, then, to distinguish two different notions of testability (Table 3–1). One refers to the *verification* of the theory regardless of its therapeutic outcome, the extent to which the theory is replicable. The other notion refers to the extent to which therapeutic outcome is related to the theory (rather than to any other factors). This kind of testability is here called *accountability*. The notions may overlap, but they are not the same. A theory may be extremely verifiable but produce very little outcome. By the same token, a theory might not be directly verifiable but produce significant therapeutic outcome.

Verification implies a fragmentation of the theory into components that can be verified one by one, such as the exercises in the appendices. *Accountability* implies a wholistic view that defies fragmentation. To be acceptable, a theory of family therapy needs to be verifiable and accountable (i.e., it must be replicable and must produce results).

Replicability implies a specificity that is not needed (or found) in the notion of accountability. A theory of therapy, even though vague and general, may conceivably produce many changes. By the same token, a very specific theory may not produce much change. Hence, both notions are necessary aspects of testability. In surveying and reviewing the field of family therapy theories (Hansen & L'Abate, 1982), one is struck by the large number of seductive, attractive, even beautiful, and interesting theories. When, however, one starts to use the criterion of testability as a necessary (but insufficient) way to evaluate a theory, a great many of these theories can fade away. They are either untestable because of the way they are stated, or they are so difficult (time consuming) and expensive to test that the result is the same: untestability.

DISCUSSION

This approach has at least five advantages: (a) it is easily reproducible and replicable; (b) it is eclectic, to the extent that this methodology can be repeated regardless of a particular viewpoint; (c) it minimizes (even though it cannot eliminate) the therapist's variability and effects; (d) it can be administered by relatively inexperienced intermediaries *under supervision*; and consequently (e) it is relatively inexpensive and downright *cheap*!

An implication of this approach, which will not be appreciated by most family therapists, is that other professionals (e.g., probation officers, family physicians) may be able to implement the use of SHWAs with a minimum of theoretical and technical preparation. This implication, of course, may have its positive and negative consequences. On the positive side, it may allow more professionals to start dealing with families without too much training and preparation. On the negative side, this lack of preparation may get unprepared professionals in trouble if they try to implement this approach during phase one of intervention rather than at phase two, where this approach is particularly useful, as discussed in the next chapter.

Another implication of this approach lies in its being possibly useful with nonclinical or with preclinical families. As our work with nonclinical volunteer undergraduate couples hopefully will demonstrate, even nonclinical couples do seem to get some benefit by applying tasks used in this approach.

A third implication of this approach may seem to decrease the role of the therapist, because of its emphasis on SHWAs. On the contrary, this possibility is far-fetched. This approach will supplement the therapist's role. The therapist will need to become more of a coach and less of a guru. One of the major uncontrollable sources of variance in psychotherapy research is the personality of the therapist (Garfield & Bergin, 1978; Gurman & Kniskern, 1981). Since such a source cannot be eliminated, perhaps its effects could be minimized. If it cannot be supplanted, then it could be supplemented by objectively measurable tasks that hopefully will work synergistically with the therapist's influence to increase the effectiveness of family therapy.

Another implication of this approach would be to "do" therapy *at a distance*. As frightening and distasteful as such a perspective may be at first blush, it should be noted that, at least experimentally, it is important to test whether the approach advocated here would work by itself with minimal personal intervention on the therapist's part. If it can be demonstrated that this approach is feasible, eventually it should be added to the therapist's influence, provided that the influence is positive. Related to this issue, the therapist also needs to consider the criterion of *expense*. Can the approach be easily administered so that it will not cost a great deal of the therapist's time and the family's money? This issue may not seem important to many family therapists. It is important, however, if we want to make family therapy available to as many families as may need it.

CONCLUSION

A systematic approach such as the one submitted here does not mean that perfection is being reached. Far from it. This is a critical attempt to bring some order and some semblance of sanity to an otherwise chaotic and disordered field. Testing this approach will take more than rhetoric and personal opinions. This approach is neither as cut-and-dried nor as simple as it may appear at first blush. However, it is testable, and it can be used with both functional and dysfunctional families (the latter only after the initial crucial phase has been successfully resolved, as explained in the next chapter).

It is easily predictable that this approach, with its emphasis on testability and generalization, will meet angry reactions from many family therapists. Nevertheless, it does make for easy and inexpensive research for a therapist so inclined or for graduate students looking for a researchable approach in family therapy.

Chapter 4

Stages of Family Therapy

As noted in the previous three chapters, a systematic approach implies that three requirements need to be fulfilled here: (a) sequential plans of family therapy, accompanied by (b) an eclectic classification of behaviors (Chapter 2), coupled with (c) an empirical methodology that makes the whole approach *testable* (Chapter 3). One area of family therapy that has not received sufficiently systematic attention is concerned with the various stages of the process of family therapy that takes place sequentially in the case of most families who want and need professional help.

The purpose of this chapter is to consider that the process of family therapy can be broken down into at least four major stages, each of which may have various phases within each stage (Table 4–1).

FIRST STAGE: STRESS REDUCTION

The purposes of the initial stage are multiple: (a) to make contact and establish trust and confidence, (b) to help reduce conflict and stress, (c) to solve or resolve a crisis, and (d) to reduce the symptomatic behavior to controllable or bearable proportions. This stage in many ways is where circular, individualized problem solving is necesary. It may last one session or up to 10 and more. Many family therapists (Haley, 1976; Selvini-Palazzoli, Boscolo, Cecchin, & Prata, 1978) conceive of this stage as being therapy and often consider symptom reduction as the goal of therapy, with nothing else added.

Because of its individualized nature, it is almost impossible to perform research at this stage. At this stage, symptom reduction and relief is the major goal. It is important to reduce the level of emotionality, acting out, or whatever behavior that brings the family in for help. At this stage one can

use whatever structurally concrete (physical arrangements, routine responsibilities, etc.), linear, circular, or metaphorical interventions may be necessary,
as will be discussed in greater detail in Section II.

At this stage it is important to emphasize activity, both for the therapist's
sake as well as for the family's. As Stahmann & Harper (1982) noted: "Our
business is to activate people. The therapist needs to instigate action that
creates behavior. Sometimes the therapist needs to be intrusive" (p. 196).
Quoting studies that support the need for activity, Stahmann and Harper
added:

> It appears that when the marital therapist is active, clients are more
> satisfied with therapy and tend to continue until their goals are
> reached. However, it is important that the therapist not confront
> tenuous family defenses too early in treatment. (p. 196)

Furthermore:

> The requirement that a family therapist be active opens up oppor-
> tunities to her or him to lay ground rules as to how the system and

Table 4–1
STAGES IN THE PROCESS OF FAMILY THERAPY

Stages	Major Therapeutic Emphases	Interventional Modality	Task Assignments

1. Engagement	Crisis resolution
	Symptomatic relief
	Relationship
	   building
		Contextual activities
		"Change" Activity
		Past issues
			Prescriptions of
			   symptoms
			Individualized
			   homework
			Depression SHWAs
			Appendix A

2. Skill training	Negotiation learning Emotional give and take	Rationality "growth" Present issues	Negotiation SHWAs Appendix B

3. Termination	Resolution of
	   unfinished
	   business
	Intimacy issues
	Loss and leaving
		Emotionality
		   "being"
		Future issues
			Intimacy SHWAs
			Appendix C

4. Follow-up	Maintenance of gains
	Spread to other
	   positive behaviors
		Multiple modalities	Checkups and
			   evidence of
			   improvements
			Appendix D

therapist will proceed. How the system responds to this structuring yields diagnostic information about the willingness and capacity of the family or couple to adapt to change. . . . The activity level of the therapist has a great deal of influence over the kind of relationship the family and the therapist develop. This kind of relationship where the therapist is active is central to the eventual outcome of therapy, as empirical studies cited later on in this chapter demonstrate. (pp. 198–199)

The importance of activity is not only relegated to the therapist. It is just as important for families to have something to do and to hang on to. There is indeed the expectation of magic, i.e., what Andolfi (1979) has called the double bind of "Change him/her but don't change us." Change the identified patient or symptom but do not change the system. Consequently, by forcing some activity on the part of the family, a therapist can gauge how cooperative or resistant a family is and can act accordingly. As discussed further in Section II, the therapist may assign some paradoxical task that will deal with the resistance, including its prescription: "For the time being, please continue doing what you have been doing. . . . It is too early at this time to try to change things. . . . I am not sure whether this family can take change."

SECOND STAGE: SKILL TRAINING AND EDUCATION

Scheflen (1981) in his last work commented on this issue in regard to families of schizophrenics. However, his comments could be applied to all families.

> I think it is imperative that we develop methods to *teach* interaction skills and linear abilities. We must learn to develop them and employ them directly and rapidly in all instances of schizophrenia before and between psychotic episodes. We must extend the principles of vocational rehabilitation. *We must not only teach physical tasks but interactional ones as well* [emphasis mine]. (pp. 159–160)

At this stage Alexander and Parsons (1982) recommend the use of linear interpersonal tasks that are (a) designed to provide an immediate sense of relief or pleasure for each family member involved; (b) so assigned to assure reciprocal payoffs among the members; (c) clearly and thoroughly explained before the family leaves the session; (d) kept simple enough to ensure success; (e) made relevant to the experience of the family; (f) easy to accept and that do not attempt to force a view of reality not shared by the family; (g) relevant for the fulfillment of both personal and familial goals; (h) graduated in complexity;

and (i) followed up routinely by the therapist. Because of its importance to the present formulation, this stage will be considered in some detail.

At this stage, provided the crisis or reason for referral has subsided or become secondary to the concerns of the family, abrupt or circular changes may no longer be necessary. Learning to negotiate conflict and acquiring skills that will help the family for the long haul may be crucial. Hence the concept of change as considered in the previous stage may not be useful. A more gradual, stepwise, incremental "growth" seems more appropriate. From initial leaps and jumps the family may need to learn to walk, and in some cases crawl! The point here is one of skill acquisition, a process that does not take place overnight.

The Homework Assignment as the Unit of Change in Family Therapy

The homework assignment is defined as the smallest (contrived) unit in which the family can interact. It may consist of a verbal ("Keep on talking while I am gone") or a nonverbal ("Divide all the loose change among yourselves") task. It may be a one-shot deal, or it may be repeated indefinitely. It can vary on many other dimensions, such as specificity-generality, concreteness-abstraction. Its purpose is to let the whole family interaction take place within the context of "practice," that is, practicing, or repeating, new behaviors until an optimum level, or criterion, of performance is achieved.

The best analogy is diet. If one wants to lose weight, one has to diet, or pay attention to food, every day, not now-and-then or hit-or-miss. If one wants to lose weight, attention must be paid to details of diet, exercise, and intake on a regular basis. By the same token, if one wants to improve physical stamina, one needs to assess oxygen intake, strength of limbs, flexibility, resistance, etc., to establish a baseline. After the baseline has been established, an ideal criterion based on norms can be established. One needs to practice to reach that criterion, repeating the behavior, no matter how many times, to reach the desired level.

An analogy closer to family therapy lies in the field of sex therapy, during which clients have to practice new skills at home, not in the therapist's office. Only through practice can one hope to change and maintain change over time. Without practice, it is doubtful whether any lasting change can take place. The Systematic Homework Assignments (SHWAs) in the appendices are easy enough for most families but difficult enough that mastering them requires a great deal of effort, problem solving, and practice.

Requirements for Homework assignments (HWAs). To assign exercises for families to practice, one needs to keep in mind certain requirements.

1) *HWAs should be easy* for most family members, applicable from a mental age of approximately 10 and up, and at most levels of functionality.

2) *HWAs should teach something new* to the family so that family members learn new ways of thinking and relating.

3) *HWAs should be progressively more complex*, going from the simplest to the most complex.

4) *HWAs should be relevant to the business of the family*; that is, they should deal with issues in such a way that families will recognize the exercises as relevant to how they feel, think, and relate.

5) *HWAs should be graduated in a natural sequence* that encompasses all the preceding points.

With these requirements in mind in the construction of HWAs, one can administer to families the SHWAs found in the appendices on a sequential basis. Exceptions can and should be made on the basis of specific issues in the course of therapy. All the SHWAs can be practiced by the family both in the office (mostly for diagnostic and demonstrative purposes) or at home (as homework assignments). As the reader will see, these SHWAs derive directly from the models presented in the next three sections. The value of models, as already noted, in addition to clarifying theories, is to link theory with practice. In fact, each model is tested through the practice of SHWAs.

Systematic Homework Assignments

Most homework assignments described in recent reviews of the field (Levant, 1984; Nichols, 1984) are administered either *ad hoc*, that is, to deal with a specific situation, or haphazardly, that is, *impromptu*, unsystematically; that is, they do not follow or derive from theory or any clinical or practical principles. Even when homework assignments are consistently used, as in the case of Phillips and Corsini (1982), for example, the relationship between theory and homework assignments seems tenuous, flimsy, or ill defined. It is the purpose of this approach to use homework assignments systematically to test the theory behind them and to administer them in a consistently sequential fashion (Appendices A, B, and C).

Systematic homework assignments are the vehicle through which the models presented here (Sections II, III, and IV) are tested dynamically, as process. In addition to testing these models, SHWAs have two major functions: (a) to increase generalization from the office to the home by learning to negotiate *without* the therapist's help, and (b) to increase the efficiency of the therapeutic process; the more these couples or families can learn at home on their own, the less time they need to spend at the office.

These SHWAs have been administered on an experimental basis to many couples and some families. The results of this research will be published elsewhere (Lutz & L'Abate, research in progress). Thus far, however, on the basis of the feedback received from both clinical and nonclinical couples and families, the following conclusions seem in order: (a) SHWAs should be assigned only after the initial crisis stage is successfully passed and the family is willing and able to learn more about negotiating with each other; (b) in some instances these SHWAs seem to succeed when other approaches seem to fail; (c) couples report being able to talk more on topics unrelated to the homework; (d) couples found it useful to discover terms that describe patterns that they were unaware of but for which they lacked appropriate terms; (e) sometimes SHWAs were useful in getting some couples unstuck from an impasse; (f) in at least one instance, where the husband was unwilling to come in for therapy, he was able to cooperate with the wife at home with the SHWAs and was actually enthusiastic about them. All in all thus far, we have found SHWAs to be an important tool in the process of therapy. This impressionistic finding needs to be bolstered by evidence.

THIRD STAGE: ISSUES OF TERMINATION

The third stage of therapy, termination, is to deal with unfinished business. One of the major goals of this stage is to deal with issues that have not been dealt with in earlier stages, among them the issue of intimacy. If issues of intimacy have not been dealt with adequately, the family lets the therapist know well enough through continuation of symptomatic behavior, complaints of dissatisfaction, inability or unwillingness to complete SHWAs, etc. This termination stage needs to be planned with the same care as the previous two stages. At this stage issues of separation, loss, dependency, individuation, and loneliness need to be checked out and dealt with both linearly and paradoxically if necessary (Section IV).

At this third and semifinal stage, the family may be ready to confront the most terrifying, frightening experience of their lives: intimacy. However, if the therapists' persuasions and biases (or defenses) have not allowed him/her to deal with this issue in their personal lives, it may be very difficult for this therapist to come to terms with issues of intimacy in the lives of families he/she wants to help. Countless therapists are as afraid of intimacy as families are!

FOURTH PHASE: FOLLOW-UP

This phase should become an intrinsic part of all forms of psychotherapy. Has the treatment done any good? Was the therapy a success, a failure, or something in between? What else does the family need? If a baseline was established at the beginning of treatment, how different from that baseline is the family now? What criteria are used to evaluate follow-up that are subjective and objective, internal and external to the *treatment* (Section V)?

DISCUSSION

Epstein and Bishop (1981) also considered four stages of family therapy consisting of (a) assessment (orientation, data gathering, problem description, clarification, and agreement on a problem list); (b) contracting (orientation, outlining options, negotiation expectations, and contract signing); (c) treatment (orientation, clarifying priorities, setting tasks, and task evaluation); and (d) closure (orientation, summary of treatment, long-term goals, and follow-up). Epstein and Bishop also represent a small group of therapists who pay attention to the importance of feelings in the process of treatment. Even though feelings need to be considered throughout the whole process of therapy, eventually they need to be confronted squarely in the third stage of treatment when the family is facing the loss (or abandonment) of the therapist, facing up to issues of mourning, grieving, and hurt.

In addition to the work of Epstein and Bishop (1981), there have been at least three other contributions to a staged view of family therapy processes. Freeman (1976) was one of the earliest contributors to a view of family therapy according to three distinct phases: (a) redefining the problem, (b) working through, and (c) terminating and letting go.

Frey (1984) more recently divided the process of therapy according to six stages, each involving associated therapist tasks. In the first stage, *referral*, the therapist deals with the initial phone call, convenes the family, and joins with the referring person. In the second stage, *joining*, the therapist needs to handle resistance, establish trust, track beliefs and perceptions, and validate family members' experiences. In the third stage, *restructuring*, the therapist increases the stress level, challenges hierarchical reversals, strengthens the parental subsystem, and pushes the family into new patterns. In the fourth stage, *consolidation*, the therapist supports parental unity, emphasizes appropriate sequences, mobilizes social network, and reduces stress. In the fifth stage, *termination*, the therapist decreases contact with family, predicts relapses, contacts the referring source, continues working with the social network of the family, and recommends individual therapy if appropriate. In the final, sixth stage, *follow-up*, the therapist reassures and supports the family, is available for crises, and assesses the outcome of therapy.

Warburton and Alexander (1985) instead divide the process of family therapy into five phases. The first phase, introduction/impression, has the goal of reinforcing the family's expectation of great changes. The therapist needs to establish credibility. In the second phase, assessment/understanding, the therapist needs to clarify what the change parameters are and needs to elicit the latent or evident structure of the family. In the third phase, induction/therapy, the goal is to produce a context for change, with the therapist becoming more directive than s/he may have been thus far. In the fourth phase, treatment/education, the goal is to produce change through linear directives.

In the fifth and final phase, generalization/termination, the goal is to maintain change and to disengage from the family.

Two important points need consideration in reviewing the authors who have contributed to a staged view of family therapy process. First, none of these authors indicates how long each stage or phase will take. Second, most of these phases imply or involve a brief therapy perspective that is mostly concerned with the short-term goal of immediate stress or symptom reduction without any concern for the family's welfare over the long haul. Only Warburton and Alexander consider a stage of education that would be equivalent to the second stage of negotiation in the present formulation. Most of the other stages, except of course, termination, would all be included into a first stage of engagement and stress reduction.

Among the many unsubstantiated myths and shibboleths of short-term therapy (Fisch, Weakland, & Segal, 1982), there is one of a "positive spiral" being instigated that eventually will produce more changes in addition to those already obtained. Yet, not one ounce of evidence is presented (Selvini-Palazzoli, Boscolo, Cecchin, & Prata, 1978) to support such a contention. We lack comparative baseline data on families treated, and there is no follow-up evidence to document objectively whether the claimed changes and "positive spirals" have indeed taken place. A therapist's or group of therapists' subjective claims are taken as "evidence," and no demands are made for empirical evidence to support claims! In fact, to ask for evidence seems to put whoever asks in the minority position, tacitly relegated to a corner for those who are not "in," implying paranoia, rigidity, and, worst, traditionalism. To ask for some degree of objectivism, for evidence external to the personal opinions of the therapist, is tantamount to mutiny and treason, punishable by scorn and rejection. Is this the point the family therapy field has reached or is this a figment of the writer's overactive imagination?

To relate these stages to theory (L'Abate, 1976), the first stage, symptom and stress reduction (Table 4–1), needs to deal with the self-presentational level of the family and its resistance (i.e., "We would be a great all-American family if it weren't for . . ."). As noted (Table 4–1), this stage can be dealt with mostly through *activity*, that is, activity on the part of the therapist and activity on the part of the family. The second stage, requiring *rationality*, would be theoretically equivalent to the phenotypical level of how the family conducts its business inside the home and without the pressure of public scrutiny. The underlying structural determinants dealing with *emotionality* would represent what L'Abate has called the genotype, whereas the *historical* determinants would represent the explanatory level together with genotypical determinants. Emotionality, the genotype of a family, is determined by historical determinants. The self-presentational and phenotypical levels would represent description, whereas genotypical and phenotypical levels would represent explanation.

CONCLUSION

In the present formulation, a sequential process of family therapy, divided into four distinct and separate stages, involves different therapeutic emphases, different interventional modalities, and different tasks or homework assignments. The first stage of family therapy will be considered in greater detail in the next section.

The First Stage: Crisis Intervention and Symptom Reduction

Chapter 5

The Tenets of Paradoxical Psychotherapy

The bee fertilizes the flower it robs.
When it's dark enough you can see the stars.

Charles Beard

From the outset we need to distinguish between two different but related sets of tenets. The first set deals with the paradoxes of human existence. The second set deals with pragmatic paradoxes or the paradoxes used for therapeutic purposes. One could subscribe or accept a paradoxical view of reality without having to use it in psychotherapy. By the same token, even though it may seem unconceivable, a therapist could use pragmatic paradoxes without knowledge or acceptance of a paradoxical view of reality.

THE PARADOXES OF HUMAN EXISTENCE

The safest assumption one can make about human existence is its variability. We are so variable, both intraindividually and interindividually, that from this variability one can derive two truisms about human nature: (a) one person's trash is another person's treasure, and (b) one person's assets can also be his/her liabilities. From these two truisms one can build on a paradoxical view of human existence and reality that is based on the derivation that, given such variability, each of us as individuals can behave contradictorily; that is, we are inconsistent in how we believe and behave verbally and nonverbally. Intraindividually we can be inconsistent and therefore contradict ourselves verbally and nonverbally, by saying something and doing something else. In addition to this intraindividual variability, we also contradict other human beings, especially other family members. Consequently, contradiction, born from our inherent variability, is the very characteristic that makes us humans rather than machines.

A paradoxical view of human nature and behavior cannot be separated from a dialectical view. Consequently, a great part of this chapter will deal with the importance of a dialectical view as part of a paradoxical perspective. In addition to a dialectical view, one would need to consider a transactional or systemic viewpoint (Hansen & L'Abate, 1982; Weeks & L'Abate, 1982) that can be found elsewhere and will not be considered here. It is difficult for this writer to separate a paradoxical from a dialectical view. Consequently, even though both views are considered separately for the purposes of exposition, their overlap will become evident in the course of this chapter. Previous feeble and incomplete attempts (L'Abate, 1976) to develop a metatheoretical position for the delivery of paradoxical injunctions have been insufficient in explaining their bases.

THEORY AND METATHEORY

It is important, for the purposes of the present discussion, to differentiate between theory and metatheory. Theory is a definite assemblage of assumptions from which postulates and models are derived. Metatheory is whatever assumption is made which is not really part of a theory but which nevertheless may color or influence the theory in some fashion: it goes beyond the theory. For instance, in previous examples at theory building (L'Abate, 1964, 1976, 1983d, 1985) a dialectical position was vaguely presented. Yet, it was never part of the theory proper, in spite of the fact that it entered in the exposition of at least one postulate of the theory (L'Abate, 1976).

Paradox: The Inherent Contradiction of Behavior

Most of us emphasize and reach for the stable, consistent, logical, and predictable aspects of human behavior. This position has been defended on the basis of the need for repeatable patterns of behavior as a basis for scientific study. This emphasis has been going on, and it will go on hopefully as one way of dealing with and making sense of behavior.

Another way of conceptualizing behavior, on the other hand, is to look at its inherent contradiction, not as polar opposites, as an engineering approach would lead us to believe, but as coexistent aspects of human nature; that is, we have the ability to be anxious and nonanxious at the same time, smart and stupid at the same time. How? Well, each of us has the capacity to be anxious about some particular aspect of our life and nonanxious about others. The issue is not one of describing us as anxious or not, but of specifying the conditions under which we are or are not anxious. As far as intelligence goes, even an individual who is extremely smart in one area can be or appear to be incompetent in other areas or at a given point in time.

The requirement of being predictable, stable, consistent, and free of contradiction laid on ourselves is not only false to the nature of human nature, but is a demand for sameness and conformity toward a mythical norm that can only dehumanize us. We are consistent and inconsistent, predictable and unpredictable, stable and unstable all at the same time: interpretation depends strictly on the time and context of observation as well as the biases of the observer himself. Contradiction is a human quality represented by incompatibility, incongruence, and inconsistency. These qualities represent the seeds of insecurity, craziness, and madness. Yet, it is the quality of going and being crazy that separates the human from the nonhuman. As human beings, we are vulnerable, variable, and contradictory. Consequently, it is the paradox of human life that the very behaviors that define us as "crazy" affirm, at the same time, our humanity. We are vulnerable, fallible human beings, not robots.

Of course, no one comprehended best the paradoxical nature of human nature than Jesus Christ in his Sermon on the Mount. Unless such a paradox is personally experienced, it is difficult to put it into words that may feel trite in comparison. Essentially, this paradox can be best conveyed through the known and repeated truism of "one person's trash is another person's treasure." Our life is what we make it, depending on how each of us wants to live it.

Hughes and Brecht (1975), in addition to a complete bibliography of literature on logical and visual paradoxes, described a logical paradox as consisting of three components: (a) self-reference, (b) contradiction, and (c) a vicious circle. Self-reference refers to the specification of location of the paradox being present in situ and nowhere else. Contradiction is any statement or proposition that is at variance with itself. "Please ignore this sign" represents a combination of self-reference and contradiction. (Incidentally, what is here called contradiction is referred to in psychoanalytic jargon as *ambivalence*, or the contemporaneous presence of two seemingly opposing feelings, e.g., love and hate.) The third component of a paradox is *vicious circularity*: the respondent is sent back to the sign and is unable to break away from the internal inconsistency of the paradox.

These three characteristics of a paradox are very important because very likely they are a clue to whatever human nature is. In information-processing terms, a paradox becomes as much of a closed feedback loop as one can find in logic. It does not allow one to get away from it through a solution. There is no solution, and whoever wants to solve it cannot win under any conditions. Thus, the attempted solution to the human paradox can only be solved by admitting our defeat and inability to solve this riddle. If we ever admit to our failure and defeat, we may be able to accept human nature for what it is, trying to deal with it according to its own paradoxical nature.

To solve the vicious circularity of self-referent contradictions, we need to look at the premises established and to the outcome obtained. When paradoxes are present, there is no growth or change possible, because of the closed feedback loop of the paradox. The only way to solve it is to think and act paradoxically, moving away from the paradox itself and considering it in its immediate context of antecedents and consequences. As Watzlawick et al. (1974) indicated, "paradox plays as important a role in problem resolution as it plays in problem formation."

THE COEXISTENCE OF OPPOSITES

One paradox of behavior that needs reflection is that we are strong when we admit our weaknesses and are weak when we deny them. For instance, in proclaiming our not needing any help, because of our presumed perfection or normality, we are subjugating ourselves to an immediate questioning of our defensiveness and our need to avoid being different. The one who "doth protest too much" is the one who becomes a source of wonder and questioning. We are at our strongest point when we can face and admit our inherent fallibility, humanness, and imperfection. The claim of normality and perfection puts us in a position of being inhuman, since no individual can be so healthy or so perfect. Admission of our weakness and failures is tantamount to an admission of our fallibility as human beings. In so doing, the seemingly weak individual is strong by facing a reality that is denied by the so-called "strong" individual.

Of course, many of the positions we take derive from cultural stereotypes that have been incorporated by an engineering approach to behavior. We have stereotypes for how strong, independent individuals behave and how weak, dependent individuals behave. We have stereotypes of masculine and feminine roles, normal and abnormal behavior, deviant or conforming norms and groups, etc. ("Strong men don't cry!") By the use of a statistical frequency distribution, dear to the heart of an engineering approach, we can place each of us on any dimension we want on the basis of measures and scores. From these measures and correlates we derive stereotypes and classifications that make sense of mythical human beings. Some good may exist in such an approach for a variety of institutional purposes. Yet, this approach falls flat on its face in applying it without contextual and situational factors that cannot be accounted for by such an approach.

A paradoxical view allows for coexistence of seemingly opposite characteristics in the same individual even at the same time, a position that would be characterized as nonsensical (or worse) from an engineering viewpoint. Yet, this approach need not see this view as antithetical to itself. A paradoxical view allows for relativity of effort, since it is aware of the multiplicity of routes available to us to reach the same goals.

Emphasis on polar opposites or antonyms stems from logical and methodological reasons that help us make sense of behavior. Yet, procedures and practices stemming from them lead us into normative generalizations that are false to behavior as seen paradoxically. What may not exist in logic—A and non-A—may indeed coexist in human behavior! We can be charitable and brutal, consistent and inconsistent, weak and strong, lazy and hard working all at the same time.

The application of logical principles essentially destroys the inherent illogicality of human behavior. Our attempts to make behavior logical and rational and make it fit into rigid verbal classes or polar extremes have put us in conceptual boxes and methodological cages that are not getting us anywhere. This criticism in no way should be taken as a dismissal of the logical and empirical approach. On the contrary, this approach is recognized as an important step in the course of evolution. Now that we are becoming aware of its shortcomings, we can use it gingerly and with a full awareness of its relative limitations inherent in any single view of behavior.

Hence, a paradoxical view of behavior tends to emphasize those aspects that have been either ignored, denied, or belittled by traditional "scientific" views. As such, it should be violently attacked and criticized by whoever subscribes to an engineering view of behavior. One of the major shortcomings of such a view lies not only in the insistence on the dimensionality and predictability of behavior but also on its finity and comprehensibility. A paradoxical view does not need to deny such a position. It only wants to consider alternatives not available otherwise. Another shortcoming of traditional engineering approaches has been the almost complete denial, in thought and action, of context as an important determinant of behavior that may help us understand what would otherwise be explained away as variability, variance, error, and randomness. It is the essential variability and inconsistency of behavior that attracts a paradoxical view.

LINEAR VERSUS CIRCULAR MODELS

A linear view of behavior assumes a gradual, step-by-step progression or decrease, such as is assumed in rote learning. A paradoxical view assumes a circular, quantum jump where no progression is relevant. Information processing assumes a feedback loop that in its circularity may allow for linear as well as nonlinear discontinuous jumps. When such circularity is applied to multiperson systems, like the family, the simplistic irrelevance of a linear view breaks down. It is impossible to handle all the complex permutations and combinations of simultaneous information processings present in everyday family life through the linear view of the laboratory. Furthermore, a circular model need not be antagonistic to linearity, since it can encompass it easily. In other words, linearity *may* take place within the context of circularity.

A linear view of behavior sees opposite polarities as mutually exclusive in describing any individual except for specifying different areas ("smart in math and dumb in English"). A paradoxical view of behavior can allow us to describe ourselves, even in the same dimension, as being at the same time both polar opposites ("smart and dumb").

In considering mechanistic and organismic linear models, Looft (1973) noted:

> The mechanistic and organismic models have been useful and have generated a vast amount of theoretical and empirical activity (and hopefully, understanding, too). Unfortunately, their historicity resides only within the persons who operate within them, they are historical in that they do not take into account the changes that have occurred in the milieus in which human beings develop. (p. 30)

On the basis of his review of the shortcomings of mechanical and organismic models, Looft proposed an alternative model that

> . . . admits to a new view of reality, one that perceives human social and mental development as the confluence of many interrelated and changing systems and subsystems, including the biological, social and cultural, and historical. The new paradigm may be given a number of different appellations by different proponents, including "rational," "general system theory," "interactional," "dialectic," or "transformational," but all of these titles imply that the model's unifying theme is *relations*; material, elemental, and organismic aspects are of secondary importance. (p. 31)

Of course, as Looft noted, this model is much more complex and methodologically more difficult than previous models. However, being aware of the complexity of the tasks allows us to be aware also of the methodological simplicity and relativity of previous linear models. But, as Looft concluded:

> The mechanistic and the organismic models of man may have served us well in the past, but our changing human needs demand a new model to guide our future activities. (p. 48)

The paradoxical stance contrasts and clashes with an engineering, physical science approach. Whereby the latter sees linearity or unilinearity and logic in behavior, assuming continuous dimensions, the paradoxical approach is unable (or unwilling) to see life and behavior according to extremities and dimensions. For instance, given a construct like anxiety, that can be operationalized into a dimension and a frequency distribution whereby individuals are then categorized at the extremes and at the middle of this distribution. From this distribution evaluative labels are derived (high-low anxiety, and so forth).

A paradoxical stance, although inclusive of such an effort, is also aware of its relativity in the sense that most of us vary in the level of anxiety we experience and most of us vary in the way we cope with and express such an anxiety. Such variability is related to individual as well as to situational characteristics that in no way can be encompassed by an engineering approach.

Furthermore, a paradoxical stance would avoid the dichotomy that derives from such a dimension in which high or low states of anxiety are related to either positive or negative correlates, traits, and dimensions. A paradoxical stance would be more appreciative of variability, vulnerability, and seeming inconsistencies than of stability, predictability, and consistencies of human behavior. It would not reject an engineering approach outright, because some good may be derived from it. In other words, seeing behavior as a paradox does not imply a nihilistic view of it. On the contrary, any positive approach to an understanding of behavior is considered. However, it needs to be considered on the basis of its *relativity* and of its *multiplicity* of alternative explanations and routes available to us.

Another way of viewing behavior is to consider that what seems to us as opposites may well represent two different interpretations of behavior which we, stuffed into our verbal cages (Rapaport, 1950, 1954), tend to dichotomize unduly. An acknowledgment of the limitations, relativity, and imperfection of our verbal labels is necessary *a priori* to understand how we think and how we misperceive.

Relativity and Multiplicity

A paradoxical view of life entails becoming aware of the relativity of our attributions and labels to describe behavior and of the multiplicity of interpretations available to us to make sense of that behavior. By the same token, this stance allows us to face the equipotentiality and equifinality of any behavior; that is, at the same time behavior can be "caused" by a variety of antecedents and the same antecedents of "causes" can have different outcomes. A paradoxical approach allows appreciation of a diversity of viewpoints and of the rewards of a pluralistic view of which eclecticism is one aspect.

POSITIVISM: AN ADJUNCT TO PARADOX

By positivism in this formulation is not meant the view of reality as a finite, unanalyzable whole. On the contrary, by positivism is meant a view closer to the philosophical position known as scientific materialism that asserts the infinite and inexhaustible nature of reality. In fact, as Bunge (1959) indicated, such a philosophical view puts limits and atomic units to reality to the point of being often called "negativism." Such a positivistic epistemology has been critically evaluated by Rickert (1962) and Popper (1959). In this formulation, by positivism is meant an approach based on seeing costs and rewards in any process, maximizing rewards, minimizing costs, and specifying the nature of reward/costs ratios. As such, it may be quite different from its synonymous philosophical position. In fact, it would be quite at odds with it.

As previously noted, another way of experiencing a paradoxical view is through an understanding of the relativity of our labels and the appreciation of multiple interpretations that any behavior can elicit. Both relativity and multiplicity of interpretations lead us into the paradox that we have choices in how we select our labels as well as our interpretations. Selection of words will be determined by our own views and perceptions of our reality. Consequently, we can choose between two seemingly opposite terms if we were to accept verbal dichotomies as representing reality (which, of course, they do not). If we do, then we can choose between positive and negative labels.

The choice of which labels and attributions to use is absolutely ours. We choose, for instance, to use positive versus negative labels. Furthermore, even in front of a seemingly negative act or event, we can choose to interpret it in positive terms. For instance, the simple perceptual act of calling a glass with 50% water "empty" or "full" is a choice that in many ways can be made in labeling behavior. When this paradoxical view is used to interpret behavior, it can guide us to consider behavior as having assets and liabilities in which a liability can be turned into an asset and an asset can be turned into a liability. Kanouse and Hanson (1971) described a "negativity bias" whereby we tend to more frequently evaluate good and bad characteristics according to "bad" more than good. Among the various explanations for such a bias, Kanouse and Hanson suggested the possibility that "life outcomes may be distributed 'automatically'," that is, "with more negative than positive outcomes than we would like to believe."

The Costs of Negative Labeling and Attributions

One of the major costs of negative labeling is psychopathology. The pervasive effect of negative labeling as present in parents vis-à-vis their children and husbands and wives in wrecking their marriages is only matched by the same kind of practices in mental health services. Negative labeling usually equates behavior performance with personality and uses emphasis on deficits rather than assets. Consider the classification of exceptional children in special education. A child without sight becomes a "blind" child. A child with low IQ scores on certain intelligence tests becomes "retarded." The child as an individual disappears in front of labels that fail to describe him and his assets. Only the deficit is considered, and the child becomes the deficit (L'Abate & Curtis, 1975).

In mental health practices, not only do negative labels abound to classify individuals according to their liabilities, but even the process of helping them has become distorted by the use of negative labels. For instance, individuals are accepted into psychotherapy because they are "neurotic," "anxious," "dependent," etc. The remote possibility that individuals seeking help may be pretty healthy and strong individuals is not even considered. Yet, most psychotherapy studies indicate the best outcome with individuals who approach normality in a variety of dimensions. No wonder mental health clinics find that motivation for psychotherapy is low! How long can anyone take negative labeling in diagnosis and treatment? It takes pretty strong individuals to withstand that process!

The costs of negative labeling on personality development, as seen in parental child-raising practices and human relations, are untold. No wonder behavior modification became such a successful fad! It came out of a context characterized by negative practices in homes, schools, and institutions. Unfortunately, even behavior modification is still unable to separate performance from personality and from learning.

The Rewards of Positive Labeling and Attributions

Positive labeling and paradoxical positivism do not need to be seen as wishy-washy pollyanna-ish attempts at denial of destructive characteristics of life. On the contrary, positive labeling means putting emphasis on assets, minimizing liabilities, and interpreting them within a context of relativity and multiplicity of practices whereby a liability can be transformed into an asset and vice versa. The daily papers are a good source of amazing feats that physically handicapped individuals perform to prove the point that a deficit need not be a handicap and that a liability can be turned into an asset; remember the case of the last man in the West Point graduating class who used his low standing to collect a dollar from everybody in higher standing than him?

Hence, positive labeling allows emphasis on assets and positive reframing of the imputed or assumed liability in terms of paradoxical reinterpretation; i.e., the oppressor is also the oppressed, the murderer is also the victim. Cherished, cultural clichés can be challenged and disputed; for example,

"Strong men don't cry" can be rephrased as "Weak men don't cry. Strong men do. I cry; therefore, I am a strong man." The same rephrasing can be applied to people who seek help: "It takes a strong person to ask for help." "How many other people out there suffer like you do, but they are not asking for help?"

Positive labeling, therefore, requires a paradoxical view of human nature that allows us to see our strengths as weaknesses and our weaknesses as strengths. It requires a conceptual and emotional change in our habits and attitudes. It gives us the ability to accept the possibility that no sense at all may be present. It gives us the possibility of giving positive meaning to what may appear a negative and senseless reality. Its major weakness may lie in its grandiose encompassibility and the fact that its claimed strengths may be its liabilities. If it is a victim of its own machinations, it accepts its role as its own victimizer!

Paradox and Change

Change, growth, and differentiation are based on our becoming aware of our inherent contradictions. Facing those contradictions allows us to go beyond and past them. Without confrontation of such contradictions we would remain stagnant. Facing the contradictions of family systems allows us to look at ourselves and change our behavior. Since contradictions are part of variability and variability is directly related to dysfunctionality, by decreasing our variability, we are reducing our dysfunctionality.

Implications. From the preceding it follows that paradoxical positivism tends to avoid rigidity and inflexibility of procedures, at either the evaluative or interventional level. By its very inclusiveness it allows us to put together methods and techniques from seemingly disparate viewpoints. Hence, any reasonably valid, professionally defensible technique becomes admissible, as long as its conclusion is based on *informed, critical, and provisionary bases.* No one should feel bound to encourage any technique based on questionable theoretical or empirical grounds (L'Abate, 1973b).

Since responsibility has greater eventual returns than irresponsibility, a paradoxical positivism would emphasize responsible practices to the point that accountability, cost analysis, and effectiveness in human applications would go without saying. An awareness of feedback on system change is acknowledged as being part of the need to evaluate, reevaluate, and change on the basis of repeated feedback. Hence, this viewpoint would support any form of reasonable accountability that would enhance and improve the quality of human services.

The awareness of the relativity of our labels and of the multiplicity of interpretations (and explanations) available to us allows one to avoid becoming involved in matters of invidious comparison of any viewpoint or method. By seeing the good in each viewpoint and method, it allows a more eclectic stance than would be possible otherwise.

Clearly, a positivistic viewpoint is also closely allied to pragmatism, adding to the sentence "It works" also "It works well under such and such conditions. However, it isn't so hot under such and such conditions." Awareness of relativity leading to a probabilistic stance forces one to be much more specific and even less grandiose than would be possible otherwise.

Consequently, it is possible to relate the dialectics of paradoxical positivism to a multiplicity of solutions in which the *plurality* or *multiplicity* of available solutions needs to be matched by *specificity* of the conditions under which conditions of one particular solution will work better or worse than others. With such a proviso, the seeming amorphousness and vagueness of paradoxical positivism becomes even more specific than other viewpoints.

For every positive there is a negative and vice versa. Consequently, it is possible to reformulate human existence in positive rather than negative terms. This is a choice we make once we become aware of the relativity of any interpretations available to us. However, once we are faced by a positive we do not need to juxtapose it with a negative. We can let the positive stand and juxtapose a negative with a positive alternative.

A negative in relationship to a worse negative can be turned into a positive. Human existence is replete with individuals whose bleak situation is brightened by the perspective of an even bleaker situation. Life becomes bearable once we are able to see others who survive under even more unbearable conditions. A seeming negative can be turned into a positive by a simple consideration of many other possible worse negatives. By the same token, any seemingly bleak situation can be reviewed as a positive by pairing it to a possible positive outcome.

Solution and Distantiation. By being able to get away from dualistic same-opposite thinking, it is possible to consider alternatives that would not have occurred otherwise. Attainment of such a position is possible when a certain degree of distancing from the prevailing circumstances has taken place. This is the unhooking that Bowen (1978) calls "emotional detriangularization," the possibility of coming up with a creative third alternative rather than a repetition of the same-opposite theme. Consideration of active alternatives comes about from an abandonment of dichotomous thinking, freedom to recast any situation in unfamiliar and often paradoxical alternatives and solutions, and exploration of rewards and costs from an altogether new viewpoint.

Eclecticism. Many of our practices tend to be unilateral, in the sense that we specialize and tend to use one single approach or one single philosophy: for instance, if one were to assume a humanistic stance, it would clash with a behavioristic stance. Or a behavioristic stance would clash, supposedly, with a psychodynamic stance. By the same token, a service approach to life clashes with a research approach or vice versa. Consequently, the definition of any approach is based on *mutual antagonism* and an external definition of a negative nature; i.e., a humanist would define himself by his/her emphasis on freedom and authenticity with a parallel criticism of the supposedly coercive practices of behaviorists. In other words, the definition of any approach is made by the similarities and differences it has with other approaches. On the other hand, more often than not, such a definition is based on opposites, since many viewpoints or approaches are viewed as being *antagonistic* to each other. Just think of the acrimony created in the psychiatric profession by the introduction of psychotherapy in the hands of psychologists or the upsurge of behavior modification techniques that threaten the status and control of patients from the hands of the medical profession!

In other words, the definition of any approach is based on *exclusivity*, how it excludes from its ideological or methodological repertoire certain concepts or techniques. By such exclusivity, usually based on *mutual antagonism*, each approach becomes limited and very likely stagnant, e.g., the present status of psychoanalysis in the delivery of human services. Without infusion of new ideas and techniques, the chances of changing are minimized. The analogy of what happens at individual and familial levels would not be amiss. We can think of professional neuroses representing collective hangups of ideologies and professions. It may take some time for this neurosis to show up, but it will be shown as soon as competition and comparison come about as the inevitable outcome of the evolutionary process. As a result of inflexibility and rigidity to new and different ideas and practices, each approach, discipline, or technology becomes quagmired in its own limitations. Change cannot take place from within the inside of the system but, as Weakland et al. (1974) have very well illustrated, from the outside.

It is clear that paradoxical positivism does not need to evolve itself in proprietary, insidious, and invidious comparisons with other viewpoints. By its very nature it is open to reconciling seemingly opposite viewpoints by treating them as different and by maximizing the inherent strengths that each viewpoint and its integration with a supposedly opposing viewpoint may bring about. If conflict comes out from the juxtaposition of thesis and antithesis, resolution comes about as a synthesis of both sides. This synthesis takes place best within the context of paradoxical positivism because of the very nature of the approach. Opposites do not need to be juxtaposed; they can be reconciled as differences!

Paradoxical Positivism and Demonstrability

Rychlack's (1968) dichotomy of dialectical versus demonstrative reasoning in the history of Western thought is taken as a jumping point to expand on the implications of a paradoxical positivistic stance. If one aspect cannot be separated from the other and if both are necessary parts of our existence, then we need to see how both work for our own good. Science and scientific description and explanation (Braithwaite, 1953; Toulmin, 1961), as representative of the demonstrative aspect, cannot be separated from the dialectic discourse, either within each scientific discipline or among or outside of scientific disciplines. Eventually, any scientific theory or results need interpretation and application in a social and cultural realm that cannot help but be dialectical. To think of science and scientific explanations as being immune to and separate from such dialectical aspects would be like denying that the atomic bomb had political, philosophical, and societal implications! Advancement and progress take place within a dialectical process of thesis and antithesis (Kuhn, 1962). By the same token, the dialectical dialogue would be meaningless without the substance of scientific demonstrations.

Each polarity is defined by an opposite reality. One is meaningless without the other. Similarly, any label used to describe and explain human behavior would be meaningless unless a dichotomy is presented (L'Abate, 1964). Yet, in dealing with human behavior, such a dichotomous approach would tend to avoid the complexity of human existence. Categorization, according to IQ scores or anxiety scores, for instance, has led to results that have only raised serious doubts and suspicions about the wisdom as well as limitations of the engineering position.

THEORETICAL IMPLICATIONS

From a paradoxical viewpoint, it is possible to accept the relativity of any theory, including the present one, and the multiplicity of available theories concerning human nature. Once these two aspects are recognized, any theory can be accepted tentatively and mostly in terms of comparative evaluation and competition with other existing theories. The ultimate "winner" will be the theory that gives the greatest rewards (economical, personal, interpersonal, etc.) with the least expense. However, since "being a winner" depends a great deal on the context, no theory can be the "ultimate winner." We can only specify under which conditions a theory is a winner or a loser and under which conditions a competing theory can do comparatively better or worse than the other theory. Consequently, this position forces each theory to a much greater degree of specificity and qualification.

Transactionalism

A transactional viewpoint is part of paradoxical positivism. It implies an appreciation of seeing any event, physical or behavioral (Dewey & Bentley, 1949; L'Abate, 1969; Spiegel, 1971), as being related to its context as well as to the observer's own biases and methods of observation. This view implies an appreciation of the multiple exchanges that occur among an event, its context, and its observer. It also implies a view of behavior as a system (L'Abate, 1969; von Bertalanffy, 1968) varying in degree of openness in its boundaries to other systems with which it is interrelated. Our appreciation of the transactional nature of human nature helps in a paradoxical appreciation of it.

Adaptive Probabilism

Rausch et al. (1974) have suggested a philosophical base for the study of human interaction called "adaptive probabilism." This position implies the uncertainty of the human condition as well as the variety of maneuvers and routes that are available in the multiplicity of events and situations of a continuously changing reality. This position acknowledges the importance of evolutionary (rather than stationary) systems (rather than individuals *in a vacuum*). From the viewpoint of paradoxical positivism it is possible to include such a stance within the context of the relativity of human existence, its vagueness and ambiguity, and the process of labeling and attribution that attempt to grasp and encompass the continuously changing ebb and flow of the human dialogue.

From the viewpoint of research, Rausch et al. (1974) emphasize the need and applicability of naturalistic observation, multivariate probabilistic methods of communication theory (L'Abate, 1969), and the use of simulation games as a more appropriate way of understanding human interaction than static experimental models more appropriate for the physical sciences.

As Rausch et al. (1974) explain:

> . . . people rarely act in a completely deterministic fashion; rather there are multiple possibilities for response to an event, and we respond to events probabilistically. The thesis thus implies that many causes may influence a single event and that a single cause may influence many effects. . . . The nature of the situation affects not only the probabilities of interactive events but also the patterning of the contingencies among them. (p. 16)

Thus, the concepts of "equipotentiality" and multidetermination are relevant to the view of behavior in systems and not *in vacuum*.

Constructive Alternativism

In many aspects paradoxical positivism is related to Kelly's (1955) *constructive alternativism* where all interpretations of the universe are subject to revision or replacement. The relativity of human interpretation and the multiplicity of alternatives available to man were indicated by Kelly in different terms but in ways closely related to the present formulation.

Technology. A positivistic, pragmatic, probabilistic stance cannot help but use technology for its own good, being perfectly aware of its side effects and possibly noxious outcomes. Emphasis on technology, then, would not be uncritical or unselective. On the contrary, it would be used within the context of *relativity* and *multiplicity*.

Method. In regard to mutually antagonistic practices and overemphasis on methodology at the expense of innovation, exploration, and originality, Buchler (1961) noted:

> When interest in a method ceases to be merely primary and becomes militantly exclusive, where regard for a method begins to be related inversely to regard for its results, a peculiar type of problem arises, belonging to the sociology and ethics of query. For this kind of inverse relation has as eventual consequence an erasure of the sense of connection between activity and its aims. The use and fruits of method become objects of disdain. Methodolatry enters the scene, and methodic activity becomes transformed into a continuing proliferation of conventions. Methodolatry is more of a cultural than an individual problem. . . . Men afflicted with methodolatry become self-righteous, and in their euphoria fancy themselves to have acquired unsuspected health. Methodic activity is identified with cultist works and virtuosity is mistaken for originality. the epidemic colony turns into a reformist party which sees itself as correcting the extravagances of the old loose ways. In time, the aridity of correctness becomes evident, even to the faithful. . . . (pp. 105–106) Method becomes inventive when it takes on the property of query. Query is that form of human experience which originates partly in a compound of imagination and wonder. (p. 114)

THE PRAGMATICS OF THERAPEUTIC PARADOXES

The variability of human existence produces tremendous contradictions that result in dysfunctionality within family systems. This dysfunctionality, as discussed in greater detail in Chapter 13, derives from our inability to share our hurts and our fears of being hurt, that is, to become aware that our very variability and inconsistency makes us fallible, vulnerable, and needy. This inability to share together with family members the bottom line of our existence produces a variety of characteristics that distinguish dysfunctional from functional family systems. These characteristics, summarized freely from the literature on family evaluation, are as follows:

Negativity. The major characteristic of dysfunctional human systems is their emphasis on negative self-attributions, as in the case of individuals labeled "depressed" or in the name calling, accusations, blaming, and vilifications found in the families of individuals labeled as 'schizophrenics." One could go on and on in listing all the evidence to support this characteristic of dysfunctional systems, but it is self-evident that no documentation is necessary for this as well as the other characteristics.

Digitality. Most dysfunctional family systems see themselves, significant others, and the whole world of reality in general in terms of simplistic dichotomous, either-or, wrong-right, true-false, friend-foe categories that are invalid in most human existence. Most problems of human relationships cannot be reduced to simple formulas based on good-bad, strong-weak, black-and-white stereotypes.

Linearity. Causality in dysfunctional systems is conceptualized in linear terms; that is, one single cause is responsible for one single result. For instance, "Jimmy is flunking in school because he is *lazy*." Cause-effect relationships are viewed according to direct, one-to-one sequences.

Acontextualism. The contextual nature of human behavior and its dysfunctionality is completely ignored, or to put it more charitably, family systems usually are unaware of the contextual nature of behavior and of its dysfunctionalities.

Uncontrollability. As considered in greater detail in Chapter 6, the runaway nature of symptoms makes them uncontrollable, unexplainable, and definitely inside the individual rather than inside the family system and also outside of the system.

Absolutism and Rigidity. On the basis of the foregoing characteristics, it is very difficult for dysfunctional family systems to be flexible, open, and relative in their ways of thinking and behaving. The world is conceived and preconceived according to set ways that are extremely intractable and unchangeable.

Defeats. Success, if one can speak of it, is achieved through continuous self-other defeats (L'Abate, 1985), whose function is to keep the family system together and unchanged.

Little If Any Humor. In these families there is little or no laughter. Life is a valley of sufferings and tears. There is no pleasure in living and certainly no pleasure in interacting with each other!

Little If Any Intimacy. As maintained earlier and as will be maintained consistently throughout this book, especially in Chapter 13, the inability to be intimate lies at the bottom of most human dysfunction.

Why are these characteristics important enough to enumerate? They are important because they serve as guidelines on how a therapist needs to behave. Given these characteristics, a therapist needs to contradict them *without appearing to contradict*! Thus, the pragmatic therapeutic paradox lies in the therapist behaving in exactly the opposite ways that characterize dysfunctionality; that is, the therapist needs to stress:

Positivity. The therapist needs to be positive about himself/herself as well as reality and the families that come for help. In other words, as discussed in Chapter 13, the therapist needs to exercise the good in how s/he sees self and other. Without this positivity, the therapist has no weapon to contradict, combat, and counterattack the family's negativity.

Analogic. The therapist is aware that most human relationships are analogic and complex. They cannot be reduced to simple dichotomies. How can the therapist convert a family to an analogic (and, hopefully, more functional) view of reality without appearing to brainwash or to show disrespect for the ways the family thinks and behaves?

Plurality. As argued at greater length elsewhere in this chapter, a therapist needs to be aware of the multidetermination and equipotentiality and equifinality of behavior. Without such a view it would be difficult to offer dysfunctional families more positive, analogic, and diverse perceptions of their set perceptions.

Contextualism. Once the symptom is linked positively to the rest of the family system, its contextual nature is affirmed without the need to affirm it! Once more, the family is contradicted without appearing to contradict!

Controllability. Once the therapist is aware that there is no way to control others, except through coersion, then one can influence families to achieve greater control over themselves. Thus, a therapist needs to control without appearing to control!

Flexibility and Relativity. A therapist needs to be flexible to survive and needs to be aware of the relativity of human perceptions, including one's own! Without both characteristics it would be very difficult to work with and help dysfunctional families.

Success. Since defeats are the very essence of dysfunctional families ("to cut one's nose to spite one's face'), the therapist needs to be ready to welcome defeating behavior (i.e., "resistance") as the best handle a family can offer. How can one succeed where success is obtained through defeats?

Sense of Humor. Without a sense of humor therapists may as well go out of business! One needs to keep that sense of humor always present, lest the family take advantage of the therapist's involvement and intanglement with the family once the sense of humor is lost! In that case, the therapist may as well quit because his/her effectiveness would be seriously impaired.

Intimacy. Very likely the present insistence on the importance of intimacy in dealing with human problems will be discounted by many therapists who see their job to intervene in as short a time and with as little effort as possible, i.e., the brief therapy movement. Insistence on the importance of this factor in the genesis of dysfunctionality and pathology and the need to deal with it in the course of therapy may well be a controversial issue to reckon with in the future.

On the basis of these characteristics, the therapist needs to contradict (a) the reason for referral; i.e., "You did not come here because so and so is 'sick' 'bad' 'incorrigible' 'uncontrollable' etc. You came here because you care about him/her," and (b) the negative nature of the symptom by exalting it and welcoming it as a friend rather than a foe (Weeks & L'Abate, 1982). This contradiction may be done directly and straightforwardly or, in some cases, indirectly and circularly. Ultimately, as we shall see (Chapter 6), the therapist needs to achieve control without appearing to control! A summary of a paradoxical position is attempted in Table 5–1. Like all summaries, it may fall short of complete exposition!

Table 5–1

I. ASSUMPTIONS ABOUT THE NATURE OF REALITY ACCORDING TO A PARADOXICAL PERSPECTIVE

1. Reality is what we make it. It is a result of our attributions that can be positive, negative, simple, or complex, etc.

2. Reality is variable in how we perceive ourselves and others. This variability leads to contradictions both within ourselves as well as among ourselves. One person's trash is another person's treasure. Our strengths are also our weaknesses. The coexistence of opposites is what makes us humans not machines.

3. Reality is complex because it is multidetermined and equipotential. Hence, reality can be interpreted in a variety of ways, pluralistically.

II. ASSUMPTIONS ABOUT THE NATURE OF DYSFUNCTIONALITY

1. Most dysfunctionality is characterized by negativity, digitality, linearity, acontextualism, rigidity, absolutism, uncontrollability, defeats and defeatism, insufficient humor, and inadequate intimacy.

2. Extreme contradictions are the watchword of dysfunctionality. The system, however, is usually not aware of these contradictions; i.e., most dysfunctional families want help but do not know how to change.

III. THERAPEUTIC IMPLICATIONS

1. The therapist needs to contradict the system in ways that will not increase its dysfunctionality.

2. The number one weapon in combating dysfunctionality is extreme, pervasive, and unrelenting positivity in thinking, actions, plans, and programs. This positivity is expressed, among other ways, through *multiple positive reframings*, as will be demonstrated in Chapter 7 in dealing with depression.

3. This positive and pluralistic view of reality needs to be corroborated by a variety of possible solutions ("There is more than one way to skin a cat!"), maximizing the family's assets and turning its liabilities into assets.

4. The reason for referral and the symptom itself need to be considered as friends rather than foes. Without them the therapist would not have any control over the family.

The therapist needs to contradict the family's dysfunctional patterns. However, such a contradiction usually cannot take place head-on, because it would elicit strong resistance on the family's part. Hence, such a contradiction often needs to be subtly indirect and cryptically circular. In other words, *the contradiction must take place without appearing to be a contradiction, lest the family react to it.* Whether the therapist challenges, confronts, or contradicts a family directly or indirectly is the main issue. Until now, most of our therapeutic techniques have been directly and straightforwardly linear. Paradoxical approaches add another dimension, not to be used exclusively, or in a mutually antagonistic fashion to linear approaches.

Paradoxical positivism is helpful in interpreting and reinterpreting the world through the use of opposites. For instance, any position taken by the patient as representing any extreme can be rephrased as representing another extreme. (Dominance means submission; helpfulness is power; strength is weakness; weakness is strength; etc.) Once this juxtaposition follows its course, it is possible to rephrase any possible negative in terms of possibly positive outcomes, comparing them to even worse negatives, or questioning the interpretation of a negative as a subjective attribution. Under these conditions, cultural stereotypes, personal attributions, and privately kept dogmas, myths, or beliefs can be questioned and often destroyed and replaced by a more relative viewpoint that allows for multiple positive viewpoints.

For every positive there is a negative and vice versa. Consequently, it is possible to reformulate human existence in positive rather than negative terms. This is a choice we make once we become aware of the relativity of any interpretations available to us. However, once we are faced by a positive we do not need to juxtapose it with a negative. We can let the positive stand and juxtapose a negative with a positive alternative.

It follows from this viewpoint that if the nature of human nature is paradoxical, we need to recognize it. We need to recognize also that behavior can be paradoxically negative or self-other destructive or self-other enhancing. If we want to intervene therapeutically in other people's lives to enhance them, we may need to fulfill at least three requirements: (a) our intervention needs to be *paradoxical* in order to allow each of us to see the contradictions in ourselves and others; (b) our intervention needs to be *positive* in order to enhance ourselves as interveners and enhance others who ask us for help; and (c) our intervention needs to be *powerful* enough to make a difference in their lives.

If the message is to be powerful enough to make such a difference, insist that our "interpretations" be done *in writing* (see appendices). These interpretations need to be written for the following reason: verbal communications can be *ignored, distorted,* or *forgotten by families. Consequently, written communications or interpretations have the advantage of becoming a written record* that permits a greater degree of precision in the quality and intensity of interpretations and interventions. From a research viewpoint, these written communications can serve as a more objective database than verbal communications. They could serve to make less ambiguous and uncertain what happens during the process of intervention. If Watzlawick et al. (1974) and Selvini-Palazzoli et al. (1978) are to be believed, they claim that with paradoxical injunctions no more than 10 therapy sessions are necessary. If this is indeed the case, then keeping track of these notes and records would allow for greater specificity and comparison of efficacy of interventions. It would allow other therapists to *duplicate* the process of intervention and check on the claim of these therapists. *If* these results cannot be duplicated, correctly or incorrectly, or *if* the method is duplicated correctly and the results are not the same as those claimed, a question about the validity of such claims can be raised. If they are reproduced incorrectly, then a written record would allow correction toward a greater similarity with the methods used by these therapists.

CONCLUSION

There are as many ways of intervening as there are therapists (Hansen & L'Abate, 1982). Maybe the words we use are different and perhaps the methods are different. However, the same therapeutic issues present with individuals remain the same with couples and families, because all of them are concerned with *change.* How can we responsibly and effectively help people change whether individually or familially? As long as change is our concern, issues will remain the same. Resistance to change is resistance to change. Whether we call it ambivalence, transference, rigidity, psychosis, or by any other name, it remains difficult to direct. How can we help clients change without appearing to want to do so? If we side openly on the side of change, such a position may be opposed. If and when there is no opposition, then our efforts are simplified. Yet, our greatest challenge lies with families who oppose us because they need our help as much as or more than families who side with us.

Chapter 6

Beyond Paradox: Confrontation, Support, and Control

The purpose of this chapter is to clarify any possible misinterpretations of paradoxical treatment by reducing it to three sets of issues: (a) issues of positive reframing, (b) issues of confrontation and support, and (c) issues of control. Since issues of circularity and positive reframing have been considered at length and in detail in Chapter 5, issues of straightforward control will be considered here in greater detail than in the past. The major characteristic of symptomatic behavior is its uncontrollability. After consideration of certain paradoxes about control, specific guidelines are given on how to achieve control by obtaining and giving it away to families. To obtain this goal the notion of control is considered within the context of positive reframing, which may well be the only "circular" procedure in the whole process of intervention.

In addition to control issues, a therapist needs to consider that therapy is a continuous dialectic (and dialogue) between confrontation and support.

We already know what patterns characterize dysfunctionality. These patterns were considered in the previous chapter. If this assumption is correct, then the purpose of therapy is to contradict these patterns and to convert them into their antonyms, i.e., from negativity to positivity, from linearity to circularity, and from digitality to analogy. Hence, the purpose of therapy is to confront, challenge, and contradict dysfunctional patterns and help clients change toward the use of more functional patterns. How can this process take place? Often, it takes place through indirect contradiction using verbal and nonverbal methods. By indirection is meant *contradicting without appearing to contradict.* Instead of facing the family head on, it is more useful to go around and intervene from the side, as it were, in a way that will not threaten the family and increase its resistance.

THE MEANING OF CONFRONTATION

Confrontation can take place in a variety of ways (Adler & Myerson, 1973). It can be done through (a) interpretation of the old garden-type variety that *explains* in some way the behaviors of the client(s); (b) clarification of patterns, what the client(s) is/are doing (which is essentially a commentary); (c) suggestions on why don't you try this or that, doing things different from the past; (d) limit setting. The pros and cons of the use of these focuses of confrontation can be found in a variety of sources supporting or criticizing the use of each approach. However, the point of considering how a client(s) can be confronted does beg the question of whether confrontation is necessary. Do we need to confront or do we not? This question brings up the additional issue of activity in therapy. How active or inactive should the therapist be in order to be effective? Some therapists would question severely whether activity or even confrontation is a therapeutic stance. On the other hand, some therapists would consider an inactive, nonconfrontive stance as antitherapeutic. Hence, the therapist is left to do what s/he is most comfortable doing or not doing, rationalizing his/her stand in the best way possible.

Cohen (1981) detailed the nature of a psychotherapeutic system he called "confrontation analysis." He defined confrontation as the "presentation to the patient of personality attributes that are consistently clinical or avoided" (p. 441).

The purpose of such an analysis, according to Cohen, "is to help the patient become aware of perceptual and behavioral distortions." After this step the therapist helps the patient deal with his/her reactions to the confrontation "in order to help modify pathological manifestations." In this kind of framework the therapist attributes negative characteristics to the patient. It is a wonder that under such negative conditions some patients are still willing to stay in therapy!

Shulman (1972) differentiated confrontation from interpretation on a here-and-now basis. An interpretation, on the other hand, is usually based on past behavior outside the therapist's office. Shulman considered 11 different categories of behaviors that should be the target of therapeutic confrontation—mood states and feeling, hidden reasons, biased apperceptions and private logic, private goals, mottos for truisms, immediate behavior, responsibility for responses of others, self-defeating behavior, existing alternatives, responsibility for change, time factors. The first six categories fit into the issue of insight—confronting the patient in order to help him become "one of something." The second purpose is to help the patient face up to his/her responsibilities and help the patient realize that the power and timing of change belongs to the patient.

Many of the issues of confrontation reviewed thus far have been dealt with by individually and linearly oriented psychotherapists. For many of them (Cohen and Shulman for instance, among others) the issue of awareness is directly linked to change; i.e., if we bring something new to the attention or awareness of the individual, then s/he will translate such an awareness into an improved behavior. In actuality, nothing is further from the truth. Most evidence indicates (as considered in Chapter 10) that awareness, like any other component of behavior, is not linearly linked to change. This relationship (or lack of it) allows behavior to change without changes in awareness. In fact, one could defend the position that behavior needs to be changed first.

Especially in dealing with families, the hope that changes in awareness can bring about changes in behavior is an illusion. If we were to write about families changing on the basis of changes in awareness, we could wait forever and it would be costly and ineffective. Better introduce or instigate changes in behavior and let awareness take care of itself!

Tamminen and Smaby (1981) quoted a variety of research studies to support their contention that

> Confrontation is one of those unaccounted for variables found in such reviews that can be thought successfully. . . . Confrontation is an invitation and a challenge to examine, modify, or control some aspect of one's behavior. It helps people to see more clearly what is happening, what the consequences are, and how they can assume responsibility for taking action to change in ways that can lead to a more effective life and better and fairer relationships with others. . . . Failure to confront when confrontation prevents the continuations of self-defeating or unreasonable behavior, inadvertently implies support for such behavior. (p. 42.)

Tamminen and Smaby (1981) viewed assertion as "a special case of confrontation." Among the various categories that make up such a technique they identified the following components: (a) verbal following, (b) summarizing, (c) open-circled question, (d) detours, (e) specificity, (f) immediacy, and (g) appropriate self-disclosure. These authors developed a scale to help trainers learn how to confront helpfully, ranging from acquiescing, scolding, and identifying ineffective behavior patterns, to recognizing feelings and negative consequences of actions and commitment to change. On the basis of this scale, Tamminen and Smaby developed a whole training program devoted to training for effective confrontation.

Hawkins (1976) defined confrontation in terms of the therapist's self-disclosure. He also quoted Douds (1967), who maintained that "the purpose of confrontation is to reduce the ambiguity and incongruities in the client's experiencing and communication" (p. 1971). Confrontation may represent a process that tends to bring families face to face with aspects of their problems or behavior that they have neither recognized nor verbalized.

Depending on one's prevalent ego state, Berne (1971) maintained that confrontation may mean different things; e.g., for a child ego state confrontation may mean criticism and reprimand, whereas to the adult ego state confrontation may mean intellectual challenge, and in the parent ego state confrontation may mean increase and interference with the parental authority. Hawkins (1976) reviewed the role of confrontation as a therapeutic activity in marriage and family counseling. He reviewed Berne's (1971) definition of confrontation:

> . . . to disconcert the patient's Parent, Child or contaminated Adult by pointing out inconsistency. The patient is stirred up and his psyche is thrown out of balance and this tends to cause a redistribution of cathesis. (p. 42)

Hawkins (1976) related five different types of therapist's confrontive styles to outcomes in therapy depending on degree of rapport (absent, moderate, and full) in the relationship. He identified these five styles as: (1) conventional, i.e., closed, low disclosure; (2) controlling verbal attack, i.e., closed, high disclosure, nonnegative; (3) controlling without verbal attack, i.e., closed, high disclosure, nonnegative; (4) speculative (open, low disclosure); and (5) contactful (open, high disclosure). With some exceptions Hawkins (1976) believed that both controlling and contactful styles are justifiable types of confrontation.

Accuracy in Confrontation

Many writers (Adler & Myerson, 1973) are concerned about the degree of force or insistence used by the therapist, which, of course, goes back to the degree of activity on the therapist's part. As Corwin (1973) noted (p. 70), "Confrontation is viewed by many as primarily an active technique." Many confrontations may be inaccurate, but do we need to be accurate to be therapeutically effective? Furthermore, by what criteria should therapeutic or confrontative accuracy be judged?

Buie and Adler (1973) defined confrontation as follows:

> . . . a technique designed to gain a patient's attention to inner experiences or perceptions of outer reality of which he is conscious or is about to be made curious. Its specific purpose is to counter

resistance to recognizing what is in fact available to awareness or about to be made available through clarification or interpretation. The purpose is not to induce or force change in the patient's attitude, decisions, or conduct. (p. 127)

Corwin (1973) considered confrontation within the continuum defined by the heroic to the routine polarities.

A heroic (dramatic) confrontation may be defined as an emotionally charged, parametric, manipulative, technical tool demanded by the development of an actual or potential situation of impasse and designed ultimately to remobilize a workable therapeutic alliance. (p. 73)

Corwin also considered how confrontation is different from interpretation. Corwin's distinction is a useful one because confrontations may differ in degree from the dramatically heroic to the mundanely routine.

In addition to this continuum, one needs to consider the continuum of improvisation-thoughtfulness that is relevant to the timing and mode of confrontation professed. As Weisman (1973) noted:

. . . our purpose in confrontation is always to recognize and respect mutual fields of reality. Whatever we do, it is to undeny, to dissipate deception, and ultimately to increase the range of options that any person has for contending with what imposes unnecessary control over him. (pp. 117–118)

Alexander and Parsons (1982) differentiated between structuring (directiveness, clarity and self-confidence) and relationship skills (affect), behavior integration, nonblaming, warmth, humor, and self-disclosure in family therapy. Supposedly the relationship between these two sets of skills is orthogonal, i.e., we need both to be effective therapists. Of the structuring skills we would choose directiveness as being related to what is here called confrontation whereas we would equate relationship skills to what here is called support.

The therapist needs to be active and confrontative as long as it does not raise the resistance level of the family to the point that the family is either lost (i.e., leaves therapy) or deteriorates. Once the decision to be active and confrontive (within a supportive context, of course) is made, then the therapist needs to ask *how* active and confrontive should one be? The answer to that question is: One should be as actively confrontive as to justify positive outcome. If this position reminds one of the Macchiavelian "The end justifies the means," so be it. However, this form of justification should be well qualified on moral, legal, and professional grounds (L'Abate, 1972).

Confrontation and Contradiction

Where is the line between confrontation and contradiction? How are these two processes related? Confrontation can take place through contradiction. Hence contradiction is one form of confrontation, i.e., challenging the way things are. We are aware that under certain conditions and with especially rigid systems, straightforward linear confrontations may increase the rigidity of the resistance of a system. Hence, we are aware that some focuses of confrontation and contradictions will need to take place indirectly or circularly. The issue here is one of distinguishing between verbal versus nonverbal contradiction. Positive reframing and relabeling could be conceived of as contractions related to the verbal, with task assignments, at least in their formal aspects of rituals; i.e., meeting at a certain time and performing certain homework assignments, at least on these formal aspects, are directed to the nonverbal. The content itself may or may not be verbal. Get-togethers on odd days to discuss goals and priorities may combine both verbal and nonverbal aspects. However, if in addition to time it is specified that everything that is discussed verbally be *written down* (L'Abate, 1981b; Weeks & L'Abate, 1982), that record helps reduce the verbal to the nonverbal (written).

CONFRONTATION AND SUPPORT

Egan (1976) considered both helpful and harmful aspects of confrontation:

> When one person (the confronter), either deliberately or inadver- tently, does something that causes or directs another person (the confronted) to advent to, reflect upon, examine, question, or change some particular aspect of his behavior . . . there are many different forms (both growthful and destructive) and many different degrees of confrontation. (pp. 293–294)

Confrontation, therefore, is desirable if it brings to the family's awareness new points of view, options, perceptions, values, attitudes, and behaviors. However, again Hawkins emphasizes the need for such a process to take place within "a concept of support, positive regard, and empathy" (p. 40).

> There is no mystery about confrontation, for it is nothing more nor less than active intervention of the marriage of family therapist in the life of the client couple; loving, encouraging, cajoling, sup- porting, persuading, questioning, arguing them toward new and more satisfying constructions of reality. (p. 411)

Most of the literature on confrontation (Adler & Myerson, 1973) does indicate that, however it may take place, it needs to be coupled with care and concern (Myerson, 1973). In other words, confrontation needs to take place within a context of support. By the same token, a supportive relationship needs to be coupled with confrontation in order to be effective. Support is not enough, just as confrontation is not enough.

However the process of confrontation may be defined (Adler & Myerson, 1973), it is a facing up to, holding a mirror up to a system, allowing it to free itself. The issue here, of course, is how is this confrontation going to take place. We know that if it is coercive, hostile, or even angry, it will not be useful. One of the critical issues of confrontation is the degree of *directness;* i.e., how direct, to the point, straightforward are we going to be? This point brings us then to consider confrontation within the context of the linear-circular continuum dear to the practice of family therapists (Madanes, 1981; Weeks & L'Abate, 1982). Confrontation can be directly straightforward at the linear extreme or cryptically indirect at the circular extreme with all possible variations in the middle of this continuum.

ISSUES OF CONTROL

One of the most important issues in family therapy is control. Who is in control of the therapy? Who is in control of the family and who should be? How much control should the therapist have and why? It will be argued that (a) the therapist needs to be in control in order for (b) the families to learn to achieve control and (c) eventually learn how to achieve control not only over the symptoms but also over their lives.

What does it mean to control? It is a means by which one expresses authority and power. It means to determine how, where, when, and for how long one or more people will behave. How can one be in control without being coercive? Can we achieve control without coercion? To avoid any implication of coercion, by control in this chapter is meant *being in charge,* a notion that implies responsibility. It is virtually impossible, philosophically, empirically, and existentially, to control anybody unless they let us. Furthermore, at best, one can control oneself but not others. Unless we are to use coercion, we need to achieve control (i.e., being in charge) to the extent that we can help others learn to control themselves, provided, of course, that they let us. The family is not going to carry out instructions that are contrary to its world view. For instance, a religious family should not be told not to go to church or to use profane language. However, if the symptomatic behavior is positively con-noted, this positivity would make it easier for the family to accept control over the symptom and to carry out the assignment. Whether positive reframing is a *sine qua non* for control remains to be seen. In fact, if control can be achieved, positive reframing may not be necessary.

It will be argued that the major circular and paradoxical intervention of less than linear nature is indeed positive reframing. Once positive reframing of the symptom has taken place, the rest of the intervention is strictly and mainly linear. Since a great deal has been said about positive reframing (Hansen & L'Abate, 1982; Weeks & L'Abate, 1982), this particular form of interpretation will not be considered here. What will be considered are issues of control, their paradoxes, and guidelines necessary, conceptually and practically, to achieve control.

Control is a major issue in therapy because it is an important issue in life. To the extent that we control ourselves as persons and as therapists, we can be successful in intervening helpfully in other people's lives. Issues of control have, of course, been considered earlier by many sources (Gibbs, 1982; Hunt, 1971; Langer, 1983). Behaviorists have given control a great deal of attention (Sidman, 1960). However, they have emphasized contingencies and consequences that reinforce behavior acontextually. Their contribution, even though relevant for an understanding of the etiology of symptoms, is too limited to encompass issues of control reviewed here.

In addition, control can be illusory and relative. As Dell (1982) has commented in this regard: "The most convincing epistemological error is believing in control. Control of anything by anybody is ontologically impossible, despite our experience to the contrary." Without having to go as far as Dell would like us to believe, perhaps instead of control one could talk about "taking responsibility" rather than control. As therapists, whether we like it or not, we need to take *some* responsibility, if not all, for whatever happens during and after therapy.

Control as a Means to an End

The goal is not to achieve control for control's sake, but to achieve control in order to give it away. There is nothing intrinsically magical about control if and when we have it, but it is extremely difficult to acquire it once it is lost!

Control as a Cosmetic

Some therapists argue that emphasis on control is illusory because control is actually a metaphor or an illusion. It may be an illusion; however, at this point we have not been able to find a more suitable metaphor or illusion. Control, as used here, is not an absolute to be bowed to. It is seen as process and as a structure to hang one's therapeutic procedures onto. It may not be the best concept to define relationships.

The metaphor of control covers a variety of behaviors; hence it may be difficult to define it precisely. It ranges from coerciveness on one hand to influence on the other. Somewhere in between these polarities there may be the concept of being in charge of oneself. It is recognized that it is an existential, empirical, and human impossibility to control anybody. Ultimately, we can only control ourselves! To be in charge of ourselves means that we can control how we behave. We may make suggestions and recommendations (i.e., homework assignments, structural changes, etc.), but it will be up to the family to follow these recommendations. Some families will, some will not, either because they do not agree with what we recommend or because these recommendations are inappropriate and untimely. Consequently, we are in control to the extent that families allow us to be. In other words, control is a two-way street. The one who is in control must be given that responsibility from the family. Hence, control may become a negotiated process. We are in control to the extent that families allow us to be.

Control is not an easy process to define or to describe. In choosing this term one is aware of the many ambiguities inherent in this term. Yet, no other term will serve a better function. We know that control is one aspect of power, but we do not really know what aspect. If one were to describe power (Chapter 8) as representing authority and responsibility, that is, making decisions and carrying them out, then control would be synonymous with authority, i.e., making decisions that the family can or should carry out (responsibility). In this sense then, control is that part of the decision-making process that represents authority. Control is achieved if there is resistance, when the resistance itself is prescribed. By prescribing the resistance, the therapist achieves control, because through the prescription he takes away control from the resister(s). By prescribing the symptom or the resistance itself, the therapist is essentially joining with the system by asking it to continue in its behavior. It also demonstrates acceptance of the system's own way of behaving. Prescription of the symptom also means asking the family to continue emitting familiar behaviors. Consequently, there is no stress because the family is asked to continue behaving in the same fashion it has been behaving and to continue in ways that are very familiar to it.

Fagan (1970) devoted a great deal of attention to the task of control for the therapist: ". . . he must be able immediately to exercise control or nothing else can follow." She defined control as "the therapist . . . being able to persuade or coerce [sic!] the patient into following the procedures he has set. . . . Unless patients do some things that therapist suggests, little will happen." In addition to the importance of achieving control, Fagan also saw dysfunctional behavior as a form of control:

> Part of the importance of control is that all symptoms represent
> indirect ways of trying to control or force others into certain patterns

of behavior. The therapist has to counter being controlled by the patient's symptom and also establish the conditions he needs to work. (p. 92)

Fagan, among others, emphasized that issues of control are important at the beginning of therapy. Controllability is one of the factors in the two dimensions of coherence and meaning within the comprehensive model of family functioning developed by McCubbin and his associates (1983).

THE UNCONTROLLABILITY OF DYSFUNCTIONALITY AND SYMPTOMS

The uncontrollability of dysfunctionality and symptoms is well supported by most of the literature in psychopathology, too long to be cited.

Powerlessness. One of the major characteristics of troubled families lies in their feelings of uncontrollability of the undesirable or symptomatic behavior. The concept of uncontrollability can be traced all the way back to Rotter's (Rotter, Chance, & Phares, 1972) external locus of control; i.e., *it controls us rather than we control it* or similar conceptions like "learned helplessness."

Involuntariness. There is clearly the implication that the symptom is not under the voluntary control of the family; that is, the dysfunctional behavior or symptoms are admitted as being outside the conscious awareness of control by the family. This particular quality of the symptom brings about the third characteristic, that the symptom is no one's responsibility (acontextualism).

Irresponsibility. A good deal of dysfunctionality is related to a lack of awareness of contextual factors that may have determined the particular dysfunctionality; that is, there is no awareness that anyone is responsible for the symptom. How can anybody be responsible when no one has the power to do anything? There is no awareness that the family environment in one way or another multiply determines that particular behavior.

Unexplainability or Unintelligibility. It is clear that a good deal of pathology is supposedly unexplained or unexplainable. This aspect of mysteriousness is present because there is no understanding of how and why that particular symptom has arisen, because of the previous characteristics mentioned, powerlessness, involuntariness, lack of responsibility—all of these together bring about the fact that there is no "rational" explanation of why the symptom should take place at the particular time or at any other time.

THE PARADOXES OF CONTROL

Control in many ways, especially in therapy, is not the goal of the therapist. There is no need to be in control, except that being in control allows the therapist to be effective. To the extent that the therapist can be therapeutic, s/he needs to be in control.

How is control to be achieved and why should we achieve it? We need to (a) help families achieve control and (b) have control in order to give it away. There are many ways of achieving control.

It is important to remember that control might not be achieved unless the symptom is positively reframed. It remains a hypothesis to be tested on whether the symptom needs to be positively reframed in order to be prescribed. How can one prescribe a negatively described behavior, as the family sees it? It is important to prescribe behavior that is nondestructive, but that is positively connoted and reframed. Once it is positively reframed, it is important that the symptom then be prescribed. At the basis of achieving control, there is the issue of prescription of the symptom. To be in control for control's sake means absolutely nothing from a therapeutic viewpoint. Consequently, we shall deal with control according to five seeming paradoxes that pervade its nature.

Control Without Appearing to Control

It is important to be in control; however, one does not need to be autocratically or dictatorially mindful of such a need. One can be in control without having to appear in control. In many cases, even though the therapist may allow himself/herself a loss of control, it is important that the therapist be in control, that is, be in charge of oneself, since it is clear that no individual can control what others do. In fact, one could argue that no one can control anybody. At the most, one can control oneself. That in itself is a very difficult goal to achieve.

Take Control to Give It Away

It is important for the therapist to have control, but the only purpose of achieving this control is to let the family have it; that is, one purpose of therapy is to give the family the feeling that they are in charge of themselves, and in charge of their destiny, and that they are indeed able to control the symptom. First, it is important for the therapist to be in control in order to model how to be in control. Second, it is important essentially to give the control away. If the therapist does not know how to be in charge, to achieve control, how can s/he teach families how to be in control? Strong and Claiborn (1982) have summarized the same point as follows: "Control of others is gained through yielding control to them" (p. 39).

Control It or It Will Control You

By "it" is meant dysfunctional behavior or symptom. The symptom needs to be controlled, and in order to control it, we need to join it rather than to fight it (Weeks & L'Abate, 1982). It is also very important to ask the symptom bearer and the surrounding system whether indeed they want to achieve such control. Without their permission and without their stated clear consent there is no sense for the therapist to try to teach the family system to achieve control. Therefore, one has to be directly asking, "Do you want to achieve control?" Only if and when the family emphatically state that indeed they do want to be in control can one proceed accordingly. To proceed accordingly, one has to be aware of two other paradoxes which follow.

Start It If You Want to Stop It

The behavioral literature has forced us for the last 20 years to look at the consequences of behavior. We have been so taken by this particular position that we have forgotten that there are other ways of achieving control, one of which is: if we really have control of a certain behavior, we can start it. A great deal of what is behind the paradoxical literature (Weeks & L'Abate, 1982) is the notion of simulation; that is, the symptom needs to be started. This is one of the major points of the Madanes (1981) "pretend" technique, role playing à la Satir (1972), the reenactment of Minuchin (1974), and many other similar techniques. Essentially all have the same characteristic, i.e., that to achieve control of the symptom, one has to start it. Once the family is aware that indeed they can start the symptom, that is already a step toward the awareness that perhaps they have something to do with its maintenance. Starting "it" is an important way of communicating to the family the fact that they are not as powerless as they say they are, that they do have some degree of control, and that perhaps they even have some responsibility over who is in charge of the symptom.

We achieve control through prescription of the symptom. Since that is the most readily available behavior to us, it is also the easier behavior to learn because it is the most prominent and preeminent. In prescribing the symptom we are essentially telling the family to *start* the symptom to stop it. The point here is: if you cannot start it, how can you stop it? Consequently, we achieve control by starting a symptom. After all, how do we achieve control over our environment, by simulating uncontrollable behavior in the laboratory and, in our case, at home. "Scientists" achieve control by making the behavior they want to control happen "under controlled conditions." What does that mean? It means, varying all the independent variables to obtain the desired or hoped-for outcome. Since such a rigid and strict method of control is not possible or even desirable in real life with families, we need to limit ourselves to a more realistic level of occurrence. Perhaps, the best analogy for this principle can be found in the practice of lobbing artillery shells or explosives in snow banks before they produce an avalanche. Essentially, an avalanche is started artificially (i.e., *under controlled conditions*) to prevent an avalanche occurring unexpectedly, when it would do the most amount of damage. Better start an avalanche when it would do the least amount of damage.

Make It Happen When It Is Naturally Happening

The principle remains the same: *Make the undesirable behavior take place where and when it is usually or naturally occurring.* By applying this principle by positive reframing and ritualistic prescriptions we can help families learn how to achieve control.

One way to do it, of course, is to have dysfunctional behavior enacted in the office. If not, have instruction or homework that will tell the family how to do it. Homework is a way of prescribing the symptom. First, prescription of the symptom covers the starting paradox; i.e., it makes the symptom occur in a different cognitive context because they are making it happen when it is usually happening. The next step is to make it happen when it is not usually or spontaneously happening. The first step is to approximate and make the symptoms take place when it is occurring most frequently. For instance, if two siblings are fighting, it is important to make the fighting take place when it is usually occurring most of the time. It is important to approximate as much as possible the natural conditions surrounding the symptom. However, by prescribing the symptom, it is no longer naturally or spontaneously taking place as the family thinks it does. Essentially, one transmits to the family the feeling that indeed there is no run-away spontaneity in the symptom and there is a good deal of voluntariness and some lawfulness in how the symptom arises.

From the preceding paradoxes of control, one can then go on to more specific guidelines for control.

GUIDELINES FOR CONTROL

We achieve control when we can specify the place, time, duration, and frequency of the behavior we want to learn to control. Once we are able to *specify* and *prearrange* for what, where, when, and how, we have taught the family how to be in control by accepting the symptom as a friend rather than an enemy. In other words, the primary prerequisite for prescribing behavior may be to label it positively. We do not or cannot prescribe negative or negatively connoted behavior for obvious ethical and practical reasons. However, we can prescribe behavior that has been labeled positively, as caring, protection, sensitivity, and so forth.

How to Achieve Control

By determining how, where, when, and for how long behavior, whether desirable or undesirable, is to take place, we achieve control. By reframing symptomatic behavior positively and prescribing it ritualistically and systemically, we achieve control. The concept of control is specific to ritualistic prescriptions. By determining *beforehand* where, when, and for how long the behavior is to take place, we are defining its spatial and temporal parameters.

There are three major characteristics to achieving control. We are in control when we know (a) where the behavior is going to take place (space), (b) when it is going to take place (time), and (c) what is going to take place (content).

Achieving Control in Space (Where)

It is important to detail where the symptom is going to take place. Whether it is going to take place in one's office, in the home, or outside the office and the home. It is important to detail where that space it—the familiar physical setting where the symptom is most likely to take place. This is the primary characteristic of control.

The best place to assign is where most normally the behavior we want to control usually takes place. It may be the bedroom, the living room, the kitchen, or the bathroom. By the same token, for the sake of drama or for practical considerations, it may be helpful to choose a place that is new or not thought of, for instance, the basement for temper tantrums or for fights.

Achieving Control in Time (When)

It is important to conceive of time in terms of frequency, duration, and intensity. These three characteristics need to be dealt with in three different ways. Time should be divided into three parts: (a) at what time the behavior should start, (b) how long it should last, and (c) how frequently it should take place (once a week, twice a week, three times a week, or every day).

Duration. It is important to have an awareness of how long the symptom takes place, and consequently, the duration should be specifically given in minutes, i.e., 5, 15, 30 minutes, or one hour, or a whole day at the most with severe depressions.

Frequency. First, the symptom has to be prescribed in terms of frequency obtained through ritualized times (once a day; one hour every other day; Monday, Wednesday, and Friday; Tuesday, Thursday, and Saturday, etc.). Control of time should be obtained through the use of an alarm clock rather than this impersonal chore being in the hands of anybody else who would make it an emotional issue.

Intensity. Intensity is difficult to control, but it is important to always understand how often this prescription can be executed over an extended period of time, whether it should be done for a week, two weeks, and so forth.

What to Control (Content)

The most clearly available and familiar behavior that the family knows well is the symptom. They need to control the symptom as the clearest frame of reference for their referral and for their coming. However, the issue of *what* to control is a thorny one. Controlling the symptom is not enough. It serves the purpose of reducing conflict and anxiety but it is not sufficient although necessary at the outset. Symptomatic relief is only the first stage of therapy, even though there are therapists who conceive of it as the goal of therapy (Hansen & L'Abate, 1982). There is more to family therapy than symptom reduction and relief. There is the issue of teaching families how to negotiate whatever issues they may face in the future (Section III).

The content of what needs to be controlled has two major aspects: (a) negotiation—power-sharing, decision-making, problem-solving skills on the one hand, and (b) on the other hand (Section III), issues of *being,* which are also called *intimacy skills,* that is, the ability to share one's neediness and fallibility—one's fears of being hurt and being found unlovable (Chapter 13).

Clearly the one in control can teach the negotiation process. One can start with the simple aspects of what they are doing and what things need to be done. When children are involved, *having* things and possessions needs to be negotiated. Eventually, though, what needs to be shared is the whole issue of being (L'Abate, Sloan, Wagner, & Malone, 1980). "Being" is the very issue that needs to be considered in therapy. How do we choose to be with one another? This is something that dysfunctional families do not seem to be able to do. Many of these families *do* have enough possessions and *do* have enough money. Many of them are employed; they *do* perform services. Yet, they do not seem to know how to love each other and feel important with each other. Therefore, what they need to learn is how to *be* with each other and how to share feelings, how to express feelings properly without judgment, how to learn problem-solving, and how to deal with intimacy issues (Chapter 13).

HOW TO ACHIEVE CONTROL

There are at least six specific ways of achieving control. Some of these are commonsensical, some have been covered in the extant literature, and some may be new. These ways are (a) changing the context of the symptom, (b) changing the direction of the symptom, (c) limiting the information flow, (d) controlling through planning, (e) controlling through appointments, and (f) controlling through writing.

Changing the Context of Symptom

There are many ways of changing the context of the symptom as suggested originally by Haley (1976). For instance, one way he suggested was to change the caretaker who was most involved with the symptomatic individual. Change the overinvolvement and let someone who is less involved take care of the symptom or of the symptom maker or identified patient. By changing this particular involvement, one changes the context. For example, the mother is overinvolved with the symptom bearer. Get her to become uninvolved and put someone else in her place, father, grandmother, etc. That is, *we change the context by changing the pattern or configurations of relationships in the family.*

This is not the only way to change context:

Behaviorally (Activity). One can change the context by giving the family new activities to do. For instance, prescription of homework assignments that involve the family coming together for specific periods of time, something they have never done before.

Cognitively (Rationality). One changes the context by the positive reframing of the symptom. If the symptom, instead of being attributed negative qualities, is now attributed positive valances, the family learns to see it in a different light. One way to do it is through written reframing of the symptoms, as in the Milano group (Hansen & L'Abate, 1982). One can do it in terms of reframing the reasons for referral, as done by L'Abate (1983).

Emotionally (Emotionality). This is probably the way people like Kempler (1981), Satir (1972), and existential therapists change the context, by essentially having people relate emotionally to each other differently from the way they have done before. Kempler (1981) changes the context by making himself available as an individual instead of an "expert."

Changing the Direction of Symptom

In addition to changing the context, we can also change the direction of the symptom, as, for instance, in the case of depression. Instead of going from the depressed person to the intimate other, i.e., the spouse or the parent (elaborated in Chapter 7), we can change the direction by asking the spouse to remind the depressed person to be depressed on schedule, at a certain time, for a certain duration, in a specific place, and according to specified routines. In other words, we achieve control when we take responsibility for making the behavior (desirable or undesirable) take place according to preestablished, prearranged plans and prescriptions.

Ways of changing the direction of the symptom are:

From the Controller to the Controlled. Essentially the caretaker is put in charge of the symptom rather than being controlled by the symptom. For instance, the child with the temper tantrum controls the parents especially if the parents become hooked by the temper tantrum and react every time the child has a temper tantrum. But when the parent is now told to make sure that the temper tantrums occur at a certain time with a certain ritualized frequency, Monday, Wednesday, Friday at a certain hour for a certain length of time, the controlled now becomes the controller because the caretaker now has control of the symptom and the controller, that is, the identified patient, no longer has the power to control everybody through the symptoms.

Generational and Hierarchical Redress. Usually the weakest and the youngest are the symptom bearers. By putting the oldest in charge of the symptom, one redresses hierarchical barriers and essentially puts the power (authority and responsibility) where it is supposed to be. It is important to follow generational lines and make sure one redresses the power structure of the family system according to age-appropriate criteria.

Break the Deadly Drama Triangle (L'Abate, 1976). This triangle seems to be the beginning of most psychopathological dysfunctions. In this triangle, to be considered in the next chapter, there is a victim, a persecutor, and a rescuer. If and when that drama triangle is evident, it should either be prescribed as is or be broken indirectly through homework assignments (see Appendix A).

Limiting Information Flow

We achieve control by limiting information either from the therapist to the family or between family members, i.e., between parents and children, as in the case of asking parents to leave the children with a babysitter without telling the children where the parents are going or what they are doing.

By not telling the family what it is supposed to do, by just giving them the assignment, by not giving all the information necessary, the therapist can be in charge as an authority. This, of course, is a favorite approach of bureaucrats, politicians, and intelligence spies. Personally, I think it is better to inform the family straight out and straightforwardly what the purpose of each exercise or assignment is, once it is agreed that control is the goal to be achieved. However, one can think of various examples or possibilities where the therapist may indeed want to limit the information flow from the therapist to the family or may give information to the older generation and have them limit the flow to the child. It may be important to achieve control by limiting the information flow, even from the therapist to the family or within the family system.

Controlling Through Planning

If the therapist can plan an intervention and it is clear about what stance to take and what to prescribe to the family with a clear sense of direction, after he/she is allowed to proceed by the family, then the planning itself indicates the level of competence of the therapist. The therapist needs to plan the various steps of an intervention and needs to have some degree of rationale that is specific to the needs of the family. Planning and assignments according to various stages and steps indicate to the family that the therapist is competent. The planned intervention is one way of indicating that s/he is in control.

Controlling Through Appointments

Progress and change occur in real life among adults according to these aspects. One is through appointments, that is, fighting by appointment as prescribed by Bach (Bach & Wyden, 1968), having marriage and family conferences, and so forth. In other words, the world progresses according to two particular procedures: (a) people, adults, meet at certain times that are preestablished, i.e., appointments, and (b) there is a running record that allows us to check on progress.

By demanding and asking that the assignments be carried out on preestablished and agreed-upon times by the family, the therapist achieves control. By carrying out the assignment according to the way the therapist outlines or plans, the family in itself learns to achieve control, because they are carrying out the assignment themselves on their own.

It is important that assignments be followed so that the family does have an appointment on a regular basis at home for marriage or for family conferences and that these conferences be recorded.

Controlling Through Writing

It is very important for families to start having running accounts of contracts, running accounts of notes of conferences, running accounts of when they are depressed, running accounts of sibling rivalry, running accounts of temper tantrums, and so forth. By putting "it" in writing (as in the case of SHWAs in the appendices), the family learns to be in charge of itself because now they have a record that they can remember and from which they can derive some lessons. Without a written record to improve on, usually there can be no assurance of improvements. These can be forgettings, distortions, and suppressions which will continue the upset in the family.

CONCLUSION

Instead of the paradox being considered as possessing mystical powers and mysterious processes of a circular nature, most paradoxical interventions can and should be reduced to linear ways of intervening stepwise, using gradual approaches to work with families. Once the problem is reduced to issues of control, the mystique of the paradox can be reduced essentially to just positive reframing. Here is where circularity is indeed present and needed. Once positive reframing has been made, the prescription and assignment of heretofore dysfunctional behavior becomes a gradual, stepwise, linear matter of control. Consequently, there is nothing about the paradox that cannot be reduced to (a) multiple positive reframings, (b) prescription of the symptomatic behavior, and (c) control that when taken by the therapist is given to our clients. This conclusion will be applied and illustrated in the next chapter.

Chapter 7

Applications to a Treatment Model of Depression

Before introducing a direct application of the foregoing considerations about (a) the need for multiple reframings of reality, (b) control issues, and (c) issues of confrontation and support in dealing with depression, it is important to lay down a framework that will serve as a theoretical basis for dealing with depression. There is no question that the literature on this subject is so extensive as to defy summary or exposition. Instead of attempting such a review, which would take one away from reduction to systematic, testable proportions, the purpose of this introductory section is to lead directly into a treatment model of depression that will be testable via SHWAs.

LIFE ROLES

Life roles can be conceptualized as triangles, that is, as visual models quite different from the use of triangles in Bowen's theory (1978). His use of the triangle is as dynamic interplay between dyads characterized by a third issue, hence, the triangle. Here, instead, the triangle is used as a structural, visual device to describe relationships among roles within each individual as well as among family members. There are six different life roles, as shown in Figure 7–1.

1. Family formation: father-mother-child
2. Ego states: parent-adult-child
3. Language: I-we-you

4. Drama triangle: victim-persecutor-rescuer
5. Family development: self-mate-parent
6. Societal structures: home-work-leisure

It would be too time consuming to elaborate on all these triangles; the most relevant of the six for family therapy and training is the Drama Triangle, as initially formulated by Karpman (1968) in his triangle of persecutor-rescuer-victim. This triangle has been mentioned by Berne (1971), Steiner (1974), and L'Abate (1976). Before entering this elaboration, one may need to consider the role of triangles in intimate relationships.

The Role of Triangles in Intimate Relationships

Anonymous (1972) had a great deal to say about the role of triangles in intimate family relationships in terms of their resiliency and stability:

> A two-person emotional system is unstable in that it forms itself into a three-person system, or triangle, under stress. A system larger than three persons becomes a series of interlocking triangles. A three-person system is one triangle; a four-person system is four primary triangles; a five-person system is nine primary triangles, etc. (p. 34)

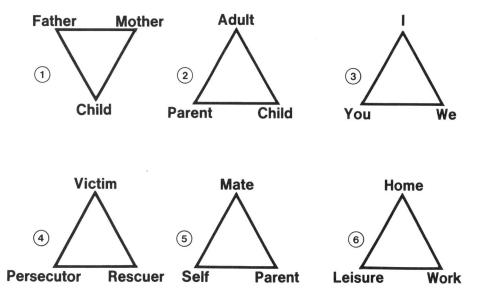

Figure 7–1. The triangles of life roles.

As Fogarty (1979) indicated:

> While two persons may shorten or lengthen the space between them, at no time is there change in the overall area of the triangle. Increased closeness between any two family members results in increased distance from the third member. Movement of persons along the lines of the triangle is reactive, often unaware, and without the free use of self-control. The triangle is a closed system with the sum of the distance between the three members remaining fixed. (p. 42)

The triangle, then, is a solid structure that keeps the status quo in the family. The less the self is present in any member of a dyad, the more likely that an issue (i.e., a symptom) will be substituted for a third member of the triangle. A longer discussion of differentiated and undifferentiated triangles can be found in Bradt (1971).

Slack (1972) conceived of triangles in terms of a problem: an individual who has the problem (P), an individual who has had the same problem (X), and a third person who has never had that problem (N). Movement from one role to another can take place if all these types of individuals are present in relationship to the problem. Another social psychologist who emphasized the triangular nature of human relationships was Heider (1958). Hence, in the notion of triangularity coalesce a variety of experimental social psychological views and clinical insights.

Of course, the triangularity of human existence is derived from the basic father-mother-child triangle and its most immediate derivative, the PAC triangle. From the eternal father-mother-child triangle, then, derive healthy as well as unhealthy relationships. The most frequently found unhealthy triangle is made up of the persecutor (or victimizer), the victim, and the rescuer. Each of these roles needs further description and elaboration. The persecutor-rescuer-victim (PRV) triangle can be seen as a direct derivative (pathological, to be sure) of the PAC triangle. The intent here is to describe how many other pathogenic roles may be derivatives of this triangle.

Triangles as Solutions to Polarities

No single dimension (i.e., a dyad) is sufficiently strong to survive by itself. Furthermore, it could be maintained that, in nature, dyads per se do not exist and that even dyads (such as marriage) have a relationship that furnishes the third element. If the relationship is less stable or permanent, the dyad is formed on the basis of an issue, be it temporary or superficial. All dyads are triangles to the extent that the relationship of the two members of the dyad is the third element of a triad. Mitroff (1974, pp. 218–250) asserted that, in science and scientific inquiry, objectivity is obtained only within the context of a triad of an observer, the object being observed, and the method of observation. Triangles, of course, are basic in navigation and in any process involving localization in space. Many theological or historical views of reality are tripartite (Father, Son, and Holy Ghost), as is Wundt's tripartite theory of emotions or the classification of behavior in terms of cognitive, affective, and conative, or volitional, aspects.

Another aspect of triangles that does not seem to be considered by the sources previously cited relates to the structure of personal pronouns; that is, the structure of personal pronouns is triangular—I, you, and we. Emphasis on the *you* of the triangle dilutes the *we*. By the same token, emphasis on the *I-we* dilutes the emphasis on the *you*. Overemphasis on the *you*, taking away from the use of the *I* and *we* pronouns, is one of the major indications of dysfunction in couples. In differentiated relationships (L'Abate, 1976), all three corners of the triangle are equally emphasized, given equal importance and weight (i.e., "I give value to you so that we can be a we"). By the same token, unequal emphasis on any one corner of the triangle (e.g., *you*—"It's all your fault") takes away from consideration of *I* and *we* in the relationship.

It should be clarified that no one individual plays an exclusive part in this triangle. From a dialectical perspective, we can all play all three parts. Some of us, however, specialize in playing one part better than we play the other two. Individuals who are a part of this kind of system may play more than one role at a time, and there may be rapid reversals of roles. The triangle has a great deal of explanatory and descriptive usefulness if one considers that these three roles may be present in all of us at different times and during different situations in the life cycle. Karpman's (1968), as well as Berne's (1971) and Steiner's (1974), analyses show that if one member of an interlocking system (a family) decides to assume one of the roles, the other members are "forced" to assume complementary roles; otherwise, the game will not work. For example, if one member assumes the role of persecutor, she/he will need someone to assume the role of victim and another to assume the role of rescuer. The role of rescuer would be what we have called the protector (L'Abate, Weeks, & Weeks, 1979).

This triangle may become a vicious circle, which ultimately results in an individual's becoming so entrenched in this kind of script that he/she extends it to persons outside the family. In fact, a child who learns this script may carry it over to his/her new family when he/she marries. Thus, from Karpman's basic triangle, we can derive the following roles, not necessarily in the same row, as shown in Table 7–1.

Variations on the Persecutor Role

We shall need to include here the roles involving evaluation (usually negative), judgments (usually hostile), and authoritarian simplification ("If we had dropped an atom bomb in Vietnam, we would have won the war"). The role of judge, jury, and executioner is evident in many marital and parent-child relationships in which revengeful, eye-for-an-eye laws are the rule. The judge acts as jury and determines the "right" and "wrong" of any issue; issues or individuals are thus dichotomized and separated into "good-bad," "right-wrong," "correct-incorrect." This is essentially the one-up position of the authoritarian, autocratic personality—the position we all assume in judging others ("Nixon was the most corrupt president we have ever had"). The policeman and detective roles are part of the same stance.

Variations on the persecutor role need elaboration. Persecution can occur through a variety of roles, for instance, the judge role. Here, one individual assumes responsibility for evaluating, in judgmental tones (usually negatively), someone else's behavior. Blaming statements, critical comments, and put-downs are all indications that one member of the family has assumed this evaluative role. Parents can do it to each other and their children, and eventually, children do it to their parents. In the juror role, we assume the position of listening to the evidence presented to us on the basis that someone is on trial before us, as in a court. After listening to the evidence, we pass judgment as to guilt or innocence. When guilt has been found, the judge metes out the sentence.

Of course, judges and jurors need evidence to arrive at a final judgment. Consequently, two more roles are used to help gather this evidence: the detective and the policeman roles. The former looks for evidence in unlikely places, sometimes undercover. The latter calls time and delimits the boundaries of acceptable behaviors, giving out tickets if the behavior is not within

Table 7–1

VARIATIONS ON KARPMAN'S BASIC PERSECUTOR-VICTIM-RESCUER TRIANGLE

Persecutor	Rescuer	Victim
Judge	Therapist	Criminal
Parent	Know-it-all or "I know better"	Defendant
Juror	Expert	Invalid
Policeman	Big daddy	Child
Patriot	Tycoon	Drug addict
Detective	Peacemaker	Servant
Preacher	Red Cross nurse or paramedic	Martyr
Executioner	Saint	Sinner
Inquisitor	Superman	Culprit
Oppressor	Superwoman	Poor-little-me
Inspector general	Connections	Oppressed
Interrogator	Wholesaler	Innocent
	Retailer	
	Band-Aid	

prescribed bounds. Eventually, after the gathering of evidence, the presentation of evidence at a trial, and the pronouncement of a sentence (on the basis of a guilty judgment), the final outcome is assumption of the role of executioner—the sentence must be executed and the guilty punished! All of us must pay for our transgressions!

Variations on the Victim Role

It takes an individual who is willing to assume the victim role to allow another to assume the role of persecutor. One cannot go without the other; both roles are present, at least potentially, in all of us. We allow ourselves to be victimized and assume the "martyr" or the "abused" role, often setting ourselves up to fulfill such a prophecy in ourselves.

There are a number of variations on the theme of victim. The most obvious are martyrs, saints, schlemiels, innocents, and helpless persons, which do not need elaboration. Let us see if we can find less obvious ones: a variation on the theme of persecutor-victim is the "I-am-innocent; s/he-is-the-culprit" variation. Here, the innocent takes the place of the persecutor by very reason of his innocence. The culprit, of course, by very reason of his defense, needs to proclaim innocence, implying, of course, that the so-called innocent one is the culprit. These positions produce an impasse—a balance that is difficult to break.

Variations on the Rescuer Role

Most rescuers are those who have resources, both tangible and intangible, real or imagined. As Foa and Foa (1974) have emphasized, there are six classes of resources (to be elaborated in Chapter 12): (1) money, (2) status, (3) knowledge, (4) goods, (5) love, and (6) services. Each of these resource classes has a role attached to it that can fit the rescuer (i.e., the tycoon, the director, the lover, the computer, the doctor, the cook, or the provider). Variations on this role would be too lengthy to be useful here. Many of us psychotherapists, however, see ourselves as rescuers since, very likely, we come from familial matrixes in which we saw ourselves as victims. We merely switch the role to another part of the triangle. If (or when) we fail in our rescuer role, we assume the persecuting stance and use evaluative judgments of a psychiatric or negative nature, explaining a behavior with another behavior but, in reality, falling into sophisticated, professionally sanctioned labeling and name calling!

The rescuer, then, needs to save others because of his/her own unresolved PRV triangle. The paradox at this point is that if we, as therapists, get over being rescuers, we may want to give up being therapists. Or if we continue the role of therapist, we continue it on a more realistic (i.e., economical and professional) basis. When the rescuer aspect is still present in the therapist, trouble begins and the therapist's effectiveness becomes questionable.

Therapeutic Applications

The turning from an unhealthy triangle to healthy relationships implies that the change agent is powerful enough to obtain such a change. It means changing negative values in each of the three corners by setting up another triangle powerful enough to offset the negatives. Such a change cannot take place unless the members of the triangle hurt enough to want to give up what they are doing and are willing to consider other possibilities of behavior not used before.

Elaborations on the Drama Triangle. In the previous discussion, I elaborated on Karpman's (1968) drama triangle, in which pathology is seen as relating to three interconnecting and interdependent roles: persecutor, rescuer, victim. This section elaborates on the clinical usefulness of this triangle in its application to therapeutic failures, in which the therapist becomes enmeshed in assuming, first, the role of rescuer for a victim and then, because of the failure to rescue the "victim," becomes either a victim or a persecutor.

The Dialectics of the Drama Triangle. The drama starts within the family; the soon-to-be-identified patient assumes the role of the victim by acting in self-debasing ways that get attention but do not break the vicious circle. Parents alternate between roles of rescuers and persecutors, while the victim succeeds in keeping his/her role unchanged.

Eventually, the victim (if, in the meantime, there has not been a suicide, or an accident, or hospitalization) will get to a therapist, either alone or with the family. The therapist, if he/she is not careful, will become enmeshed enough to assume a rescuing role, that is, by using techniques and methods that will not produce any change, either in the victim or in the family system, or both. The therapist will be defeated; whether this defeat takes place objectively or subjectively, the therapist can then switch from the role of rescuer to the role of either victim or persecutor. She/he may end up feeling frustrated, cheated, essentially questioning his/her ability and competence as a therapist. From this role, the therapist may turn to a persecutor role, branding the victim as a "patient" with a psychiatric label to justify the failure to help.

The Denouement of the Drama Triangle. Another development in the drama triangle takes place, especially when the victim is a woman. An adolescent with an unhappy home, where the parents are perceived and probably behave as persecutors and rescuers, will eventually marry a husband who has become a rescuer to save her from her family. However, the victim brings with her the role, as shown in depression, hysteria, etc.

The husband, who until now has enjoyed the role of rescuer, is unable to cope with the role of victim played by the wife (crying, complaining). Eventually, no matter how patient or controlled he may be, he will become the persecutor, criticizing or blaming the wife or, in extreme cases, hitting or battering her, further reinforcing the role of victim.

She may then find a therapist who will enter into a collusion with her against a past or present persecutor (i.e., her parents and/or her husband). In doing so (i.e., accepting her perception of their destructiveness as persecutors), the therapist then starts to assume the role of rescuer. The victim will continue to enjoy her role, externalizing most responsibility for her behavior toward her husband and/or her parents but essentially not changing. Eventually, the therapist may get bored or tired of the repetitiveness of the woman's complaints and her inability to assume this continuation on therapeutic grounds (it will take a long time to change her need for support, for example). As the therapist, however, starts to see the victim for other than straight therapeutic reasons, she will start to feel taken advantage of, cheated, frustrated. The victim may terminate therapy or, because of the ineffectiveness of therapy thus far, drop out or seek another therapist. The therapist may feel victimized and start being critical of the woman for her inability to change; this criticism eventually becomes manifest in the ultimate rejection—the psychiatric label (i.e., "She cannot change because she is depressed, psychotic, etc.").

If (or when) the therapist is unable to cope, she/he may begin to terminate, or the victim herself, already sensitive to criticism and failure in her previous interactions with parents or husband, may drop out herself, joining the thousands of therapeutic failures who float from one therapist to another.

The victim has few alternatives left by the time she meets a therapist who is able to get her out of the victim role and to assume a more constructive and creative outlook on herself and her relationships. Alternatively, she may go through the full circle and rejoin her parents in the original triangle.

When the victim is a male, he may choose a woman who will assume the role of rescuer first and persecutor second, assuming the transgenerational continuation of the drama triangle.

Often the victim may switch roles and become a persectuor, forcing a polarization in the parents (i.e., one becomes the rescuer and the other the persecutor, alternating both roles), while the child keeps the victim role as long as it is convenient.

Thus, the drama triangle becomes a useful device not only to understand certain aspects, mostly transactional, of family psychopathology, but to understand therapeutic failures in which the drama triangle is reenacted with the help of the therapist.

This introduction serves to see depression as the result of the expression of interplays among the various parts of two triangles. One is the drama triangle already considered. The other triangle is concerned with how distance is maintained in the family through the use of roles like distancer, pursuer, and distance regulator (Barton & Alexander, 1981). The distancer avoids closeness, the pursuer actively wants it, and the distance regulator plays the "ambivalent" approach-avoidance game ("Come here, go away"; "Help me but not in the way you do it"). Of course, no one wins in these triangles, and the person labeled "depressed" usually has incorporated both triangles with special emphasis on playing the victim role and the distance regulator part (see Appendix A).

Of course, these parts are interchangeable. Anyone can play all six parts at any given time. For instance, a husband may be playing the distancer part emotionally but the pursuer sexually. By the same token, the wife may play the pursuer part emotionally and the distancer part sexually. Most of us play all these roles, hit-switching from one to the other, keeping these triangles alive and our families together and, naturally, unchanged!

THE PARADOXICAL TREATMENT OF (MARITAL) DEPRESSION

This section details in specific steps the paradoxical treatment of depression in the light of the arguments presented in Chapters 5 and 6.

Depression, specifically marital depression, is a very resistant pattern, because of the rigid adherence to keeping it and maintaining it in spite of the onslaught of various therapeutic approaches. In many cases, in spite of a variety of linear frontal attacks, the depression is not given up and the individual resists any possible therapeutic intervention. Consequently, it is important to follow a definite sequence of four steps: (a) multiple positive reframings, (b) prescription of the depression in (c) a ritualized fashion, and (d) systematically linked (Appendix A).

MULTIPLE POSITIVE REFRAMINGS

In many cases of depression one single positive reframing of the symptom is insufficient. Consequently the symptom needs to be elevated to the highest possible common denominator of goodness and usefulness. To obtain this goal at least nine different positive reframings are necessary to convince the depressed individual. It is important that the therapist him/herself believe in the validity of these statements in order to deliver them convincingly, concisely, and constructively.

Statement No. 1. "I am glad to hear you are depressed, because if you were not, I doubt whether you would have sought professional help." This statement essentially reframes positively the reason for asking for help (L'Abate, 1975a).

Statement No. 2. "I am glad to hear you are depressed. There are a lot of people who are unwilling or unable to recognize or accept their depressions. These people are unable or unwilling to ask for help and end up in hospitals, jails, morgues, and cemeteries." This statement differentiates between people who ask for help and those who do not and makes depression a positive and constructive motivation for therapy.

Statement No. 3. "We are all depressed individuals. We only vary in the degree we are willing or able to recognize and accept depression in ourselves. We cannot live and not be depressed, because we all are vulnerable to hurts as fallible and needy human beings" (L'Abate & L'Abate, 1979).

Statement No. 4. "I am glad to hear you are depressed because then we can do something about it. If you were depressed and did not admit it, you might be doing something destructive, like drinking, gambling, or driving fast cars." Although this statement may seem repetitious of previous statements, especially No. 2, it is a somewhat different refrain, or a variation on the same theme. It is also a hopeful statement.

Statement No. 5. "Depression can be used and eventually, if you use it right, you may even learn to enjoy it." This is a rather startling reframing of the symptom and is perhaps one of the most attention getting of all these statements.

Statement No. 6. "Up to now you have considered depression as an enemy and a foe to fight and to avoid. It is the black hole of Calcutta to run away from. I suggest, instead, that you start thinking of depression as a friend, something you want to join, use well, and eventually learn to live with and enjoy." This statement is also rather useful in getting attention, and in many ways reflects the convictions of this writer about depression, like all the previous statements.

Statement No. 7. "Up to now depression has controlled you, your life, and perhaps your marriage and your family. Now you need to choose, do you want the depression to control you or do you want to control it?" This statement is the logical extension of all the previous statements. Although some of the previous statements could be skipped according to the therapist's individual style, the last two statements are crucial in the reframing because they lend direction to the prescription of the symptom.

Statement No. 8. Sometimes additional positive statements about depression have been found useful; for example, "Depression as the royal road to self and selfhood. I can only learn more about myself when I am by myself and allow myself to be with my depression so that I can listen to it." Here the therapist can model for the client the value of being depressed, in words that indicate that the experience of depression is familiar to him/her and not foreign or uncommon.

Statement No. 9. "When I am depressed, I am being honest with myself because depression is a truth teller and it can tell me a lot about myself that I would not know if I were not depressed." A variation on this statement would be: "I am together and honest with myself when I am depressed. When I deny or reject depression, I am phony and I despise myself."

These statements convey to the client(s) all the multiple attributions that can be given to depression. It is somewhat arrogant for some of us to think that one single statement, no matter how positive, can convince our clients. It is important, therefore, to resort to a wide range of positive reframings that in some way reflect the therapist's convictions and beliefs.

Symptom Prescription

Once the cognitive spadework is done and the client(s) is/are convinced of the validity of this position, it follows from the foregoing statements that it is the function of the therapist to help the client(s) reach the goal of controlling the symptom. The principle behind this prescription is a basic one already considered in the previous chapter; i.e., *we need to make the depression occur when it is naturally occurring* (that is, the therapist achieves control of the symptom, i.e., the depression, by helping the client achieve that control). The control is achieved by following all four steps outlined here.

It follows from the principle above that through symptom prescription the therapist makes the depression take place when it is normally and usually occurring through a change of the sequence in the occurrence and in the context, both cognitive and external. If the client wants to achieve control, then it follows that the prescription should be obeyed because it is through this joining with the symptom, rather than avoidance, that control is obtained. Consequently, "being depressed," whatever it may mean to the client, is *the desired state of being* rather than otherwise. "Go be depressed. I need you to be depressed at certain times of our own choosing and in certain places of our own choosing." Here the therapist conveys to the client that s/he needs to become friends with the symptom and to start learning from it: "I want you to become depressed whenever you are alone or whenever it is possible for you to be by yourself and be depressed without interruptions." It is important here to convey the notion that being depressed needs to take place at *prearranged times and prearranged places*. "So that if you have any depressed thoughts or feelings before that time you learn to put some of those thoughts or feelings aside until you have a proper time and place for them."

Ritualized Tasks and Assignments

Five different rituals will be considered in this section: (a) choosing the frequency (alternate days like Monday, Wednesday, and Friday, or Tuesday, Thursday, and Saturday); (b) choosing the time of day to be depressed (usually in the evening before going to bed or at any other time when the client can be alone and undisturbed); (c) choosing the length of time to be depressed (any time from 15 to 30 minutes has been found to be sufficient); (d) setting an alarm clock or kitchen timer for the desired and agreed-upon interval; and

(e) concentrating on being depressed and writing down every thought and feeling that comes through one's head during that time. Of course, these notes are to be brought to the therapist for reading and discussion so that the goal of learning from the depression is reached.

Systemic Linkage

Unless the individual lives alone and help cannot be obtained from other sources, the foregoing prescriptions need to be systematically linked with the individual who is most involved with the symptoms, i.e., spouse, partners, parents, etc.—the involved intimate. The function of this linkage is to change *the sequence* of symptom occurrence; that is, usually the depressed individual uses the symptom to attract sympathy, support, and succor. However, as soon as this is about to happen, avoidance sets in and the caring intimate involved, usually (naively?) well intentioned, is rebuffed, rejected, or discounted. Otherwise, the caring intimate feels helpless in dealing with the symptom and is or feels victimized by it. The direction, however, is from the symptom bearer to the involved intimate. A systemic linkage puts the involved intimate in charge, so to speak, of the symptom. It is up to him/her to *remind* the symptom bearer that s/he has to be depressed and under what conditions. Now the sequence is changed. Instead of going from the symptom to the involved intimate, control is going from the involved intimate to the symptom. By changing *multiple* contexts, within both the individuals and the relationship involved, the symptom is also changed.

DISCUSSION

One of the major implications of this form of treatment is theoretical. What is paradoxical about the steps and substeps outlined here? Are the multiple positive reframings paradoxical if the therapist wholly believes in their validity? Most of the task assignments are linear and straightforward. Is being positive in one's thinking and reframing paradoxical? At this time, no definite conclusion has been reached by this writer, except to raise these qustions to wonder whether any circularly complex and multiply determined and equipotential reality can, should, and needs to be reduced to a linear progression. Certainly, this is one of the challenges facing paradoxical psychotherapy.

This formulation leads to at least two therapeutic implications, one about timing and the other about resistance. In regard to the former, it is important to have established a relationship with the client and his/her supporting system (involved intimates). It is within this context that information about the nature of the depression and of the overall functioning needs to be gathered. One needs to evaluate secondary gains and how much distance regulation the symptom exerts on the whole system. Hence, it is important to gather a great deal of pertinent information and in so doing form a trusting relationship with whoever is involved in the symptom.

Occasionally, especially with drug addicts, one will find individuals who are so afraid and fearful of depression that they will resist doing the homework. For many of them depression means loss of control, reality, and even life. Consequently, one may need to wait longer and not insist that homework assignments be followed as a condition for continuing therapy. Instead, one needs to wait patiently and show that as bouts of depression repeat themselves, the client is helped to approach depression slowly, eventually helping him/her arrive at a positive, rather than a bleak, black, and burdensome, view of depression. Once this cognitive restructuring takes place (and often it may take a few weeks), then the next step of symptom prescription can take place. Hence, the therapist needs to keep his/her position clear and constant, without, however, harassing the client with it: "We have tried it your way. Does it work for you? Are you ready to try it my way?" The option of symptoms control, and of course personal responsibility, is difficult for some people to accept, especially if powerlessness, helplessness, and hopelessness have been the main characteristics of their life-style. Eventually, once it is demonstrated that fighting depression does not work, they can be helped in joining it (Appendix A).

CONCLUSION

This approach has been used with a variety of clients, single, married, and in families. Its logical and empirical validity has been assessed already (Jessee & L'Abate, 1985), but greater empirical validation is necessary.

The Second Stage: Systematic Homework Assignments

Chapter 8

Negotiation: Decision Making and Problem Solving in the Family

The purpose of this chapter is to consider a model of negotiation in the family that would lend itself to applicability and testability. This model consists of three components: (a) power sharing or division of labor, (b) task assignments, and (c) negotiation potential. Chapter 6 considered control and influence as one aspect of power. In this chapter, power will be considered in terms of decision making and problem solving. A summary of this model is found in Table 8–1 and the SHWAs derived from it are in Appendix B.

As Beavers and Voeller (1983) commented, negotiation skills are the most important skills that most dysfunctional families lack:

> Individual and family functioning can be related on at least two observable dimensions, negotiation skills and boundary clarity. An individual's skills in defining self limits and negotiating with others are tied to how skillfully that individual's family is able to handle those tasks. (p. 96)

THE PROCESS OF NEGOTIATION

Most of the literature on negotiation has been reviewed elsewhere (L'Abate, Ganahl, & Hansen, 1986). Consequently, this section will present the model and supporting references.

The role of motivational factors has been reviewed by Zantman (1976) and especially by Druckman (1977). The latter presented the most complete available model of negotiation, comprising antecedent preconditions (goals, incentives, and power/dependency relations) and background factors (cognitive and ideological differences, bargaining orientation, attitudes between parties, and the personalities and roles of the negotiators). In concurrent processes, Druckman distinguished among bargaining tactics and strategies, persuasive debate, coercive tactics (e.g., threats, punishments, commitments), and phases defined by concessions and cooperation/competition. In concurrent conditions, Druckman distinguished among openers, secret parading, monitoring feedback, number of coalitions, third parties, mediational mechanisms, stresses, complexity, context, and external events. Among outcomes, Druckman listed type of agreement, satisfaction with agreement, and the range of possible outcomes and new alternatives.

Hermann and Kogan (1977), studying the effects of negotiators' "personalities" on negotiation behavior, found what may well be the antecedent characteristics to suggest that functionality and successful problem solving go hand in hand in families.

> Subjects with a cooperative orientation toward negotiation were high in anxiety, moderate in cognitive complexity, high in conciliation, and low in self-esteem. Subjects with an exploitive orientation were low in anxiety, high in cognitive complexity, low in conciliation, and moderate in self-esteem. Subjects with a competitive orientation were moderate in conciliation and high in self-esteem. . . . Subjects whose strategy focused on their own self-

Table 8–1

SUMMARY OF A MODEL OF NEGOTIATION AND NEGOTIATION POTENTIAL
IN THE FAMILY

A. Power sharing and division of labor
   1. Authority—Who makes the decisions about what?
   2. Responsibility—Who carries the decisions out and how are these decisions carried out?
B. Task assignments
   1. Orchestration—Who makes the *big* decisions and how are they carried out?
   2. Instrumentation—Who carries out the *little* decisions and how are they carried out?
C. Negotiation potential = ill × skill × will
   1. *Ill* means the level of functionality-dysfunctionality to negotiate available to the family. This level is defined by the family's style (Chapter 9).
   2. *Skill* means the level of ability-disability to negotiate available to the family. This level is defined by the family's competence (Chapters 10 & 11).
   3. *Will* means the level of motivation to negotiate available to the family. This level is defined by the family's priorities (Chapter 12).

---

interests were more authoritarian than were subjects whose strategy focused on mutual interests. (Hermann & Kogan, 1977, pp. 262–263)

From these results, Hermann and Kogan concluded:

The mesh of predispositions of the opponents can help determine how each perceives the other's moves and intentions and how sensitive each will be to the other's behavior. . . . Interpersonality sensitivity (in negotiation) depends on the personality characteristics of both members of a dyad. (p. 276)

This study forges possibly the strongest link between individual personality factors and dyadic interactions, suggesting a relationship between functionality and problem solving: the healthier the individual members of a family, the more successful their problem-solving negotiation, decision making, and conflict resolution strategies will be (Lewis, Beavers, Gossett, & Phillips, 1976).

A MODEL OF NEGOTIATION

If the goal of family therapy is to improve the negotiating competence of a family, we need to know more about the process of negotiation and its components. Unfortunately, existing models of negotiation, decision making, and problem solving (L'Abate, Ganahl, & Hansen, 1986) are incomplete (they do not include emotions as a component, for instance), irrelevant (because they apply to short-lived, contrived situations), or ineffective (because they apply to homogeneous groups of managers, not to heterogeneous groups such as the family). A relevant, effective model of negotiation needs to separate the observable components of the negotiation process, giving a diagnostic notion of the process as it breaks down and also how it applies to clinical and nonclinical families.

RESISTANCE TO NEGOTIATION

Some of the stickiest problems in helping families negotiate are (a) motivating them to negotiate and (b) teaching them how to negotiate by acquiring completely new skills. In this regard, the confrontation of issues must be presented as a sine qua non for change; that is, without confrontation of conflictual issues, there will be no change. Consequently, the resistant member(s) needs to be confronted with the idea that refusal to face issues keeps the family unchanged. In this situation, it is important to elaborate the costs and rewards of such a position. After this analysis has been completed, the individual is congratulated for his/her concern for and protection of the family and asked to choose the position s/he wants, with full awareness of the consequences (e.g., polarization, rejection, expulsion).

The next issue in resistance to negotiation is the amount of emotionality aroused by confronting conflictual issues; that is, the emotionality may become so intense that negotiation cannot proceed. At this point, the therapist should point out the essential distinction between feelings (how one feels about the issue) and actions (what can be done about the issue). Often the aroused individual, on the basis of past experiences, has developed a great deal of emotionality; thus, it is important at this point to deal with the whole issue of forgiveness (L'Abate, 1975a). Can the past be let go? Beyond the unwillingness to negotiate and the accompanying inability to negotiate, one is bound to find, more often than not, frustration, despair, hopelessness, and helplessness. All of these, and other attendant feelings, need to be brought out and expressed. Again, the therapist here needs to remind the family of the basic separation between feelings and actions. Until now, family members have perhaps thought in terms of a linear, single-causality model; that is, only one course of action is possible. Instead, the family needs to learn that given certain feelings—whatever they are, however limited they may be—countless actions and options are available to them.

A third necessary issue in the beginning stages of negotiation relates to establishing common ground rules for the whole process. Ground rules may be (a) avoiding accusations and recriminations; (b) avoiding the pronoun "You" and using "I" or "We"; that is, expression of feelings in a nonjudgmental and nonhurtful fashion; and (c) following common rules of courtesy, such as waiting for a person to finish, and abiding as much as possible by the Golden Rule. After all members accept these common ground rules, the therapist needs to clarify (a) the goals of the negotiation, (b) the processes to be followed in reaching the common goals, and (c) realistic outcomes that match the goals.

All the preceding illustrates the therapist's major role in teaching negotiation skills to families—to help them switch from a climate of emotionality to a climate of rationality (Bowen, 1978), with distinct boundaries around emotion and how it can be expressed, the rational process of creative discussion, and action separate from emotionality and rationality. Without these boundaries, it is almost impossible for the process of negotiation to proceed to a successful outcome. Skillfully used, the emotionality aroused by confrontation can become the motivation to negotiate successfully.

During this process, the therapist should be aware of the role that defeats and defeating behaviors play in keeping the family close and unchanged (L'Abate, 1985). Without a positive reframing of these defeats and the desire to transform them into victories, the process may falter.

WHAT IS POWER?

McDonald's exhaustive review (1980) covered most of the theoretical and methodological issues relating to power. Views about power vary from overuse (Haley, 1976) to a nihilistic denial that such a concept is even needed (Foa & Foa, 1974). Little would be accomplished by restating McDonald's arguments, breaking down family power into marital, parental, offspring, sibling, and kinship relationships. The resources that McDonald considered the bases of power are normative authority, economics, affect, personality, and cognition. Control is attempted through influence, persuasion, and assertiveness. The outcomes are attained through decision making, implementation, and definition of social/family realities.

Instead of following McDonald's concepts and models, this chapter presents a different theoretical model that has been useful in understanding families structurally as well as processually. This model rephrases existing models concerning the overlap and similarity among decision making, conflict resolution, problem solving, and negotiation (L'Abate, Ganahl, & Hansen, 1986). The original feature of this model is that one may consider its information processing with significantly separate, clearly identifiable steps and invariant sequences.

Despite the profusion of research literature on power in the family (Alkire, 1972; Bahr, Bowerman, & Gecas, 1974; Bowerman & Bahr, 1973; Cromwell & Olson, 1975; McDonald, 1980; Swingle, 1976) and the importance of this concept in family functioning and decision making (Haley, 1976), very little of this literature has filtered into the everyday language of family therapists. Reasons for such neglect are perhaps irrelevant to the issue at hand: *Whatever power exists in the family, it must be negotiated, but to negotiate power, everyone in the family must share it.* To achieve this goal, one needs a clear definition of power. A variety of definitions of power in the interpersonal context (Schopler, 1965) have been proffered. Power has been equated with energy in the physical realm but, as such, it is difficult to define and to assess. Some people suggest abandoning this concept as too vague and too difficult to assess (L'Abate, 1976). Others consider it the basic ingredient of decision making (French & Raven, 1959; Haley, 1976).

Perhaps this construct would become useful if we define power as having two components—authority and responsibility. *Authority* refers to who has the power to make decisions, and *responsibility* refers to who has the power to carry out those decisions. Thus, authority is the process of decision making, whereas responsibility is the process of implementing such decisions. Often, both authority and responsibility reside in the same individual (e.g., when one makes strictly self-relating decisions). On the other hand, a variety of decisions involve more than one person. More specifically, in marriage, a variety of decisions need to be carried out, for instance, housecleaning, cooking, child care, and finances.

In such circumstances, authority and responsibility often become split; that is, one individual may have all the decision-making powers while the other has all the responsibility to carry out decisions. Furthermore, the spouse who has the authority, but not the responsibility, is the one who wants to retain such an arrangement. Under these conditions, the marriage becomes a boss-servant relationship rather than a partnership. Depending on how ingrained and rigid this arrangement is, it may or may not be functional for the persons involved. Although the split between authority and responsibility is commonly seen in spouses, it can be found also in parent-child relationships in which the parent wants the authority but the child takes (or refuses) responsibility by conforming to (or opposing) the parental decision making. If the authority is inconsistent, coercive, or rigid, the child may develop oppositional or rebellious behaviors that question the parental authority (L'Abate, 1976). Thus a vague concept, power, can be reduced to specifically visible processes of decision making, or authority, and the execution of decisions, or responsibility. Dysfunctionality occurs when both processes have not been satisfactorily negotiated.

Supposedly, authority is commensurate with responsibility. However, this is not always the case, especially in intimate relationships. Often (L'Abate, 1976), fathers want the authority but not the responsibility, and some wives collude in this arrangement. By the same token, some men may relinquish decision-making authority to avoid assuming responsibility. Conflict about power issues may ensue; unresolved conflict will produce dysfunctionality.

Power becomes a highly visible and observable concept when it is reduced to who more often makes the decisions about what issues (authority) and who translates such decisions into tasks and chores (responsibility). For instance, in analyses of household chores, many supposedly egalitarian couples claim equal responsibility. When one observes who does what, however, the woman is very likely the one who completes these chores. The issue here is that power, like most anything else in life, needs to be negotiated.

WHO DOES WHAT?

A second component of this model lies in the structure of the task or issue at hand; deciding to move or buy a home may be a different issue from deciding to go to a movie or a restaurant. Dysfunctional families may find it difficult to participate at all levels of decision making and become as upset by minor decisions as by major ones. Functional families may be upset more by major than by minor decisions. Furthermore, functional families would be clearer on not leaving one single member stuck rigidly in any one role.

In dysfunctional families, roles of who decides what may be more rigid than in functional families, giving rise to greater confusion about who does what and when it is done.

Levin (1976) differentiated two levels of power on the basis of the importance and the frequency of decisions. Rule-setting decisions that determine the family life-style were defined as *orchestrational*. Frequent administrative decisions necessary for the ongoing life of the family were defined as *instrumentational*. For the purposes of this model, we shall call Levin's levels of power *task assignments*. In the analysis of 140 couples interviewed through a specially derived questionnaire, Levin found that the partner who had the greater ratio of resources had the greater authority to make orchestration decisions and to relegate such authority. Orchestration-level decisions were found to be male-dominant, whereas instrumentation-level decisions were female-dominant. Levin's differentiation adds to the model in understanding the sharing of power in the family.

NEGOTIATION POTENTIAL

Inability to negotiate derives from feelings of inadequacy and powerlessness. A genuine lack of appropriate skills is the outcome of prolonged social deviance and/or isolation. Thus, a third component of this model, negotiation potential (NP), is the outcome of the following multiplicative factors: (health $\times$ ability $\times$ motivation); that is, NP = (ill $\times$ skill $\times$ will).

NP involves three characteristics as the minimum necessary conditions to start the process of negotiation, i.e., the degree of health-functionality (ill) existing at the time (Chapter 9), which may or may not be related to the amount of skill available (Chapters 10 and 11) and to the degree of motivation (will) necessary to want to negotiate (Chapter 12). Negotiation, then, cannot take place unless a certain degree of functionality (as yet unknown), a certain amount of skill (also unknown), and a certain degree of motivation are available in the family.

THE FUNCTIONS OF A NEGOTIATION MODEL

As discussed in the next four chapters, this model has various functions: (a) It synthesizes and integrates a wide range of knowledge, schools, and theories, showing how each school, theory, or approach impinges on and emphasizes one particular component of an information-processing chain. (b) This model not only outlines the steps of a negotiation process but specifies the competencies that are necessary for negotiation (i.e., a deficit in any one of the three areas can break down the whole process). (c) These components are relevant to a life-cycle view of negotiation, identifying (1) personal career (emotionality and awareness); (2) educational career (self-concept); (3) occupational career (activity); and (4) priorities and contextual careers (in-laws, children, siblings, friends, neighbors). How this model applies to the actual teaching of negotiation can be found in L'Abate's (1981b) discussion of the role of family conferences as a step toward learning negotiation skills.

Diagnosis

This model, in its static and structural characteristics, has mostly a descriptive, diagnostic function. From this model, it is relatively easy for the therapist to ask the family relevant questions and discover who has the authority (if any), who has the responsibility, what kind of decisions are made on major and minor matters, and who makes them. More inferentially, the therapist needs to assess the functionality, ability, and motivation of the family to gauge their potential to negotiate, more or less successfully, issues of having, doing, and being (Chapter 12). Sharing this information directly, through focused questioning, directs therapy toward helping family members to learn to negotiate successfully, starting perhaps with easy, concrete issues and going on to more complex ones.

Therapy

Teaching power-sharing and negotiation skills to couples and families implies a much more active role than some therapists are willing to assume. Levenson (1972) predicted:

> A new therapy is emerging, along with a new therapist and new patient, oriented more to participation than understanding, sensitivity and design rather than to insight and formulation. Psychoanalysis, to remain an enterprise of true sensibility, must be a bit ahead of its time seeing into the future and embracing it. This is not mere modishness, although it moves toward it, but rather a quite necessary vitality. *What "works" pragmatically in one period will not work in the next.* (pp. 222–223)

Garfield (1981), commenting on changing phases in psychotherapy, noted that one trend may be shorter and more active therapies. He mentioned Herzberg (1946) and Thorne (1946) as two of the pioneers in this area. Herzberg (1946) was among the first therapists to indicate how to exert direct influence on the patient's personal environment by removing, or transferring, the patient from it. He also assigned tasks directed against (a) impulses that maintain the neurosis, (b) obstacles to satisfaction, (c) essential predispositions (to failure), (d) gains (secondary), and (e) delaying factors.

Thus, the role of the therapist in power sharing and negotiation is much more active than previously thought or taught. Family members are asked to (a) set aside one hour a week for couple or family conferences (L'Abate, 1981a); (b) carry note pads in which they jot down what happens outside and inside those meetings; and (c) show an active involvement outside the therapy session to demonstrate that they are indeed involved in the process of change—they cannot change lying down!

A therapist, however, can only be as effective as his/her conceptual tools. If his/her tools are outdated, vague, and inappropriate, therapeutic effectiveness will slow down. Since a therapist needs to be clear about what is going on, the therapist's first function is diagnostic. S/he needs to assess very clearly how power is shared. Who has the authority for what? Who has the responsibility? Who makes major decisions? Who makes minor ones? How are those decisions negotiated (if they are negotiated)? Are they haphazard and last-minute? Or are they clearly planned, prepared, and implemented? What resources are negotiated? Why?

The goal of the family therapist, then, is to help families learn how to share and negotiate power equitably and harmoniously. To attain this goal, the therapist must understand the nature of power and actively help families to negotiate it.

CONCLUSION

Most family therapy literature has not paid sufficient and necessary attention to invariant steps and sequences involved in the process of negotiation. Negotiation is a crucial process that is present in most if not all aspects of our lives. However, most of us, personally and professionally, have had little if no experience with it (is this why family therapists also get divorced?). Power, defined here as authority and responsibility, needs to be negotiated in the family (as well as outside it). A model of decision making and problem solving is submitted to identify and clarify the various component sequences of this process. This model lends itself to SHWAs that can be applied to test it.

Chapter 9

Styles in Intimate Relationships

A previous theoretical presentation (L'Abate, 1976) omitted the linking of internal personality differentiation to external patterns of interpersonal style. It is the purpose of this chapter to correct that omission and to link certain characteristics to visible interpersonal patterns, suggesting three basic styles in intimate (close and prolonged) relationships. These basic styles are apathy, reactivity, and conductivity. Apathy *(A)* stands for (a) *autism* (maximal distance from people), (b) *alienation* (feeling apart and isolated from others), (c) *atrophy* in emotional expressiveness, and (d) *abuse,* among others (see Table 9–1). Reactivity *(R)* stands for (a) *reaction,* (b) *repetition* of the same or opposite pattern, and (c) *rebuttals,* among others. Conductivity *(C)* stands for (a) *creativity,* (b) *congruence,* and (c) *commitment* to change in intimate relationships, among others. Apathy means "doing nothing" through withdrawal, turning away, and either not participating in an interaction or reaction with violent or abusive actions. Reactivity means following the initiative of someone else, doing something in sequence and secondarily to what someone else has already said, stated, or done. Conductivity means taking initiative, responsibility, and leadership ahead of someone else, getting out of the trenches, so to speak, showing one's true colors and acting in accord with one's sense of being in charge, caring, and necessity. Each of these styles has direct consequences for interpersonal relationships. A list of synonymous terms for these three styles is found in Table 9–1.

This model has been taken to characterize most intimate relationships even though Beels and Ferber (1969) originally used parts of it (reactivity and conductivity) to characterize schools of family therapy and therapists. It will be used to describe intimate relationships between parents and children, between spouses, and between therapists and clients. This model has been found useful in its derivation from a theory of personality development in the

Table 9–1
A GLOSSARY FOR THE *A-R-C* MODEL

Apathy

A: This letter stands for an abusive absence or atrophy of activity, with an aggressive or acrimonious acerbation, avoidance, and aggravation of relationships.

abusive—physical, pharmacological, or verbal
absence of activity—passivity with
atrophy—inability to respond
aggressive—aimed at physical pain with
acrimonious—bitter and sour acts
acerbation—designed to make worse the
avoidance—withdrawal from a situation
aggravation—guaranteed to deteriorate through *alienation, autism, addiction*

Reactivity

R: This letter stands for repetitive retaliations or revengeful rebuttals designed to keep a relationship the same or refractory to change.

rigidity—inability or unwillingness to change, with a
repetitive—pattern of repetitious sameness or oppositeness
retaliation—to pay back in kind with an
rebuttal—immediate answer
restricted—limited or
revengeful—angry put-down
refractory—unchanging or difficult to change, with redundant reiteration and
reversals—role shifts from one position to another, producing inconsistent and contradictory patterns, taking place especially when individuals subscribe to a digital (either-or, black-white, true-false, right-wrong) view of reality, and
recriminations—accusations and blaming through which a culprit, victim, or perpetrator is "found" and "labeled"

Conductivity

C: This letter stands for caring and compassionate concern and commitment to creative change through confrontation and clarification of content and context.

constructive—positive
commitment—determination to
creative—be different
change—in improving the
context—surroundings, through
contact—actual seeing and hearing
confrontation—involving all parties
congruent—matching words with deeds through
circular—surprising and suddenly positive
cryptic—reframing of issues concerning
change—oneself and interactions involving
competence—an ability to negotiate

family (L'Abate, 1976) and in its application to most clinical problems found in dyadic and multiperson systems.

It is important at the outset to define what is meant by "style." Parloff, Waskow, and Wolfe (1978) defined style as a range of dimensions: (a) non-lexical properties of speechlike inflection, fluency, loudness, and pitch; (b) lexical aspects, such as infrequently used words; (c) kinesis—body movements and gestures; (d) technical emphasis, such as directive and supportive; (e) connotative meanings inferred from both verbal and nonverbal patterns. These meanings represent the context relevant to the personality of the individual, going beyond the technical aspects but dealing with a more atmospheric orientation (e.g., permissive, authoritarian). In fact, according to Parloff et al. (1978), only the last dimension of style—connotative meaning—has shown any positive relationship to outcome. The authors also cited Lieberman, Yalom, and Miles' study (1973), in which four clusters seem to be related to positive outcome (i.e., a leadership style that involves moderate level of stimulation, high caring, frequent clarification of feelings, and a moderate executive function).

In addition, McCall and Simmons (1966) stressed the importance of role identities and of the self as determinants of actions. The differentiation of role identity has a great deal to do with how we intervene in our intimate relationships. We can choose to define ourselves as *apathetic* (and we all may be, at times), as *reactive* (and we all may be, at times), or as *conductive* (and we all may well be, at times). Yet, as will become clear during the presentation of this model, the conductive style is the professional ideal, *if* one is oriented toward change rather than toward repetition or stagnation in a relationship.

PERSONALITY DIFFERENTIATION AND INTIMATE STYLES

L'Abate (1976) serves as the theoretical backdrop and connection between personality characteristics and interpersonal styles encompassed by the *A-R-C* model, as shown in Table 9–2, according to a continuum of likeness in personality differentiation. This dialectical continuum spreads along six ranges of likeness: symbiosis-autism at the two extreme ends; sameness-oppositeness on either side of the center; and the center, which is made up of the two ranges of similarity and differentness. This continuum was used to deal with attraction, mate selection, family formation, functioning, and dysfunctioning (L'Abate, 1976) and is compressed here into the three different styles.

Personality states accompanying the various ranges in the likeness continuum (see Table 9–2) represent verbalized and nonverbalized shorthand statements that define the self as characterized by the self. The dialectic polarities of symbiosis-autism *(A)* cover extremes of attachment, such as *folies-à-deux* on one hand and extreme examples of isolation and autism on the other.

Table 9–2

PERSONALITY CORRELATES OF THE *A-R-C* MODEL IN RELATIONSHIPS

Interpersonal Styles	Degree of Functionality	Level of Differentiation (Likeness)	Internal States	Degree of Fusion	Degree of Distance	Level of Activity	Problem Solving: Degree of Change
Apathetic-abusive	Minimal	Symbiotic-autistic-alienated	"I am you"—"I am not"	Extremely diffused-confused	From minimal to maximal	Extremely variable	Almost nonexistent: deteriorating
Reactive-repetitive	Borderline to "normal"	Sameness-oppositeness	"I am like you"—"I am the opposite of you"	Moderately fused	Fixed to rigidly variable	Less variable than above	Digital or dichotomous; contradictory permanence
Conductive-creative	Maximal	Similarity-differentness	"I am somewhat like you"—but "I am also different from you"	Autonomous-interdependent	Optimal-articulated	Balanced-focused	Analogical and diversified: improvement

Polarities of sameness-oppositeness *(R)* are most represented in repetitive and conflictual spouse-spouse *and* parent-child (adolescent) interactions; integration of similarities and differentness *(C)* are found in most functional interpersonal relationships with a greater potential for intimacy, change, and growth.

APATHY *(A)*

Apathy is a context of hopelessness and helplessness in relationships, the ultimate outcome of which may be deterioration to the point of breakdown, suicide, death, "accidental" destruction, or irresponsible and irreparable physical negation. Apathy is one of the major characteristics found in drug-abusing families, who have strong resistance to treatment (Stanton, 1979). The self-destructive and suicidal aspects of drug usage within a family context indicate one of the major outcomes of apathy (i.e., deterioration), with or without therapeutic intervention.

In apathy, there is little motivation toward or interest in change. Most of the time, especially without intervention, one can predict deterioration as the major outcome. Part of this style is the lack of effective emotional, cognitive, or behavioral repertoire that the individual(s) can use to overcome the apathy. Eventually, reaching rock bottom may motivate some individuals to seek change through either internal or external intervention. Apathy can be found in very close—very distant relationships and can best be exemplified by the apathy of the addict (Jaffe, Peterson, & Hodgson, 1980) who becomes too enmeshed with the addiction to do anything else. Symbolically, this addiction, as discussed by Peele and Brodsky (1975), can be generalized to symbiotic love relationships that, in extremes, become *folies-à-deux,* in which the dialectical opposite of symbiosis is or becomes autism and alienation. Apathy is usually based on omission (i.e., the failure to do anything about one's destructiveness), even to the point of denying or being unaware of one's destructiveness or the destructiveness of a relationship, as found in *folies-à-deux,* addictions, extreme deprivations, and depressions (Feuerlicht, 1978).

Most of the evidence converging on the concept of apathy *(A)* is theoretical. Earlier in this chapter, apathy was defined in terms of autism, alienation, and atrophy. To these three qualities can be added the following: (a) passivity, (b) indifference, (c) lack of initiative, and (d) extreme intensities of delay or discharge, as found in at least two previous theoretical statements (L'Abate, 1964, 1976). *Apathy* and *passivity* as index entries in the literature are infrequent. Neither of these entries is considered in more recent studies of psychotherapy with upper-class patients (Applebaum, 1977) or schizophrenics (Rogers, 1967). Passivity as a whole has been considered a "sex-typed behavior within the context of active males and passive females" (Janis, Mahl, Kagan, & Holt, 1969).

Concepts of apathy or passivity are not found frequently, either in general psychological literature, surprisingly enough, or even in the psychotherapeutic literature. The most that can be found (Bergin & Garfield, 1971) is "apathy" in reference to schizophrenia (p. 621) or as a characteristic of schizophrenic behavior (p. 62). A more recent version (Garfield & Bergin, 1978) contains no reference to either apathy or passivity except for one entry, "passive resistance." Considering how many references and entries we have for inferred concepts such as "anxiety," one cannot help but wonder why we cannot conceptually deal with apathy as the extreme on a continuum of activity. L'Abate (1964, 1976) dealt with this dimension through extremes in delay-discharge on a temporal continuum. The opposite extreme of apathy would be impulsivity or hyperactivity.

Sullivan (1953) considered the dynamism of apathy and nonviolent detachment, in which "all the tensions of needs are markedly attentuated" (p. 55). He differentiated nonviolent detachment from apathy: the former, a protective dynamism called out by prolonged and severe anxiety, in contrast to apathy, a protectivee dynanism called forth by unfilled needs.

May (1969) has been more concerned with the importance of apathy than anyone reviewed here. He considered apathy as (a) a state of affectlessness, (b) a withdrawal of will and love, (c) a statement of "it does not matter," (d) a suspension of commitment, and (e) an adamant and rigid coolness that refuses to admit the genuinely tragic in one's existence. As May acknowledged: "There is a dialectical relationship between apathy and violence. To live in apathy provokes violence, and . . . violence promotes apathy. Violence is the ultimate destructive substitute which swings in to fill the vacuum where there is no relatedness" (p. 30). May also quoted Sullivan, who viewed apathy as a magic way of protecting oneself (Sullivan, 1954, p. 184).

Meyerson (1974) discussed several forms of apathy. Psychiatrically, it is a pathologically low level of activity. In its religious sense, the Catholic Church defines it as a sin (of sloth) of inaction. In democratic societies, political apathy is reprehensible, and *apathy* is often used pejoratively to accuse those who do not share the special interests and commitments of a group. Sociologically, groups living under extreme deprivation may exhibit apathy, such as societies lacking strong institutions or suffering from extreme economic deprivations.

Brody (1964) conceptualized a continuum of passivity-activity, of which apathy is a component. As she noted, the concept of passivity "has not adequately been studied and it is important to define it" (p. 64). She used Rapaport's definition of passivity: (a) a state of abeyance, (b) helplessness in dealing with the flood of drives and impulses, and (c) extreme delay and avoidance of discharge (as in L'Abate, 1964, 1976). She defined it as "a state or a quality of readiness to be acted upon by external forces, or by internal forces beyond the control of the conscious ego" (p. 66). She attempted to differentiate between normal and neurotic passivity. In this context, passivity is considered one aspect of apathy and is therefore destructive. What Brody would consider "normal" passivity would here be considered nonreactivity and, therefore, one specific aspect of conductivity: the quality of being sufficiently in charge to know how and when to mind one's own business (nonreactivity thus being the most constructive course of action in some situations). As Brody herself qualified: "Normal passivity may be regarded as an achievement of the mature ego. It grows out of a capacity for delay, it makes receptivity and leaning possible, and it is a prerequisite for creative thinking." Passivity, according to Brody, has an additional quality of surrender, a submission to wills and forces outside the self: "Passivity and passive aims become pathological when they advance sadomasochistic gratifications" (p. 67).

Fried (1970) insisted that the passive-active continuum is the crucial psychological dimension. She viewed "activeness" as a necessity of life, the correlates of which are (a) positive self-esteem and (b) confrontation of reality and vitality. She debunked the myth of female passivity and gave a great many illustrations of passive males. She related passivity to anxiety, equated it with (a) apathy, (b) inertia, (c) lack of initiative, and (d) inactivity, and saw it as allowing exploitation of others. Passivity implies paralysis and atrophy of feelings, with a consequent concentration of feeling artificially produced through props (e.g., drugs, alcohol). "Passivity is an offense of omission rather than commission" (p. 174). Fried considered the subjective advantages of passivity: (a) "The world owes me indemnity," (b) "I will get revenge through passive resistance and sulking," (c) "I can be excused (because of my passivity)," and (d) "My passivity is one way of dealing with my murderous and destructive wishes." Clichés and truisms are often indications of such indolence.

Boszormenyi-Nagy and Ulrich (1981) used the concept of "stagnation" in much the same way that we use apathy. They listed the ways stagnation (i.e., apathy) can be manifested clinically, through (a) denial and/or avoidance of issues; (b) lack of expectations, when no demands are made of self and intimate others; (c) giving up, as shown by self-destructive and self-defeating behaviors; (d) accepting uncritically the status quo as the only available way of being for oneself and for intimate others; or (e) terminal thinking about the hopelessness and changelessness of the existing situation ("Nothing can be done; that's the way it is"), such as forgetting about the past and learning nothing from it.

Support for the validity of a concept of apathy is provided by the work with neglectful parents done by Polanski and his associates (Polanski, Chalmers, Butterwieser, & Williams, 1981), with their key concept of the "apathy-futility syndrome," meaning that these parents are enmeshed in a long-lasting style of social isolation. They have few or no friends and show no involvement in neighborhood or civic groups. Their isolation goes back all the way to childhood and adolescence and seems to stem from a personal philosophy of life and a style of relating to the world that sets them apart from normal social relations. The isolation escalates and multiples their feelings of social and interpersonal inadequacy. All these factors tend to render these parents extremely infantile in their interpersonal relationships and unable to fulfill even simple social relationships. The outcome is of extreme dependency on external sources, with underlying feelings of hopelessness, helplessness, and frustration, which Polanski has called "apathy-futility" and which makes it very difficult for many social agencies to help these parents in any way.* The vicious circle is repeated with the children of such parents. The emotional deprivation in early childhood leads to impaired intellectual functioning, social detachment, and withdrawal.

Passivity is thus seen as one way, by no means the only way, to define apathy; indifference, "not caring," and withdrawal being other aspects of the same kind of behavior (i.e., the individual's inability and unwillingness to seek or strive for change and his/her helplessness when faced with attempts from external forces toward change.

REACTIVITY *(R)*

Reactivity means a context of disqualifications, or defeating vicious circles, whereby most of the relationship follows a same-opposite dialectic designed to keep it completely unchanged. Reactivity can produce a continuation of the same behavior or can result in opposite behavior. For instance, the literature on child abuse indicates that more abusive parents were themselves abused children (Lefkowitz, Huesmann, & Eron, 1978). By the same token, a great deal of juvenile delinquency seems the outcome of unclear and permissive parental practices. Thus, apathy takes place in a context of confusion and chaos, both personal and interpersonal, whereas reactivity takes place in a context of rigidity, both personal and interpersonal.

Reactivity, then, is defined as an immediate rebuttal, a swift reaction to someone else's behavior, resulting in a vicious repetition of the same-opposite dialectic, with no change in the relationship. Reactivity is frequently the only kind of response to come out of a context of apathy (i.e., many individuals are usually stimulated to respond from their apathetic stance by a partner, parent, or caretaker, who elicits, usually and at best, a reactive response). Thus, apathy and reactivity are more closely linked and related to each other than to conductivity. The first two come from a context of dependence,

---

*This whole issue of dependency and dysfunctionality is considered in greater detail in L'Abate (1985a).

whereas the latter comes from a context of integrated and balanced autonomy (L'Abate, 1976). It is thus much more difficult to shift from a reactive to a conductive style than to shift from apathy to reactivity.

In reactivity, the motivation, or interest, to change is limited and therefore held rigidly to the immediacy of the interation. The larger context is not considered; under these conditions, one would predict no change in the relationship in which *repetition* of the same-opposite behavior becomes the hallmark. This repetitious cycle is evident in some intimate, marital, parent-child, and some ineffective therapeutic relationships. Under conditions of reactivity, individuals surrender personal responsibility for their behaviors to another, explaining their reactions in terms of *the other's* behavior (or the devil or the monster): "The 'bad one' made me do it." Personal responsibility is thus externalized to a target or source that justifies or condones one's behavior. "I behaved this way because s/he did this . . . or that. . . ." The "s/he" can be a spouse/spouse, a parent/child, a therapist/client, or a teacher/student dyad.

Reactivity is usually based on a destructive commission or commitment to doing something in response to someone else's behavior, as found in examples of physical and verbal abuse or verbal demeaning and discounting, with no awareness or consideration of a larger context. Here, oneself and the other's self are denied, along with the context (Satir, Stachowiak, & Taschman, 1975). Under reactive relationships, one would consider what Haley (1976) called "recurring unproductive sequences," as exemplified by the roles of the drama triangle—victim-persecutor-rescuer (L'Abate, Weeks, & Weeks, 1979) or by Satir's incongruent stances (L'Abate, 1976)—blaming-placating-computing-distracting (i.e., repetitiously rigid patterns that are difficult to break up internally or externally).

To avoid reacting, an individual needs to delay responsibity and come up with something new and different, which will in some way acknowledge the contextual similarity of the triggering stimulus. Thus, the first step in switching from a reactive to a conductive stance is to (a) stop and nonreact, (b) think through a reactive answer that one knows would escalate the interchange, and (c) substitute for the original reactive answer a different and positive response that will not "hook up" negatively the original producer of the initial stimulus. Here, one needs to be committed positively to creative change. Positive change implies *progression* rather than *status quo* (reactivity) or *regression* (apathy).

CONDUCTIVITY *(C)*

Conductivity means a positive approach designed to improve, affirm, enhance, and enrich a relationship so that each person involved in it will define him/herself as autonomous but interdependent. Conductivity also stands for correction, or corrective experiences that allow us to change. Change takes place within a context of mastery, not within reactive or apathetic styles. Thus, conductivity *(C)* is defined as the creative commitment to change through awareness and knowledge of the context surrounding a relationship. It is usually based on constructive commission of acts that will improve a relationship, enhancing self, the other's self, and the context of the relationship. In reactivity, the "I" and "You" are viewed as being in opposition to each other; whereas in conductivity, the "We" acknowledges and affirms the importance of the relationship and of cooperation rather than competition.

Conductivity, then, implies (a) awareness of larger spatial and temporal contexts (L'Abate, 1976); (b) initiative and responsibility in decision making and problem solving; (c) being in charge of oneself to the extent of determining whether, when, and how one is to respond to produce the greatest good with a minimum of effort (cost-reward analysis). Awareness of larger contexts also involves an orientation of relativity (L'Abate, 1957), in which one is aware of alternatives, relative cost/reward ratios of alternatives, and some projection of what desirable outcomes may be, with an awareness that change is not an absolute process but involves going through various problem-solving steps that include feedback, further confrontation, and continuous consideration.

Indifference is found in apathy, immediacy in reactivity, and delaying of a response in conductivity. In the first, one does not care and does not confront, nor does one consider an issue important; consequently, there is denial of self and context. In the second, there is denial of self or other. In the third, there is care and there is a continuous awareness and affirmation of the importance of context. In reactivity, there may be neither denial nor affirmation of context—just omission (Satir et al., 1975).

Conductivity implies most of the characteristics of healthy development that Heath (1980) listed as symbolization, allocentrism, integration, stability, and autonomy. In conductive relationships, more positive feelings are present, and distracting detours are shorter. Refractory periods and intensities of feelings are also less explosive and short-lived, with a successful resolution; thus, negative feelings from past transactions do not enter (Bach & Wyden, 1968). In reactive relationships, past behaviors influence the present ("gunny-sacking," in Bach and Wyden's terms). In conductive relationships, attention is given to the present and the future. The past has either been forgiven, or it is not allowed to enter to influence the present.

Conductivity is especially relevant to role conflicts in the home. How can one partner be in charge (selfhood) without intruding on the selfhood of the other partner? Issues of authority, responsibility, and power shared-assumed-delegated-negotiated need to be looked upon as issues of conductivity. These are issues of integrating similarities and differences between patterns that need to be confronted and negotiated in any intimate relationship. A conductive style implies ability to confront, negotiate, let go, and assume role responsibilities and interpersonal competencies that bear awesome consequences for ourselves and our clients. We have no choice but to strengthen our conductivity and let go of our apathy and reactivity!

A line of research that would help us understand the distinction between reactive and conductive styles is the distinction of children who differ in impulsive versus reflective styles (Kagan, 1965). *Reactive* essentially means an impulsive immediacy without reflection, whereas *conductive* implies a reflective style characterized by forethought and planning. To reflect on a situation means essentially to reflect on all of its aspects, pros and cons, consequences, context, and one's previous experiences, answering them in the most positive and constructive manner one can possibly assume, selected from among all the possible constructive and destructive alternatives. This dimension of impulsivity-reflectivity has been subsumed by L'Abate (1964, 1976) under the two extremes of a temporal continuum defined by delay on one hand and discharge on the other. Readance and Bleau (1978), for instance, found that this cognitive style is a significant characteristic in learning. Learners using an impulsive-cognitive style are at a seeming disadvantage in problem-solving situations. Procedures designed to change such a style show that reflective modeling, instruction in meaning of strategies, and training in discrimination of distinctive features aid impulsive learners to become more reflective and to improve problem-solving strategies. The use of reflective modeling, as shown by the work of Rupert and Baird (1979), does tend to slow children and help them decrease their error rates. It will be relevant to study adult consequences of cognitive styles. Will impulsive children grow up to become reactive partners or parents? Do, indeed, reflective children grow up to become more conductive persons, partners, or parents?

Conductivity and Intimacy

Intimacy, the sharing of both hurt and sad feelings, as well as pleasurable, pleasant, and positive feelings, can take place mainly in the context of a conductive, not a reactive, relationship.* Intimacy can be found only in conductive relationships, in which both individuals are sufficiently in charge of themselves to be able to be separate yet together at the same time (L'Abate & L'Abate, 1979). It is virtually impossible to be intimate in apathetic relationships, in which diffusion is more likely to be present, or in reactive relationships, in which fusion is more likely to be present (see Table 9–3).

Conductivity, Context, and Second-Order Change

The major characteristic of conductivity that makes it qualitatively and quantitatively different and, hopefully, superior to reactivity and apathy is

---

*These issues are considered in greater detail in Chapter 10.

an *increased awareness of contextual factors* (i.e., those factors which go above and beyond the immediate situation). Reactivity is usually considered an immediate, usually unreflective response, whereas conductivity is usually concerned with waiting, delaying, and postponing a reaction until most of the information necessary and relevant to an appropriate and constructive response has been gathered. Thus, when a conductive response is given, it is designed to take into consideration a temporal perspective that is part of the context. Delaying a response assures being in control and thinking of various alternatives that will allow the most creative and helpful response with the least amount of energy expenditure.

Another difference between conductivity and reactivity deals with Watzlawick, Weakland, and Fisch's (1974) distinction between first- versus second-order change. First-order change is directly related and immediately limited to the situation, whereas second-order change implies a broader perspective that goes above and beyond the specific situation at hand. Another way of differentiating among the three parts of this model, then, is to say that apathy implies no change, reactivity implies first-order change or repetition, and conductivity implies a discontinuous jump that is related to the whole context of the transaction rather than to the immediate specifics of it, as in the case of reactivity. This discontinuous jump implies an analogical rather than a digital perspective, the difference between being "hooked" or "unhooked" by a situation.

In summary, in apathy, options are neither visible nor contemplated. In reactivity, options to problem solving are limited or dichotomous ("You are

Table 9–3
CORRELATES OF INTIMATE STYLES

Apathy	Reactivity	Conductivity
Passivity	Defensive-oppositional	Supportive
Indifference	Incongruent	Congruent
Chaotic-violent	Blaming	Equalitarian-democratic
and explosive	Placating	Transactional
behaviors:	Distracting	Relational
Suicidal-homicidal	Computing	Contextual
Alcoholic-addicted	Rigid, i.e., drama triangle	Flexible
Symbiotic-autistic	Rescuing	Spontaneously unpredicta-
Alienated-abusive (phys-	Persecuting	ble
ically, pharmaceuti-	Victimizing	Effective-reflective
cally and verbally)	Authoritarian-permissive	Parallel
	Impulsive-compulsive	Intimate
	Complementary-symmetrical	

Note: These correlates are taken from a variety of sources, most, but not all, of which are contained in the references and discussed in the body of this book.

either my friend or my foe"). In conductivity, options are many, diverse, and analogical (both/and). Apathy in interpersonal relations means giving up, withdrawing, with unconcerned or impotent insensibility, not intervening, as shown by indifference, inane reactions, or actual distance. Reactivity means a conflictful dichotomy in which behavior is elicited in response to other behavior, producing a repetitive cycle of unchanging patterns. The level of activity in apathy may range from extreme passivity and inactivity to extremes of goalless and ineffective hyperactivity. Distance between people may range from extreme closeness to extreme distance. The range of activity in reactivity is less extreme and less variable than in apathy, whereas distance may vary from close to inconsistently variable. Activity in conductivity is efficiently goal directed; in reactivity, it is wasteful and goalless because of its repetitiveness. In conductivity, distance between individuals is optimal and flexible, allowing persons to be distant enough to be close (L'Abate & L'Abate, 1979).

Although these three steps could be considered to lie on a continuum from maximal dysfunctionality in apathy to maximal functionality in conductivity, there is a discontinuous jump necessary in going from *R* to *C* since each of the three steps has characteristics of its own that make it difficult, without intervention, to progress from *A* to *R* to *C*. These postulated relationships among *A-R-C* components and other aspects of behavior allow us to understand most clinical problems as falling in the apathy-reactivity ranges. Problems in the reactivity range furnish the bulk of most outpatient and private practice cases, whereas problems in the apathy range may be seen in inpatient treatment settings (as well as in jails, morgues, hospitals) and, occasionally, by a variety of different therapists since therapeutic progress in this style *(A)* is extremely problematic.

APPLICATIONS OF THE MODEL

This section will apply the *A-R-C* model to three major intimate relationships: (1) parent-child relationships, (2) marital interactions, and (3) families as a whole.

Parent-Child Relationships

In this section, various strands of evidence that support the validity of the *A-R-C* model in parent-child relationships need to be considered. For instance, Gordon's (1970) differentiation of three models (i.e., authoritarian, permissive, and effective) is another way in which both authoritarian-permissive models are most related to apathy and reactivity, whereas effectiveness is one aspect of conductivity. By the same token, Baumrind (1971) distinguished among authoritative, permissive, and authoritarian parenting styles. The first (authoritative) falls in the conductive style, and the last two are examples of reactive categories.

Schaffer and Crook (1980) observed 24 children, aged between 15 and 24 months, playing with their mothers in a structural situation. In spite of considered variations, the best maternal strategy was described as one that went beyond the specifics of the task assignment but also involved a sequential attention-action strategy designed to manipulate the child's involvement state. In other words, this maternal style involved a conductive stance, whereby the mother was able to respond to the context of the relationship rather than to the immediate, narrow, specific demands of the child.

Hoffman (1979) concluded that moral internalization in children is fostered when (a) the parent frequently uses inductive disciplinary techniques à la Aronfreed (1968), which suggest to the child the harmful consequences of his/her behavior for others, and (b) the parent frequently expresses affection *outside* the disciplinary encounter (i.e., the parent takes the initiative for a positive experience for the child, using conductive rather than reactive techniques).

As Wahler (1980) indicated, opposition (oppositeness in L'Abate's 1976 theory) may be passive (through noncompliance) or aggressive fighting. Wahler observed that such an opposition comes out of a *reactive* context, very much in line with the present contention. As Wahler described it, "Both parents and child react to each other in verbal and non-verbal ways that observers can agree are either aversive (e.g., whine, yell) or non-aversive (e.g., smile, talk quietly)" (p. 31). Wahler agreed with Patterson's observations that in difficult families the probability is very high that aversive behavior will be immediately followed by some response from the other person. The solution from a behavioral viewpoint, of course, is to diminish the coercive process by altering reinforcement contingencies.

The characteristics that Wahler attributed to the parents (usually of the lower SES level) of more oppositional children were (a) insularity and (b) entrapment (i.e., these parents feel cut off from the community and live in a rut from which they see themselves as victimized and unable to get out). Both these characteristics support the position of the present model that reactivity comes out of a context of apathy, if one can consider insularity and entrapment two characteristics of apathy.

In one of the earliest studies of parent-child relationships, Sears, Maccoby, and Levin (1957) differentiated between (a) love-oriented and (b) object-oriented parental styles. The former consisted of praise as a means of reward, isolation as punishment, and withdrawal of love or punishment, with reasoning. Object-oriented styles consisted of tangible rewards or incentives. Since Sears et al.'s work, a plethora of studies on parental styles have produced a variety of theoretical models (Martin, 1975). Most of the literature on infant development (Osofsky, 1979) points out the presence of at least two general styles of maternal behavior in reaction to the infant's requests: (a) the mother simply reacts if and when the infant needs it *(R)*; and (b) in addition to attending to the infant's needs, the mother takes responsibility for making the interaction pleasant by eliciting smiling, pleasant responses from the infant *(C)*.

Aronfreed (1968) classified disciplinary practices into two major categories: (1) inductive and (2) sensitizing. In addition to conceptual differences that would be too lengthy to summarize here, Aronfreed attached specific techniques to what he saw as two extremes of a continuum. For instance, indirection consists of (a) withdrawal of affection, with rejection, isolation, expression of disappointment, deprivation of physical contact, and telling the child that s/he should feel "bad"; (b) examination of the child's responsibility in accounting for (explaining) his/her behavior, repairing whatever was done, and encouraging the child to define transgressions and to initiate personal moral responsibility; and (c) explanation of relevant standards, with a description of consequences of actions, suggesting to the child appropriate actions, telling the child what aspects of the behavior were unacceptable, reasoning, and talking things over. Sensitization, on the other hand, consists of verbal assaults (yelling, screaming, bawling, shaming, scolding, ridiculing) and physical punishment.

On the basis of this description, it would appear that both techniques would cover the whole *A-R-C* waterfront, ranging from apathetic, in the case of sensitization, to parts of induction that are reactive (a) and parts that are conductive (b and c).

Aronfreed's position is supported by Martin's review (1975) of parent-child relations. He found that:

> Internalized reactions to transgressions (self-blame, guilt, and world conceptions of right and wrong) in children are correlated with maternal warmth and with disciplinary practices characterized by cognitive structuring (clear statement of expectations, abstract moral principles, and consequences to others) and use of the affective relationship. (pp. 503–504)

As for independent behavior in children, Martin concluded:

> The most convincing evidence at this time indicates that independent behavior is associated with a pattern of parent-child interaction in which the parent demands age-appropriate behavior, enforces rules firmly and consistently; encourages, listens to, and

is occasionally influenced by communications from the child, and provides a generous measure of affection and approval. (pp. 508–509)

By the same token, Martin concluded that "parental punishment and unacceptance have consistently shown a positive relationship to child aggression at all age levels" (p. 515).

The same kind of relationship to aggression is also found with parental permissiveness and laxity, supporting Gordon's (1970) position. Warmth and acceptance are both related to love-oriented approaches to discipline that lead toward internalization, whereas parental nonacceptance is related to both antisocial behavior and to withdrawn neurotic behavior across a wide age range. Hence, it would seem that parental techniques based on negative orientations and inconsistency (from laxity to punishment) would be found in both apathetic and reactive styles. Love-oriented techniques would be part of a conductive style.

Martin concluded his review by noting:

> Sensitivity in responding to the child's needs and the honest expression of the parents' feelings without continuous nagging and criticism as emphasized in the approaches of Gordon and Ginott, is supported by the almost universally found correlation of parental acceptance with the child's general adjustment. It is reassuring to see a growing congruence between research findings and popular, contemporary child-rearing literature. (p. 529)

Bradbard and Endsley (1978) found that "adults can be instrumental in fostering and maintaining children's curiosity by being attentive, sensitive and supportive of children's needs to explore by answering children's questions informatively and by displaying positive characteristics of curious people." Olmstead (1977) reviewed 25 selected studies of parental teaching strategies. She found that general information, positive feedback, and expansiveness were positively related to scores on Stanford-Binet, Peabody Picture Vocabulary Test, and verbal and manual performance on a Block test, whereas specific information, negative feedback, and performance demands were negatively correlated to the scores on the same tests. Olmstead also isolated 10 desirable teaching behaviors in parents, such as explanation, encouragement, praise. She found that these behaviors were positively related to children's advancement in the classroom. In addition, Olmstead's research with mothers and their infants (1979) found two distinct styles: one she called "initiating," which seems to be related to the use here of the conducting style, and the other she called "a primarily responsive style," similar to the reactive style.

Most of these studies seem to support the notion that parent-child relationships could be described according to an *A-R-C* model. Of course, the bias of the theorist is evident here!

Couples

There is a relationship between the *A-R-C* model and the theory of logical types—symmetrical and complementary—developed from Whitehead and Russell (1950). This theory was used by Bateson (1972), Haley (1963), and more recently tested by Scoresby and his associates (Harper, Scoresby, & Boyce, 1977; Christensen & Scoresby, 1975, 1976). It was used initially by Lederer and Jackson (1968) to describe conflictual marital relationships. Symmetry is found in relationships characterized by repetition and escalation of the same pattern *(A);* complementary implies the same-opposite dialectic *(R).* A third, parallel style, as described by some of these investigators (Harper et al., 1977) appears strongly similar to a conductive style.

Another source of support for the present model is found in the work of Bernal and Baker (1979). They identified five levels of interaction among couples: (I) object interaction, focused on an object or issue; (II) individual interactions, focused on the individual, including mutual accusations and blaming since each partner views the other as the reason for his/her behavior: *"Members of the couple view their own actions as reactions"* (emphasis mine); (III) transactional interactions, focused on patterns of relating (you and I); (IV) relational—"us" and "we"; and (V) contextual, with discussion of psycho-historical materials and even intergenerational processes. Distressed couples tend to use predominantly Levels I and II, whereas nondistressed couples tend to use predominantly Levels III, IV, and V. Consequently, although it is not clear from the authors' presentation whether their Level I corresponds to apathy, it is very clear that their Level II corresponds well to reactivity:

> Agreement on a dispositional, casual view of each other's and mutual ascriptions of responsibility occurred with couples that were locked into an interactional impasse involving mutual blaming and accusations; this was characteristic of Level II interactions, more frequently occurring with the distressed than with the nondistressed couples. (p. 299)

Bernal and Baker's classification helps also to identify at least three different subtypes of conductive style (i.e., transactional, relational, and contextual). If those three functional levels and the other two more dysfunctional ones are related to the circumplex model of Olson, Sprenkle, and Russell (1979), a great step forward in theory construction may be accomplished.

In their study of couples, using the consensus Rorschach test, Pontalti,

Arnetoli, Dastoli, Martini, Stoppa, and Colamonico (1979) used Bales' (1951) classification scheme to distinguish positive emotional reactions, which manifest (a) solidarity, improving the other person's morale, helping and giving pleasure; (b) reduction of tension, laughing, kidding around, and showing personal satisfaction; (c) consensus, accepting positively, understanding, contributing, and giving in. Except for the last category in "c" (giving in would not be considered a conductive characteristic), the rest would qualify for inclusion in a conductive style. The same authors classified negative emotional reactions as showing (a) disagreement, passive resistance, formalization, and refusal to help; (b) tension, asking for help, and withdrawal; and (c) antagonism, lowering the other person's morale, defensive (A). A third category contains emotionally neutral acts which are, however, helpful for task solution and also qualify as conductive in style, provided there is no coupling with negative affect: (a) giving suggestions and directions, involving respect for the autonomy of the other; (b) giving opinions, judgments, analyses, and expressing sentiments and wishes; (c) giving orientation and information, repeating, clarifying, confirming; (d) asking for orientation, introduction, repetition, and confirmation; (e) asking for opinions, judgments, analyses, and expression of achievements; (f) asking for suggestions, directions, and possible alternatives for achievement.

In their typology of divorcing couples, Kessell, Jaffee, Tuchman, Watson, and Deutsch (1980) found that enmeshed, on one hand, and autistic patterns of divorce, on the other, were the most difficult to mediate and had the poorest postdivorce adjustment. Direct conflict patterns (characterized by frequent and open communication between spouses about the probability of divorce) and a disengaged pattern (low conflict and high communication), both less intense than the enmeshed and autistic patterns, showed better mediation outcome and postdivorce adjustment. It seems that enmeshed and autistic patterns would fit into the apathetic style because they are described by these investigators as "chaotic" in nature, with a great deal of inconsistency, contradiction, and reversals. The autistic pattern, the antithesis of the enmeshed type, was characterized by extreme physical and emotional disturbance, very much in line with the use of the same term in L'Abate's theory (1976). Hence, it seems that the direct and disengaged patterns fit into the reactive style. Apparently, the conductive style should be able to reduce conflict by more constructive communication and conflict resolution, offering a greater possibility of achieving intimacy. If and when this style is used, the chances of divorce should therefore be less.

Mettetal and Gottman (1980) postulated that the two concepts of reciprocity and dominance are responsible for the variance in marital relationships. What they found, in agreement with many other investigators, is that in distressed couples, there is a great deal of "reciprocity of displeasurable behaviors," which they called negative reciprocity and which characterized distressed couples more than nondistressed couples. This lack of negative reciprocity in nondistressed couples was attributed to the wife's nonreacting to the husband's negative behavior.

Netzer (1980) described case studies of extremely symbiotic couples in a way that supports Mettetal and Gottman's findings:

> In pathological couples, repetition is continual and rigid, the only movement is toward escalation and occurs only for hubric reasons, that is, to have one's own positions triumph once and for all and irrevocably, whatever the cost. (p. 19)

Coleman (1980) described reports of conjugal violence that took place in most cases in "chaotic" circumstances and in a state of chronic dissatisfaction. Retaliation, both physical and verbal, and extreme jealousy about past and present extramarital partners were frequent: "Intense marital symbiosis is a major factor in the eruption of violence." As discussed previously, symbiosis and alienation are two aspects of apathy, whereas sameness-oppositeness are two aspects of reactivity.

Tamashiro (1978) conceptualized marriage from a perspective of developmental stages that is relevant to this chapter because the marriage concepts ranged from (a) magical to (b) idealized-conventional, (c) individualistic, and (d) affirmational stages. From this model, it appears that the magical stage would be found in the apathetic style. The idealized-conventional stage would more likely be found among reactive styles, whereas the individualistic and affirmational stages would more likely be found among conductive styles or vice versa (i.e., the three different styles would be found at various stages of marriage, with the possibility of persons' improving their styles as they "grow up" after marriage and through the struggles of marriage).

The most evidence to support the present model comes from the work of Gottman (1979), whose detailed research of nondistressed couples remains exemplary in an otherwise empirically barren field. Among the many findings, those specifically relevant to the proposed model are: (a) stressed couples show more reactive than conductive interaction (as predicted from this model); (b) stressed couples exhibit more cross-complaining about each other's behavior without positive resolution but with, instead, a continuation and the usual escalation; (c) counterproposals, which, in Gottman's language, suggest the same-opposite dialectic that stymies, and interaction without resolution; (d) cycles of negative affects; and (e) editive function, to the extent that one partner feels free to correct the other in how s/he should think, feel, or act (A and R).

Essentially, Gottman's data point toward two different types of interactions, differentiating reactive (stressed) from conductive (nonstressed) couples. In the former, there is an adversary escalation of interactions without completion or resolution; in the latter, there is a positive context of friendship and understanding, with a successful deferral of any flair-up of negative affect. Nonstressed couples respond to convey empathy, understanding, positive regard, and affect to the point that any potentially abrasive situation is turned into a mutually satisfactory outcome for both partners.

Another line of research that supports the validity of these three different styles of intimate relating comes from the work of Fitzpatrick and Best (1979), Fitzpatrick, Fallis, and Vance (1982), and Sillars, (1980). These investigators distinguished among three conflict resolution strategies used by marital partners, which were used in coding actual protocols obtained by various groups of couples:

1) There is an avoidance of discussion of conflictual issues (A) as measured by antisocial, simple, or extended denial of conflict, underresponsiveness to the other, topic shifting, and avoidance; abstraction, semantic and process focus; joking, fogging, ambivalence, and pessimism. Essentially, strategies to distract or detract from the issue need to be confronted.

2) Competitive acts are clearly antisocial communicative strategies (R) that include faulting or blaming the partner, rejection, hostile questioning, hostile joking or sarcasm, presumptive attributions, compliance, seeking and avoiding responsibility.

3) Cooperative acts (C) are designed to find mutual, prosocial outcomes in a conflict and include nonevaluative description of the conflict, with underresponsiveness to the other, qualifications, personal disclosure, soliciting disclosure, emphasizing support and commonalities, accepting responsibilities, and initiating problem solving.

It seems that these three different strategies of conflict resolution fit rather well into the present model: avoidance would correspond to apathy, competition would fit a reactive style, and cooperation would be one aspect of conductivity.

Families

A source of support for the A-R-C model can be found in the work of Lewis, Beavers, Gossett, and Phillips (1976), who evaluated families along the whole continuum of functionality-dysfunctionality. On the basis of their results, these investigators differentiated three degrees of functionality: (a) severely dysfunctional families, presenting chaotic structures; (b) midrange (moderate dysfunctionality) families, presenting rigid structure; and (c) most competent and functional families, presenting flexible structures. From these three types of relationships, one can link chaos to apathy, rigidity to reactivity, and flexibility to conductivity. Characteristics that distinguished competent from rigid or chaotic families were (a) an affiliative (versus an oppositional) attitude about human encounter; (b) respect for one's own and the subjective world view of others; (c) openness in communication versus distancing, obscurity, and confusing mechanizers; (d) a fine parental coalition without evidence of competing parent-child coalitions; (e) an understanding of varied and complex human motivations versus a simplistic, linear, or controlling orientation; (f) spontaneity versus rigid stereotyped interactions; (g) *high levels of initiative versus passivity* (emphasis mine); and (h) encouragement of the unique versus the bland human characteristics.

Three other characteristics that were especially related to optimal family functioning were (a) a high degree of shared and flexible leadership provided by parental coalitions, (b) closeness with clear separateness and boundaries among members versus considerable distancing in midrange families, and (c) respectful negotiations that allowed for individual opinions and personal autonomy. Another characteristic of conductivity that is supported by the work of Lewis et al. (1976) is *unpredictable spontaneity*, or the ability to come up with a variety or wide range of behaviors and options, in contrast to the other two styles, in which options become fewer and fewer, hence, more stereotyped and repetitious. Surprise, joy, and excitement in living, with humor and laughter, seem to be part of this characteristic. By the same token, the ability to enjoy cannot be fully exercised unless one has been able to feel and express fully one's pain, sorrow, and grief. Trollope (1959) put it well a long time ago:

> Sorrow should not be killed too quickly. I always think that those who are impervious to grief must be impervious also to happiness. If you have feelings capable of the one, you must have them capable also of the other! (pp. 426–427)

To conclude this brief overview, Lewis et al.'s (1976) study identified three different degrees of functionality among families. Optimal families showed predominantly *conductive* styles, midrange families (characterized especially by opposition to each other) showed predominantly *reactive* styles, and least functional ("chaotic") families showed predominantly *apathetic* styles. Lest the reader think this a biased interpretation of the results, s/he should consult Lewis et al. to decide whether or not this interpretation is tenable.

Most of the empirical evidence about families relates most directly to the two concepts of reactivity and conductivity. However, the presence of a three-step continuum defined by the present model is also affirmed by the same evidence. For instance, Burgess and Conger (1978) studied whether there would be distinctive patterns in day-to-day interactions that would distinguish abusive and neglectful families from families without histories of either abuse or neglect. Observational data, rated with the Oregon's Behavioral Observation

Scoring System and collected in the homes of 17 abusive, 17 neglectful, and 19 control families, indicated that the abusive and neglectful parents demonstrated lower rates of interaction (apathy?) and were more likely to emphasize the negative (reactivity?) in their relationships with their children. Control families were able to use more positive and constructive (conductivity?) methods of interaction.

Another source of support for differentiating between reactive and conductive styles derives from the work of Alexander and Barton (1976) with families of juvenile delinquents. They found that families of normal adolescents, in contrast to those of juvenile delinquents, used more supportive (conductive) methods of interaction, whereas the latter used more defensive methods (apathetic or reactive).

IMPLICATIONS OF THE *A-R-C* MODEL

One major issue brought about by the *A-R-C* model relates to the stability or variability of these patterns. Does apathy in intimate styles mean apathy in other interpersonal situations? The answer to this question should be noncategorical and qualified. This model stresses intimate relationships (i.e., close and prolonged). This model does not deal with superficial, short-lived, or brief social interpersonal relations, for which this model has either no or very little validity. Possibly, the person who is apathetic in intimate relationships is a lion in business activities. Consequently, one should not attempt to generalize from this model, whose limits have been stated from the very outset, or to extrapolate to any relationships other than those stated (i.e., parent-child, spouse-spouse, families).

One further qualification should be made. It is possible that, under stress, persons in short-lived, superficial social situations may revert (regress?) to their more intimate styles. Is it under stress that the "true colors" emerge? One could think of intimate relationships as stressful since they continuously confront, challenge, and chafe the very core of one's being. Of course, intimate relationships in and of themselves need not be inherently stressful. One can make them so by not knowing how to deal with intimate issues of hurt, caring, and self-assertion (L'Abate, Weeks, & Weeks, 1977, 1979). To the extent that we do not know how to deal with those issues, an intimate relationship can be stressful. Most of us do not know how to share intimate issues of feelings and self-definition. How can we if our models, our parents, are no better than we are? We need, then, to learn how to deal with intimate others through trial and error. In therapy, if the therapist has not dealt with these issues in him/herself, it is very unlikely that they will be resolved in the client. Poor outcome, prolonged and homeostatic therapeutic relationships, and the need for repeated therapeutic relationships are thus present when conductivity in the relationship is unsatisfactory. How can our clients learn to deal with intimacy if we have not? Substantial training efforts should be directed toward intimacy issues, which are at the core of one's very existence and which can be resolved only within a conductive relationship.

Diagnostic Implications

Developmentally, apathy is found in individuals, couples, or families characterized by a great deal of mistrust, expedient self-centeredness, uncooperativeness, and resistant behaviors and who are stuck, fixated, or regressed to incorporating static or impulsive stages of development. Reactivity includes individual, dyadic, or multipersonal systems characterized by guilt, inferiority, or identity diffusion, in which uncritical and unquestioned conformity to external rules is demanded, producing dialectically related patterns of negativism, rebelliousness, and questioning of power and control. Conductivity characterizes individuals in the upper stages of development, maturationally and cognitively (Aubrey, 1980) or constructively-developmentally (Kegan, 1980).

Cognitively (Cooney & Selman, 1980), apathy is present in relationships at a stage in which friendships and peer relations are characterized by momentary, short-lived physical connections (through toys) as is also found in relationships of addicts. Reactivity, in social-cognitive terms, is found in Stage 1 relationships characterized by one-way assistance and unilateral decisions. In Stage 2, reactivity is characterized by fair-weather cooperation and some bilateral partnerships. Conductivity is found in Stages 3 and 4, characterized by stable and complex self-systems, intimate mutual sharing, autonomous interdependence, and pluralistic orientation in the system.

Affectively, the difference between reactive and conductive transactions lies in the presence of negative (anger, pain, fear) rather than positive (excitement, joy) and intense (explosive) rather than soft (intimate) feelings. Reactive relationships usually do not allow a successful completion of interaction; the "same" (negative) feelings are not successfully worked out so that nothing is resolved (i.e., the same feelings exist and the same type of interaction goes on).

One of the major areas of overlap between this and other models (L'Abate, 1983d) lies in the area of emotionality (Chapter 10). It should be clear by now that, in apathy, emotions are either completely avoided or short-circuited, resulting in impulsive and often destructive activity, or they are directed in obsessive maneuvers that heighten rationality to destructive extremes, to the point at which no activity of any kind takes place. If and when emotions are felt in the reactive style, they are used either to placate or to blame external targets, with an inability to assume personal responsibility in the securing and exposing of emotions. Consequently, feelings, if expressed, are communicated in negative fashion. Usually, no limit is found for their control and positive expression. It follows that the only constructive and articulated expression of deep and soft emotions can be found in the conductive style: the individual can use the personal pronoun "I" to share with another what is deeply felt without putting down one's partner or making the other person feel guilty or "bad." In this style *(C)* feelings *(E)* are clearly distinguished from thought *(R)* or actions *(A)*. The individual in this style can reflect, introspect, and cogitate about the nature of the feeling. If and when appropriate, these feelings are expressed as they are, accepted without apologies.

Therapeutic Implications

The major implication of this model is that therapists need to behave conductively rather than reactively or apathetically, as suggested by Gurman (1979) in his review of the therapist's roles and functions. Another implication of this model is that therapists need to behave as conductors regardless of theoretical orientation, picking up whatever conductive techniques one finds congenial to one's personality and temperament. What therapists cannot do is remain apathetic or reactive.

Most models of individual psychotherapy and some models of family therapy, as Beels and Ferber (1969) discussed, fall within the class of reactivity, whereas most structural, strategic, and systematic approaches (Haley, 1976; Minuchin, 1974; Selvini-Palazzoli, Boscolo, Cecchin, & Prata, 1980) fit within the range of conductivity. This model, of course, supports more active, innovative forms of intervention such as are found in the brief therapy literature of the Palo Alto group (Watzlawick, Weakland, & Fisch, 1974), the Milano group (Selvini-Palazzoli, Boscolo, Cecchin, & Prata, 1978), or the ex-Philadelphia contingent (Haley, 1976; Minuchin, 1974). Action for the sake of action is, of course, just as fruitless. Focused, goal-directed, systematically active, confrontive, and circular (rather than linear) interventions, as found in Erickson's example (Haley, 1976) indicate that the days of complacent passivity and acceptance, without active direction, and simple *reactive* reflection of feelings (and very little of that!) may be behind us. This model suggests the picture of the counselor or therapist as a conductor or innovator, actively involved in intervening at various levels of interaction, with the goal of producing positive change and not unduly prolonging a fruitless relationship in the name of "growth" or "personal experience" (terminology used to cover up personal and professional inadequacies and to justify the lack of any positive changes and progress in our clients).

The conductive model implies not only active participation but also *active initiation* on the part of the therapist or counselor to take charge, lead, and direct toward change, to help more people move from apathetic and reactive positions to higher levels of conductivity. To help people learn how to be in charge of themselves and to help them transform themselves into responsible human beings, we need to help them become more like ourselves! Ultimately, then, the goal of any therapeutic relationship is for our clients to be like us in some respects (similarity) and to be themselves to conduct their business in the most creative fashion that is comfortable for them (differentness). Whatever the outcome, it remains an awesome responsibility, requiring all our creativity and conductivity. As Levenson (1972) noted, "Therapists, like the rest of us, are given to saying absolutely the right thing at the wrong time, for the wrong reasons" (p. 203). Levenson considered how important it is for the therapist to become immersed in a system in order to work one's way out of that system (p. 174). He concluded that "a new therapy is emerging, along with a new therapist and new patient, oriented more to participation than understanding, to sensitivity and design rather than to insight and formulation" (p. 222).

Therapeutically, one can assume a more conductive system in relationships if and when one becomes aware of (a) repetitiveness in one's relationship or general therapeutic modus operandi; (b) the possibility of admitting one's fallibility in a relationship and the need for improvement and change; and (c) personal discomfort and dissatisfaction in one's repetitive behavior and the need to make a clean break to improve the relationship.

To obtain change in our clients, we need to be (a) more active; (b) more aware of the immediate contexts of our clients (usually, this context is the family); (c) more focused on actual changes in the client's context rather than in his/her verbal behavior; and (d) more demanding of ourselves and of our clients in the realization that changes do take place, if and when the words go with the music. Often, we claim apathetically that in just listening to our clients and responding to their immediate verbal statements (Hart & Tomlinson, 1970), we are being therapeutic. Where does therapy end and being "dumped on" start? Are we allowing our clients to dump on us if we just reinforce their verbal behaviors without asking for congruence (that their acts go with their words)? In asking more of our clients, however, we need to ask more of ourselves. We cannot remain satisfied merely to respond to the immediate needs of our clients. We need to support their options, give each option its cost/reward ratio, and help our clients go out and try to use some of those options. Without tasks and homework assignments, our clients may even get the idea that simply talking will produce changes. This model implies that just talking will not produce change—it takes more than talking!

Therapists become "hooked" to clients just as the other way around, especially if they have been taught to react, as in the case of some nondirective practices, rather than to conduct. A therapist may become so absorbed by the immediate needs of clients that s/he avoids dealing with their larger contexts. Therapeutic practices that, in some instances, may have involved a reactive therapeutic orientation may include (a) nondirective counseling and (b) behavior modification. In the first instance, the student is taught to take the last response of the client and answer that specific response—but usually nothing else! One can find some of the early manuals (Porter, 1950) or even more recent developments (Carkhuff, 1972) that represent such an approach.

Any practicing counselor experiences a good share of reactive relationships. It is very easy to become engulfed, get hooked, and remain immersed in any client's immediate problems, losing sight of any larger issue (i.e., teaching individuals, dyads, families, and groups to become conductors rather than to remain apathetic or reactive). Often, we remain reactive and meet therapeutic failure out of our own personal passivity, our professional training, and our failure to consider more active alternatives that would get us out of repitively prolonged, fruitless interactions with our intimates and our clients.

The reactive approach in behavior modification may be found especially in some training of parents. The parent is taught to answer a child's behavior immediately, without consideration or value given to the larger spatial or temporal context. Thus, *immediacy* is one of the characteristics of reactivity, and it is on this very dimension that one can differentiate conductivity from reactivity. The conductor bides his/her time and waits to get out of the trenches, to speak or act until the moment is right, and s/he is more aware of the response that needs to be made to improve the situation. Thus, another difference between reacting and conducting is *delaying* (i.e., waiting and using one's time to obtain more information and to plan a specific strategy and tactic that will change a situation for the better). This is the hallmark of conductors such as Haley (1976), Minuchin (1974), the Palo Alto group (Watzlawick et al., 1974; Watzlawick, 1978), the Milano group (Selvini-Palazzoli et al., 1980), or Andolfi (1979). If and when the response of a conductor seems immediate, it is because s/he has been able to evaluate the situation enough to be aware of factors other than those immediately at hand; that is, the conductor is aware of the larger context, to the point that the most active therapists of the last decade have been, not by chance, family therapists!

One major way of "blasting" an apathetic system out of its indifferent posture is to make it angry, as in cases described by the Milano group (Selvini-Palazzoli et al., 1978). Only by provoking anger, dealing with it appropriately ("I am glad you are angry with me. I prefer anger to indifference or apathy. Why are you angry?"), and using it can one learn more about how a system operates. In addition to anger, which is more readily available, one may be able to use hurt (L'Abate, & L'Abate, 1979). As Vincent (1980) conclued about therapists' skills, two major dimensions have been identified as having clear relationships to outcome: (a) *structuring* skills (made up of directness, clarity, and self-confidence), which accounted for 36% of the variance in outcome measures, and (b) *relationship* skills (made up of affect, behavior integrations, warmth, and humor), which accounted for 45% of the variance in outcome measures. These therapist characteristics accounted for about 60% of the variance in treatment effectiveness. These results support the position of the therapist as a "warm conductor" rather than an aloof and "neutral" executive, as envisioned by the Milano group (Selvini-Palazzoli et al., 1980).

Kimberlin and Friesen (1980) found that empathic responses were related to the conceptual level of "helpers," as measured by the Paragraph Completion Test. It is important to note here that empathic training per se does not a therapist make. Criticism leveled against both nondirective and behavior modification approaches are especially relevant when one defines counselor training as a mechanical, routine, uncritical application of "empathic" response that may make our students assume that "being nice" to our clients will make them change! Behavioral approaches have received the very criticism that I have already made—failure to acknowledge and deal with context. The fact that behavioral approaches are too limited and simplistic in this sense and that all is not well with their applications has recently been admitted by traditional behavioral proponents (Patterson, 1985; Vincent, 1980).

For change to take place, we need to do *something positively different* from what we have been doing in the past. Whatever is done differently from the past needs to be sufficiently similar to fit into a temporal and spatial context (L'Abate, 1976), yet sufficiently *new* and *novel* to be different from what we have done before. It is this peculiar integration of similarity and differentness (i.e., *positively* different) that brings about change. Often the devil we have is better than the devil we may get. Change is difficult to the extent that it implies acquiring or expressing new and unfamiliar responses. We all are afraid of the new, the unfamiliar, and the novel. To change, we need to do or say something positive, something we may never have done or said before!

The controversy between "growth" and "change" (Haley, 1976) could be eliminated if we (a) look at this issue in terms of progression versus regression; (b) use an analogical (both/and) rather than digital (either/or) position; and (c) consider that *both* concepts are relevant to progression, which can take place continuously (growth) or discontinuously (change). Thus, both growth and change are different routes or different aspects of the same process (i.e., progression). We need to be mindful that progression does occur within a context of conductivity, not reactivity or apathy. Going forward (i.e., progression) implies using new and different ways of dealing with intimate others; regression implies falling back into the same old ways, essentially deteriorating, as in apathy, or staying the same, as in reactivity. Regression, therefore, can comprise two different routes or aspects: deterioration (i.e., relationships become worse), or stasis (homeostasis or sameness), in which there is neither progression nor deterioration—no growth and no change.

As Strupp (1973) considered for individuals (and it applies to couples and families): "Every neurotic patient is unconsciously committed to maintain the *status quo,* and psychotherapy, particularly if aimed at confronting the patient with his inner conflicts, proceeds against the obstacle of powerful unconscious resistance" (p. 494). Strupp went on to comment that "motivation for therapy" (i.e., change) is "a global and highly complex variable." It is a well-known finding that coercive participation in psychotherapy tends to produce a negative outcome. There are groups of individuals, couples, and families that are apathetic (i.e., "resistant to therapeutic approaches"). Hence, we need to consider, as many others have done (Strupp, 1973): What are the components or characteristics of this "resistance to change" found in a good percentage of our clients before, during, and after intake?

The trick is to help clients go from apathy to reactivity to conductivity. Some basic issues here should be: (a) Can these shifts be accomplished? How? and (b) Can we help clients skip from apathy to conductivity without going through experiencing and using reactivity? These and other issues raised by this model will be tested in future work. Whether one can jump from apathy to conductivity, skipping reactivity, remains to be seen. Supposedly, paradoxical injunctions, positive reframing, symptom prescription, and task assignments may jolt rigid or chaotic systems into a more positive and conductive stances than would be possible otherwise, using more linear techniques. Prescriptions, positive redefinitions, and reframing of symptoms and behaviors may lead to sudden states of confusion, disorganization, and anger until "new" rules are established.

The issue of helping clients become more conductive is answered by pointing to the area of ritualized instructions for the family to learn *not to react* to each other (Selvini-Palazzoli et al., 1980). Another prescription (a version of the Milano group's task) that I find useful in my practice is to have family members utter "I" statements of a feeling nature for five minutes without interruptions from other family members. A third possibility is to teach families to conduct family conferences (L'Abate, 1981b). Moving people from an apathetic or a reactive style to a conductive style may thus imply using linear, circular, and metaphorical approaches that make the therapist into a conductor.

Research Implications

A line of research that helps distinguish between reactive and conductive styles is the work of Worthy (1974), who was able to identify at least two different styles in sports, finding that dark-eyed athletes seem to do well in mostly reactive sports, such as tennis or basketball, whereas blue-eyed athletes seem to do better in nonreactive sports, such as golf, or excel in conductive positions, such as quarterback in football (a sport at which dark-eyed athletes excel in reactive positions, e.g., receiver). One could therefore attribute differences in reactivity to certain inborn characteristics, differentiating between volatile, exuberant, expressive Southern Mediterranean stocks versus controlled, calculating, inhibited Northern Scandinavians, with room, of course, for sufficient variability to find exceptions in either case.

Another line of research—social learning theory (Bandura, 1982)—tends to support the validity of this model. Bandura, through the concept of self-efficacy, has found that individuals high on this dimension tend to do better in a variety of learning and problem-solving tasks than individuals low on the same dimension. In addition, he considered environmental responsiveness. When these two dimensions (self-efficacy judgment and environmental outcome judgment) are dichotomized, a 2 × 2 table is obtained (p. 140), on which two of the bottom quadrants are (a) apathy and resignation and (b) self-devaluation and despondency. At the opposite and positive quadrant, there is "assured, opportune action," whereas, in the middle, the fourth quadrant is characterized by social activism, protests, and grievances. The first two quadrants seem to fit into the apathetic style, the third the conductive, and the fourth the reactive style.

At present, the evidence for this model is indirect even though the trends and strands from various sources suggest a certain degree of validity, if not usefulness. As for research, one of the major issues raised by this model is whether we, indeed, are reactors or conductors, or do we have reactive or conductive relationships? Some of us get more "hooked" than others under certain conditions of stress and confrontation. Furthermore, how can we classify individuals in either of the three categories unless we take samples of the ways they interact with intimate others? Hence, this is a dynamic model. It does not lend itself to reduction to paper-and-pencil statements of how an individual would answer under certain interactions. More often than not, individuals using any one of the three styles would not have any awareness of what they are saying or doing. In fact, one wonders whether many therapists themselves are aware of how they respond to their clients. Again, it would be impossible to classify individuals unless we sample repeatedly how they interact with intimate others. Determination of any of the three styles needs to be made by (a) verbal responses in terms of irrelevant and distracting characteristics that would seem indirectly to indicate apathy as well as responses that would directly indicate it; (b) verbal responses indicating immediacy and negative feelings, which would represent reactivity; and (c) responses that indicate an awareness of context and conductive styles.

Of course, this model would predict that individuals in the lower levels of cognitive, developmental (Aubrey, 1980; Cooney & Selman, 1980; Kegan, 1980), and social maturity (Heath, 1980) would use mostly apathetic styles, whereas individuals in the upper levels should be using mostly conductive styles. Thus, a direct connection between this model and various theories, including the one on which this model is based (L'Abate, 1976), could be tested empirically.

CONCLUSION

Willems and Stuart (1980) rhapsodized about the beauties of taxonomies (pp. 121–122). Among the eight different advantages that these authors offered were the advantages of pinpointing well-established results and clarifying confusing, contradictory results. As far as family systems are concerned, Willems and Stuart emphasized that theory in this area "has been weak. Few adequate studies exist for clarifying the phenomenon of family systems . . . [;] much work needs to be done in defining and classifying variables and processes of interest to the family theoretician" (p. 122). We hope that the *A-R-C* model, combined with other models (Chapters 10, 11, 12, and 13), is one step in the "right" direction, as requested by Willems and Stuart. Evidence to support it in family relations, spouse-spouse, and parent-child relationships has been reviewed. The task of the future will be to find evidence that negates the validity of this model and to develop a more refined classification of substyles within each major style.

In closing, a theory-derived model is proposed that takes into account indifference, repetitiveness, and creativity in intimate relationships. This model allows us to make sense of prolonged but fruitless therapeutic and interpersonal relationships without successful resolution or culmination. Perhaps in the future, one may be able to make finer distinctions among various types and functions of apathy, reactivity, and conductivity. For the present, we will be content with validating the present formulation.

Chapter 10

Competence in Families

At least three major components must be understood to break down the process of negotiation in families. The first component has already been dealt with in the preceding chapter on styles. A conductive style is a primary *sine qua non* condition for a satisfactory intimate relationship. The second component will be dealt with in this chapter and Chapter 11 through an information-processing model of family competence. The third component, priorities, will be presented in Chapter 12.

A MODEL OF FAMILY COMPETENCE

The framework presented here deals with competence in intimate relationships, especially family relationships. Relationships are governed, controlled, determined, if you will, by at least five subcomponent parts (see Table 10-1). An intimate relationship needs to be broken down into (1) a *structure*, which is spatial and nonverbal (L'Abate, 1976); (2) a *function* which is processed over time; (3) an *outcome*, or result, of the process; (4) a *change mechanism*, or whatever may account for change or no change in the relationship; and (5) a *context* of the relationship, which is physical (i.e., the surroundings) and human (i.e., the people who, with varying degrees of participation are involved in it).

Using a different language, an integrative model for intimate (close and prolonged) relationships (as shown in Figure 10–1) needs at least the following components: emotionality, rationality, activity, and awareness, all of which take place within a context. A satisfactory model of intimate relationships must consider all aspects of the model proposed here equally important and relevant. Satisfactory intimate relationships are defined by a satisfactory aware-

Table 10–1
THE NECESSARY COMPONENTS FOR AN UNDERSTANDING OF INTIMATE
RELATIONSHIPS

General Language	Information Processing	Language Used Here
Structure	Input	Emotionality
Function	Throughput	Rationality
Outcome	Output	Activity
Change mechanism	Feedback	Awareness
Context	Context	Context

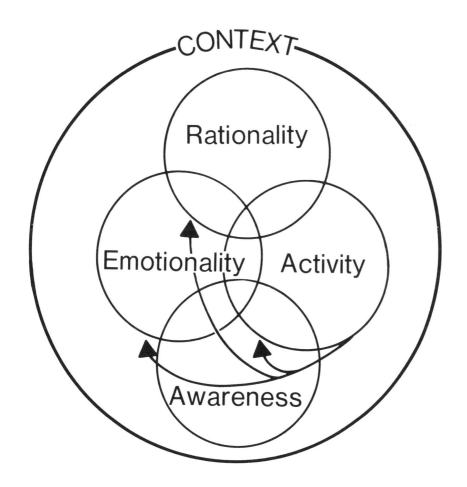

Figure 10–1. The *E-R-A-Aw-C* model.

ness of one's feelings, thoughts, and actions, and the adequacy and appropriateness of their expression in a context. Awareness is used to pinpoint one's feelings; emotionality, to experience and share them; and rationality, to consider them when negotiating an activity.

To understand intimate relationships, one needs to consider at least these five components. As Table 10–1 shows, these components can be considered within three language systems: a general one, an information-processing one, and the language peculiar to this monograph. Within the language of information processing, *emotionality (E)* is relevant to inputs or recognition of information, *rationality (R)* is relevant to linking of inputs to outputs, while *activity (A)* is relevant to the process of output, or expressions of the information received. The issue of change and feedback is dealt with through *awareness (Aw)*. As Figure 10–1 shows, this process takes place in a *context (C)*.

Any skipping, bypassing, or short-circuiting of any of these components will produce an imbalance in the process; that is, if or when E is bypassed, overreliance on R or A may result in an overloading of either component. In addition, if or when Aw is short-circuited or bypassed, an overloading of E or direct routing to R or A may take place. For example, if we are now aware of how we feel about an issue, either we may tend to overrationalize obsessively about it or we may overreact to it impulsively. Hence, all components need to be paid equal attention or an imbalance in the circular process will take place.

Emotionality influences more directly nonverbal activities, primarily in the face (smiles, cries), and content-free verbal utterances (pauses, interruptions, speech and voice breaks, speed and frequency of breathing). Rationality influences the content, sequence, and meaning of verbal activities of language. Awareness includes both nonverbal and verbal activities. Awareness involves a reflective understanding of one's activity, rationality, and emotionality as they have taken place in a specific context.

Emotionality is the primary basis—the structure—of intimate relationships and refers to the related concepts of intimacy (Chapter 13) and approach-avoidance. The concern of emotionality is the present, and it is related to the career of the "real" self. Rationality is, of course, cognitive and is thus concerned with cause and effect and with time—delay-discharge. Rationality is analogous to the career of the intellect, or education. Activity refers to behavior and to one's career, or occupation. Awareness affects all three components: E, R, and A. Context is mainly responsible for the career within one's family of origin (parents, siblings, relatives) and with in-laws, friends, and neighbors (i.e., one's closest context). A larger context, the institutional community, which includes one's school, church, agencies, government, will not be dealt with in this book even though its influence is acknowledged.

APPLICATION OF THE MODEL TO FAMILY RELATIONSHIPS

This model has implications for negotiation between and among intimate or close relationships. As elaborated in Appendix B, if proper and creative negotiations are to take place, (a) feelings have to be recognized, expressed, and shared; (b) various alternatives need to be considered, taking into account the various and different feelings of the parties involved; and (c) whatever is agreed upon by both parties can then be translated into activity, or trying out a course of action. Evaluation of costs and rewards, consequences, alternatives, choice points—the whole process of negotiation—is usually accompanied and paralleled by awareness and changes in awareness concerning E, R, A, and the specific context surrounding the situation.

On the basis of this model, therefore, a satisfactory intimate relationship is defined as the ability to negotiate in close and prolonged relationships, achieving intimacy, emotionally; developing a positive self-concept, cognitively; acting congruently and conductively; and becoming aware of one's strengths and weaknesses in each of these areas and admitting them to oneself and to others. To deal with these complex behaviors, we need complex models, such as the one to be presented here.

This model has been used to classify various theories of individual therapy (L'Abate, 1981b), family therapy (Hansen & L'Abate, 1982; L'Abate, 1983c; L'Abate & Frey, 1981; L'Abate, Frey, & Wagner, 1982), and various types of treatment modalities (Ulrici, L'Abate, & Wagner, 1981). As we shall see, this model can also fulfill other diagnostic and historical functions, allowing the integration of various philosophical and therapeutic stands. The plan of this chapter and the next is to consider separately each component of the model and then show how the model as a whole can be applied to the following: (a) functional and dysfunctional aspects of relationships, (b) a classification of psychotherapeutic theories, and (c) a classification of psychotherapeutic methods.

EMOTIONALITY (E)

Under the rubric of E will be considered those aspects of behavior which deal with *distance* between and among individuals. As shown in Figure 10–2, the center of E is intimacy, with all its attendant difficulties and paradoxes (L'Abate, 1977; L'Abate & L'Abate, 1979).

It would be impossible to discuss and defend the specific choice of all the minute elements making up this figure. We will attempt, however, to define E and clarify its functions.

Definitions. E is a class of variables that have been called at various times and in various sources (a) affects, (b) emotions, (c) feelings, (d) moods, and (e) sentiments. This component represents the subjective, receptive extreme of a continuum, defined at one extreme by passivity and at the other extreme by activity *(A)*. Thus, *E* represents the passive aspect of our behavior because *E* is something that happens to us. It is usually experienced subjectively and internally. *E* begins the chain of information processing and is therefore an input component. *The function of E is to regulate distances between and among individuals.* On the basis of our feelings of love-hate, liking-disliking, attraction-repulsion, we approach or avoid certain individuals.

Bowen (1978) and one of his students, Fogarty (1980), distinguished between feelings and emotions. Emotion is the overall armamentarium of subjective awareness from which, depending on the situation, a variety of emotions may be aroused or recruited. Emotionality represents the area that includes all emotions, feelings, moods, and affects.

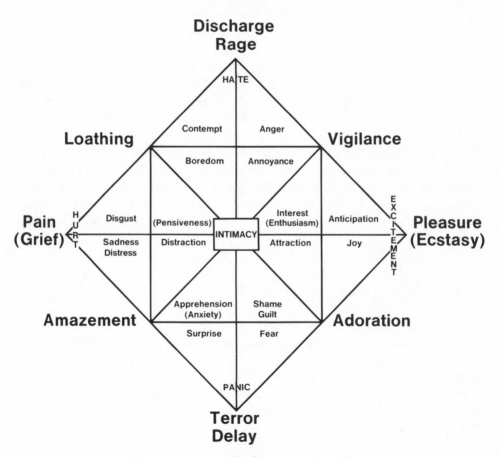

Figure 10–2. A model for emotionality (*E*).

According to Fogarty (1980), "There are basically three moves one can make in life. [One] can pursue others; [one] can stand still and accept the present position as his [her] lot in life; or [one] can keep distance from others" (p. 58). These moves are regulated by feelings and emotions.

Fogarty differentiated between feelings and emotions in a way that makes sense: Feelings are reactions to actions of others or of oneself. In other words, feelings are *reactive*. Emotions, on the other hand, represent the overall "baggage" of reactions that we carry around with us and from which, depending on the circumstances, various feelings may come forth. For instance, *guilt* would be reactive, therefore a feeling, whereas, shame, from which guilt derives, would be an emotion. *Emotionality* means a tendency to use feelings as a way of relating to intimates.

Emotions, whatever they may be, *are* and must be accepted as specific givens (Davitz, 1969) with properties of their own, separate and independent, both conceptually and experientially, from rationality, activity, awareness, and context. Lacking a logical scheme to evaluate, clarify, and eventually understand emotions, we have been unable to capture their essentially existential nature and have attempted to distort them by reducing them to rational schemes or, even more simplistically, to "nothing but" external behavior.

Whether we have indulged in the rational or the behavioristic fallacy (i.e., the tendency to emphasize R or A at the expense of E), we have been unable to consider E important, in its own right, to an understanding of human competence. We may have focused too much on our rational and intellectual development and on our interpersonal skills, perhaps omitting emotions as relevant to an understanding of ourselves.

Functions of E. Emotionality has energizing, motivating, and directing functions pointing us toward or away from what we like or dislike. Affects (or E) are the ultimate result of the pleasure-pain continuum that is part of the basic existential tasks of life. Joy, pride, excitement, sadness, anger, hurt are all part of this aspect. As we have already noted (L'Abate & Frey, 1981), often affects are fused, diffused, or confused with cognition (R) or behaviors (A). Whenever affects are not independent of cognitions or behavior, a dangerous short-circuiting takes place (i.e., obsessive, repetitive, impulsive, or explosive behaviors result). The need to keep affects separate from cognitions or behaviors is illustrated by the fact that, as we shall see again and again, the relationships among awareness, affects, cognitions, or behaviors are not linear but, on the contrary, circular and complex. Given the same feeling (e.g., anger), a variety of cognitive formulations can take place: (a) externalizing the anger—"You made me mad"; (b) internalizing it—"I wonder why I feel angry"; (c) generalizing it—"You made me mad"; or (d) specifying it—"I like you, but what you just did aroused some feelings of anger in me." If cognitions do not take place or take place adequately, affects are often translated directly into behaviors, such as impulsive murders ("I shot him because he made me mad").

In other words, given a specific feeling (e.g., anger), there are an almost infinite number of ways to rationalize it or to act about it, depending a great deal on how *aware* an individual is and how balanced the relative independence of affects, cognitions, and behaviors is.

Both awareness and affects have input functions; that is, they are responsible for receiving information from both inside and outside the body. They are responsible for which stimuli are admitted to one's awareness and affectivity and which stimuli are not. Both components are the gatekeepers of consciousness.

Averill (1980) viewed emotions as "socially constituted ways of solving certain types of problems and conflicts," differentiating emotions as passions and subjective experiences that happen to us from actions as something we do. As Averill (1980) noted, "Psychoanalytic theory does not have a great deal to say about standard emotional reactions" (p. 161). Actually, emotions have either been ignored or belittled by cognitive and behavioral theorists alike. For instance, Schachtel (1959), a psychoanalyst himself, was quite critical of how emotions had been dealt with by Freud as well as other psychoanalytic writers:

> There is a widespread tendency to look upon the universal human phenomenon of emotion as something negative, as a disturbance or a disorganizing influence on behavior. Often this view is propounded by contrasting affect with reason, emotional with reasonable behavior.
>
> The view of affect as a disturbance is prevalent also in the young science of psychology. (p. 19)

Schachtel went on to review how Freud viewed emotionality as "hysteria" and also mutually exclusive with action. In contrast to this position, Schachtel took a position that parallels very closely the one presented here:

> I believe that there is no action without affect, to be sure, not always an intense, dramatic affect as in an action of impulsive rage, but more usually, a total, sometimes quite marked, sometimes very subtle and hardly noticeable mood, which nevertheless constitutes any essential background of every action. (pp. 20–21)

Schachtel went on to suggest what would today be called a systems view of emotions:

> The function of affect can be fully grasped only if we do not confine our viewpoint to what goes on in the individual organism but take

as the object of study the *life-scene* in which the affect arises and in which it affects not only the body of the isolated organism, but other organisms/animals/men who perceive the expression of affect and react to it. (p. 23)

As a result of this position, Schachtel proceeded to consider emotions, in their relationships to actions, both integrative and disintegrative "forces" in human behavior.

Phillips' (1968) only reference to emotionality is in terms of "intimacy"; from there, the reader is referred to emotionality as synonymous with "interpersonal skills." Another Phillips (1978) does consider feelings in their relation to behavior. He is just as quick, however, to discuss their importance (pp. 165–169) through the fallacy of short-circuiting them and equating them with behavior: "Whether statements or actions about one's feelings, or about others' feelings, occur, they are *all* [emphasis mine] references to behavior" (p. 169). Phillips and many other behaviorists missed the point that, given the same feeling ("I hate you"), a variety of behaviors may follow, from destructive to constructive; therefore, the relationship between feelings *(E)* and actions *(A)* is not linear, but circular. As Phillips himself admitted:

> Since feelings seem so omnipresent in human affairs, so integrally related to behavior, whether or not we attempt to separate feelings and behavior in a conceptual sense, a theory posing a major, qualitative difference has to account for this difference in neurophysical and behavioral terms. This might not be a fruitful undertaking. (Phillips, 1978, p. 165)

No theory has to reduce emotions and feelings to neurophysiological or behavioral terms. In fact, a theory of emotions *qua* emotions would need to consider the roles of both external and internal cultural factors.

In addition to short-circuiting emotions for behavior, emotions have been short-circuited for rationality; that is, we have attempted to *understand* emotions by using rational or logical, usually digital (either-or, wrong-right, etc.), changes, perhaps using, as Watzlawick (1978) would have it, our left, language-related hemisphere instead of the more intuitive, more space-related right hemisphere. It has been difficult for us to accept that.

E and Passivity

Averill (1979) is one of the few "feeling" theorists who relates *(E)* to passivity. Averill considered what he called two metaphors of emotions: (a) as *syndrome,* that is, any set of responses that convey information in a systematic fashion; and (b) as *transitory social roles or scripts*. He emphasized that emotions are usually "something that happens to us (passions) and not something we do (actions)." Therefore, emotions relate those aspects of us that are passive and receptive to another aspect at the other end of a continuum—*activities*. Hence, the model poses two rather passive sides—*E* and *Aw,* in their receptivity—and two more active sides—*R* and *A,* in their instrumentality.

Averill (1979) classified emotion into three categories: (a) transcendental, such as anxiety and mystical experiences; (b) impulsive, such as grief, joy, and fear; and (c) conflictive, such as anger and hysterical reactions. As interesting as this classification may be, it does put together radically different emotions—grief, anger, fear—in a single category, a shortcoming that raises some questions about the heuristic usefulness of this classification.

Averill's thorough and unique presentation of anger, in spite of some possible shortcomings, remains an important contribution to a crucial but, unfortunately, understudied area of research. His model for anger (pp. 64–65) remains one of the most complete, and probably the most important, available in the literature on emotions. He factor-analyzed 11 motives for anger, yielding three major factor loadings that are relevant to this model: (a) malevolence *(E)*, (b) fractiousness *(Aw),* and (c) constructiveness *(A),* relating more to the qualities of the angry person than to the external qualities of the precipitating incident.

Zajonc's (1980) position is extremely helpful to the present model in the primacy of *E* over *R*. First, he castigated more cognitive theorists for "simply" ignoring affects (p. 152), illustrating his conclusion by the lack of references to affects in the cognitive literature. Second, he emphasized the primary role of feelings over thinking in most forms of information processing, reviewing a host of experimental findings to support this position. Third, he maintained that affective reactions are (a) primary, in ontogeny and philogeny, (b) basic, (c) inescapable, (d) irrevocable, (e) implicative of the self, (f) difficult to verbalize (because they take place in the world of space rather than the world of time), (g) not necessarily dependent on cognition, and (h) separable from content (cognition). He suggested a two-system view in which *both* affect and cognition are coequal and different, as maintained here. He concluded his review, as follows:

> If we stop to consider just how much variance in the course of our lives is controlled by cognitive processes and how much by affect, and how much the one and the other influence the important outcomes in our lives, we cannot but agree that affective phenomena deserve far more attention than they have received from cognitive psychologists and a closer cognitive scrutiny from social psychologists. (p. 172)

Facts and Fallacies About Emotionality

It is tempting to reduce emotions to by-products of reasoning or to explain them as actions. In fact, philosophers have in the main avoided feelings while emphasizing rationality and action. Sartre (1977), for instance, reached this conclusion: "There is no reality except in action. Man is the sum of his actions. He is what his life is" (p. 61). When motives and causes are considered (Urmson, 1968), "desiring" is the most "emotional" concept that philosophers will allow to enter into their conceptual schemes (Prichard, 1968).

It is no accident that actions are linked to thinking but not to feelings and emotions. This essential quality seems derived by psychologists and philosophers alike. For instance, Ausne (1977) is a more recent reviewer who excluded feelings and emotions from consideration. At best, intentions, volitions (voluntary-involuntary), and deliberations are allowed to creep in as motivational concepts (Hampshire, 1967; White, 1968).

Pronko (1951) differentiated feelings from emotions on the basis of covert (visceral) versus overt (facial) expression. Both are diffuse, organismic reactions. He reserved the label "emotion" for "disrupted or disorganized behaviors" (p. 306), a definition accepted by Hill (1981), who qualified this definition by adding the characteristic of "failure of a stimulus-response coordination" or "no response activities" (p. 323). In other words, both authors saw emotion as "breakdown of the individual's behavioral equipment" (Hill, 1981, p. 325).

In contrast to such a definition, we need to consider feelings and emotions from a completely opposite viewpoint, that is, as energizing, directing, motivating, and focusing reactions that allow us to respond viscerally as well as facially and motorically. We need to differentiate emotions and feelings as subjective rather than objective response. Both Pronko and Hill as well as other psychologists equated feeling and emotions with external, visible activity; in the present context, such an equation is inappropriate and inaccurate. There are deep-seated emotions (e.g., shame, guilt, envy, hostility, pain) that can remain completely covert and often are never manifested, in some cases never even felt or admitted into the awareness of the individual. In fact, there is a whole field of medicine (psychosomatic medicine, that is) in which strong repression of feelings and the overuse of other defensive maneuvers produce reactions inside the body (obesity, high blood pressure, ulcers) that otherwise fail to be expressed externally. Pronko and Hill exemplify well the negative view of emotions and feelings that would deny any positive quality and/or outcome to feelings and emotions. To redress this view, I propose a more positive and constructive view of emotions as *resources*, which, however, many of us do not know how to use well.

There appears to be a conceptual push to reduce both emotions and rationality to action. Schafer (1976a,b), for instance, among others (Case &

Landesman, 1968; Hampshire, 1967), conceived of thoughts, wishes, and emotions as actions, all of which should be so designated in verbal forms denoting action. He is unwilling to separate the definition of a situation (feedback) from the definition of a reaction to it (input, i.e., feelings) because they are both "correlative." According to Schafer, reasons and rationality are specifications about the intelligibility of actions. The meaning of an action is given by "its reasons."

Thus, the connecting link of action to rationality and then back to emotions, as best as one can deduce from many writers (Case & Landesman, 1968), is *volition*. The action that is considered can fall within the voluntary-involuntary continuum. Most actions are "rational"; their "reasons" or "causes" can then also be rational. Hence, one is drawn to conclude that "irrationality" does not belong or relate to the realm of actions or that there is no room for irrationality in any existent theory of actions (Case & Landesman, 1968).

This view of human behavior as a rational "computer" leaves no room for a view of man as a "feeling" animal. Apparently, emotions cannot be digested by either computers (human or otherwise) or philosophers! It may be that the essential lack of linearity in emotions and the inherent association of them with "weakness" or "femininity" are threatening.

It is also tempting to reduce emotions to simplistic dichotomies, such as good-bad, pleasant-unpleasant, happy-sad, positive-negative. Unfortunately, such polarities fall far short of capturing the complexities and nuances of the emotional system. These dichotomies are usually the outcome of a cognitive or behavioral definition of emotions. Instead of polarizing the dimensions of emotion, we just accept them: "Emotions are." This acceptance alleviates the theoretical and therapeutic problems of justifying why we have emotions. It also, perhaps, leaves us with a more answerable set of questions with implications for theory; i.e., how can we use emotions in conjunction with, not instead of, our *R, A,* and *Aw?* Theoretically, then, we believe it is important to demonstrate the value of accepting emotions rather than isolating them from reasoning and actions or dimensionalizing them into polarities. Furthermore, despite the prevalence of cognitive and behavioral approaches to emotions in the clinic, there is an impressive array of "heavy-weight" theoretical positions and research data that justifies regarding emotions on an equal basis as reasoning and action and that points out how complex emotions actually are.

The issue of negative-positive attributions is so ingrained even in major theorists (Dienstbier, 1978) that this dichotomy is blithely accepted and uncritically taken for granted; that is, that there are "negative" and "positive" emotions, without differentiation between an emotional state (e.g., fear, anger, joy) and the actions that may or may not follow that emotional state. Why is *fear* or *anger* any more negative than *joy?* What is it about these feelings that makes them negative?

It is unfortunate that even among major emotional theorists, such a distinction is accepted and used, making most theorizing about *E,* if or when such a distinction is used, rather questionable. Tomkins (1978), Izard (1977), and Tomkins and Izard (1965) argued that affects are the primary motives of man. Tomkins' theory, which provided the base for the more complex and useful theory developed by Izard, essentially links emotion with motivation. He maintained that the emotions are reflected in facial responses, which are organized and innate, and triggered by subcortical neural mechanisms. These responses from the face provide conscious feedback that is either rewarding or punishing. Tomkins regarded eight emotions as primary: interest/excitement, enjoyment/joy, surprise/startle, distress/anguish, disgust/contempt, anger/rage, shame/humiliation, and fear/terror.

In general, Tomkins presented a rather broad-ranging theory, ingenious but idiosyncratic and not well tied to empirical data. Nevertheless, he did assume that the primacy of the emotional system is demonstrable in five ways. First, he maintained that, to motivate behavior, drives require amplification from the affects; however, in the absence of drive, any affect is a sufficient motivator of behavior. For example, one must experience the emotion of excitement to be sexually aroused, but one need not be sexually aroused to experience excitement. Second, the drive system is cyclical, depending on the temporal rhythms of the biological functions; however, since the affect system has "generality of time," it is not dependent on tissue deficits or the cycles of the drive states. Thus, affects are not limited to activation by temporal needs—and their activation with respect to time places them in a central role to motivate human behavior. (Tomkins [1978] did state that pain as an avoidance drive is midway between affect and drive in that it has generality of time.) Third, drives must be satisfied by specific behaviors (e.g., if I am hungry, I eat). Affects, however, can be linked to virtually any object or behavior (e.g., anger can be dealt with through violence, assertions, or self-reproach). Fourth and fifth, affects are capable of greater generality of intensity and modulation; that is, they are more flexible than drives in both their urgency and fluctuations.

Izard's attempts (1977) to build a theoretical framework for emotions around motivational considerations have their beginnings in Tomkins' theory. His theory, however, accounts for more than motivation, attempting to encompass the complexity of emotions through neural, glandular, visceral, and psychophysiological activity, subjective experience, and the innate and learned characteristics of emotions and patterns of emotional-cognitive-motor responses (Strongman, 1978).

Izard called his theory the "differential emotions theory" (1977), describing 10 primary, separate emotions: interest, enjoyment, surprise, distress, disgust, anger, shame, guilt, fear, and contempt. Like Tomkins, Izard emphasized the role of facial expression in emotions, along with their interactions with neural activity, postural cues, and subjective experience. Izard's rather grand scheme of the emotions thus implicates virtually every major organismic system: perception, efferent neural transmission, brainstem reticular arousing system, hypothalamus, facial-postural patterns, and feedback, limbic cortex, endocrine, visceral, cardiovascular, and respiratory systems, subjective experience, and emotion-cognition-motor interactions.

Izard defined emotions on three levels: (1) neurochemical activity, which is innate and patterned for the discrete emotions; (2) neuromuscular activity, which primarily occurs in the striate muscles of the face and relays to the brain feedback about postural activity; and (3) the subjective, or phenomenological, experience of the emotion. Izard maintained that these activities are independent of cognition but that cognition interacts almost continually with them.

In scope, research, and organization, Izard's theory is commendable. It is a wide-ranging theory that accounts for the complexities of neurophysiological involvement with behavioral/expressive and phenomenological experience. Much of this theory is backed up by creditable empirical evidence; the remainder, given appropriate technology, is more than likely testable. The theory places E in a central role in human behavior and accords it an equal status alongside R and A, without too much attention to Aw.

Plutchik (1980) proposed a classification of eight emotional states, maintaining that there is a relationship with one of eight primary emotions: fear, anger, joy, sadness, acceptance, disgust, anticipation, and surprise. *Fear*, for instance, is linked with a behavioral act *(escape)*; with a functional aspect *(protection)*; with a personality trait associated with it *(timid)*; and even with an ego-defense mechanism *(repression)*. As Plutchik himself acknowledged, there have been and will continue to be various classifications of emotions. Among them, his is probably as sophisticated as one can find; however, something is missing from his as well as others' classifications.

Pain and Hurt. One misses, in these classifications, pain and hurt and the avoidance of them as important and very fundamental emotions. At best, Plutchik used "sadness," "grief," and "disgust," which combine into "remorse," while "surprise" combined with "sadness" produce "disappointment." Perhaps pain and hurt may show themselves as sadness and disgust or any of the other emotional states. Pain and hurt are such fundamental and difficult emotions to reach that many of us (even researchers of emotions) go to great lengths to avoid dealing with them. (Chapter 13).

Developmental View. Plutchik's and other attempts at classification (Izard, 1977) miss a developmental view of emotions that might indicate which emotions are related to which developmental stages in the course of the life cycle. This shortcoming has been corrected by Sroufe (1979).

Range and Depth of Emotional Experience Relative to Personality. Although

Plutchik does attempt a link between emotional states and personality types (and sex difference), what is the relationship of range and depth of emotional experience to personality? Are the beautiful people whom Maslow (1968) claimed to be self-actualizing capable of a wider and deeper repertoire of emotions than are individuals lower in the developmental scale? To put it another way, are differentiated individuals able to get in touch with and express a wider and deeper range of emotions than are less differentiated individuals?

Emotions in a Vacuum. Plutchik and other researchers (like other personality researchers) have studied emotions in a vacuum. Emotions do not take place in a vacuum. They take place in relationships! Hence, any attempt to study emotions by artificious and artificial means (e.g., pencil-and-paper tests) are destined to fail in dealing with the raw stuff of emotions that take place in relationships, not in pencils and self-reports.

Chain of Emotional Reactions. I disagree with Plutchik's chain of emotional reactions. He started with a stimulus event followed by cognition, followed by a feeling, followed by behavior, then followed by a "function." Emotions are more bound to our bodies; therefore, they are developmentally and situationally primary in receiving, encoding, and selecting information. Information that is affectively neutral (one doubts that there is such a thing) may directly stimulate cognition. If the information is affectively and cognitively neutral, it will affect actions, as in the movements of an athlete. Thus, instead of stimulus event, or "function," one would tend to emphasize "feedback" loops, which differentiate to emotionality, rationality, or activity, two out of three or all three (see Figure 10–1).

The age-old argument of whether affect or cognition comes first, like the chicken or the egg, fails to differentiate among different functions of feedback. There is feedback (i.e., Plutchik's stimulus events) that goes directly to feelings, some to cognition, and some to behavior, as shown in Figure 10–1. Once our view of feedback functions has been differentiated, we do not need to argue which of the two—affect or cognition—is primary in a chain. Yet, one could argue that feedback to either cognition or behavior, as primary in the chain, is still monitored to some extent by emotions. For instance, we do not tend to read material if it is boring, nor do we persist in an activity that is boring. Hence, all three aspects of behavior are recruited in different sequences, *depending on the nature of the task:* that is, a physical activity will be pleasant for its own sake; yet, associated with it will be the feeling of "good," "exciting," etc. Cognition in this case may run a distant third even though it will still be necessary to depend on it in playing strategies, temporal and spatial judgments, etc. Reading a technical book, on the other hand, may tend to feedback to cognitive more than to the other two aspects. Yet, one will read with greater interest and concentration if the material is interesting and relevant to one's pattern of attitudes and expectations, depending secondarily on affective components and only thirdly on behavior. Reading as activity could take place on an easy chair or a couch, with little other physical activity. Hence, each of the three aspects of behavior could be primary, according to the kind of task one is performing (i.e., lovemaking is a pleasurable activity with very few rational components!).

Linear Simplicity. Plutchik assumes, as already considered, a linear relationship between a stimulus event and the cognition, feeling, and behavior associated with it. Yet, in different terms, one must stress that in reality such linear simplicity does not take place. The threat of an enemy and the danger and the fear derived from that enemy do not always produce "escape," as Plutchik indicates. To protect oneself (Plutchik's "function"), one could decide to fight back and defend oneself! The loss of a loved one does not always produce isolation, sadness, a cry for help. One can use that loss to reach and be reached by other loved ones so that no isolation is experienced! Thus, Plutchik assumed linearity when none is present. The statement "I don't like you," said for whatever reasons, could be followed by a whole spectrum of reactions, ranging from turning around and walking away to picking up a gun and shooting.

Another difference between the present model and Plutchik's model is that he considers all eight major emotions equal, whereas in the present model (Figure 10–2), rage, terror, ecstasy, and grief are considered the four major extremes, while the other four emotions, though they may be just as intense, occur relatively less frequently.

One of the major controversies about E is the *dimensionality* view shared by investigators such as Plutchik (1980) and Izard (1977, 1978) versus the general view of others (Mehrabian, 1977) who consider characteristics of E without content, so to speak. The first view reasons and catalogues emotions, whereas the second view tries to give E directionality, intensity, and duration regardless of specific dimensions. The present model (Figure 10–2) attempts to find a solution that comprises both views. First, *intensity* increases from the center to the periphery: the most intense emotions are on the outside of the figure, and the less intense ones are inside. One needs to be aware that there is an inverse relationship between intensity and duration in E, to the extent that the more enduring feelings, such as love and devotion or a sense of commitment, although strong, may not be as intense as a temper tantrum, a sudden panic, or the ecstasy of an orgasm. The vertical dimension in this model deals with intensity ranging from extreme discharge in rage to extreme delay in panic and terror. Second, this model has *dimensionality*. The horizontal dimension ranges from avoidance of pain at one extreme to approach toward pleasure at the other. Third, as indicated earlier, *duration* is accounted for by the periphery versus centrality in an inverse temporal relationship.

Emotionality and Space

The thesis of this section is that if E governs distance between us, it works at the very beginning of information that we usually receive through our eyes and other sense organs. We approach people we like. We avoid people we dislike. The liking-disliking continuum, therefore, is controlled by our initial processing of information, which is usually emotional unless one would hide, for other reasons, one's liking or disliking someone. We may dislike the boss, but we will not share that feeling with him/her.

Another distinction needs to be made: E is related to space, and R is related to time (L'Abate, 1964, 1976). If E consists of physical, paralinguistic, kinetic, and proxemic responses, as previously reviewed (Figure 10–1), it should be easy to see that those movements, gestures, and responses take place in space. No one needs words to see a sad person cry, an agitated individual move about aimlessly, a desperate person attack. Most, if not all, emotional experiences and expressions are nonverbal.

Wilbur and Wilbur (1980) reviewed categories of nonverbal behavior that are relevant to emotionality: (a) kinesics, (b) eye contact, (c) paralanguage, (d) proxemics, and (e) touching. These are all forms of assessing emotional experience that takes place in space (L'Abate, 1964, 1976), whereas R takes place in time. We can thus differentiate emotional experience and expression, which is controlled by the right hemisphere, from thinking, which is more dominated by the left hemisphere (L'Abate & Gale, 1969; Watzlawick, 1978; Zajonc, 1980).

Schlenker (1980) distinguished three classes of nonverbal behaviors: (a) body language, (b) space use, and (c) paralanguage. The first comprises body positions (e.g., posture and facial expression) and body movements (e.g., gestures and changes in facial expression); space use comprises interpersonal distancing (close/far), seating arrangements, and territorial claims; paralanguage refers to spoken information that is void of content or menaing (e.g., tone of voice, speed or slowness of speech, hesitation and pauses). The mediation of these behaviors takes place through space or, as L'Abate has maintained, through the eyes (1964, 1976). As Schlenker wrote, "the eyes universally symbolize affect" (p. 258), adding that "body language, space-use behaviors, and paralanguage expose feelings and images on the two major dimensions of social interaction—power and evaluation" (p. 266). He went on to elaborate how nonverbal behaviors are related to our liking or disliking others by how we communicate these feelings directly, facially as well as verbally.

Ruesch (1977) argued:

> Nonverbal expressions fulfill two communicative functions. First,
> because body movements and vocal sounds are the principal ways

through which emotions are expressed, they become the principal route through which feelings are explored. Second, because it is universally understood, action language also serves as instruction for verbal communication. The relationship between verbal and nonverbal components of a message is explained in the notion of metacommunication, which indicates that any message has two aspects—the statement proper (p. 5) and the explanations pertaining to the interpretation of the statement. Thus, when a statement is phrased verbally, instructions tend to be given nonverbally; and if the statement is nonverbal, verbal explanations usually follow. Although most people learn to communicate in both verbal and nonverbal terms, there exists a segment of the population that is more nonverbally oriented, and among these persons are many bearers of psychosomatic conditions. They have difficulty with digital-verbal methods, and prefer object or action language for purposes of expression. (p. 35)

By the same token, most of R is linguistic and, therefore, based mainly on time, following the characteristics of temporal processing described elsewhere (L'Abate, 1964, 1976).

Emotional Distance. This is the most ephemeral and difficult distance to evaluate and measure; however, it is indeed the most important. We could be thousands of miles away and many years may have passed, but we remain attached to and involved with our families of origin. Most of the time, the family is a unit of individuals who are physically, legally, and emotionally close to each other. This closeness can be used by the family to enhance or to debase each individual. How they relate to each other emotionally, therefore, has to do with how differentiated from the others each individual is. Each family has tacit and unwritten rules about how close or how far each individual can be from the rest of the family.

How close we are with another individual and how close we want to be is reflected in legal contracts, such as marriage certificates, wills, agreements, and all kinds of written or unwritten contracts and understandings. In functional families, this closeness is negotiated and flexibly used to the greatest advantage of each individual within the family context. In dysfunctional families, this closeness is denied, rejected, abused, distorted, and usually used to bind and "hook" each individual in ways that will not allow him/her to become autonomous in the individual's own eyes. Functionality usually results in self-determination and differentiation in the family system and in individuals making up the system. Dysfunctionality usually results in the inability to determine, define, and differentiate oneself independently from the family's own repetitive ways of defeating one another (L'Abate, 1985).

Perception and Emotionality. There is a great deal of evidence (Jenkin, 1957) that our perceptions are influenced by emotional processes. In fact, interpersonal perception is even more influenced by affect than is perception of inanimate objects. It will be argued here that most of our interpersonal perceptions are emotional and that, indeed, emotionality governs, controls, and determines our perception of interpersonal situations, especially intimate ones. Falling in love, loving, liking, and disliking are all determined by affective processes. Interpersonal distance, how close or far we keep or stay from others, is a matter of how we perceive others on the basis of purely affective decisions (i.e., boring-nonboring, liking-nonliking-disliking). We are closer to those we love and distance ourselves from those we do not. What is more affective than loving and liking?

Davitz (1969) found that reports of emotional experiences in monozygotic twins contained, on the average, about 20% identical categories, whereas reports of dizygotic twins contained an average of 15%, and unrelated siblings 13%. The differences between the first and the last two groups were statistically significant. Even on a checklist of shared activities, monozygotic twins reported that they shared significantly more activities, friends, etc., than did the dizygotic twins. These activities were independent of their reports of emotional experiences. On the basis of these and many other results not reported here, Davitz concluded that "physiological similarity between people is positively related to similarity of their emotional experiences" (p. 57). Since the measurement of physiological activity in Davitz's work leaves much to be desired, it could be argued just as well that similarity of environmental experience is related to similarity of emotional experience, a conclusion that Davitz also reached.

One of the strongest links in the conceptualization and research to support the primacy of emotionality in the initial decoding of interpersonal information can be found in the work of Sifneos (Sifneos et al., 1977), who coined the term *alexithymic* to describe individuals who are unable to express their feelings verbally. In a series of studies, Sifneos and his collaborators found that psychosomatic patients were more likely to exhibit alexithymic characteristics than were their controls. To check further on Sifneos' hypothesis, Anderson (1981) examined the relationship between physiological responses to stressful stimulation and self-reported ratings of stress. She used five groups of 10 subjects each (normal controls, persons who suffered from migraine headaches, tension headaches, essential hypertensives, and arthritics), who were exposed to physical (exercise) and psychological (mental arithmetic) stressors. Various physiological measures were recorded during stress tests. Each subject was asked to rate each stress activity on a five-point scale, from extremely pleasant, euphoric, to extremely unpleasant, very disagreeable. The results showed that three of seven correlations between ratings and mean physiological levels were statistically significant, indicating a negative relationship between physiological responses (forearm muscle tension, electrodermal response, and systolic blood pressure) and reported degree of unpleasantness. The author interpreted these results as suggesting that the more unpleasant the stress, the lower the subject's physiological level of activation. On the basis of this and other interpretations, Anderson advanced the possibility that impairment in the expression of affect is a necessary but insufficient factor for the development of psychosomatic disorders.

Emotionality and Development. Sroufe (1979) reviewed the literature on the ontogeny and development of emotions from birth to 36 months of age, when recognizable and distinguishable emotional patterns appear. He postulated eight different stages of development in this period, with special attention to what he considers the three basic affective systems: (a) pleasure-joy, (b) wariness-fear, and (c) rage-anger. He viewed attachment as an affect and bond that determine future affective patterns and competence as a combination of affective and cognitive components. However, he considered the relationship between these two components linear rather than nonlinear.

Another developmental psychologist (Yarrow, 1979) stated:

> Many theoretical and methodological lines have converged to bring about a resurgence of interest in emotions. Among these convergent influences are ethology and its uncovering of the evolutionary roots of emotional expression; the shift from normative description of cognitive development to a search for underlying processes; the growing recognition of the essential interrelatedness among emotions, cognition, and motivation; the refinement of technology from measuring the neurophysiological concomitants of emotion; and an emerging awareness that understanding of emotions cannot be obtained simply from the viewpoint of an outside observer but requires input from the individual about his or her own feelings.
>
> Just as we have come to question the value of the broad concept of intelligence and have found it meaningful to study component cognitive functions, it might be similarly liberating to differentiate the global concept of emotion and to examine the different forms and levels of expression separately.
>
> Although emotion is evidenced in many different kinds of behavior, it seems to have a dynamic unity. Emotions are activated in similar ways by intense or incongruous stimuli. Sharper definition is needed of the dimensions of affective behavior and of the electrophysiological criteria used. Moreover, we must be aware of the possibility of developmental changes in the relationships among measures; the relationships may differ at different points. . . . Feelings are frequently at a subliminal level of awareness and are difficult to bring to full consciousness. . . . To increase our understanding of emotions, it is imperative that we move from the microscopic

to the integrative level. Ultimately, it may even be necessary to try to make inferences about the meaning of the patterns of behavior observed, to judge when a frown is an expression of fear, of anger, or of uncertainty.

We still know relatively little about effects on emotional development of variations in normal environments. Although we have some knowledge of the patterns that facilitate a child's affective adaptation, the definitive findings are sparse and our understanding of the processes that mediate effects is limited.

Emotions in developmental psychology have had a rather checkered history. Although emotions were a cornerstone of psychoanalytic theories of adult psychopathology, for a time in academic psychology, the study of emotions was almost isolated from feelings. Feelings have increasingly become legitimate foci of study. Aside from clinical studies that have linked adult psychopathology to intense emotional experiences in early infancy, we have very few data on the relation between early emotions and later adaptation. We are very much in need of longitudinal research to investigate continuities and transformations in emotional expression, as well as the conditions under which emotional experiences in infancy may increase personality development and later capacity to cope with stressful experiences.

Many of our data are based on studies of negative emotions—fear, anger, depression. Consequently, we know less about the conditions associated with positive emotional outcomes. . . . We need to take a fresh look at our implicit models of emotional development, how emotions are acquired and how they relate to other aspects of development. For a long time, theories of learning were based on the notion that the organism strives to reduce tension and restore equilibrium—we do not yet understand relative contributions of biological and environmental factors in the expression of emotions. The fact that we are able to identify these differentiated questions suggests progress; it also emphasizes that we still have far to go. (pp. 955–956)*

Sex Differences in Emotionality

Most of the psychological literature on sex differences in emotionality has either ignored them (Maccoby & Jacklin, 1974) or considered them negligible (L'Abate, 1980). Balswick (1979) has been extremely vocal in pointing out

---

*Copyright © 1979 by the American Psychological Association. Reprinted by permission of the publisher.

repeatedly what L'Abate (1960) found out a long time ago; that is, boys are much more unwilling or unable to admit to fears and anxiety. Consequently, they are much more defensive about emotional issues. For boys to admit issues of emotionality is to admit weakness and inadequacy. The opposite is valid for girls. It is all right for a girl or woman to admit being afraid, anxious, and vulnerable. Socially, it is permissible, indeed expected, for girls to admit to weakness as a feminine attribute. Girls can cry; "strong men" do not cry. It is role-appropriate for girls to deal with emotionality, whereas the contrary is true for boys, whose admission of vulnerability would be considered inappropriate and indicative of feminine traits.

Lineham and Egan (1979), in their comparison of skills between males and females, studied whether men are more assertive than women, but in the expression of feelings, they quoted a study of Barron (1971), supporting the findings that the content of men's and women's verbalizations differs, suggesting that women appear more assertive than men in the expression of feelings. Men are more self-oriented and are more concerned with action, problem solving, and projection of themselves and the environment. Women, on the other hand, talk significantly more about their feelings and the feelings of others and are concerned with bringing another member of the group into the conversation. In considering the implication of expressing ideas (rationality versus emotionality), Linehan and Egan brought out the possibility that expression of feelings in contrast to expression of ideas, is characteristic of the low-powered individual. Subordinates in work situations are more likely to express feelings than ideas. In fact, many assertion studies do not even include expression of feelings as assertive behavior; expression of feelings is clearly not related to the objective effectiveness of standing up for one's rights and may even be contraindicated. They suggested, however, that expression of feelings be included in assertion training programs to meet the need of men rather than of women.

Safir (1981) studied the issue of sex and hemispheric differences in relation to accessibility of verbal codes to recognize emotional expressions on faces. He presented six facial expressions of emotions (happiness, surprise, anger, fear, sadness, and disgust) to both right and left visual fields of 120 undergraduates. He replicated the study with another sample to control for surface characteristics. His conclusions are worth quoting:

> In summary, Experiments 1 and 2 provide evidence of a sex difference in hemispheric specialization for recognizing emotional expressions. Males were particularly inaccurate in recognizing emotional expressions presented to the left hemisphere and thus showed a clear right-hemisphere specialization [for recognizing emotional expressions]. (p. 98)

Females showed no hemispheric difference in recognizing emotional expressions. This sex difference is not merely a difference in visual acuity or in the ability to make spatial judgments since both sexes showed a substantial right-hemisphere superiority for recognizing faces. The sex difference was interpreted to mean that males have limited access to verbal codes for decoding information from the representation of an emotional expression. More generally, males, in contrast to females, appear to have relatively limited access to verbal codes for emotion. Females' relatively superior access to left-hemisphere verbal codes for emotion suggests less segregation between their emotional feelings and language. Males may lack verbal codes for emotion, or, more likely, thay lack connections between verbal codes for emotion and imagery, and motor codes for emotion. Thus, males have the vocabulary and the emotional feelings but lack skill in connecting words to feelings.

Emotionality and Psychopathology. Pathology in emotions results from our inability to become aware of emotions and to express them properly, neither too little nor too much. This disproportionate deficit or abuse tends to fuse with either reasons (obsessiveness, compulsivity) or actions (impulsiveness, volatility). Under conditions of inadequate differentiation, the three may become fused, confused, and selectively defused so that one aspect takes primacy over the other two and, in so doing, becomes dependent and linked to the very aspect it seeks to suppress or avoid. For instance, the individual who becomes either compulsive or impulsive by direct avoidance, denial, repression, or suppression of feelings may actually become controlled by them to the very extent that the more anxious, scorned, sad, or mad she/he becomes, the more impulsive or compulsive she/he will become.

We train ourselves in intellectual, academic, and interpersonal pursuits and have vested institutions that accomplish such goals. Yet, we have left out training in the affective area. Even though some feeble attempts have been made to educate children affectively, how can such training "take" if the child is continuously subjected to inadequate models of E, mostly in the home and in the neighborhood? In other words, we have assumed that the family is the agency or institution responsible for such training, without consideration of safeguards to guarantee a satisfactory level of performance. Furthermore, we sanction physical punishment to the point that only when it reaches violent extremes can legal agencies intervene.

As recent research (Lewis, Beavers, Gossett, & Phillips, 1976) has demonstrated, there are optimal families in which individual members are respected, enhanced, and regarded positively, mostly because their individual feelings are respected. Each member is allowed to express feelings freely, without fear of retaliation or reprisal. In contrast to these families are less than optimal familes in which individual feelings are either repressed or denied, or, if expressed, they are distorted or acted out negatively. Thus, emotional development is essentially adventitious and accidental. It parallels closely the kind of emotional development reached by our families of origin. It is well nigh impossible to do any better than our family of origin has done! We are emotional prisoners of our families. We learn to deal with emotions from our parents and siblings. No matter how well these models may have taught us, we learn how to deal with emotions as we learned language, automatically, without differentiating a variety of ways of experiencing and expressing emotional states to enhance others as well as ourselves.

Jacobs and Willens (1970), in a series of very promising studies, developed first an adjective checklist that was factor-analyzed after administration to a large sample of undergraduates. On the basis of these factor analyses, Jacobs suggested a number of hypotheses, which bear repeating after a decade of research, about the dimensions of emotions (pp. 134–135). Jacobs proceeded to make further analyses of his adjective checklist and the nature of emotions derived from it. On the basis of these analyses, he suggested the following scheme (p. 135). Earlier than other psychologists such as Averill (1979), he expressed surprise at psychologists' "preoccupation with negative affect" and relative neglect of passive emotions. Consequently, Jacobs proceeded to study emotions in normal and pathological populations, finding, as he had predicted, that the latter abound in more negative than positive emotions. He trained students in abnormal psychology classes to work with these patients, using role playing, companionship, and story telling as methods of elevating the patients' usually negative moods. Most of these studies, still tentative and incomplete, suggested that his procedures were worthy of further applications and study.

The inability to express feelings not only has profound psychosomatic implications, as Sifneos and associates (1977) and Waring (1980a,b) have shown, it also has implications for substance abuse and addictions. All these dysfunctional maneuvers can be interpreted as stemming from the same source: the inability to express feelings constructively has one direct interpersonal manifestation; that is, it does not allow one to get close to others. Thus, abuse and addiction can be interpreted as being related to an inability to express feelings (L'Abate, 1977; L'Abate, Weeks, & Weeks, 1979).

All these maneuvers, whether psychosomatic or abusive (both internal and external, i.e., aggression), represent a form of avoidance and an attempt to maintain distance. Thus, the management of interpersonal distance is one of the major tasks of life, just as important as being able to tell time. We conclude, then, that interpersonal distance is controlled and governed by our emotions (i.e., how we like or dislike somebody) but is modulated and mediated by our rationality (i.e., we may dislike a person in authority but have no recourse other than to keep our feelings to ourselves).

Families' Affective Rules. This area pertains to the study of family affective rules by Gross and his co-workers (Middleberg & Gross, 1979; Turner &

Gross, 1976), who supported Satir's (1972) emphasis on feelings and emotions to fulfill individual and family growth needs. On the basis of questionnaire data, Middelberg and Gross found that family members do share common rules on how to handle feelings and present a variety of conceptual and technical ideas that are worthy, in their testability, of further attention and replication.

Doane, Golstein, and Rodnick (1981) replicated a study by Vaughn and Leff (1976) of an index of negative affective style, used by the parents of adolescents at risk for schizophrenic or psychiatric breakdown. This index is made up of (a) unnecessarily harsh or personalized criticism, (b) guilt induction, and (c) overly intrusive as well as supportive behavior. The first two negative affective styles were thought to reflect various measures of emotions. They were studied across settings (benign or negative across settings). A positive affective style predicted a positive outcome, whereas a predominantly negative pattern predicted a poor outcome. An inconsistent pattern was not useful in predicting either outcome. Even when the styles for both parents differed, one benign and one negative, the outcome was poor.

> Thus, in viewing both parents as equally involved in setting the affective tone of the family, there is clear evidence that the more consistent the parental pair are in a negative affective style, the greater the effect on the probability of a schizophrenic's spectrum outcome in the offspring. (p. 345)

Intimacy and Emotionality

Most of the evidence in support of intimacy indicates that most partners need to deal with their closeness-distance dimension, which different sources have called "togetherness-separateness" (Rosenblatt, Titus, Nevaldine, & Cunningham, 1979), "separation-individualization" (Farley, 1979), or integration of their similarities and differences (L'Abate, 1976).

Smither (1977) maintained that the study of empathy is handicapped by the inadequacy of theories about emotions. Most of the literature on empathy seems to be related to the four major, easily observable emotions: happiness, sadness, anger, and fear. There is a need to understand the individual's appraisal of the situations through less visible emotions such as pride, remorse, jealousy, envy, and shame. Furthermore, most emotions cannot be understood unless there is a *contextual understanding* of their occurrence. Smither also emphasized an important distinction that is repeatedly made here, that is, the need to keep emotions as subjective experiences separate from their expression as activities. What we feel is one matter. What we do about our feelings is another. The two should not be confused. In fact, a great deal of pathology does result from the fusing, or meshing, of the two. Of course, one's ability to appraise, recognize, and label does depend on one's level of cognitive development, which, however, is here considered secondary, sequentially, to the appearance of feelings.

Feelings and Communication

Communication is a basic requirement for the development and maintenance of *any* interpersonal relationship. Marriage is a relationship in which disclosure is expected to be far higher than in most other relationships. Marriages, however, differ considerably, both in the degree to which partners communicate with one another and in the areas in which communication takes place. Communication breakdown is often one of the major reasons that a couple seeks help from the family therapist.

There appears to be virtually uniform agreement that communication is a key concept in a successful marriage. Rogers stated that "good communication within and between men is always therapeutic" and likened a successful marriage to psychotherapy. He wrote: "Ideally, marriage should support one's mental health by allowing openness and honesty through good communication. Psychotherapy in its broadest sense is the interaction of two personalities leading to an improvement in function in both partners" (cited in Powell, 1969, p. 86). One important reason for this improvement mentioned by Rogers is that sharing of feelings results in a more clearly defined sense of self. It is a psychological truism that one understands only as much of oneself as one is willing to communicate to another. Powell maintained: "If you and I can honestly tell each other who we are, that is, what we think, judge, feel, value, love, honor and esteem, hate, fear, desire, hope for, believe in, and are committed to, then and only then can each of us grow" (p. 92).

Communication, then, is a dynamic force capable of profoundly influencing and affecting the degree of interpersonal closeness in a relationship. Because it can be used to draw others closer, to repel, to help, or to hurt, communication is of vital importance to the family and/or marital therapist. In fact, the sharing of feelings is one of the major tasks of such therapy. In particular, the family often must be helped to learn to share such feelings as hurt, guilt and shame, helplessness and hopelessness, and anger (Chapter 13).

Cox (1967) pointed out that before one can discuss communication between individuals, one must examine the individual because free and open communication begins within the individual. One of the most common reasons for not revealing emotions is the fear that others will not think well of us or will reject us. In his book *Why Am I Afraid to Tell You Who I Am?* Powell (1969) wrote:

> I am afraid to tell you who I am, because if I tell you who I am, you may not like who I am, and it's all that I have. . . . All of us have our secret past, our secret shames and broken dreams, and our

secret hopes. Over and against the need and desire to share these secrets and to be understood, every one of us must weigh fear and risk. . . . In some of us it is the fear of breaking down, of sobbing like a child. Others of us feel restrained by the fear that the other person will not sense the tremendous importance of my secret to me. We usually anticipate how deep the pain would be if my secret were met with apathy, misunderstanding, shock, anger, or ridicule. My confidant might reveal my secret to others for whom it was not intended. (p. 102)

Often, the individual has had just such a learning experience in the past and is (understandably) reluctant to go back for more.

Feelings and Individual Differences

Reasons of a more or less sociological nature also influence disclosure of feelings. A person's ability to empathize with another may be determined by the degree or kind of similarity between two individuals and upon similarities of experience between the two persons. The process of "self-revelation" is dependent upon building rapport between the partners, and this relationship is best facilitated when the couple shares a similar sociocultural background. Lewis (1971) also has found that "individuals who come from similar socio-cultural backgrounds are better able to reveal themselves clearly to each other, become then more dependent upon one another, and thereby discover in each other the fulfillment of their needs" (p. 45). A closely related point is Coombs's (1966) finding that the greater the value consensus among individuals, the greater the ease of communication.

As noted earlier in this chapter, another factor that influences disclosure of feelings is sex differences. Several research studies have shown that men reveal less personal information about themselves than do women. Wives, more than husbands, tend to disclose their hurtful feelings. Wives reveal their anxieties more frequently to their husbands than do the latter in return (Adams, 1971).

In our culture, most men are trained not to cry or show their feelings—to do so might be considered a weakness. Paradoxically, however, it is only in allowing himself to be weak that a man can be strong. Strength does not lie in denying one's hurt; rather, real strength lies in acknowledging it and using it to avoid self-defeat. It is thus incumbent upon the helper to deal with this feeling from the onset—"You are here because you hurt and because you care? Is that right?" Another cogent point is that both care and hurt are demonstrations of love: "If you don't hurt for each other, how do you know you care? *We hurt for and with those we love.*"

Another feeling that must be dealt with in the initial interview and throughout the process of enhancement is hopelessness (or helplessness). Hopelessness, or helplessness, can be very self-defeating since it may persist to the point at which it is accepted as a final given. The therapist must therefore recognize and acknowledge this behavior: "I can see how you can feel hopeless and helpless, but that does not mean you can control and defeat everybody with those feelings." "If you want to go on feeling hopeless, you can do it all by yourself. If you want to consider other positive ways to live with yourself, we can suggest a few. If you want to continue working with us, you may need to give up hopelessness and helplessness." The control and manipulatory aspects of one's claimed helplessness and inadequacy also need to be brought to the fore, as does the fact that people who ask for help are not as helpless as they think they are. In fact, their helplessness is a strength, in that it motivated them to seek assistance and to do something about their situation.

Two other feelings that the individual or family frequently brings into therapy are guilt and shame. Guilt means the awareness of one's "wrongness," having done wrong, that is, having committed an error. Shame means awareness of one's "badness," of being bad and being exposed to one's badness. According to Lewis (1971):

> In the experience of guilt, the self is doing the judging; the experience is thus self-contained and self-propelled. Guilt is about something specific about which the self is critical, in contrast to shame, where criticism or disapproval seems to emanate from "the other." (p. 74)

She further pointed out that the focus of experience in guilt is *thoughts;* shame tends to be a wordless, acute *feeling.*

The desire to please and to learn from someone often helps us to alter our punitive attitudes toward ourselves, thus alleviating some of the feelings of guilt and shame. Suggestion and correction of misconception can soften the effects of a too-strict conscience on the patient. "You really kick yourself around, don't you? What has feeling guilty gotten you thus far? You set your standards too high with your perfectionism—that's a guaranteed formula for being miserable."

Another feeling that commonly causes difficulty in both the individual and the family is anger—either overt or covert. The ability to feel and act out anger is learned early in life. According to Sullivan (1953), the child learns rage behavior from angry, punishing parents. Depending on the particular development of the child and the cultural frame in which he/she grows up, the responses to frustration or anxiety-provoking situations change from diffuse rage to more specific patterns of anger, aggression, hostility, and hate, as well as resentment and apathy.

As Bird (1955) pointed out, strong, unexpressed feelings, of whatever kind, can play havoc with logical thinking and reasonable behavior. Therefore, the therapist's initial task is to help the patient accept him/herself as feeling angry. At this stage, many patients need some reassurance that anger is a common feeling and is acceptable to the therapist. The next two operations involve helping the patient find out, in a constructive way, why he/she feels angry. For instance, what situations in the family bring on anger? If they cannot be changed, what alternatives are there for dealing with them?

It is generally agreed that any intimate relationship (particularly marriage) will inevitably generate some hostility and conflict because of the intense interaction. The question, then, is: How are marital conflicts best handled? Deutsch (1973) identified two types of interpersonal conflict: constructive and destructive. Destructive conflicts are typified by a tendency to expand the area of conflict and by tactics of threat, which leads to increased mutual distrust and lack of communication. Constructive conflicts, on the other hand, are characterized by a mutual recognition of each other's interests, open and honest communication of information, and a trusting and friendly attitude, which allows both persons the flexibility to find creative solutions to the conflict (Barry, 1970).

Although there is a need for freedom and openness in marital relationships so that any emotion may be expressed, Powell (1969) noted that there also needs to be intelligent self-control. Continued and uncontrolled expression of negative emotions is extremely trying and eventually leads to severe conflicts within the marriage. Cutler and Dyer (cited in Adams, 1971) found that talking openly about the violations of expectations does not lead to adjustment. Likewise, Komarovsky (cited in Adams, 1971) reported that, among working-class couples, there is no correlation between self-disclosure and marital happiness. Adams noted that "some men don't want to be told too much; some achieve happiness precisely because they achieve some privacy" (p. 345).

Communication can also be problem-producing (destructive) if couples resort to screaming at each other and hurling invectives. Exchanging insults ("I know you have homosexual tendencies even if you don't know it") or labeling the partner "alcoholic" or "mother-fixated" is what Bach and Wyden (1968) call "bad-fighting." They warned:

> There are limits of tolerance in every fight. . . . The power to inflict major psychological and social damage is always in the hands of intimates. Inevitably, they come to know so much about each other's weaknesses that they can pinpoint quite precisely where to hurt the partner. Such "hitting below the belt" inflicts needless injury. It is also dangerous because it invites a needlessly vicious counterattack if the cornered partner panics. (pp. 72–73)

Powell (1969) concurred, noting that "the vocation of putting people straight, of tearing off their masks, of forcing them to face the repressed truth, is a highly dangerous and destructive calling," and he cited Eric Berne's warning against disillusioning people about their "games." "It may be that they just can't take it. They sought out some role, began playing some game, took to wearing some mask precisely because this would make life livable and more tolerable" (p. 117). The therapist who indulges in direct confrontations with the family must consider these questions: If the psychological pieces become unglued, who will pick them up and put them back together again? Can I?

Bach and Wyden (1968) acknowledged that many psychiatrists and psychologists believe that fighting between husbands and wives is an "outrageous and dangerous" idea. Their experience, however, has shown that "couples who fight together are couples who stay together" *provided* they know how to fight properly. Bach and Wyden recommended first, that the best way to get constructive results from intimate hostilities is to fight by appointment only—the more calmly and deliberately the partner can organize thoughts before an engagement, the more likely it is that the arguments will be persuasive and that the fight, instead of ricocheting, will be confined to one issue.

Other "fundamentals of communication" that couples in therapy should be taught, according to Bach and Wyden, are as follows:

1) Obtain the attention of your receiver. Prepare him/her to receive your message.

2) Send your message clearly, with a minimum of extraneous static. Stake out your own area of interest and stick to its limits.

> The aggressor should make as clear a statement as possible of his demands or expectations; of the rational basis for his goals; and of realistic ways for his opponent to meet these demands. The aggressor should specify precisely what's at stake, what it would mean for him to lose the fight, and how the changes that he seeks will benefit both fighters. (p. 55)

3) Keep yourself and your receiver focused on the joint interest area.

4) Obtain feedback to check how your message has been received.

Role playing is another useful tool for improving communication in family and/or marital therapy. Cox (1967) noted that stepping into the shoes of another person will increase the possibility for empathy as well as intellectual understanding.

In summary, one would expect that the real test of a couple's unity could be the degree to which the spouses can discuss unpleasant matters. The research, however, indicates that marital satisfaction is less related to the proportion of unpleasant than to the proportion of pleasant disclosure. In fact, frequency of unpleasant disclosure is far higher in the unhappily married than in the happily married (Gottman, 1979; Levinger, 1965). Satisfied spouses showed less tendency to discuss negative feelings, particularly when those feelings pertained to their mates. Those same spouses, however, were more likely than were the less satisfied ones to discuss unpleasant feelings about external events, such as a bad day at work. Marriage partners also ranked the communication of positive feelings as far more important than the communication of negative feelings (L'Abate & McHenry, 1983).

Perhaps, then, "talking about one's feelings" does not necessarily mean spilling everything. For the average couple, selective disclosure of feelings seems more beneficial to marital harmony than does indiscriminate catharsis (Levinger & Senn, 1967).

RATIONALITY (R)

As Mandler (1975) recognized, "any consistent view of man . . . must find a place for phenomena other than purely cognitive ones" (p. 3). Acknowledging his "increasing unhappiness with the illusions and inadequacies of some current philosophical work that pretends to provide . . . explanations of human action, thought, and emotion," he unfortunately attempted to give a "cognitive interpretation of emotions" (p. 5), rather than accepting emotions as givens, separate and independent from rational thought. He gave some attention to the arousal of emotions but limited the major emotion to "anxiety," leaving out joyful, painful, or fearful situations and anger.

Definitions of R. R covers a variety of terms that need definition and differentiation: (a) reasoning, (b) thinking, (c) cognition, (d) logic, (e) planning, (f) problem solving, (g) brainstorming, and (h) decision making. Rationality represents a stance in which one uses logic and very logical ways to deal with intimate relationships.

Functions of R. The R modulates the relationship between E and A through *controls.* It links E with A, allowing processing of E and a slowdown of A. R therefore usually has a *delay* function, whereas E has mostly a *discharge* function. A, of course, is modulated by both E and R. *Decrease,* or belittlement, of R in the model would produce an increase in E and in A, as seen in hyperactivity, hysteria, and impulsivity. One of the major functions of E is to heighten or to reduce A; one of the major functions of R is to modulate such a relationship. Another function of E is to motivate us for A, almost like the trigger of a gun or the quarter in a jukebox. R, instead, processes stimuli admitted into one's awareness by rules of logic, comparing, contrasting, categorizing, and clarifying them in relation to past and present similar or dissimilar stimuli. Hence, R deals with information storage (i.e., memory, verbal processing, linguistic rules and habits). In addition, R serves as a moderating factor to affective stimuli, interpreting them according to their spatial and temporal contexts. R is responsible for translating into thoughts, sensory awareness and affects. These thoughts are then translated into words or deeds. Hence, R serves as connecting link between affects and behaviors. R encourages intentions, beliefs, motives, information, planning, and programmatic problem solving (Figure 10–3).

One important distinction that is a source of confusion and misunderstanding concerns the difference between R and Aw. This model makes the distinction quite clear: R *precedes* A and links E with A, whereas Aw *follows* A and links it with E in a circular (nonlinear) relationship within a context.

Again, it would be almost impossible to justify inclusion of the elements of R shown in Figure 10–3. Let us assume for the time being that these elements are a reasonable (no pun intended) approximation of whatever is needed to make up R, both dynamically and statically.

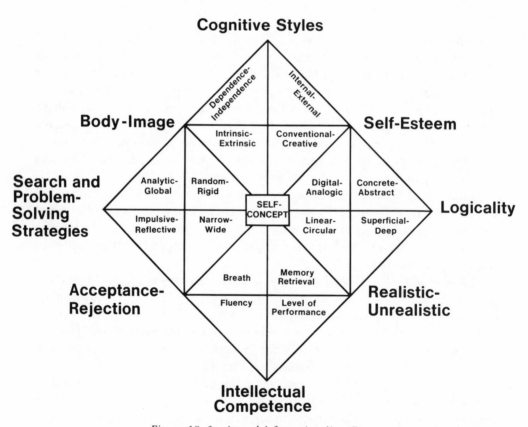

Figure 10–3. A model for rationality (R).

The bottom line of this component, as is intimacy in the case of E, is self-concept. It is assumed that how we think of ourselves has a great deal to do with how we learn to deal with interpersonal interactions. This position is clearly in agreement with that of Lindsay (1978).

Cognition and Rationality

The reason for choosing and using the notion of rationality instead of cognition lies in the following arguments: Rationality is a definite stance, a choice we make and assume about how to use our cognitive resources. We choose to be rational or "irrational" in how we conduct ourselves with others. A rational stance means an emphasis on wanting to be logical and as much in control as possible in our dealings with ourselves and others. It could be argued that rationality is a form of manipulation to the extent that we choose to consider rationality the best way to conduct ourselves with others. By the same token, a rational stance implies relegating emotions and feelings to a secondary position and, in some individuals, to a tertiary position, after activity.

Cognition, on the other hand, represents the overall extent of our intellectual, informational, and problem-solving apparatus that we use in learning, performance, and achievement, educational and occupational. We use the term "irrational" when we behave in ways that do not make sense, that are out of control, and void of any logical or contextual understanding. Rationality, then, is a form of control, of checks and balances to our own impulses, desires, and wishes. It is Freud's superego, Berne's adult, and has the supreme representation in the computer as an all-knowing, logically controlled resource.

We shall argue that as important and relevant as this stance of rationality may be in problem-solving situations (in which it may be a distinct asset), it may become a liability in interpersonal situations, especially intimate ones. In many ways, a rational stance may be dehumanizing because it stresses a logic of relationships based on computer printouts rather than actual human conditions. It dehumanizes us to the extent that in such computerlike logic, there is no room for error; errors are not acceptable (are not computed) because they diminish one's humanness. This logic stands in contrast to a view of humans as fallible, imperfect beings and errors as inevitable in human nature.

This section is admittedly shorter than the earlier section on E or the section to come on Aw. Perhaps there is less controversy about the centrality of R, even though there may be some controversy about its equality or parity with E or Aw. Perhaps this is one way of evening the score, if one needs to be evened? We have not even begun to review how distortions of R may cover the whole pathological range. Yet, as this model makes clear, there may be distortions in E, distortions in R, and distortions in both.

Emotionality and Rationality

As Shapiro and Weber (1981) have noted:

> It is becoming commonplace to express discomfort with recent
> preoccupation with cognition, a preoccupation that has led to a
> narrow, even exclusive, focus on cognitive phenomena at the expense
> of other aspects of development. Currently, there are many signs
> of renewed attention in theory and research to social and emotional
> development and their interrelations with cognition. At the same
> time, there has been a new appreciation of the importance of con-
> textual influences and of the interdependency of individuals and
> their environments. The pursuit of an integrative view of devel-
> opment seems particularly timely. (p. vii)

Sampson (1981) has been extremely critical of what he considers a major
danger in social, personality, and developmental psychology—cognition. He
questioned the ideological and empirical bases on the following grounds:

> It is my contention that the cognitionist perspective offers a portrait
> of people who are free to engage in internal mental activity, to
> plan, decide, wish, think, organize, reconcile, and transform con-
> flicts and contradictions within their heads—and yet who remain
> relatively impotent or apparently unconcerned (in psychology's
> world view) about producing actual changes in their objective social
> world. In substituting thought for action, mental transformations
> for real world transformations, cognitivism veils the objective
> sources and bases of social life and relegates individual potency to
> the inner world of mental gymnastics. (p. 735)

The controversy about the primacy of emotions over cognition has been
rekindled by Lazarus's (1982) most cogent arguments in favor of the primacy
of cognitive processes over emotions. Rather than repeat his as well as Zajonc's
(1980) evidence and opposing arguments, the E-R-A-Aw-C model suggests
that both writers are right and that both are wrong. When one introduces
the concept of human variability and individual differences, one finds that
for some individuals, emotions come before cognition (as in the case of impulsive, passionate acts); in some individuals, cognition comes before emotion
(as in the case of intellectuals, college professors, and astronauts). Most individuals usually balance both processes according to situations and contexts.
Even the most impulsive individual may restrain behavior in front of a policeman, and the most intellectualized individual may lose restraints after
drinking a few. This position, then, would argue for the inherent orthogonality
of emotions and cognitions, with some individuals at the extremes, showing

too little or too much of either one, and the majority, according to situations, balancing the two.

What is the evidence in favor of individual differences? There is a great deal of evidence, not cited by either Lazarus (1982) or Zajonc (1980), that bears on this point. Four sources will be briefly presented and cited: (a) Sifneos et al.'s (1977) discovery of alexithymic individuals, who are unable to process emotions; (b) Waring's (1980 a,b,c, 1981) discovery of couples who avoid emotions and, consequently, intimacy in their marriages, presenting instead, as Sifneos has also found, a plethora of psychosomatic symptoms, or symptoms without physical basis; (c) Brown, Birley, and Wing's (1972) findings that families of schizophrenics use "negative" feelings in their interactions, a finding replicated by the UCLA-Rochester studies (Doane et al., 1982; Wynne, 1983); and (d) learning (Bower, 1981).

My collaborators and I (L'Abate, 1983d; L'Abate, Frey, and Wagner, 1982) have argued for the primacy of emotions over cognition on a variety of philosophical, developmental, and taxonomic grounds. One point that we have stressed indirectly (that both Lazarus and Zajonc seem to avoid) is whether the object of our emotions and cognition is animate (human) or inanimate. In intimate relationships, we have argued that emotions are the basis of the modulation of interpersonal distance; therefore, they precede cognitions, as in love, falling in love, liking and disliking people, and most interpersonal relationships, both intimate (private) and public. Thus, interpersonally speaking, we tend to favor Zajonc's position more than that of Lazarus. By the same token, we are willing to concede to Lazarus the primacy of cognitions over emotions in interactions with inanimate objects. Yet, even this position is questioned by the experimental work of Bower (1981) on mood and memory.

We would, thus, like to congratulate both opponents for the importance of this controversy for theory construction as well as for its practical implications in personality development and therapy with families. From the viewpoint of human variability, both are right and should win prizes; both are wrong and should pay penance to the god (goddess) of human variability, contradiction, and paradox.

ACTIVITY *(A)*

A is the outcome of a chain of information received by *E*, processed by *R*, and resulting ultimately in *A*. Dynamically, it has been shown to be classifiable into various categories. Statistically, its major elements are describable and reproducible (see Figure 10–4).

Definition of A. *A* covers a variety of terms that will need to be defined and differentiated: (a) behavior, (b) acts, (c) actions, and (d) deeds. Although *A* and action have a certain degree of overlap in meaning, *A* has a further implication of quick movements, whereas actions may be clearly separated into words and deeds. *A* usually refers to verbal and nonverbal aspects. Actions may include a verbal component to the extent that words and actions are usually used as separate terms. Shotter (1975) defined action as "movement informed by knowledge and possessing both internal (mostly reasoning) and external determinants" (p. 23). In fact, for Shotter, psychology should be "the science of moral action" in which subjective experiencing, responsibility, and involvement in the world would be the real focus of interest. Behavior, as defined by behaviorists, is strictly externally determined.

Activity has more implications of sequentiality and patterning; actions seem to imply finite and somewhat fragmented or interrupted deeds. Consequently, we chose to use activity *(A)* over actions. There is a difference between *A* and behavior. As used here, *A* means *both* the internal and the external components of any act; whereas, behavior assumes only external, observable components, nothing else.

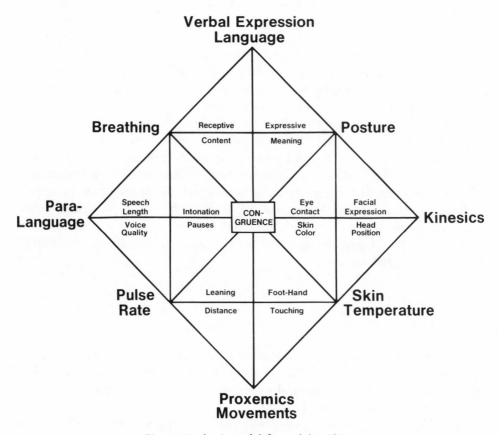

Figure 10–4. A model for activity (A).

As Bateson (1977) asked:

> What constitutes an action? An action is a piece cut from the flow
> of behavior, by the observer, a piece of the behavior of one "indi-
> vidual" cut out from the flow of interaction of two or more indi-
> viduals. . . . Where the cut is made is obscure, why there and not
> elsewhere? Do jackasses see the flow as divided up into actions?
> (p. 336)

Yudlin (1976) outlined five functions in which the notion of "activity"
figures in the context of scientific thinking: (a) activity as an explanatory
principle (a methodological and philosophical idea expressing a universal characteristic of the human world); (b) activity as the subject matter of objective
research (something that can be reproduced within the theory of a scientific
discipline in keeping with its methodological principles, tasks, and basic
ideas); (c) activity as a subject of control (a thing that can be organized in a
functioning system); (d) activity as a subject of design (i.e., investigating
methods and conditions for implementing definite, predominantly new types
of activity); and (e) activity as a value (analysis of the role of activity in different
cultural systems). Rubinstein (1977) summarized the various theoretical approaches to the concept of action and concluded, following L. Wittgenstein,
that the prevailing sociological model of action as behavior plus a subjective
component is fundamentally misconceived. An alternative view is presented
in which the meaning of an act is a function of the social context rather than
the subjective experience of the actor. In this model, the causal antecedents
of A are Aw, E, and R, but not necessarily in that order.

Argyle (1980) considered actions to take place in "interactions," which
have the following features: (a) goal structure, (b) repertoire of elements, (c)
rules, (d) sequences of behavior, (e) concepts, (f) environmental setting, (g)
roles, and (h) skills and difficulties. Rules are developed to fulfill goals set
in situations through (a) maintaining communication, (b) preventing withdrawal, (c) preventing aggression, (d) coordinating behavior, and (e) achieving
cooperation. Difficulties in skills can be dealt with through social skills training (SST).

As Ginsburg (1980) concluded:

> Human action is situated temporally and hierarchically structured
> and meaningful, but modifiably so. The action of interest often is
> *joint* action, produced by the coordinated activity of two or more
> people, and not explainable in terms of any one of them. . . . To
> understand an action, it is necessary to understand the situation of

its occurrence, and also to identify the temporal and hierarchical structure of the action—that is, its sequential linkages and its act/action relationships, the meaningful units it contains, and the meanings it carries in the instance of interest. (p. 343)

Functions of A. A is the ultimate discharge into words or deeds of the chain of information starting with Aw (which could be bypassed), E (which could be bypassed), and R (which could be bypassed). A is the outcome of this information-processing chain that will start another link with and to Aw, completing the circle. Certain activities, such as many nonverbal actions of gymnasts, athletes, dancers, and painters, have almost no feedback to either affects or cognitions; that is, behaviors are corrected on the basis of immediate sensory feedback (visual, auditory, kinesthetic, or skin), almost completely devoid of affects (E) or cognition (R). The dancer or the athlete "concentrates" (i.e., focuses awareness) on his/her body acts, in which almost no affects or cognitions are necessary. If and when they intrude, they may produce lapses in awareness and in performance. A has a variety of other functions that differentiate it from the other components: (a) survival, (b) judgment, and (c) congruence.

Ultimately, what we do is more important than what we say. We need to act (move, do, etc.) to survive physically. We are, ultimately, also judged by what we have done or by the threats or promises we make about our future actions. The heart of A is congruence: (a) how our deeds (nonverbal actions) match our words; (b) how our A expresses or fails to express E and R, constructively or destructively; and (c) how we have changed A on the basis of our Aw; that is, how we have learned from past experience.

CONCLUSION

E, R, and A are important components and determinants of behavior. By themselves, however, either alone or in combination, they are incomplete without the help of two other components, which are to be elaborated in Chapter 11.

Chapter 11

The Model Continued and Applied

The purpose of this chapter is to continue elaborating on the information-processing model of family competence presented in the preceding chapter and to show how this model can be applied to (a) functionality and dysfunctionality in families and (b) a classification of psychotherapeutic theories and methods. Appendix B shows how this model has been applied to the process of negotiation.

AWARENESS *(Aw)*

One cannot consider the concept of awareness without resuscitating the old operant-awareness controversy of the 1960s (Murray & Jacobson, 1971), in which learning and awareness were considered necessary if change is to take place. The major shift that has occurred since then is the apparent lack of references to the role of awareness. In fact, the latest edition of the *Handbook of Psychotherapy and Behavior Change* (Garfield & Bergin, 1978) does not even include an index entry for this topic. Despite this exclusion, the concept of awareness is indeed considered in this handbook! Even without an index entry, the concept of awareness has a way of coming up in a variety of references. For instance, Orlinsky and Howard (1978), considering therapy as experience (in addition to therapy as activity, dramatic interpretation, and association), believed that two major aspects

> may differentiate psychotherapy from most other social situations, so far as the patient's perception is concerned. First, the therapist

is likely to be an unusually influential focus of *awareness* [emphasis mine] for the patient, especially in individual therapy where the therapist is virtually the sole occupant of the patient's "object world." Second, the patient's own self-perceptions are likely to be brought more forcefully into the foreground of awareness than in most other social situations. Both of these factors should heighten sensitivity to the impact of the experiential aspects of the relationship on the patient. (p. 296)

In reviewing research related to awareness of feelings and outcome in psychotherapy, Orlinsky and Howard concluded that "more research in this area (*awareness of feelings* [emphasis mine]) of patients' self-experience seems indicated by the few findings accumulated thus far" (p. 297). These authors also reviewed studies pertaining to therapists' self-perceptions and their *awareness* of instrumental participation with patients. Their conclusion, at the end of this section (pp. 302–303), was that "this is an area that has barely been opened to research."

The notion of the operation of complex psychological processing outside awareness has traditionally been associated with the concept of the unconscious as used by psychodynamically oriented clinicians. This notion, however, has not found an equivalent place in the mainstream of American experimental psychology. These authors cited mounting evidence from disparate areas of empirical research, such as selective attention, cortically evoked potentials, and subliminal perception, which provide support for such a concept. In fact, explanatory concepts of a nature similar to that of the unconscious have been included in several models of perceptual processing although there may be an extremely large gap between clinically based and experimentally based conceptions about the nature of unconscious processes. These very processes may provide an interface between clinical and experimental approaches to an understanding of personality.

One can only ask why awareness has faded from interest and attention in psychological research and why it is necessary to reconsider its role in competence. At this point, only speculative conjectures can be brought forth. One will need to review the literature to research whether or not anyone has improved on the controversy of the 1960s, which, incidentally, referred to the role of awareness in operant learning, *not* in traditional psychotherapy. Why has awareness fallen into disfavor? Is it a "bad" term, reminiscent of "insight"? Is awareness a variable or state so difficult to measure that consideration of it is useless? Most of the research relevant to the role of awareness in learning was based on asking the subjects (or parents?) whether or not they were aware of the contingencies in whatever reinforcement paradigm they were involved in. Thus, the definition of awareness as used in those days and as used here is considerably different. Awareness then was considered in an extremely limited fashion (i.e., knowledge of experimental contingencies).

In reconsidering the role of awareness in intimate relationships, we need to ask ourselves why its role has declined. Why does awareness not have the place it deserves if its role is as important as it is purported to be? Among the shortcomings that have plagued the concept of awareness are the following: first, definitional inadequacies; that is, often, awareness has been equated to insight or to "understanding." This is an improper equation; awareness as defined here is *not* equivalent to insight. Awareness as considered here implies knowledge of self-behavior—insight, if you will—plus a better understanding of one's functionality and dysfunctionality in relationship to internal and external contingencies. Awareness as defined here thus encompasses the old-fashioned concepts of "expanded consciousness," "expanded insight," and "expanded understanding." It is important, however, to realize that such an *awareness may or may not be related to change in activity*. In other words, awareness is one component of the overall chain of information processing. Whether such a supposedly expanded awareness results in improved behavior does not necessarily follow because awareness and A are not necessarily linked to each other in any isomorphic or linear function. Changes in A may, in fact, be negatively related to awareness. Only if one subscribes to the notion of functional independence of Aw and A can one make sense or and reconcile some of those seemingly contradictory findings (Applebaum, 1977).

Perhaps awareness may be equivalent to what some people call "growth," which usually means a different perspective, thinking in a way that is different from the way in which one has been accustomed to thinking. Unfortunately, the term *growth* may have other connotations (e.g., "Do your thing regardless of whom you hurt"—encounter and marathon groups) so that such an equation, even if valid, is unsatisfactory: plants grow; humans progress, regress, or mostly stay the same—regardless of what we say!

In referring to Aw, we mean specifically the *awareness* of oneself *in relationship to others*, not awareness of self in a *vacuum*. Yet, this awareness represents also the feedback we receive from our internal feelings, our overt thoughts, and our more overt actions, all of which impinge on our awareness. This awareness implies also how we perceive ourselves in secret, the secret self that most of us safeguard from others, including our intimates. Ideally, in most differentiated individuals (L'Abate, 1976; L'Abate & Frey, 1981), E, R, and A are functionally separate from each other and need to be balanced *equally*, no one of the three components assuming priority over the others. If E is "repressed," "suppressed," or "denied," compulsivity in R or impulsivity in A may be the outcome. If thoughts are "repressed," "suppressed," or "denied," E and A increase and heighten to the level of what is usually called "irrationality" and/or hysteria. If A's are "repressed," "suppressed," and controlled and/or delayed, fantasy and, eventually, hallucinations and withdrawal may be the outcome.

Aw, which in most cases has been classified in the cognitive-reasoning area, could just as well be considered within the area of emotions and feelings. In fact, the most difficult awareness to achieve in life is the awareness of one's own feelings of hurt and fears of being hurt (L'Abate, 1973a, 1977). *Aw* is a condition that encompasses and pervades all three components of intimate relationships—*E, R,* and *A*—rather than one component and/or *E*. The important differentiation is that all four components are kept separate but, at the same time, allow a continuous and clear flow from one to another; that is, awareness of different feelings and/or thoughts *may* lead to different states of awareness, which *may* lead to different actions.

Since awareness has thus far not been adequately conceptualized with an operational definition, it follows that, as yet, we really do not know whether or not (a) awareness increases or improves with changes in any of the other three components, and (b) an increase in awareness, whatever it may be, can or should produce *ipso facto* a change in behavior. If the aspects are functionally unrelated, one would not expect that behavioral change per se should be related to changes in awareness. In fact, there is some tentative evidence that suggests the contrary (i.e., the two are not related). Change in one aspect does not necessarily imply change in the other (Woodward, Santa-Barbara, Levin, & Epstein, 1978; Slipp & Kressel, 1978). Second, awareness has been equated with a momentary state rather than seen as a *process of becoming aware*, as in the study of verbal learning.

Definitions of Awareness

Among the various ways in which awareness (*Aw*) may be defined, we need to distinguish among continua of (a) consciousness, (b) arousal, (c) vigilance, (d) alertness, and (e) openness, along which *Aw* may vary.

One of the best definitions of awareness, one that seems to encompass the meaning and functions of this concept, was given by Jurkovic and Selman (1980). They considered it "a reflective understanding of intrapsychic processes" (p. 92). In this context, of course, one would also add *reflective understanding of intrapsychic and interpersonal processes after they happen.* Jurkovic and Selman, in addition, considered four "intrapsychic" issues: (a) *subjectivity*, or awareness of conflicting thoughts, feelings, and motives; (b) *self-awareness*, or awareness of the relation between the self as observer and the self as observed; (c) *personality*, or awareness of inner attitudes, beliefs, and values as a coherent system; and (d) *personality change*, or awareness of the nature of transformations in the basic nature of the self. They used these concepts to suggest a developmental progressing of increasing differentiation.

The Functions of *Aw* as Feedback

Aw functions to (a) keep the individual alert to internal and external stimuli and clues; (b) receive these cues and allow entry to the individual through thresholds of arousal, which vary from individual to individual and from situation to situation; and (c) route this information to the various components that seem most relevant to the information, whether *E-R-A* and/or the whole context of the relationship.

This feedback loop may be specific to one component (i.e., *E, R,* or *A*), to more than one, or to all three *plus context*. It is this component of the model that, more than any other, relates to physiological and physical factors.

The major function of awareness is *corrective*. Yet, one needs to remember that the relationship among components in this model is *nonlinear*. Consequently, one cannot predict that changes in *Aw* will result in changes in *E, R,* or *A* any more than that changes in any of these components will bring about changes in *Aw*.

It is this very nonlinearity (i.e., independence) that makes the characteristic so important. Without this characteristic, there would be overlap and it would therefore be necessary to consider one component separate and separable from any other component. The relative independence of these components does not deny their intrinsic overlap at the center (see Figure 10–1). The issue is as follows: How much overlap is functional and how much is dysfunctional? The degree of overlap (among components) depends on the strength of the boundaries: the stronger and more impermeable the boundaries, the less overlap. The weaker and more permeable the boundaries, the greater the overlap will be (see Figure 10–3). *Aw* performs separate feedback functions to affect *(E)*, cognition *(R)*, and behavior *(A)*. This feedback can be narrow, short, strong, weak, diffuse, or specific. It can be directed backward to affects or cognitions or behaviors, affecting one, two, three, or none of these aspects. *Aw*, depending on its characteristics, can serve positive (reinforcing of homeostasis) or negative (correcting and changing homeostasis) functions in any of the three aspects. In this sense, we should be speaking of awarenesses rather than awareness.

Aw can bypass *E* and produce feedback directly to *R*, as, for instance, in the case of intellectual presentations, business deals, and negotiations in which impersonal rationality tends to dominate and in which affects *(E)* would only interfere. Thus, there are a great many behaviors, especially verbal ones, that produce feedback into *R*, in contrast to many nonverbal behaviors in which the feedback is most immediate to *E* (i.e., shorter and more direct). Ultimately, *A* produces feedback to *E*: One reacts to how one has behaved in terms of feeling good, bad, or proud of one's performance, depending on the effect that the behavior has had on others or on oneself. The feedback loop to *E* can be longer and more indirect than to *R* or to *A*. One may become quickly aware of a feeling or one may become aware of how one felt under past circumstances only after some time (even years) has elapsed. Sometimes, a period of incubation is necessary. Sometimes we do not become aware of our feelings because we have suppressed or repressed (i.e., avoided) them.

It follows from this nonlinear relationship, as shown by the amount of overlap between and among components (see Figure 10–1), that awareness, even though functioning as correction, does not work 100 percent as correction. It is neither possible nor desirable to expect or assume such an eventuality. The extent of recruitment and use of each component and its elements depend on the extent of usage (size of circle), strength of boundaries (permeability), and amount of overlap with the other three components.

Awareness implies a knowledge of the results of one's A upon others and of knowledge of the results of others' A on us. Thus, it does possess many of the characteristics of feedback as reviewed by Annet (1969). This impact could be based on our feelings, our thoughts, or our actions. Thus, if (or when) awareness is viewed as feedback, it becomes an independent dimension that cuts across feelings, thoughts, and actions, possessing characteristics of width and depth that will be elaborated later.

Aw and Consciousness

These terms—Aw and *consciousness*—are not considered synonymous. One needs, of course, to be conscious if one is to be aware. Consciousness, then, is the larger context in which awareness is embedded. Consciousness is content-free and generic. Awareness is content-related, usually specifically related to a feeling, to a topic, or to a reaction set.

Negotiating with the Self

How can one negotiate with oneself when negotiation is an interpersonal process? Easily. One needs to be able to look at oneself confronting oneself as objectively as possible and to go through exactly the same steps in negotiation that one follows in negotiating with others. Thus, we have three different levels of negotiation: (a) private, within oneself; (b) public, with intimates; and (c) public, with relative strangers or nonintimates. If one can negotiate with oneself and intimate others, one should (this is a qualified *should!*) be able to negotiate successfully with nonintimate others in relatively short-lived and somewhat distant, superficial relationships.

Awareness of What?

Aw relates to sequential steps necessary in the information-processing loop that proceed through (a) input, (b) processing or mediations, (c) outputs, and

(d) feedback (Annet, 1969). Each of these aspects of awareness indicates its encompassing quality and its importance. Yet, *Aw* is a concept as elusive as we believe it to be relevant.

Whatever *Aw* may be, we "know" that (a) it varies profoundly from individual to individual; (b) within individuals, it varies from time to time; and (c) it may increase or expand with age. Beyond these three basic conclusions, we would have a hard time specifying (a) what awareness is, (b) what it relates to, and (c) what it leads to. We postulate it as a hypothetical construct inside the skin of individuals. We know that it exists, but somehow we do not know how to get hold of it. We also "know" that it is an important part of our human experience and existence. Yet, it shares one of the qualities of the weather: everybody talks about it, but nobody does anything about it.

As difficult as this concept may be, its importance is matched only by its elusiveness. Any statement about *Aw* can only be made with much tentativeness and humility. Attempts have been made, and many (this writer among them) have been seduced by this concept. Nevertheless, we can conclude that (a) although *Aw* seems to possess a great deal of relevance for an understanding of behavior, its relevance has been matched by its elusiveness; (b) although many theorists have been seduced by its relevance, they have been just as frustrated by its elusiveness; and (c) the very qualities of seductive elusiveness make awareness a very appealing, yet frustrating, subject to approach. Interest and involvement may not necessarily lead to fulfillment and communication. Anyone attempting to deal with *Aw* will do so at his/her own peril. Energy investment may not lead to just or equitable results. One can take a chance with open eyes and fall just as hard as one whose eyes are closed. Here goes another idealist, as a lover to a rendezvous, fascinated by this concept.

Klinger (1977) had this to say concerning awareness:

> Introspective awareness is a matter of responding to inner events and is therefore very much subject to both refinement and distortion. Awareness of the meaning of one's inner life can greatly improve one's self-communication, a benefit long ago pointed out by Jung but largely ignored by systematic researchers. (p. 101)

Yet, if *Aw* is so important, why is it not related to human emotions, except as "self-awareness" (Izard, 1977) or as "consciousness"? As Izard noted:

> There seems to be no useful distinction between the concepts of subjective experience, consciousness, and awareness, and all these terms seem to imply an existential dichotomy—experiencing-not experiencing, conscious-unconscious, aware-unaware. (p. 142)

In rejecting these dichotomies, Izard cited Snygg and Combs' (1949) distinction of *levels of awareness* in consciousness. He concluded, however: "As a rule, the level of awareness of a phenomenon is an index of its motivational value for ongoing behavior" (p. 143). Hence, Izard made *Aw* one of the conditions *sine qua non* to the energizing, mobilizing, and initiating behavioral sequences. Can such sequences be initiated, however, without *Aw*? There is some evidence that one can have changes in behavior without changes in *Aw* (Slipp & Kressel, 1978; Woodward et al., 1978).

Aw and Knowledge

Aw is that part of consciousness that "knows" something about oneself and other selves. *Aw* is thus important from the viewpoint of epistemology since *Aw* and knowing are linked to each other. Knowledge, then, becomes the important dimension of awareness, to the point that "Know thyself" means essentially "Be aware of yourself" and "Be sensitive to what goes on inside and outside yourself." If, then, awareness is knowledge, does it mean that awareness is a cognitive process? Not at all. One can be aware of a tight knot in the stomach, but one may or may not be aware that the tightness has been produced by a particular stressful situation that one has just encountered. Being aware of that tightness and "knowing" some of its antecedents or correlates does not necessarily mean cognitive emphasis. One may not be aware of one's bodily changes but still be aware of one's stressful circumstances. The two processes—internal and external—may not necessarily be integrated. Both may be blotted out completely, or both may be "remembered" partially, or just some part of one may have left a trace in *Aw*. Thus, even though *Aw* may be related to a process of knowing, that process does not mean a cognitive relationship—it may have internal components as well as external ones. Knowing is best conceived as kinetic inquiry (Bentley, 1950), as a transaction in which the observer is part of the whole field.

Aw as an Insufficient Condition to Change Behavior

The fact that *Aw* is not sufficient for change does not imply its irrelevance. On the contrary, the fact that the relationship between *Aw* and intimate relationships is nonlinear indicates that under certain conditions, yet to be specified, *Aw may be directly related to intimate relationships*. Its nonlinear relationship with *E, R,* and *A* does suggest that it is independent of and dependent on these components under conditions that need specification. *Aw* is worthy of study for its own sake. Why? As Gendlin (1978) pointed out, a repression-linked view of *Aw* would lead us to view it as a restricted "unconscious," narrowed by painful blocks and traumas in one's own developmental history. His view is much more acceptable here: the conscious-unconscious distinctions can be linked to the completeness of the experiencing process, as defined by Gendlin. Consequently, *Aw* can never be complete—to the extent that human experience cannot be complete. To this extent, then, all of us are faced by different degrees of *Aw* that depend a great deal on how much experiencing and focusing we ourselves exercise. *Aw*, then, is a matter of practice. The more we practice it, the more aware we may become. We must be careful, however, not to equate or expect that changes in *Aw* per se will lead to behavioral changes. It takes more than *Aw* to change, and *Aw* per se may not be sufficient to change behavior.

If this is the case, why should we be concerned with *Aw*? Just because it may not be related to external behavior, it is not necessarily unimportant. Internal changes are still relevant, if not from a phenomenological viewpoint, from an empirical viewpoint. Lieberman (1979) called for a return to inspection(ism) on a variety of logical and epistemological and empirical grounds:

> If introspective reports are sometimes wrong or misleading, however, there is equally compelling evidence that in some instances they may provide information of truly impressive accuracy and reliability. . . . Introspection is limited in what it can achieve, but an acknowledgment of its limitations does not thereby require its total proscription. . . . It is clear that one of the major sources of information for predicting (and thus potentially modifying) behavior are people's introspective reports. (p. 319)

Past and Present Conceptualizations of Awareness

A review of the literature on the theories and research on awareness would lead us astray from our major goal of linking *Aw* with intimate relationships, within the framework of a model of information processing.

A recent theory of self-awareness (Duval & Wicklund, 1972), even though experimentally fruitful, defined awareness as experience, making it difficult to relate to the kind of awareness one deals with in psychotherapy. Perhaps, width of awareness or something akin to cognitive complexity may describe *in part* the kind of awareness being considered here. Another formulation worthy of consideration is that of Luft and the Johari model of awareness (1969), consisting of what is known/not known to us and what is known/not known to others.

Applebaum (1977), in the report of the Menninger Foundation's 20-year (and $1 million!) testing of the effects of psychotherapy, defined *insight* as "a change in some aspects of the patient's functioning, brought about through and related to some increase in self-awareness. *Insights, then, involve new self-awareness that results in change*" (p. 34). There are at least two shortcomings in this definition and the assessment of it in this report. First, one cannot logically expect that increased self-awareness is linearly related to change in behavior. In fact, there is no evidence whatever in the literature on psychotherapy that the two aspects are related to each other, either linearly or isomorphically. Second, in this project, raters evaluated and rated awareness *indirectly* but never directly, as far as the reader can tell, on the basis of an overall review of all the individual's responses to various test materials (pp. 84–89). In other words, self-awareness was *inferred* rather than evaluated by a specific instrument. Thus, on both logical and empirical grounds, the Menninger report leaves much to be desired.

As Bochner (1978) suggested, no analysis of interpersonal communication can be complete without reference to three classes of concepts—intrapersonal, interpersonal, and situational—a classification that is reminiscent of Satir's (1972) distinction of self (intrapersonal), other (interpersonal), and context (situational). Schofield and Abbuhl (1975) maintained that body movement exercises can and do have beneficial effects on understanding and self-awareness as measured through a projective task. Nonverbal activities (insofar as insight and self-awareness are concerned) could have the same beneficial effects as role playing. Barrilleaux and Bauer (1976) failed to find any significant increase in awareness as a result of Gestalt awareness training. Fisher's (1976) use of subliminal inputs in body-boundary awareness may be an experimental approach to manipulation of awareness. Armstead's (1977) results supported this line of research. As Poe and Mills (1972) found, interpersonal attraction is significantly related to similarity of personal needs and to awareness of others. Miller, Nunnally, and Wackman (1975) developed an awareness wheel consisting of five radii: (a) sensing, (b) thinking, (c) feeling, (d) wanting, and (e) doing. This wheel is part of a whole theoretical framework underlying the Minnesota Couples Communication Program, of which awareness is the base.

Awareness, of course, has been the favorite term for most humanistic (Gendlin, 1978), existential, and human potentials movements (Otto & Mann, 1969), in contrast to the term *insight*, which is used preferentially by the psychodynamic (Applebaum, 1977) school. The former implies emphasis on awareness of the emotional and irrational aspects of human nature. The latter implies emphasis on the awareness of the rational, logical aspects of human beings. Both schools emphasize awareness as a hypothetical variable relevant to personality change. Both schools, thus far, seem to have failed in operationalizing this variable and building a nomological network around it that should lead to further empirical testing and comparisons.

Gibb and Gibb (1969) made some statements about "growth" in people (not in plants!) that can apply just as well to "awareness." Their statements are quoted almost verbatim, but the term *growth* has been changed to *awareness*: (a) Human awareness is essentially a socially interdependent process. Emphasis here is on awareness as process, not as a static state or condition separate and independent from other beings. (b) Awareness is a process of identifying one's own intrinsic emerging motivations and of maintaining a life style in congruence with these motivations. Emphasis here is on motivation—Why do we do as we do? (c) Awareness is a process of increasing the depth and validity of communications with the self and with others. Emphasis here is on *depth* and *validity*. (d) To achieve productive changes in personal awareness, we must confront the issues of the preceding statements in contrast to and comparison with the awareness of intimate others. Emphasis here is on *confrontation, contrast,* and *comparison* so that change may take place in awareness. L'Abate, Weeks, and Weeks (1979) also made awareness, especially awareness of one's hurt feelings and fears of being hurt, a construct necessary to constructive change.

Curle (1972) related awareness to identity in assuming that "identity can be either a sense of knowing who one is, based upon awareness (that is, awareness-identity); or, what is more usual, a sense of belonging (that is, belonging identity), and both of these can be stronger or weaker" (p. 8). Curle went on to classify individuals according to their standing (high or low) on both factors: awareness and identity. Curle defined awareness as self-awareness, or our consciousness of our own being. In this sense, he paralleled the present conceptualization of being, which is based on awareness and emotionality. When Curle described one's identity, he seemed to refer to what is here described as emotionality. To be aware of one's identity means to be aware of one's innermost feelings and thoughts as well as reactions to one's own words and deeds (Chapter 13). Curle also warned about the dangers of becoming too wrapped up in one's awareness, as in cults that promote self-awareness as a way of life and a supreme goal. Thus, self-awareness may become self-absorption and at this point interfere with anything else an individual may think or do, leading one essentially to deny the context of one's existence. Curle's *belonging identity* is comparable to the references here to intimacy, being, and feeling close to someone we love. Curle used the concept of mask and mirage to describe what we put on to fool others (masks) and what we follow to fool ourselves (mirage).

Shur (1976) has been one of the harshest critics of the expansion of awareness by the humanistic movement, viewing much of the human potentials movement's emphasis on awareness as dangerous and misguided. He questioned whether an expanded consciousness, or awareness (he used both terms interchangeably), would actually promote the kind of action and behavior necessary to change existing social conditions. He criticized the human potentials movement especially for its (a) antiintellectual stance, (b) the artificiality of its procedures, (c) excessive claims not backed by sufficient or satisfactory evidence, and (d) the possibility of considerable danger of misuse and abuse. Essentially, he questioned the use of shortcuts and pat formulas for achieving personal comfort and success ("Do your thing") that do not heed the social and personal consequences of hurt inflicted on intimate others. The hedonistic and content-free (all process) emphasis on "being" and "experiencing," with a belittlement of traditional social values and a neglect of socioeconomic differences is a criticism made by L'Abate (1972). In spite of the harshness of these criticisms, some of the points made by Shur bear on points to be made here: (a) awareness cannot be equated with action or, for that matter, with either emotions or reasoning, and (b) awareness is not a sufficient or necessary prerequisite for behavioral change.

Therapeutic Implications

A therapist who wishes to do so may well concentrate on awareness. If one wants behavioral change, however, one cannot assume that (a) changes in awareness will take place as a result of therapeutic interventions, and (b) these changes, if any, will lead to behavior change. If behavioral change is desired, one will need to use different techniques and methods to bring it about. Increased or expanded awareness does not necessarily lead to behavior change, just as behavior change does not necessarily lead to expanded awareness (Selvini-Palazzoli, Boscolo, Cecchin, & Prata, 1978). Whence comes awareness? Do we need this construct? Why? Some possibly therapeutic outcomes are (a) changes in awareness without changes in behavior, (b) changes in behavior without changes in awareness, (c) no change in awareness and no change in behavior, and (d) changes in awareness accompanied by changes in behavior. Assuming that change is for the better, possibility c is more likely to take place without intervention or with incompetent intervention. The other three possibilities can take place if or when the therapist stresses them explicitly and systematically, without expecting them to be related to each other.

It is important for family therapists, therefore, to become aware that techniques directed toward expansion of awareness are not enough and that it is just as important to emphasize responsible and practical exercises *outside* the therapist's office (as suggested in the appendices). In fact, all three major aspects of family functioning—E, R, and A—need to be stressed equally (i.e., if an individual, couple, or family emphasizes thinking and reasoning at the expense of action, the therapist may stress action and/or feelings).

Research Implications

We will need to discover whether there are studies that link awareness, however defined, with psychotherapy; if such studies are not available, we need a study that can test the present formulation. Another relationship that will need development is the linking of awareness to emotions and to emotionality. What is the relationship, if any, between these two areas? Thus far, awareness has been considered a part of cognition. Is awareness indeed the link between feelings and cognition? Two specific areas to which awareness can apply are the notions of (a) "feedback" in communication-information theory and (b) "knowledge of results."

In their chapter on the evaluation of therapeutic outcomes, Bergin and Lambert (1978) concluded with a variety of recommendations for measurements that can assess psychotherapy outcomes. Their second conclusion is particularly relevant here: *Changes in both behavior and internal states are important* (p. 173).

> Changes in overt behavior, when targeted as criteria, are currently very popular and, because they are more easily assessed, they are more inexpensive than phenomenological changes, though not necessarily more important. The problem of measuring experiential phenomena with adequacy and precision remains a crucial test for future research in criterion development. (p. 173)

They recommended a variety of measures. They did not, however, specify the nature or characteristics of the phenomenological changes derived.

Another avenue of research is suggested by the work of Weissman (1979) and her associates. This typology distinguishes between descriptive and reflective communications. The former deal with explanatory (affective, ventilative, and anecdotal) statements. The latter include statements that indicate awareness of one's behavior, modification of thinking, or consideration of alternative explanations and/or courses of action. The ratio of descriptive versus reflective statements, according to Weissman, seems to be related to the course of therapy. The more reflective the communication, the more positive the psychotherapeutic outcome.

Perhaps one of the most promising approaches to awareness (one that has direct links and relations to the present proposal) can be found in the work of Selman, Jaquette, and Lavin (1977), representing an encompassing definition and specification of different levels of awareness related to interpersonal consequences, on a level unsurpassed in conceptualizations of awareness. Unfortunately, for this approach, the operationalization of awareness is loosely based on a few focused questions and a great deal of subjectivity on a rater's or an interviewer's part. If there were ways and means to start measuring the processes considered in such a viewpoint, however, one would have a decided advantage in measuring changes in awareness as a result of traditional psychotherapeutic intervention.

A significant possibility in the measurement of awareness in depth, width, and specificity would lie in linking it to ego development as defined by Loevinger (1976). Developmentally, she identified, through a sentence-completion test, various stages and levels of what she called "ego development." Yet, this ego development refers to how one conceptualizes the self in relationship to others. In addition, she linked her stages of ego development to

Rogers' (1961) stages of process in psychotherapy. In either formulation, the construct being assessed is not behavior, or thinking, or feelings, but how and how much each individual is aware of the self. Of course, such a link is offered tentatively; yet, it would not be untenable to say that one could validly claim awareness, instead of ego development, as a synonymous construct.

Guerney (1977) and his associates have developed a self-feeling awareness scale (SFAS), which allows one to quantify the degree and type of feeling awareness a speaker may have (pp. 371–377), and an awareness questionnaire, which allows one to assess changes in awareness in two areas: awareness of another's feelings and awareness of another's ideas.

Awareness, unfortunately, cannot be packaged in a neat box or sorted into a convenient classification. Somehow, awareness seems to defeat any attempt at definition that lends itself to clear operational definitions.

Awareness Training: Change or Growth?

We need to distinguish very clearly between these two concepts because therapists of various theoretical persuasions use both. Generally, humanistic therapists, such as Perls or, for that matter, Satir, strive for growth as a linear, step-by-step process. The same view may be found in psychodynamic therapists. Change, on the other hand, seems to be a more nonlinear, discontinuous, and probably circular process. One can change without changes in awareness, and changes in awareness do not necessarily lead to external changes. Hence, awareness may be neither sufficient nor necessary as an ingredient of change: change in behavior can take place without changes in awareness.

The concept of awareness may be relevant to individual growth. Nevertheless, one must ask: How relevant is this concept to marriage and family therapy? Do changes in awareness indeed produce changes in behavior? On the basis of our clinical experience, the answer to this question must be a strong, clear, and emphatic NO! I agree with Haley (1976) in questioning the value of this construct for changes in marriage and the family. In fact, the evidence presented by the MacMaster group (Woodward et al., 1978) suggests an almost reverse relationship between change and awareness. The least aware (in some cases, hostile) families were those who evidenced the most change, as assessed by their children's behavior in school. Thus, at least as far as marriage and family therapy is concerned, increased awareness is not necessarily related to change.

A Tentative Model for Research on Awareness

Most of the preceding thoughts and observations could be summarized into a tentative model (see Figure 11–1) that attempts to consider as many as possible of the relevant aspects of awareness. The three major aspects of this

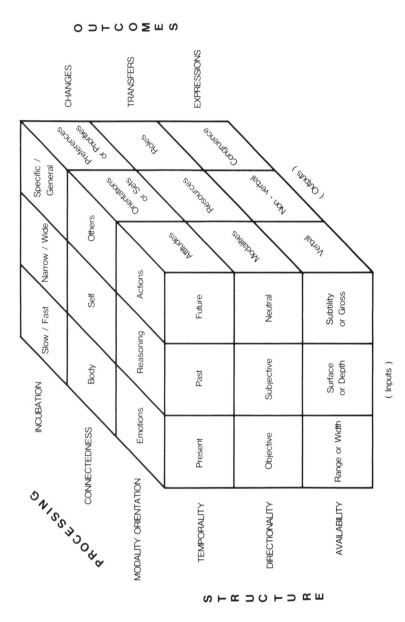

Figure 11–1. A model for research on awareness.

model are (a) structure, (b) meaning, and (c) outcome, following essentially an information-processing enumeration of three sequential stages (i.e., input, processing, and output). One important note concerning outcome, or output, as it relates to awareness is that *there may not be an output*! Awareness may change. If, however, we assume a nonlinear relationship between awareness and actions, it is almost impossible to postulate a direct link between changes in awareness and changes in behavior. A change in awareness that takes place today may not manifest itself in action until two years from now, maybe never. The process of incubation and translation into action, if any, is thus an arduous and tortuous one.

The tentativeness and limitations of this model should be stressed, despite its seeming grandiosity. If nothing else, it should serve as a basis for debate and controversy, the only means through which we shall be able to clarify what awareness is all about. Our ideas will not change unless we submit them to public scrutiny and debate. A critical evaluation of this model will allow a further refinement that may bring about more precise definitions and specifications.

Conclusion

The last word on awareness has not been said. Its sporadic appearance in the psychological literature cries out for systematic reformulation, refinement, and measurement. What is the relationship between awareness and intimate behavior? Which kind of awareness leads to behavior change and which kind does not? These and many other questions stress the need for a major research program in this area.

CONTEXT *(C)*

What is context? Most psychologists talk about "situation" or "environment"; the most advanced of them talk about person-situation interaction! Context can be physical and can be human. Without devaluing the role of the physical surroundings and their influence on human relationships, this term will be used here specifically to denote the human surroundings that impinge on and influence us the most. Those surroundings are the family! When we use the term *family*, we mean the direct stream, web, and fabric of intimate relationships that are formed by blood or by decree—people who live or have lived together under one roof for prolonged periods (years) of time.

Schaefer (1976), in his testimony to the U.S. Senate and House of Representatives, emphasized research on the networks of family relationships among father, mother, child and sibling strengthening and supporting family care through parent-centered programs. A broader scope of research suggested by a social ecological analysis of influences on child development and a focus upon the professions and institutions as well as upon families and children would contribute substantially to future intervention and to more effective child care, child health, and education professions and institutions. (p. 1528)

Broffenbrenner (1976), in the same joint hearings, reviewed most of the parent-intervention programs, finding them as a whole "disappointing" but emphasizing the need for family support systems.

Lewis, Beavers, Gossett, and Phillips' (1976) study validated two major constructs about the family that are relevant to the process of therapy: (1) the primary importance of communication variables in conceptualizing and assessing family functioning; and (2) the cardinal role of the parental coalition in establishing the level of functioning of the total family. There is, then, a need to focus on the level of intimacy established by the parents and to consider it the ultimate goal of family therapy, in which most families must face (a) congruence, (b) self-regard, and (c) intimacy.

ELABORATION OF THE $E-R-A-Aw-C$ MODEL

Probably the most promising approach to understanding the nature of emotions is the "shotgun" model—attempting to account for as much as possible across different organismic modalities rather than focusing on one or two key facets. Rather than identifying specific neural pathways or particular behavioral expressions, or looking for physiological states associated with particular cognitive activity, a broader and more molar view of emotions seems warranted. To a large extent, Izard (1977, 1978) seems to have attempted this approach.

In one way or another, he focused on a tripartite model, roughly separating emotions, cognitions, and behaviors. Izard has been clearer and more forceful about this issue than have other emotion theorists, maintaining that it is the interaction of the emotion, cognition, and motor subsystems, as separate and independent subsystems, which guarantees our basic freedoms as human beings. He also maintained that, as a separate subsystem, emotions may represent an organizing component, or resource, for thought and action. He borrowed this idea from Leeper (1970), arguing that "if an emotion mobilizes energy, has an organizing effect on behavior, and motivates thought and action, it seems reasonable that the emotions are important human resources"

(p. 108). He further stated that we must capitalize on the adaptive functions of emotions, allowing them to influence thought and action immediately, to modulate them when necessary, but, we must remain able, when feasible, to think and act congruently with them.

Data from research on attitudes also seem to corroborate a tripartite view of behavior. Baggozzi (1978) used an analysis of covariance and found that a tripartite division of attitudes into affective, behavioral, and cognitive components was theoretically valid. Jaccard and Crawford (1983) also presented evidence to suggest that attitudes can be conceptualized as comprising three aspects: affects, beliefs, and intentional behavior.

Woolfolk (1976) also stated that "no one conceptualization can satisfactorily account for all human emotion" (p. 58). In fact, he argued from the "multimodal" position of Lazarus (1976) that emotions are but one of five intrapersonal psychological modalities comprising behaviors, affect (emotion), sensation, imagery, and cognition. Woolfolk cited several studies that uphold his contention. Lang (1971) presented data to suggest that behaviors, emotions, and sensations each represent separate dimensions of our response systems: the behavioral, the phenomenological, and the physiological systems. He studied the effects of desensitization of phobias and found that each of these systems was manipulated in lessening phobic reactions. He further found very little correlation across these systems when they were used to assess treatment, indicating that they are independent of one another. Woolfolk also pointed out two studies that he claimed demonstrate a dichotomy in consciousness between verbal cognitions and visual-spatial cognitions (imagery). Woolfolk stated that the modalities of "cognition and imagery directly correspond to the verbal-processing mode (left-side) and visual-spatial processing mode (right-side), respectively" (p. 61).

Hutchins (1982) applied his thinking-feelings-actions model to a taxonomy of behavior types based on a ranking of these three aspects, obtaining 15 different permutations and combinations from these three basic aspects. Hershenson (1982) used both Hutchins (1979) and L'Abate (1981a) to integrate both Maslow's and Erikson's hierarchies into a six-step developmental scheme consisting of (a) survival, (b) growth, (c) communication, (d) recognition, (e) mastery, and (f) understanding.

In summary, arguments from emotion, attitude, and clinical perspectives suggest a multifocused approach to intrapersonal psychological functioning. These perspectives point to a tripartite division of functioning at a minimum, with some evidence suggesting that a division into finer parts may be warranted. All these perspectives suggest that, to understand emotions, one must approach them as a separate and independent response system, coequal in functioning with R, A, and Aw. Furthermore, to begin to understand behavior, we must learn how each of these parts interacts with the others.

Clearly, E-R-A can be broken down further. In addition to the analysis of the preceding chapter (Chapter 10, Figures 10–2, 10–3, 10–4), it is possible to elaborate on how each of these components is broken down, as shown in Figure 11–2.

There is very little that can be added to the analysis shown in the figure, except to note that without feedback function and contextual factors, there would be little meaning in this circular elaboration.

FUNCTIONAL AND DYSFUNCTIONAL ASPECTS OF E-R-A-Aw-C

Figure 11–3 attempts to show how the E-R-A-Aw-C model can be applied to a visual representation of functionality and dysfunctionality in individual, marital, and familial systems. One needs to keep in mind that in addition to the *content* of this model, one needs to consider the following characteristics: (a) size of the component part; that is, if E is enlarged, another component—R, A, or Aw—may shrink; (b) amount of overlap among components may vary from almost none, as in A., to a great deal, as in C.; and (c) permeability of boundaries defining each component may be rigidly impermeable, as in A., to extremely permeable and ill defined, as in C. B., then, describes the functional system, with balanced boundaries, satisfactory overlap among parts, and sufficient separation among parts to ensure proper balance.

As discussed in detail elsewhere (L'Abate, Frey, & Wagner, 1982), this model can be used diagnostically as well as therapeutically. Ideally, the sequence given by the model describes how information should flow from E to R to A to Aw, C being omnipresent. Most systems, however, do not always function ideally in the processing of information. In dysfunctionality, often, E is either greatly enlarged at the expense of the other components or is belittled, the other parts becoming enlarged. Another possibility is that the sequence may change: Instead of E's appearing at the beginning, immediate acting out may take place, coupled with a great deal of emotionality. Thus, the ideal sequence is changed to A-E-$R(Aw$-$C)$. The letters in parentheses indicate that other component factors (i.e., Aw and C) may not even be considered or be part of the sequence.

By the same token, in an extremely intellectualizing system, R may be the incoming part and E may be relegated to a later position, i.e., R-A-$E(Aw$-$C)$. Thus, the model can be used to describe traditional nosologies. For instance, an obsessive-compulsive system could be described by an R-Aw-C-A-E sequence. A hysterical system may be described by an E-A-$R(Aw$-$C)$ sequence, etc. Hence, the first function of this model is strictly diagnostic. It is important to evaluate how each system uses or fails to use these components.

Therapeutically, the system allows one to see how one can interweave the five components. Supposedly, one could start with C, but by changing it

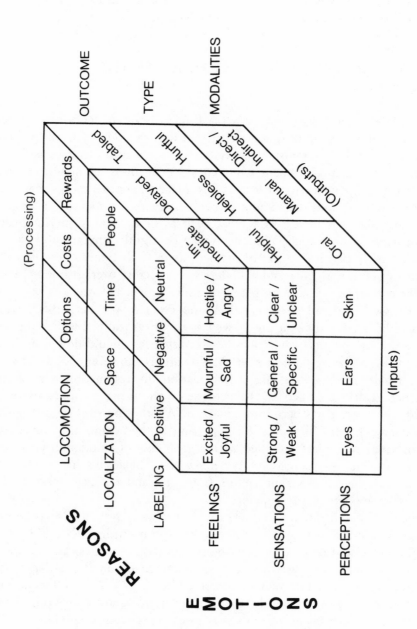

Figure 11-2. Elaboration of the *E-R-Au-C* model.

A. Rigid Boundaries

1. Denial of context

2. Minimum Overlap Among Parts

3. Maximum Separation of Parts

B. Balanced Boundaries

1. Awareness of context

2. Adequate Differentiation of Parts

3. Appropriate Separation of Parts

C. Permeable Boundaries

1. Overintrusion of context

2. Maximum Overlap Among Parts

3. Minimum Separation of Parts

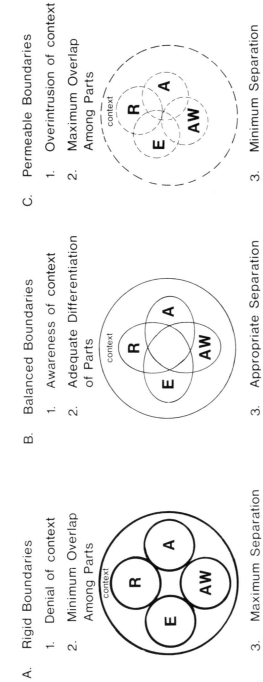

Figure 11–3. Functional and dysfunctional aspects of the *E-R-Au-C* model.

through positive reframing, one could then assign tasks that deal with A and Aw at the outset of therapy. Toward the intermediate and final stages of therapy, one will need to deal with E and, ultimately, with intimacy among the members of the family system. This sequence will be elaborated further in the next sections of this chapter.

A CLASSIFICATION OF THERAPEUTIC THEORIES

This classification, using the model, can be found in Table 11–1. The contents of the table are basically self-explanatory.

Very briefly, I shall elaborate on how this classification applies to present-day family therapy theorists, some of whom are listed in the table. For a more detailed explanation of these lists, the reader may refer to Hansen and L'Abate (1982).

Humanism in Family Therapy

Kempler (1981), along with Bockus (1980) and Whitaker (Neill & Kniskern, 1982), can best illustrate the experiential approach, which, with the phenomenological (Rogers) and existential approaches, would make up the humanistic movement (Hansen & L'Abate, 1982). Kempler emphasized this approach as "ahistorical" (p. 8) and focused mainly, but not exclusively, on "the immediate, the present," an approach characterized by "exploration, experiment and spontaneity." The what and how of behavior in its "beingness" is more important than the why, since verbal understanding without accompanying somatic and bodily correlates is seen not only as futile, but as an obstacle to growth. Action is seen as necessary to expand awareness and ultimately to obtain cathartic release and, supposedly, relief. The encounter between the individual and the therapist is seen as the major vehicle of growth (rather than change): (a) "I-ness" or clear expression of where one is at any given time; (b) a sensitive appraisal of others and of the context surrounding one ("I") and others; (c) the therapist's admittedly manipulative skills to get what s/he wants from the encounter; and (d) the ability to finish and complete an encounter successfully—without unfinished business.

Theory per se is downgraded because of its potential for restrictive and constrictive outcomes (p. 45). The individual's subjective experience is more important than any theoretical assumptions. Theory, like contrived techniques, can be a means of increasing distance between the therapist and the family. Mental health is judged by (a) whether each person "can clearly state who he is and what he wants from our encounter" (p. 176); and (b) the individual's ability to remain in the here and now, especially in dealing with painful issues. The same position has been taken by Whitaker, who sees theory as indoctrination and, as such, unduly constrictive and "constipating." He

Table 11–1

FIVE MAJOR THEORETICAL FORCES FROM AN *E-R-A-Au-C* VIEWPOINT
(Adapted from Korchin, 1976, and Lazarus & Monat, 1979)

Characteristics	Emotionality (Input) Humanism	Rationality (Throughput) Psychoanalysis	Activity (Output) Behaviorism	Awareness (Feedback) Various Trends	Context Family Therapies
Basic human nature	Man has free will, choice, and purpose; he has the capacity for self-determination and self-actualization.	Biological instincts, primarily sexual and aggressive, press for immediate release, bringing man into conflict with social reality.	Like other animals, man is born only with the capacity for learning, which develops in terms of the same basic principles in all species.	Same characteristics as found in emotionality. However, the stress here is on how and how much each individual is aware of the self and others. Supposedly, awareness is directly related to how an individual behaves.	Individual behavior is part of a system, and it is this system, the family, that is mainly responsible for how each individual learns to respond, constructively or destructively.
Normal human development	A unique self-system develops from birth on. The individual develops his personally characteristic modes of perceiving, feeling, etc.	Growth occurs through resolution of conflicts during successive developmental crises and psychosexual stages. Through identification and internalization, more mature ego controls and character structures emerge.	Adaptive behaviors are learned through reinforcement and imitation.	Reflection, meditation, correction.	Normality is not a useful term in a system. Functionality, how a system works or fails to work, is more important than any notion of normality.
Personality determinants	The person transcends instinctual and environmental forces. Emphasis is on biologically rooted forces such as self-actualizing tendency and inherited "potentialities" rather than on tissue drives or deficits, but emergent self-concept is	Behavior is lawful and completely determined. Biological forces (e.g., sexual and aggressive instincts and an inherited, predetermined, developmental sequence) are heavily emphasized, though social forces also are important in shaping	Behavior is lawful and completely determined. Environmental/social forces are the prime shapers of personality. Biological drives (e.g., hunger, thirst, sex) are downplayed: their importance, according to some who adopt this ap-	Awareness and consciousness are the major determinants of behavior. Although consciousness may vary from individual to individual, it does grow, with age, depending on the kind of experiences the individual is subjected to.	The family system determines how each individual develops in his/her own unique way. Yet each individual, no matter how unique, possesses characteristics that have been learned in the family system in which s/he grew up.

(cont'd)

201

Table 11-1 (continued)

Characteristics	Emotionality (Input) Humanism	Rationality (Throughput) Psychoanalysis	Activity (Output) Behaviorism	Awareness (Feedback) Various Trends	Context Family Therapies
Personality determinants (cont'd)	shaped mainly by social forces.	personality. Contemporary versions of this approach acknowledge a greater balance in the interplay of both biological and social determinants.	proach, is that biological drive satisfaction, when associated with social stimuli, establishes influential social motives.		
Personality description (structure)	The major structure of personality is the self, which consists of the individual's private images of what s/he is and would like to be.	Id, ego, and superego compose the structures of personality, along with various levels of the psyche (conscious, preconscious, and unconscious).	Personality structure consists of a collection of habitual responses or learned behavior patterns. Emphasis is on respondent and operant behaviors, though recent approaches also stress "person variables," such as cognitive styles and strategies.	The most important aspect of personality is how insightful, aware, conscious, alert one is to both internal and external cues.	The characteristics of the family system, mainly structural (rather than historical), will be shared in different ways by the individuals making up that system.
Personality dynamics (process)	"Force-for-growth" and tension production are psychological processes of most importance, along with congruency between the self and experience. When incongruency exists, threat and anxiety result and lead to defensive reactions. A search for meaning and purpose also motivates much human behavior.	Tension-reduction ("pleasure principle") and the interplay between the expression and the inhibition of the life and death instincts constitute the main processes of personality.	Environment/behavior relationships are emphasized, along with "principles of learning" related to respondent and operant conditioning and modeling. Tension reduction is a major motivational concept for some behavioral theorists but largely irrelevant for others.	Inner growth, i.e., development of self-other awareness, is to be strived for through a variety of means not usually given by our culture (i.e., meditation, fantasy trips, etc.)	Personality development is a constant differentiation of the self from the family system, starting with undifferentiated and becoming progressively more differentiated.

202

Table 11-1 (continued)

Characteristics	Emotionality (Input) Humanism	Rationality (Throughput) Psychoanalysis	Activity (Output) Behaviorism	Awareness (Feedback) Various Trends	Context Family Therapies
Personality development	The growth of a unique self-system, which influences characteristic ways of acting, thinking, and perceiving, is emphasized. Interactions between the person, with his or her need for positive regard, and significant others, who may freely or conditionally give positive regard, greatly affect the emergent self-system.	Growth is exhibited as a biological unfolding of stages or developmental landmarks and crises. Successful resolution of these developmental landmarks leads to a more mature ego, while unsuccessful resolution may lead to character traits, or to inadequate personality functioning.	There is no guiding concept of inherited and unfolding developmental stages or crises. Growth is a function of reinforcement and imitation. Schedules of reinforcement, stimulus generalization and discrimination, shaping, and social learning are key concepts that affect the production of habits and therefore create personality.	Growth in insight and awareness is always qualitative, chancy, and uneven. Development is characterized by impasses, plateaus, and sudden spurts of revelations, insights, and surprises. Development is both inward and outward, but predominantly inward.	The individual is differentiated and integrated at the same level as the system s/he is part of. If the system is rigid and unbending, the individual may learn to become another part of that system or develop opposite tendencies (i.e., acting out, rebelliousness, etc.).
Time orientation	Focus on present phenomenal experience; the here-and-now.	Oriented to discovering and interpreting past conflicts and repressed feelings, to examine them in light of present situation.	Little or no concern with past history or ethnology. Present behavior is examined and treated.	Awareness of the present is paramount to past and future.	The present and the future are better indicators of how a system works than is the past. Present is what counts. It encapsulates the past.
Role of unconscious material	Though recognized by some, emphasis is on conscious experience.	Primary in classical psychoanalysis, less emphasized by neo-Freudians and ego psychologists. To all, of great conceptual importance.	No concern with unconscious processes or, indeed, with subjective experience even in conscious realm. Subjective experience shunned as unscientific.	The larger the breadth and the deeper the consciousness, the more one can get in contact with unconscious material.	Mostly irrelevant but not thrown out of hand if given. Its presence gives information on how the system works or fails to work.

203

Table 11-1 (continued)

Characteristics	Emotionality (Input) Humanism	Rationality (Throughput) Psychoanalysis	Activity (Output) Behaviorism	Awareness (Feedback) Various Trends	Context Family Therapies
Psychological realm emphasized	Perceptions, meanings, values. For some, sensory and motor processes.	Motives and feelings, fantasies and cognitions; minimum concern with motor behavior and action outside therapy.	Behavior and observable feelings and actions. Emphasis on extratherapeutic actions.	Internal cues, bodily cues, breathing, temperature, heart beat are important cues.	Organizations, coalitions, subsystems, alliances, nonverbal behavior, relationships among family members.
Role of insight	More emphasis on awareness, the "how" and "what" questions rather than the "why."	Central, though conceived not just as intellectual understanding but as it emerges in "corrective emotional experiences."	Irrelevant and/or unnecessary.	More important than external behavior.	Minimal if it does not bring about system changes. Oftentimes, interfering with "real" changes. Not to be taken at face value.
Psychopathology	Pathology reflects great incongruency between the self and experience, and a rigid, defensive support of a restrictive self-image. Anxiety threatens the person, and if defenses fail altogether, total personality disorganization ("psychosis") results. A sense of purposelessness or meaninglessness may also lead to pathology. Incongruency exists between the depreciated self and	Symptoms reflect underlying conflicts and defensive reactions to anxiety. Fixations and regression under stress result in inadequate (too weak or too strong) development of ego and superego. Pathology reflects inadequate conflict resolutions and fixations in earlier development, which leaves overly strong impulses and/or weak controls. Symptoms are partial adaptations or	Pathology is based on faulty learning. Symptoms are viewed as the problem to be treated, rather than as signs of pervasive underlying conflict or "disease."	Too divided or too undefined, unfocused, and widespread awareness may become so intense that no external behavior is possible or no adequate link between insight and appropriate behavior can be made.	Rigidity or chaotic relationships among family members. Enmeshment or indifference of family members. One member scapegoated and made into the identified patient for the purpose of keeping the system intact or unchanged.

Table 11-1 (continued)

Characteristics	Emotionality (Input) Humanism	Rationality (Throughput) Psychoanalysis	Activity (Output) Behaviorism	Awareness (Feedback) Various Trends	Context Family Therapies
	the potential, desired self. The person is overly dependent on others for gratification and self-esteem.	substitute gratifications, defensive responses to anxiety.			
Personality change (psychotherapy)	Change is highly probable, given the proper "atmosphere" of congruence, unconditional positive regard, and empathic understanding. Therapy emphasizes the "client's" perceptions of personal experiences, as well as his/her own innate tendencies and responsibility for healing and growth. Client is encouraged to discuss the here-and-now and to gain insight into his/her own functioning. Therapist facilitates growth (e.g., expanding awareness) by providing the proper atmosphere noted above and by reflecting and clarifying the client's feelings and meanings.	Adult personality change is difficult but possible with a highly trained and objective therapist. Resolution of unconscious conflict through insight is the prime goal, along with the strengthening of ego functions. Techniques such as free association and the therapist's analysis of patient's resistances, dreams, and transference help uncover the patient's past difficulties and illuminate their operation in the present.	Behavior is highly malleable and under the control of environmental contingencies, and hence is readily capable of alteration. Behavior modification techniques emphasize the present rather than the past and concentrate on overt behaviors, though cognitive and emotional (covert) variables are often manipulated and changed too. Highly specialized techniques rely on numerous procedures such as extinction, positive reinforcement, desensitization, cognitive restructuring, and modeling. Because goal of therapy is to teach patient to unlearn problem	Personality changes to the extent that the individual is aware of both internal and external conditions. The greater the insight, the better the chances of personality growth. Client is encouraged to describe in detail sensations, perceptions, fantasies, dreams, and daydreams because all of these are relevant to understanding of the self.	Change means that the system ceases behaving in destructive ways and learns to behave so that everybody in the system "wins" and nobody "loses." Old patterns of organization, coalitions, and alliances and splits are changed into a more intergenerational hierarchy with clearly defined boundaries for parents, children, in-laws, etc. Problem solving is effective and the family learns to work as a unit.

Table 11-1 (continued)

Characteristics	Emotionality (Input) Humanism	Rationality (Throughput) Psychoanalysis	Activity (Output) Behaviorism	Awareness (Feedback) Various Trends	Context Family Therapies
Personality change (psychotherapy) (cont'd)			behaviors and/or to learn more adaptable ones, insight into possible underlying and unconscious processes is irrelevant.		
Goal of therapy	Foster self-determination, authenticity, and integration by releasing human potential and expanding awareness.	Attainment of psychosexual maturity, strengthened ego functions, reduced control by unconscious and repressed impulses.	Relieve symptomatic behavior by suppressing or replacing maladaptive behaviors.	To make individuals aware of themselves and others.	To increase the functionality of a family in whatever ways the family finds functional for itself.
Role of therapist	An "authentic person" in true encounter with patient, sharing experience. Facilitates patient's growth potential. Transference discounted or minimized.	An "investigator," searching out root conflicts and resistances; detached, neutral, and nondirective, to facilitate transference reactions.	A "trainer," helping patient unlearn old behavior and/or learn new ones. Control of reinforcement is important; interpersonal relation is of minor concern.	The more "insightful" the therapist, the better. The therapist is a "master" of awareness and the model for the clients to emulate.	Extremely active, but the family loses because no changes have been produced if the therapist is inactive.
Necessary qualifications and skills	Personal integrity and empathy valued over professional training and formal knowledge.	Highly trained in theory and supervised practice; much technical and professional knowledge. Must have firm self-knowledge to avert dangers of countertransference.	Knowledge of learning principles primary; understanding of personality theory and psychopathology secondary; no concern with self-knowledge. Actual interventions can be done by nonprofessional assistant.	Personal analysis focused on self-awareness and awareness of others. Experiential training in yoga, transcendental meditation, fantasy and consciousness-raising exercises, art, diary keeping, dreams and daydreams.	Knowledge of family structures, functions, and dysfunctions. May or may not have received therapy for self and family of origin. Effective in helping families change without appearing to effect such changes.

Table 11-1 (continued)

Characteristics	Emotionality (Input) Humanism	Rationality (Throughput) Psychoanalysis	Activity (Output) Behaviorism	Awareness (Feedback) Various Trends	Context Family Therapies
Representative schools (from Hansen and L'Abate, 1982)	Phenomenology Existentialism Experientialism Logotherapy	Orthodox Adaptational Ego psychology Object relations Reality therapy Rational-emotive therapy			
Representative theorists in the family field (from Hansen and L'Abate, 1982)	T. Gordon B. G. Guerney, Jr. R. F. Levant C. Whitaker G. Napier V. Satir F. and B. Duhl L. Constantine W. Kempler	N. W. Ackerman M. Bowen I. Boszormenyi-Nagy J. Framo H. Stierlin	G. Patterson R. Stuart F. J. Thomas R. C. Weiss N. S. Jacobson R. Liberman	F. Perls* A. Watts R. Selman Eastern Philosophers	A. Adler S. Minuchin P. Watzlawick and the Palo Alto group J. Haley M. Selvini-Palazzoli C. Madanes J. Alexander

*Most of these therapists here are individually- rather than family-oriented.

sees "being" as the most difficult goal, one that "doing" usually detracts from.

Thus, in experiential therapy, primary importance is given to the therapist as an individual being, not as an expert, since theoretical and technical expertise only helps to distance the therapist from the family.

Humanism, therefore, represents an overall term for a variety of viewpoints whose commonality is found in their emphasis on the importance and value of subjective experience as the most relevant given of human existence. The key to this experience is being able to be in touch with one's feelings and emotions.

Rationality in Family Therapy

Within this rubric are various theories that emphasize logical sequences (versus the importance of irrationality in the humanistic tradition) based on linear, cognitive, progressive understanding through historical reconstruction, through the study of the family of origin, one's history, and the history of a relationship back to two generations (Boszormenyi-Nagy & Spark, 1973; Bowen, 1978; Framo, 1982). Here, the past is supreme in one's understanding of the present; the present as a manifestation of the past is meaningful only through a detailed reconstruction of past events and sequences. This school, of course, owes its own theoretical and technical roots to Freud and the psychoanalytic and psychodynamic schools. Here, the therapist is an expert who needs to know theory and the self, not as an affective chameleon, as in the case of Kempler and Whitaker, but as a knowledgeable, controlled, and insightful representative of theoretical givens that are translated into allegedly well-defined techniques. The therapist's style is studied and delayed, where, in the humanistic tradition, affective immediacy and open expression are valued as more important than intellectual knowledge.

Behaviorism in Family Therapy

The major contribution of this school to the field of family therapy is methodological, in the sense that this school has developed methods of observation and analysis that remain unparalleled in the other theoretical schools. In fact, one could say that research done in the field of family therapy is done by investigators of a behavioristic persuasion. What the field is now experiencing, however, is an integration of behavioral with structural and strategic approaches (Alexander & Parsons, 1982; Weiss, 1980).

DISCUSSION

The comparative testing of these various approaches has been going on for the past 20 years. There have been, however, few attempts to compare experiential and psychodynamic theories. A study by Beutler and Mitchell (1981) attempted to compare experiential and psychoanalytic therapeutic procedures with depressed-internalizing ($n = 24$) and impulsive-externalizing patients ($n = 16$), as defined by symptoms, history, and MMMPI scores. They were treated by either experiential or analytic therapists. The experiential therapists' approach was characterized by (a) the use of guided fantasy and imagery; (b) an emphasis on the here and now; (c) being more self-disclosing and personal; (d) having relatively greater verbal and physical activity; and (d) placing a relatively stronger emphasis on feelings, as opposed to insight. Analytic therapists, on the other hand, (a) used verbal interpretative rather than imagery techniques, (b) emphasized unconscious and childhood processes, (c) avoided self-disclosure, (d) were relatively nonverbal and inactive, and (e) discussed historical insights rather than current feelings. Two major effects were found on outcome: depressed-internalizing patients obtained more benefit from both treatments than did impulsive-externalizing patients, and experiential psychotherapy showed a clear superiority over analytic treatment. In addition to these two findings, a positive relationship was found between emphasis on current feelings and subsequent therapeutic outcome; a negative relationship was found between outcome and therapist's use of imagery and guided fantasy. According to the authors, these findings failed to support the hypothesis that experiential and psychoanalytic treatment might exert differentially powerful affects on the two types of patient groups treated in this study.

CLASSIFICATION OF THERAPEUTIC METHODS

The *E-R-A-Aw-C* model allows us to clarify most therapeutic methods, as shown in Table 11–2. A more detailed and specific elaboration of this table can be found in the original article by Ulrici, Wagner, and L'Abate (1981), more recently reprinted in a collection (L'Abate, 1983d).

CONCLUSION

This chapter has completed the two remaining parts of a circular model of family competence originally presented in Chapter 10. It elaborated on the model and applied it to classification of therapeutic theories and methods according to five different aspects of interpersonal competence: emotionality, rationality, activity, awareness, and context.

Table 11–2

CLASSIFICATION OF THERAPEUTIC METHODS ACCORDING TO THE *E-R-A-Aw-C* MODEL

(Adapted from Ulrici, Wagner, and L'Abate, 1981)

Emotionality	Rationality	Activity (Behavioral)	Awareness	Context
Methods focus on experiential exercises that differentiate feeling states of solitude and solidarity.	Methods focus on the conscious understanding that differentiate reality-based control.	Methods focus on the application of scientific principles to shape and control behavior.	Methods are oriented toward providing a greater degree of *reflection* on one's bodily sensations.	Methods focus on adjusting dimensions of cohesion and adaptability, which maintain family functioning.
Developing intrapersonal awareness through individual exercises of meditation, fantasy trips, imaginary dialogues, here-and-now awareness.	Teaching new concepts and theories through lectures, readings, and discussions.	Solving behavioral problems through experimental analysis —quantifying behavior, determining controls, implementing interventions, and evaluating.	Transcendental meditation, either (a) focused (on a mantra) or (b) unfocused; fantasy trips; body positions designed to increase body control and awareness (i.e., yoga); dreams and daydreams; metaphors and the metaphors of behavior.	Establishing appropriate boundaries for cohesion and autonomy through: (a) directives given in session, e.g., spatial rearrangements, reenactments of events, demanding specific interactions, blocking others, bringing members of the social network; (b) behavior assignments for daily context, e.g., rituals, paradoxical exercises, age-appropriate tasks, activities to support coalitions or limit enmeshment.
Developing awareness of interpersonal relationships through interactional tasks of role play, sculpting, etc.	Relating past influence to present functioning through cognitive re-creation of past events, e.g., psychoanalytic dialogues, genograms, rational reevaluations.	Teaching and increasing desired behavior and extinguishing inappropriate behavior through techniques: (a) respondent conditioning, e.g., stimulus pairing, desensitization; (b) operant conditioning, e.g., positive reinforcement, punishment.		
Focus on immediacy of feelings and spontaneity of emotional expression.	Developing insight to differentiate feelings from actions through analysis of one's present and past relationships, e.g., working through transference, understanding defense operations and ego controls.	Teaching desired behavior through social learning, e.g., modeling, films.		

Table 11-2 (continued)

Emotionality	Rationality	Activity (Behavioral)	Awareness	Context
Teaching skills of interpersonal sensitivity and communication through lectures, readings, demonstrations, and practical exercises.	Teaching skills of rational thinking and ego control through lectures, discussions, and practice at rational problem solving and decision making.	Increasing and maintaining behavior through evaluative feedback. Practicing application of learned behavior through role play and simulated exercises. Implementing desired behavior or its approximation through behavioral tasks performed in daily context. Teaching behavioral principles through lectures, models, and practice exercises with feedback or by programmed instruction.		Restructuring operations in response to situational stress and/or developmental change through: (a) assigning linear task to directly change operations, e.g., rescheduling, assigning family duties; (b) assigning paradoxical task that emphasizes operational problems, e.g., role reversals, behavioral extremes.

Chapter 12

Priorities in the Family

The issue of priorities in the family has been bypassed by the family therapy literature because individuals often have priorities, unspoken priorities, while family systems, even though they may have them, do not speak about them. Yet, this area is extremely important from the viewpoint of personality development in the family (L'Abate, 1976) because it deals essentially with the whole issue of motivation, energy investment, and expenditure. Furthermore, this area is theoretically crucial in connecting what one could consider individual functioning to overall family functioning. The contribution of individual priorities, developed, of course, from family-community interactions, to the well-being of the family will be considered in this chapter through three separate and distinct models: (1) a model of intrafamily priorities, (2) a model of interpersonal priorities (the *A-B-C* model), and (3) a model of resource exchange. These three models are summarized in Table 12–1, and their application to SHWAs can be found in Lesson 7 of the Negotiation Series in Appendix B.

PRIORITIES AND MOTIVATION

The field of motivation in monadic psychology is very broad, including vaguely defined concepts such as "drives," "needs," and "expectations." In reading this literature one becomes aware that a great deal, if not most, of the theorizing and research in this area is completely ignorant or unaware that most of our motivation, development, substinence, reinforcement, ups and downs, etc., are related to and derived from our families, in one way or another. The complete bypassing of the family as the matrix of personal motivation reduces traditional considerations of this subject to irrelevant platitudes and useless subject matter. As harsh as this judgment may appear, it does express the continuous dissatisfaction that results from a failure to find relevance in an area that is generally distant to the concerns of family therapy. Once the subject of motivation is recouched in terms of priorities, then a great deal of relevance is obtained because individuals in families usually recognize their importance to the overall family functioning.

INTRAFAMILIAL PRIORITIES

The original definition of this concept in its relationship to similar concepts in the family therapy literature can be found in the earlier formulation of the theory underlying all the models reviewed thus far (L'Abate, 1976). Briefly and operationally, a priority does not exist in and by itself. It receives meaning in comparison with and contrast to other priorities. For instance, the priority of personhood, the cornerstone of all other priorities, has meaning to the extent that being a person and defining oneself as a human being needs to be done within the context of other priorities, i.e., partnership, parenthood, etc. How do we choose to define ourselves in relation to ourselves and those we love and who love us? Priorities, therefore, represent choices we make in how we choose to spend our energies (defined in terms of how much time we spend cultivating that particular aspect of ourselves at the expense of or to the advantage of other priorities) (Nock & Kingston, 1984). We can choose one priority at the expense of other priorities, or we can cultivate one priority

Table 12–1
SUMMARY OF PRIORITY MODELS FOR FAMILIES
(See Lesson 7, Appendix B)

A. Familial and Intrafamilial Priorities
   1. Personhood
   2. Partnership
   3. Parenthood
   4. Relatives
   5. Work
   6. Friends
   7. Leisure
B. Interpersonal priorities (the *A-B-C* model)
   1. Attachments
   2. Beliefs and values
   3. Commitments
C. Resource exchange: The triangle of living
   1. Having
   2. Doing
   3. Being

to recognize, affirm, and enhance other priorities. If one's self-definition, for instance, is at the expense of the marital partnership, then in the long range the marital relationship would eventually suffer. Thus, the matter of priorities is a difficult balancing act that we need to deal with throughout the lifespan. How can we enhance ourselves and others at the same time?

Intrafamily priorities, in order of importance, are as follows: (a) personhood, (b) partnership, (c) parenthood, (d) relatives (parents, in-laws, and siblings, i.e., kinfolks), (e) work, (f) friends, and (g) leisure. Each of them will be considered in as much detail as possible.

Personhood

By personhood is meant a variety of concepts that in the literature are usually recognized as (a) selfhood, (b) personality, (c) identity, (d) self-concept, (e) self-esteem and self-actualization, and the like. In addition to similarity to all these concepts, by personhood is also meant (f) one's sense of personal competence and effectiveness as an individual, as well as one's self appraisals, self-definitions, and sense of personal worth. In a way, personhood represents how much we like and love ourselves (warts and all) and how important we think we are to ourselves and to those we love and who love us.

Personhood, therefore, represents all the many attributions we make to ourselves and how we choose to manifest and express them outwardly toward those we love and who love us. A great deal of this importance is communicated in our use of the personal pronoun "I" when we are able to express to others how we feel about important, emotional issues in the family, without making any unkind and judgmental conclusions about others (Tiedeman, 1978). In this regard we need to consider four different issues relating to personhood: (a) issues of selfhood versus selfishness, (b) issues of reciprocity, (c) issues of responsibility, and (d) issues of perfectionism.

Selfhood and Selfishness. Among the many conditionings we receive in growing up, one of the most pernicious refers to the confusion of selfhood with selfishness (Kreilkamp, 1976); that is, in asserting the importance of the self, self-affirmation is viewed as deleterious to the goals of the family and sometimes of society. It is important to distinguish one concept from the other by defining selfhood as any kind of self-affirmation that does not take place at the expense of intimate others; i.e., "I win, you win."

"Do Ut Des." Selfishness, by the same token, implies a different process; that is, self-affirmation and expression takes place at the expense of someone else, usually a loved one: "I win, you lose." For instance, a person's love of gambling would reduce the amount of money available to the rest of the family. A person's moonlighting may bring necessary income into the family but deprive the family of emotional presence and support. The whole issue of selfhood is also linked to the next set of issues.

Personhood and Reciprocity. Most dysfunctional families have completely let go (forgotten, ignored, left out, etc.) the importance of the Golden Rule, not only in interpersonal relationships, but especially on how family members will conduct themselves with each other. In fact, it is not infrequent to find families who do follow this rule *outside* the family but are unable to follow it *inside* the family. Indeed, this rule is so important that one could conclude that a great deal of dysfunctionality derives from our failure to follow it inside our families. Because of its importance a separate optional homework assignment (Appendix B) has been written to be administered to families who have forgotten its importance.

Personhood and Perfectionism. A great many dysfunctions in families derive from the practice of perfectionism (i.e., to be reframed as "high standards") requiring perfection of one's self and loved ones and making love conditional; that is, "I love myself and others to the extent that they perform to my standards." This topic will turn up again in the next chapter in relation to forgiveness. Suffice it to say that demands for perfectionism rob us of our humanness to the extent that a misguided equation is being used, and that is: to be perfect means to be "good." Consequently, to be imperfect means to be "bad." This is not only a dehumanizing dichotomously digital equation but is also a source of a great deal of unhappiness (Watzlawick, 1977). When has anybody found a happy perfectionist? The more functional human and analogical equation, of course, sees perfectionism as heavenly and not of this earth, while being imperfect means to be human! Our errors and imperfections confirm us as human beings rather than machines.

Personhood and Responsibility. Taking responsibility for oneself is a very difficult process that many of us abdicate in making others responsible for our behavior, as done mainly in the abusive and reactive relationships (Chapter 9). Assuming responsibility means speaking up for oneself in a way that will not degrade, denigrate, or dehumanize others. Again, taking responsibility for our feelings, thoughts, and actions implies a process of differentiation that most families do not provide. How can we take responsibility for ourselves if the importance of our feelings is denied, discounted, and often deleted from most of our interactions? We learn to deny our feelings and in so doing we fail to make them available for consideration in any family business, and most family businesses are emotional.

Partnership

We learn how to become therapists, engineers, physicians, etc., but no one teaches us to become partners in marriage. The only partnership we may have observed intensively and extensively was the one our parents had (and in the future less and less of us will have had that privilege!). No matter how good (effective, creative, positive, etc.) that partnership may have been, we cannot apply it wholesale to our marriage, assuming that we are marrying spouses who are different from our parents. Not only do we marry different individuals, but the cultural context has changed. The demands that were culturally sanctioned in the past have changed. We can no longer expect, for instance, a single-earner family, a lifetime marital commitment, or an inflexible division of labor.

Of course, how we choose to define ourselves has a great deal to do with whom we choose to marry (and vice versa). Hence, a great deal of how we work out our marital partnership depends on our personhood. How can a bridge exist without pillars? Relationships are based on persons, and persons are responsible for how they will behave inside their families. Consequently, to work with families without paying attention to the individuals involved means considering only one aspect of family functioning. It means looking at how a bridge works without looking at the pillars! Competent individuals will tend to marry similarly competent individuals with whom they will be able to negotiate a working partnership. Since, however, many of us are not that competent, we will marry similar others who, being unclear and incomplete about themselves, like most human beings are, will also be unable to be clear about what is involved in being and becoming a partner.

Parenthood

Becoming a parent implies having a partnership, in which our spouse supposedly (and ideally) would be our best friend, our lover, our companion, and our most loving critic. If and when this partnership is inadequate and not working, for whatever reasons, parenthood will be in some way impaired. This impairment in turn will affect how the children will be raised. If personhood is originally defective, the marital choice will in some way reflect the defect in how both partners will work out or fail to work out their relationship. The outcome, eventually, will be an impaired parental relationship. For instance, if the father chooses an occupational self-definition and considers work (success, money, achievement, etc.) as being more important than the family, he will be unable to negotiate a successful or even working marital partnership. The result may make the mother become more involved in issues of child raising without the necessary support and input of the husband. In this case priorities will be confused. The father will consider work as a substitute for self-definition whereas the wife will make children more important than the marriage or the self.

Furthermore, many of us fall prey to the misguided religious or romantic notion that the self needs to be given up for the sake of others! Again, how can bridges exist without pillars? The self then becomes the very cornerstone of our partnership and of parenthood. Once its importance is denied or belittled, the whole process becomes distorted, and eventually it will topple down! (L'Abate, 1976).

Relatives (Parents, In-Laws, and Siblings)

The influence of relatives on our emotional well-being cannot be denied. If we try to ignore them or belittle them, they, in one way or another, will make their presence felt. Their importance cannot be denied. With time most of us realize, sometimes too late, that we have only one set of parents and one set of siblings. They in one way or another will affect us as much as we affect them. They need to be recognized as one of the important priorities of our lives, responsible for a great deal of our happiness and unhappiness over the family life cycle.

Work

Work can fill and fulfill a great many inadequacies, most of them human. If we are ill defined personally and maritally, we may find satisfaction in our work, achieving, consequently, a modicum of self-respect we may be unable to achieve as individuals and as marriage partners. Work, therefore, may fill personal emptiness and social inadequacies, because we were taught how to work but no one taught us how to behave as human beings. Most of us learned the hard way! Our assumption of competence as human beings (however incorrect) is carried out in our marital and family responsibilities. We learn to be truck drivers and engineers, but no one teaches us to become partners and parents!

The definition of ourselves according to work roles and responsibilities, to cover up personal inadequacies, produces an imbalance once the marital partnership requires us to reciprocate to our spouses an involvement with house chores and responsibilities. Men especially have to shift from a work role, no matter how high and mighty on the corporate ladder, to attend to banal and mundane matters of taking care of children, changing their diapers, attending to roof leaks, cutting grass, etc. If our self-definition is in terms of our occupational role, how can we fulfill demands that contrast with that role?

When the self is filled with one's concept of work, other more primary self-definitions become secondary, including the self itself, defined in human terms rather than in occupational terms. After all, if I am a professor, how can this title be secondary to the title of human being, marital partner, and parent? Work, then, may become so primary to the self's survival that other primary roles are relegated to secondary status, producing a conflict of priorities between self, spouse, and children (L'Abate & L'Abate, 1979). No other avenue of survival, except one's work, seems available to the self. Under these conditions, then, work becomes so important that all other commitments become secondary.

Many of these conflicts have been studied in the literature (Bohen & Viveros-Long, 1981; Cramer, 1985; Geerken & Gove, 1983). Consequently, they will not be reviewed here. The presence of so many studies in this area, however, attests to the importance of work in conflict with other family priorities. Work is fifth!

Friends

Friends become our support group when relatives are not available. One single friend may make the difference between our survival and our demise. In fact, a pet sometimes may fill some of our loneliness and keep us alive! Friends are as important to our self-survival as our work. If and when we have no work, these friends may become even more important. Work may be necessary for our economical survival, but spouses, chidren, relatives, and friends are vital for our emotional survival. Which of these is more important? We can change jobs relatively easily, if we are skilled and feel competent. However, how many wives or children do we want or can we replace like disposable goods? Furthermore, considering that most of us cannot have more than a handful of friends over a lifetime, we need to cultivate them as well as our relatives, because they may become just as important (Derlega, Wilson, & Chalkin, 1976; Kandel, 1978; Weiss & Lowenthal, 1975).

Leisure

All of the foregoing priorities bear on our use of our leisure time. Shall we use that time with extra work? Should we use it to enjoy our spouses and children? Should we go on vacation to the seashore or visit our relatives? Should I spend the evenings watching TV guzzling beer or should I go downstairs in the workshop to be by myself? These are continuous choices we all make every day and every living hour. How do we want to spend our time, with whom and how (Young & Willmott, 1975)?

Priorities Over the Family Life Cycle

Of course, priorities *do* change over the family life-span. The issue here is whether priorities were functional to begin with and whether they were corrected over time. Certainly flexibility needs to be exercised so that sometimes we do go to the seashore but sometimes we do go to see relatives. Of course, work is important and sometimes we may need to work extra time to finish a project. The issue here is one of basic commitment. A wife will not mind the husband working extra time occasionally, provided she is convinced of his basic commitment to her and to the children, and that he will devote extra time to them to make up for time given away somewhere else.

INTERPERSONAL PRIORITIES

In addition to familial and intrafamilial priorities, there are at least three other sets of priorities that influence most of us and influence how we behave both inside and outside our families. These priorities include our (a) attachments, (b) beliefs and values, and (c) commitments. Each of these topics has a long history in developmental and social psychology. Unfortunately, as noted earlier in this chapter, most of these topics have been considered acontextually, that is, as if they developed in a vacuum, outside the sphere of influence of the family. We need to review them from the viewpoint of the family, making them part of what motivates us to want to negotiate or not negotiate family issues.

Attachments

This area has been the subject of extensive theorizing and research (Ainsworth, 1979; Bowlby, 1982; Henderson, 1977; Parkes & Stevenson-Hinde, 1982; Waters, Wippman, and Sroufe, 1979). In reviewing this concept within the context of dependence, L'Abate (1985) proposes a model of attachments and dependencies that views victories and defeats in the family as distance regulators, making early attachments the matrix for subsequent functioning or dysfunctioning.

Beliefs and Values

Again to review the whole field of research and theories in this area would take one far afield from the major focus of priorities. Suffice it to say that in dealing with families, the therapist needs to become aware of the family's as well as the individuals' beliefs and values in regard to themselves, each other, religion, politics, work, etc. A therapist needs to know how each member of the family perceives reality, as defined by most of the priorities reviewed thus far.

Commitments

What is each individual committed to? Is there any commitment to self and others? Is the individual committed to self-destruction or self-enhancement? Does the individual say one thing and then do another? How congruent are individual members in their beliefs and values? Beliefs and values refer to what they think, but their commitments may speak louder than words. A son may claim to be dedicated to the welfare of the family, but he may smoke pot on the side. What is his *real* commitment? He may say one thing but he may do another. Thus commitments are not only what individuals claim they do, but what they *actually* do. Unfortunately, the literature on commitment is rather sparse (Johnson, 1973). Hence, a great deal of what family members write in their SHWAs should also serve as the basis for discussion and learning about the importance of commitments in family life.

RESOURCE EXCHANGE: THE TRIANGLE OF LIFE

In addition to intrafamily and interpersonal priorities, there is an additional set of resources that need to be exchanged in the family. These resources, adapted from the Foa and Foa (1974) resource exchange theory, consist of love, status, services, information, money, and goods. L'Abate, Sloan, Wagner, and Malone (1980) compressed these six classes of resources into three major resources: being, which includes love and status; doing, which includes services and information; and having, which includes goods and money. This model is shown in Figure 12–1. Questions that follow from the model are shown in Table 12–2.

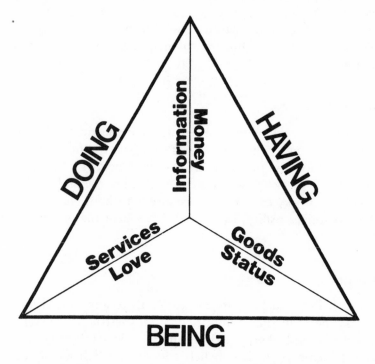

Figure 12-1. The triangle of living (adapted from Foá and Foá, 1974).

Doing

Major family conflicts focus on all these resources, and power rests with whoever controls access to these resources. Who controls incoming and outgoing information? How is the information received in the family processed and imparted among family members? What services (chores, jobs, responsibilities, etc.) are rendered by which member of the family? Since the doing—who does what, when, and how—is a major source of conflict among family members, it needs to be negotiated; that is, everyone should have some responsibilities relevant to age and ability, and no one should be exempt from sharing these responsibilities unless handicapped or incapacitated. How is this sharing accomplished in the family? Effectively? Autocratically? Democratically? Randomly?

Having

What goods should be bought? How much money is there in the family and how is it allocated? Will the parents share the same bank account or have two separate ones? Will the children receive allowances free from any strings or is money used coercively—to reward or to punish? Who decides which goods are bought and how much they should cost? Are bills paid on time? How does the family negotiate decisions over goods and money?

Regardless of the conflicts families may have over doing and having, these are pseudoconflicts to the extent that any conflict in the area of doing and having suggests an inability to come to terms with and deal with issues of being. In fact, one would assert that most issues of dysfunctionality in families stem from families being unable to love and to give status to themselves and to each other unconditionally.

Being

This resource is probably the most difficult, often impossible, resource to exchange. How is love expressed in the family? Verbally? Nonverbally? Through services? Through money or goods? Is love a commodity for bribe and blackmail? Is self-acceptance and acceptance of other family members an easy or difficult process? Status means affirmation of importance of self and others, as discussed earlier under the rubric of selfhood. Most of the families we see in therapy have jobs and job-related competences. They also have sufficient goods in terms of house, car(s), clothes, etc. They have also mastered doing by acquiring an education and providing some kind of service through work.

Ultimately, therefore, most conflicts over doing and having are distractions from the family's inability to deal with issues of being. How to be, how to love oneself and others without demands for perfection or for performance, is one of the crucial issues of living. No amount of work and no amount of money can make up for deficits in being. This topic will receive further attention in the next chapter, dealing with intimacy, because issues of being involve issues of closeness-distance also.

How does one negotiate being? Goods, money, services, and information can and need to be negotiated, but how can being be negotiated? Can one negotiate love and status? The answer to this question, of course, is negative because being cannot be negotiated. It needs to be shared, and the process of sharing being requires a certain degree of style, skill, and motivation that most clinical families do not possess. It takes a great deal of functionality to share being because it requires a level of development that is not present at

Table 12–2

THE TRIANGLE OF LIVING: QUESTIONS THAT FOLLOW FROM THE MODEL

A. Having
    1. What does money mean to (you, marriage, or family)?
    2. What kinds of conflicts are there about money?
    3. What do goods, possessions, and material things mean to (you, marriage, or family)?
    4. What kinds of conflicts are there about goods (gifts, things, or purchases)?

B. Doing
    1. Who performs what chores (or services) in this (marriage, family)?
    2. How does this arrangement work for this (marriage, family)?
    3. What kinds of information is allowed in this (marriage, family)?
        a. TV programs and movies (what kind? for how long?)
        b. Newspapers and/or magazines
        c. Books (who reads what?)
        d. Relatives (get-togethers, frequency of meetings, feelings surrounding visits, etc.)
        e. Friends and/or neighbors
        f. Others (visitors, drop-ins, entertainment, etc.)
    4. Which of these are more important? To whom? How? Why?

C. Being
    1. What does love mean to this (marriage, family)?
    2. How is love shown or demonstrated?
    3. Is love used as a commodity to bribe/blackmail family members?
    4. How important are each of you to yourself and to others in the family?
    5. How is this importance shown or expressed inside the family?
    6. How is this importance shown or expressed outside the family?
    7. How do you fail to show your individual importance?

D. Balance of having-doing-being
    1. Which of these (having, doing, or being) is more important to you?
    2. Why? (i.e., what does it get you?)
    3. Are you satisfied with the way you rank these resources?
    4. If you are, why?
    5. If you are not (satisfied), why not?
    6. How could each of you do better?

If necessary, these questions could be written up into a SHWA format and assigned as an additional homework assignment (see Lesson 7, Appendix B).

the beginning of therapy. In fact, this sharing requires that in the process of therapy a third stage needs to be reached, the stage of intimacy.

CONCLUSION

Priorities are an important, albeit unspoken, motivational component of family functioning and dysfunctioning. While these priorities need to be brought into the open and discussed, their negotiation needs to take place *both* at home and in the therapist's office. They are an important, mostly implicit aspect of family life that ultimately depends on whether the family wants to negotiate or not. The family's inability to negotiate concrete issues of doing and having bespeaks its inability to come to terms with issues of being and of intimacy, a topic that will be considered in the next chapter.

The Third Stage: Issues of Intimacy

Chapter 13

Intimacy: The Sharing of Hurts

When joys are shared they are doubled. When troubles are shared, they are halved. (Old German proverb)

The purpose of this chapter is to stress the importance of intimacy in family relationships and to suggest ways and means of helping families achieve greater intimacy. Most of the literature on intimacy (Sloan & L'Abate, 1985) has avoided dealing with its applications, and most of the literature on family therapy (Levant, 1984; Nichols, 1984) has avoided dealing with this topic altogether.

THE IMPORTANCE OF INTIMACY IN FAMILY RELATIONSHIPS

Intimacy is not only important to family relationships, it is the necessary, albeit not sufficient, ingredient for human survival. Intimacy is the basic interpersonal variable necessary for the maintenance and prolongation of close relationships, both inside and outside the family, as in friendships. Its presence increases the chances (but does not guarantee them) that greater lasting relationships will also be present (Waring, 1980a). Its absence implies that most forms of psychopathology derive from our inability or unwillingness to share our hurts with those we love and who love us. In fact, Jessee and L'Abate (1985) have argued that intimacy is the very antidote for depression in marriage and the family.

Intimacy has received a great deal of interest recently in terms of what could be called multifactorial theories; that is, intimacy is defined according to a variety of factors, such as physical, intellectual, and emotional intimacy (Sloan and L'Abate, 1985). In the present context, intimacy is defined according to one factor and one factor alone; that is, *intimacy is the sharing of our hurts and of our fears of being hurt.* This definition, then, impinges on the meaning of hurt. What is meant by hurt? By hurt is meant our vulnerabilities and neediness, that is, our fallibilities, foibles, failures, frustrations, and frailties. From this definition, which will be expanded later in this chapter, derive three paradoxes that will explain, at least in part, why intimacy is so difficult to achieve: (a) we need to be separate as individuals to be together with intimate others; (b) we only hurt the ones we love; since hurt and love are intertwined, love means giving the ones we love and who love us the power to hurt; and (3) we need to seek comfort and nurturance from the very ones we have hurt and who have hurt us (Sloan & L'Abate, 1985; L'Abate, 1983a; Patton & Waring, 1984).

In fact, intimacy is the most difficult commodity to achieve in this life. Indeed, most dysfunctionalities in families are related to one's inability to be intimate with one other (L'Abate, Weeks, & Weeks, 1979; Patton & Waring, 1984) and to be available to one other in sharing our hurts and our fears of being hurt. Sharing our hurts is the single most difficult act facing us as human beings and as family members. The most difficult words to say in the English language are "I hurt" or "It hurts me." It is not easy to perform this act, and it takes a certain developmental level to be able to self-disclose our hurts and fears of being hurt (L'Abate, 1983d).

Intimacy, as defined here, can be achieved only when a relatively well-developed, -differentiated and -integrated sense of self is present. We need to have a sense of self to share it with intimate others. To be intimate, therefore, we need to (a) have achieved a certain level of conductivity in our style with family members (Chapter 9), (b) be aware of and in touch with our emotionality (Chapters 10 and 11), and (c) be aware of our priorities and the balance of being with doing and having (Chapter 12). As already considered in Chapter 9, intimacy is possible in the conductive-creative style and not in the abusive-apathetic or reactive-repetitive style. Emotionally (Chapter 10), intimacy can be obtained once we are able to distinguish and differentiate our feelings from our reasonability and our activities, avoiding obsessing compulsively with our thoughts or jumping impulsively, immediately, or drivenly into action; that is, experiencing feelings is one thing, expressing them is another. Given all these paradoxes and requirements, it is no small wonder that intimacy is so difficult to achieve.

Hence, we cannot expect intimacy to be available from the outset of therapy from families who seek our help. We will need to help them (a) solve immediate problems (Section II, Appendix A) and (b) learn skills to negotiate and solve problems over the long haul (Section III, Appendix B). Once they have achieved a modicum of conductivity in their styles and competence in how they solve problems and make decisions, then and only then will they be able to deal with issues of being and with issues of intimacy.

ISSUES OF BEING

Through the last two chapters the need to come to terms with issues of being has been alluded to without qualification. It is important, therefore, to explain what is meant by "issues of being." According to the triangle of living presented in the previous chapter (Figure 12–1), being is made up by the ability to love and by the status, that is, the feeling of self-importance and of self-efficacy. What is love? By love is meant at least three different processes: (1) caring, (2) seeing the good, and (3) forgiveness (L'Abate, 1975a, 1983d). According to the *E-R-A-Aw-C* model of competence (Chapters 10 and 11), caring represents activity, while seeing the good and forgiveness represent rationality, because both processes represent rational decisions we make when not seeing the good in ourselves and others and not forgiving ourselves and others would be more expensive than seeing the good and forgiving! Sharing of hurt, of course, is a thoroughly emotional process and as such takes place only as a by-product of the first three steps of caring, seeing the good, and forgiving (Appendix C).

Caring. To care for oneself and others means to be concerned for our own and their physical, economic, and emotional welfare (Gaylin, 1979). Caring, therefore, in its coarsest expression represents our willingness to change the diaper of our baby and carry the bedpan of our sick spouse, parent, or loved one. Caring is implicit in the initial provider role, but that role is insufficient to deal with extraeconomical factors. It is not enough to bring the bacon home—one needs to know how to cook it and share it with others in the family! Caring is shown every minute of our lives in how we take care of our bodies through diet, exercise, and social interactions, with our loved ones, relatives, and friends. Caring means paying attention to our feelings and to the feelings of those we love. Caring therefore is the most direct, universal communication of our love. This love is given unconditionally when we accept ourselves and intimates in spite of our warts and errors, without requirements for performance or for perfection. When this process is distorted by conditionality ("I love you if . . ."), then love is distorted and rejection of the self and of others may be the outcome.

Seeing the Good. This process goes back to the arguments of Chapter 5 concerning the importance of assuming a positive stance not only as persons, partners, and parents, but as professionals. If we cannot see the good in ourselves, how can we see the good in others? How can we be effective therapists if we cannot affirm families by going out of our way to find positives in their reason for referral and in the symptom(s) itself? A glass with 50% water, according to an overabused cliché, can be called either "empty" or "full." What we want to call it is entirely our choice.

Forgiveness. Little if anything has been written about forgiveness in the family therapy literature as well as in the psychotherapy literature at large.

Yet, this is an extremely crucial human process. If we cannot forgive ourselves for our stupidities, how can we learn from them and how can we forgive others? We do not learn from our successes except to become rigidly attached to the past ways that have brought those successes about. We learn from our errors as well as our successes. These conclusions apply to us as individuals as well as family therapists. Our failures keep us humble and our errors keep us alive and alert not to repeat them. How can we teach families forgiveness if we have not practiced it ourselves?

ISSUES OF INTIMACY

Intimacy as Hurt Sharing

We hurt for those we love. If we care about ourselves, find ourselves unable to change, and are helpless to do anything about changing, we then hurt. If those we love hurt, we hurt too; hence, hurt is the result of caring. We find it very difficult, if not impossible, to hurt for those we do not care about. It is difficult, well-nigh impossible, for the professional helper to help others if s/he is unable or unwilling to deal with his/her own personal hurt. Denial of personal hurt implies the inability to get in touch with and be aware of the inevitable hurt that results from the very fact of existence. We cannot live and not be hurt, or if we have been protected from hurt, how can we deal with it when we inevitably face it in the course of living? It is no wonder that if one is to be "normal," some degree of loss and conflict is necessary, since without them and the inevitable hurt that losses and conflicts bring us, we would be unable to cope. "Adjustment" could not conceivably occur without ability and willingness to cope with hurt. This hurt needs to be shared with those who care for us, and it should be part of the focus of the third stage of family therapy.

Sharing joys and victories is a process that can occur easily with anyone. We are, most of the time, willing and able to share anyone's victory. Are we, however, able to share our hurt and pain? It is difficult to achieve awareness of our personal hurt and awareness of hurt in those we love. How can we share our personal hurt with someone else if we deny it or are unaware of its presence in ourselves?

Sharing hurt means being present, being available, listening, and feeling what a loved one is feeling. There is no requirement that the listener remedy a situation that is beyond his/her power to change.

Recognition of Helplessness

One can do nothing in the face of hurtful and self-destructive behavior except point it out, recognizing it for what it is and acknowledging the little gain that is achieved from that recognition. The individual has the choice of continuing to behave destructively or becoming available to learning helpful behavior:

"If you want to go on destroying yourself (or your marriage, or your family), you can do it without help. If you want to change and behave helpfully, you can count on us. What will it be?"

"You will need to decide how you want to spend your life. We cannot and will not make the decision for you."

"It costs as much to get a lawyer to destroy this marriage as it costs to help you build this marriage. However, the decision as to which it will be us up to you."

It is important to recognize one's helplessness in the presence of hurt and hurtful behavior, refusing to accept this behavior as a given:

"I can see how you can feel hopeless and helpless, but that does not mean that you can control and defeat everybody with your behavior. You are entitled to your feelings, but you are not entitled to express your feelings destructively."

"If you want to consider other, positive ways to live with yourself, we can suggest a few."

Helplessness as Control

The manipulatory aspects of one's claimed helplessness and inadequacy need to be brought to the fore: "You are as helpless as a ten-ton truck." "You are as weak as an army tank." We need to be convinced that when we ask for help we are not as helpless as they think or feel we are. In fact, awareness of helplessness is a strength, because helplessness is what motivated us to ask for help and to do something about our situation. "It takes a strong person to admit helplessness. It takes a strong man to cry; you are lucky that you can cry. I have met many weak people who, unfortunately, can't. I wish I could say the same thing about your mate (child, etc.). Apparently, s/he feels so weak that s/he cannot cry."

Turning Anger or Guilt into Hurt

Anger may well be externalized guilt or feelings of helplessness. Regardless of its possible structural or historical antecedents, a great deal of anger may derive from frustration, defeat, and the hurt that accompanies any loss of self-esteem. Anger may be like sand and smoke—it renders us blind to our hurt and to the hurt of those we love. It is important to help convert anger into hurt about one's failure to help oneself and others: "I can see that you are very angry with each other. Are you hurting, too?" "You seem furious with her (him), but who is your worst enemy? If you are your worst enemy, who should you be angry at? What's underneath that anger? If you feel guilty, does it mean you hurt for yourself? If you hurt, does it mean you care for yourself and those you love?"

Another fear is that emotional honesty in communication may hurt the other person or that such communication may tend to be divisive. Sometimes, a partner or parent withholds information in the name of tact or protectiveness. This is especially true when it comes to sharing information about sexual preferences. "Tact," however, is often a cover-up to avoid possible confrontation and feedback from the mate. Many couples fear that they cannot afford to fight. They worry that if one partner raises his/her voice, the other must do so. There might be tears, loss of control, rejection, even separation.

How family members feel about each other has an important bearing on what they communicate to each other and how they respond to what is communicated. In studying interpersonal trust as a factor in communication, Mellinger (1956) found that the primary goal of communication with a distrusted person becomes reduction of one's own anxiety, rather than the accurate transmission of ideas. Therefore, a communicator who does not trust the recipient of the communication tends to conceal his/her own feelings about an issue through evasive, compliant, or aggressive communications, or through distracting, placating, or blaming and other reactive measures.

INTIMACY AND SELF-DISCLOSURE

In breaking down the process whereby families obtain some degree of intimacy, there needs to be a modicum of (a) empathy, (b) self-disclosure, and (c) sharing. Each of these three steps needs to be looked at in greater detail.

Empathy

The ability to put oneself in the place of another, especially another loved one, requires a certain degree of so-called "ego-strength" (Carlozzi, Gaa, & Liberman, 1983) and all the qualities that Davis (1983) in his review condensed into (a) social functioning, (b) self-esteem, (c) emotionality, and (d) sensitivity to others. These characteristics are in keeping with the arguments of the present formulation: at a certain degree of functionality (i.e., social functioning) as assessed by the family's style (Chapter 9), plus competence (i.e., emotionality) as in Chapters 10 and 12, plus self-esteem as in priorities (Chapter 12). The basic issue here brings us back to the importance of emotionality (Chapter 10) and what Zajonc (1984) has called "the primacy of affect." One cannot feel for others if one cannot feel for oneself.

Self-Disclosure

To review the literature on self-disclosure would be irrelevant here (Tolstedt & Stokes, 1984). Suffice it to say that self-disclosure is one of the prerequisites for sharing hurt. However, if we are unable or unwilling to share and to give of ourselves, the process of intimacy cannot take place (Derlega, 1984; Waring, 1980b). Hence, one of the goals of family therapy is to help family members disclose more about themselves, as shown in Table 13–1 or as done in Appendix C.

Sharing

Sharing, especially the sharing of hurtful feelings, is the foundation block of an intimate relationship. Typically, two persons' increasing commitment to each other leads to increased communication between them. Thus, the most intimate relationships are those characterized by the greatest disclosure of feelings. In fact, according to Jourard (1958), "self-disclosure of personal information is an index of 'closeness' in the relationship, and of the affection, love, or trust that prevails between two people" (p. 208).

There are at least two positions that allow us to share part of ourselves: (1) as already noted, we need a sense of self to share it, and (2) we need to subscribe to a notion of selfhood rather than selfishness to follow and practice the law of reciprocity, as discussed in Chapter 12. Some of these issues have been considered by Wallach and Wallach (1983) and by Goethals (1984) in a review of that book. We cannot give of ourselves unless we trust those we love to give parts of themselves to us.

Intimacy and Depression

Depression, as discussed in Chapter 7, is a very complex condition that results from a variety of personal and interpersonal factors. Among them is (a) low self-esteem (Battle, 1978; Gardner & Loei, 1981), which may be the outcome of (b) perceived parental rejection (Lefkowitz & Tesiny, 1984), (c) real or perceived losses (Roy, 1981), and ultimately (d) the inability to reach into one's emotions and grieve with someone who is willing and able to share our grief with us. After all, how do we know we love someone and are loved in return? When we are able to hurt when they are hurting and when they hurt when we do.

Hurt and Grief. Under the category of grief are also included (a) bereavement and (b) mourning. It is left to the reader to distinguish differences among these three concepts! Grief is the outcome of a loss, be that of a parent in childhood, of a spouse, or of self-esteem (Frantz, 1984; Moriarty, 1967; Schneider, 1984; Worden, 1982). Unresolved grief, that is, grief that is not

Table 13–1
TWO INVARIABLE EXERCISES FOR CLOSENESS-AVOIDANT COUPLES AND FAMILIES

In our work with the concept of past and present griefs and sharing our fears of possible hurts and griefs (L'Abate, 1983a) with its concomitant paradoxes, we have attempted to help couples become more intimate either on a group basis, through intimacy workshops (L'Abate & Sloan, 1984), or through intimacy letters (L'Abate & Samples, 1983) in a more circular and cryptic fashion.

The purpose of this table is to describe two straightforward exercises that in our clinical practice have been used to help couples and families to share their feelings of hurt and grief more directly.

Exercise for Couples

The couples should face each other with their eyes closed, holding hands. The following instructions are given:

> Please keep your eyes closed. Get in touch and concentrate on all the pain, hurt, and grief that you have accumulated over the years. Let these feelings of pain, hurt, and grief grow inside of yourself. Whenever you are ready say, "I hurt." Keep on saying it until you feel sure that you have heard the same message from your partner.

As the message is given the therapist should correct whatever incongruent or incongruous expression may accompany the expression of these feelings (i.e., smiling or anger). Accept tears and encourage their value as being the true expression of honesty and congruous expression of one's sad feelings. As these feelings are expressed, encourage whatever dialogue may ensue between the partners, focusing on the proper and direct expression of hurt feelings and sharing as a way of becoming clearer about oneself and closer to one's partner.

One of the major issues in the avoidance of closeness is the fact that each partner very likely needs to seek comfort from the very person who has hurt him/her the most (L'Abate & L'Abate, 1979). This paradox makes it even more difficult for the couple to get closer together. Mention this and other paradoxes to the couple if you think it may help them.

Exercise for Intimacy-Avoidant Families

In this exercise, which can either be administered in the therapist's office or assigned as a homework task (Appendix B, Exercise 3), the family is given a list of feelings items starting with "I" statements. Each family member is to complete each statement avoiding any reference requiring the "you" pronoun. Only "I" statements are acceptable.

Each member should be given as much time as is necessary to complete all the statements on this list.

Note: One of the major issues in the administration or assignment of either exercise is, of course, *whether* they are *relevant* to the needs of the couple or family, and *when* it is the most appropriate *time* to introduce them in the treatment. In both cases, it is suggested that either exercise be introduced after the therapist becomes convinced that the couple and the family are avoiding closeness and intimacy and that no other approach is available to the therapist to achieve this goal.

shared satisfactorily, can play havoc with oneself and with the self's relationships with others, including loved ones.

Bereavement. Most of the research on bereavement (Jacobs & Ostfeld, 1977; Kaffman & Elizur, 1979; Rubin, 1981; Sanders, 1979–80; Schoenberg et al., 1970; Vachon et al., 1976; Zisook, Devaul, & Click, 1982; supports the importance of dealing with grief and bereavement *when or as soon as* they take place. If grief and bereavement are not dealt with properly, i.e., they are not shared with loved ones, they remain a cancer in the individual's life and the individual's family.

Mourning. Evans (1976) reported two cases of unresolved mourning, where mourning was not overtly acknowledged within the family, thus becoming a secret. As the author describes them, in each family a child became openly dysfunctional producing a spiral of progressive intrafamilial alienation. Gardner and Pritchard (1977) emphasized with appropriate case reports the importance of rituals (like funerals and general family grieving) to minimize the development of severely pathological conditions. Naylor (1982) reported how failure to mourn a sickness or a defect discovered in newborns can have untold consequences for their mothers.

In addition to most obvious losses, like death, illness, and accidents, there are also a variety of less evident or obvious conditions that hurt us just as much and that need to be shared within the family in order for the family to function properly. These conditions are inherent in human nature, and they are (a) our vulnerability as human beings, (b) our fallibility, and (c) our need for other human beings as seen in loneliness.

Vulnerability. To share one's feelings is to become very vulnerable. One also becomes vulnerable in sharing the hurts of another. Only recently have social psychologists dealt with issues of vulnerability (Derlega, 1984). We all are vulnerable to death, sickness, accidents, and disability. We men are especially vulnerable to being unable to share our vulnerability. As Lewis (1978) has argued, we need to compete and not to show weaknesses (how could we go to the moon otherwise?), we lack adequate role models to show and share our vulnerabilities, and we are conditioned to ride on our horses without showing our emotions and, even worse, without crying. L'Abate, Hastrup, and Frey (submitted for publication) have argued, in fact, that crying is really the last taboo, personally, manfully, parentally, professionally, and therapeutically. Crying is the full integration and expression of our grief and of our fears of being hurt (L'Abate, 1977, 1983d). We may admit to our vulnerability only in the face of evident losses like death of a loved one, a poor marriage, or unemployment (Roy, 1981).

Fallibility. Very little can be found in the literature on this concept, except for Brandsma (1975). As he argued, our errors remind us of our humanness. As argued already in Chapter 12 concerning self and perfectionism, errors are inevitable in the course of our existence. The issue here is not whether we err but whether we learn and even profit from our mistakes. This concept is intrinsically interwoven with the whole issue of forgiveness, which is a condition *sine qua non* for our admission into the human race. As noted earlier, forgiving our errors allows us (a) to forgive the errors of those we love and (b) to learn from our mistakes. Without forgiveness it is doubtful whether progress can take place toward sharing of hurts. In fact, Hunter (1978) considers forgiveness as a contributing factor in the attainment of emotional maturity. This factor is so important that one entire lesson (Appendix C) is devoted to it.

Loneliness. One could argue that loneliness is part of the human condition. By the same token, just because we are born and die alone, it does not mean that we should live alone! We could live in the middle of a crowd and still feel lonely (Goev, 1976; Mijuskovic, 1977). The inevitable outcome of a loss is an increasing sense of loneliness. Whether we lose a spouse through death or divorce, many of us are becoming either single parents or aged widow(er)s. Through the life cycle for shorter or longer periods, all of us will experience loneliness. Some of us are absolutely terrified by it (Beattle & Viney, 1981; Kubistant, 1981; Margolis & Derlega, 1982). Some of us welcome it as relief from external stress.

CONCLUSION

Intimacy is the forgotten area of family therapy. Yet, it is the most powerful determinant of functionality if shared and of dysfunctionality when avoided. In fact, intimacy is so threatening that even some family therapists avoid it. Families themselves are so afraid of it that they will drop out of therapy to avoid it.

The Fourth Stage: Issues of Follow-Up

Chapter 14

The Importance of Follow-Ups

Family therapy is not terminated once the family's hurts are shared and, hopefully, set aside after a discussion of how the family can avoid repeating hurting itself. It takes more than hurt sharing to solve family problems. As argued here, it also takes a great deal of negotiation training that most clinical families do not have.

Once most family problems have been successfully dealt with (Stages 1 and 2), and a certain degree of intimacy is obtained (Stage 3), the issue of termination needs to be considered by both the therapist and the family.

THERAPEUTIC CONSIDERATIONS

Termination of family therapy (a) should not take place abruptly and (b) should contain the message that the family, in a way, is still not out of the woods and, therefore, still "on trial" to the extent that it still needs to demonstrate that it has profited by the therapy process. ("I am not sure I have done any good for this family until you have been on your own for at least six months.") In other words, the family still has the responsibility to apply whatever training it has received, like keeping up family meetings, showing maintenance of gains, and spreading positive effects to other aspects of family living (Chapter 3, Table 3–1).

In terminating without the contract of follow-up, there is always the possibility that some families may let go of themselves and regress. Hence, the contract of follow-up tends to help families consolidate their gains because they need to keep aware of and alert for the changes that need to be implemented over time. By becoming aware that they are still on trial, so to speak, and not yet out of the woods, they will become much more aware of themselves than they would otherwise, that is, without a follow-up contract.

PROFESSIONAL ISSUES

When we take the family pet to the veterinarian because of sickness or discomfort, the pet may receive treatment in the form of surgery, shots, or drugs. Usually, the veterinarian will ask (and in some cases insist) that the pet be brought back for an evaluation of whether the treatment did any good or not, and to check on whether additional or different treatment is necessary. This professionally responsible practice is also followed by the medical profession (with exceptions, of course). Apparently, however, veterinarians have higher standards than we family therapists do, because most of us are satisfied with reaching short-term goals (i.e., symptomatic relief, crisis resolution, etc.), considered here as the *first* stage of family therapy, and *nothing else*! Apparently, we are assuming (without evidence) that clinical families already have available all the problem-solving and decision-making skills they will need in the future. Therefore, they do not need any negotiation training and certainly no hurt sharing. As one prominent therapist of this persuasion put it (arrogantly, one could say): "All that intimacy stuff is just ethnic," implying quite clearly that this emphasis was cultural rather than universal and more specific to the author's peculiar ethnic background rather than something present in all families, dismissing (rather peremptorily, one could say) the crucial importance of hurt sharing in the process and termination of family therapy (and, of course, soundly discounting its author!).

We need to follow up the maintenance of gains and spread of positive effects not only for the therapeutic considerations already discussed, but also to show directly to families that *we do care*. Without any clear contract of follow-up, the family can reasonably construe that the therapist may have done all that s/he could do. Consequently, termination without follow-up could suggest to some families that, if they are in trouble again, they will need to go somewhere else for help, since the therapist, by bidding "good bye" and "fare thee well" may have communicated to the family that s/he has done whatever s/he could do and that nothing else can be done. If this is not the case, why are there families who go from one therapist to another?

Termination with a six-month follow-up appointment tells the family: "I care for this family and I will be and will stay interested in its welfare and I will continue remaining interested in you." To facilitate the process of follow-up, a questionnaire made up from a variety of sources (Appendix D) is submitted to help family therapists use it verbally as an interview schedule when families come back for a follow-up. If and when a family is unwilling or unable (it is important for the therapist to determine which is which) to come back for such a follow-up appointment, then this process could be performed by phone or by mail (with a stamped, preaddressed envelope). How expensive could these alternatives be? Even a secretary or an assistant could implement this module.

Could it be that follow-up procedures are not part of family therapy practices because family therapists do not want to know how effective they are and prefer to maintain their practices undisturbed from any possible negative feedback? In other words, without feedback of any kind, there is no possibility of change about how family therapy is practiced. Then, if family therapists cannot change their practices on the basis of necessary and welcome feedback, how can they help families change? If we do not know what outcome we produce in families, how do we know whether the theory (or theories) we follow are valid or applicable? Without follow-up we close ourselves within our theoretical and therapeutic cocoons, blind to any improvements in our therapeutic practices as well as to our personal rigidities and biases.

RESEARCH IMPLICATIONS

In his review of therapists' behavior for the prediction of outcome (mostly based on research on individual psychotherapy), Schaffer (1982) concluded:

> I believe that the most serious impediment to the development of measures of [therapeutic] skillfulness is the lack of "specificity" of most theories and measures. . . . theories that lack specificity describe how to do therapy in terms that are abstract, vague, and global. Highly specific theories are more concrete. They are expressed in terms of observable therapist's behavior that is recommended in specific instances. (p. 678)

This conclusion implies that therapists of all persuasions and specializations need to check on the validity of their clinical practices and the effectiveness of their therapeutic efforts not only on the basis of claimed personal satisfaction but also on the basis of definite and specific behavioral gains in the families they claim to help. Therapeutic popularity, either in the therapist's personality and style or in the enthusiasm of some family members, is not enough. Time needs to intervene to check on whether the enthusiasm and popularity have produced significant changes and gains.

In their review of the literature on follow-up to evaluate the outcome of *individual* psychotherapy, Nicholson and Berman (1983) argued that "information at follow-up often added little to that obtained at the end of treatment" (p. 261). They interpreted these findings as supporting the conclusion that "general durability of gains achieved during psychotherapy suggest[s] that costly follow-up procedures may be used more selectively" (p. 261).

From a family therapy standpoint one could argue with the validity of these findings (they cannot be generalized to family therapy) or the conclusion reached on the basis of the findings. In the first place, these findings were based on records obtained through self-report, which is usually the main source of information in individual psychotherapy research. Self-reports void of contextual corrections are subject to unknown biases and likely distortions, since there is no one else external to be informant to confirm or disagree with the self-report. When, however, the nature of follow-up reports is contextual, taking into account the views and opinions of family members, this report usually represents a process of monitoring, evaluating, and correcting individual opinions (verbally and nonverbally), producing a response and a report that hopefully would be more "objective" because it is based on consensus of family members and not on individual opinion.

Second, follow-up procedures need not be costly, as the authors concluded. If a therapist is really interested in how each family is doing after completion (not termination) of the third stage of therapy, then there are a variety of steps that could be taken. If the fee is too expensive, it could be reduced, or, as suggested above, follow-up could be conducted by phone, by mail, or by a secretary or an assistant (Appendix D). Where there is a will there is a way! How expensive could these alternatives be? Consequently, one needs to conclude that most family therapists are not interested in follow-ups because they are inherently convinced of the validity and usefulness of their theory(ies) and of their therapeutic practices.

CONCLUSION

The importance of follow-up procedures in family therapy has been stressed on therapeutic, professional, and research grounds. These grounds will be insufficient to help therapists improve their practices and their effectiveness. It will take more than the arguments to help therapists change. Certainly, change will not take place on the basis of evidence, because, as argued in Chapter 1, change is a dialectical process. Feedback on the other hand, belongs in the demonstrative realm, something to be avoided by "real" family therapists.

SECTION VI

Conclusion

Chapter 15

Toward a Technology of Family Interventions

The purposes of this final chapter are (a) to present arguments in favor of a technology for marriage and family interventions and (b) to prognosticate on the future of a systematic approach to family therapy.

TECHNOLOGY AND TECHNIQUE

As considered at length in Chapter 1, techniques consist of one-of-a-kind sleight-of-hands, magical gimmicks, that derive from the mystique of the guru-therapist. As magical laying-on-of-hands they are nonrepeatable events and consequently they cannot be studied in any systematic fashion. The variance of outcomes in therapy is still in great part relatable to relationships skills (aesthetic style). Fortunately, part of the outcome of therapy can be traced back also to structuring skills, that is, those methodological tasks that are repeatable from therapist to therapist and that represent the technological baggage of our field. Neither style without method nor method without style is sufficient to produce outcome. *Both* are necessary, and, of course, often in our work *both* are insufficient. We all have our share of failures (Coleman, 1985).

Hence, the first word of the title of this chapter, "Toward," could be understood to mean "In favor of." Being in favor of an approach does not mean its exclusive use. It only means that a pragmatic, technological, demonstrative approach needs to be given *at least equal time* as an aesthetic, dialectic, stylistic, relationship approach. A technology implies that for almost every negative human problem there are systematic and testable ways of solving it.

The key words in technology are *standard operating procedures*. Without standard (repetitive) procedures, a technology becomes a technique.

According to Webster, the term "technology" has at least two meanings, as "systematic treatment" and as "applied science." Both meanings can be subsumed under the rubric of method, that is, any approach that is replicable and that leads to observable and measurable results and to cumulative knowledge. Either as a systematic treatment or as applied science, this term needs to be differentiated sharply from "technique." By technique is meant an approach that depends in great part on the individual using it as synonymous with "style." Technique would represent the aesthetic aspect emphasized by Keeney and Sprenkle (1982), whereas technology would represent the other side of the aesthetic coin, that is, the pragmatic emphasis on methods that work and that produce results.

Since the field of family therapy is replete with techniques (Gurman & Kniskern, 1981; Hansen & L'Abate, 1982), the purpose of this book has been to emphasize the importance and relevance of technology, not in contrast but *in addition* to aesthetic emphasis. Success in therapy consists of "technique × technology" or "style × method" or "relationship skills × structuring skills." Hence emphasis in this book has been in part on demonstrative, pragmatic, structured approaches in interventions with couples and families.

The Fear of Technology

The field of family therapy is especially phobic of any approach that in any form comes close to "scientific" respectability. Research is limited to a few individuals or centers, and if and when it is conducted, it is with a large grant. Consequently, a great many research projects, like the Timberlawn project (Lewis, Beavers, Gossett, & Phillips, 1976) or Gottman (1979) or Minuchin's work (1974), are so expensive that only researchers receiving the grant initially can replicate themselves, since no one would qualify to receive a grant to replicate somebody else's work.

Why is this field so phobic about research? As a whole, the entire mental health enterprise has been extremely resistant to any notion of accountability, verifiability, and testability (Chapter 3). Therefore, it is not surprising that the field of family therapy is just as resistant. This phobic resistance can be counted in the number of dialectical (aesthetic), impressionistic clinical papers that are published in trade journals against the number of research reports. One does not need to demonstrate this point with data, but it would not be surprising to obtain a ratio of five to one for clinical versus research papers (at least)!

Technology in whatever form has been a favorite whipping boy (girl?) of humanists, yet we use it all the time in our daily lives (Sarason, 1984; Strupp, 1973). We go to the moon with it. Yet, for unfathomable reasons we consider it a monster in human affairs, a necessary evil that needs to be *resisted*, lest it control us more than it is doing already.

Research is feared and is considered a "dirty" word as not being different from the fear of technology that pervades part of the American culture (Rybzynski, 1983), as will be discussed at geater length elsewhere (L'Abate, in preparation). Apparently, we are not afraid of technology as an abstract noun representing a variety of mechanical activities. However, we seem to be afraid of technology as a threat to the status quo, a discounting of our way of life and loss of control over the environment and our lives, as Rybzynski (1983) has convincingly argued.

THE FUTURE OF SYSTEMATIC FAMILY THERAPY

The approach formulated here is seen as a complement and a supplement to family therapy. It does not detract from the therapist's effectiveness, personal style, and competence. It is designed to add to all these characteristics synergistically. SHWAs can be used informally in the therapist's office to serve as information outlines for interviews, or the same modules can be administered to couples and families at the appropriate stage and time during the process of therapy. Naturally not all families will be able to use and follow the instructions as written in these modules (see appendices). Adolescents especially will be resistant to the idea of "homework" as being too reminiscent of schoolwork. There will be at least one resistant family member who will refuse to spend time working on SHWAs. In this case, the resistance needs to be discussed in the therapy sessions, and perhaps some of the SHWAs can be conducted in the therapist's office rather than at home. Of course, it would help the process if the therapist were fully acquainted with the theory and rationale for the SHWAs, starting to administer them to the most cooperative families and branching out to the most resistant ones *after the first stage.*

There is nothing sacred about these SHWAs. They are not set in stone. The creative therapist could change the wording, simplifying it or making it more complex. The research therapist will find that the methodology advocated here can apply to any kind of model that can be reduced to the written instructions of a module. Give us your models and we shall apply them! Naturally, the greatest implication of the present approach lies in the ease with which SHWAs can be administered not only to clinical families, as a supplement to therapy, but also in the ease with which these SHWAs can be administered to nonclinical families, volunteer families in search of enrichment, and even individuals in search of additional experiences above and beyond the therapeutic experience.

From a research standpoint, the crucial experiments to check on the validity and usefulness of this approach will consider at least three experimental groups of families. One group would receive SHWAs alone, a second group would receive therapy alone, and a third group would receive both SHWAs and therapy. At the present time, research going on in the author's laboratory is attempting to determine whether these SHWAs are useful under two conditions, i.e., with maximum therapist's time; that is, volunteer undergraduate couples do answer these modules in front of a "therapist" (45 minutes) while another group answers these modules at home and spends just enough time with the "therapist" to report on the progress and receive the module for the next lesson (15 minutes). In addition, these modules are being administered to undergraduates in abnormal psychology classes to find out more about their range of applicability (Chapter 3).

ADVANTAGES OF SHWAs

As outlined in Chapter 3, there are distinct advantages to the application of SHWAs to families. Among these advantages the following are the most distinct: (a) reproduction and replicability is easy, (b) the eclectic nature of these SHWAs allows them to be administered to families regardless of the theoretical viewpoint held by the therapist, (c) SHWAs are an additional avenue of intervention available to therapists, and (d) SHWAs can be administered by relatively inexperienced therapists.

Ease of Reproduction and Replicability

As long as these modules are not used for commercial purposes, violating the copyright laws, therapists and student therapists are allowed to use them for purposes of research. Any results coming out of the author's laboratory would be suspect, unless, of course, these results were negative! Therapists could easily accumulate cases where these SHWAs were administered to families with some kind of pre-post-therapy objective evaluation and follow-up (Chapter 13, Appendix D).

Eclectic Natue of SHWAs

The eclectic nature of these SHWAs should make them acceptable to a variety of therapists with a variety of theoretical persuasions. Eventually, SHWAs derived from the models presented here will need to be compared with SHWAs derived from competing theoretical models. The comparability of competing models should eventually allow us to test each model's validity as well as usefulness. If therapists do not like these models, they are welcome to create their own and reduce them to written format to test them.

Additional Avenues of Intervention

Conceivably, SHWAs could be administered to families long distance, so to speak. Thus far we have found that resistant members of some families are willing to work on SHWAs even though they may not be willing to join their families in therapy sessions! If resistant family members can see other family members work together on these assignments and get some pleasure out of them, they may decide to join them. Hence, a therapist should not allow a resistant member to sabotage the administration of SHWAs, but should work alongside the family to allow the resistant family member to be included in these SHWAs, if and when the opportunity arises. What about couples and families who live overseas or in rural areas unreachable by mental health facilities?

Ease of Administration

SHWAs are the fourth application of what this author has called *The Laboratory Method in Clinical Psychology* (L'Abate, 1973b, in preparation). Previous areas of application for this method were (a) evaluation of children, couples, and families (L'Abate, 1968, 1972, L'Abate & Wagner, 1985), (b) monitored play therapy with children (L'Abate, 1979), and (c) structured enrichment programs for couples and families (L'Abate, 1973b). This method implies application of standard operating procedures (like SHWAs) in the hands of less experienced intermediary personnel under supervision and support of a more experienced professional. This method lowers considerably the cost of intervening with couples and families, because the bulk of treatment would be in the hands of less experienced intermediaries.

DISADVANTAGES OF SHWAs

Naturally, there are limitations to how and when SHWAs can be administered to families. There are chaotic and chronic families whose first stage of treatment may last over a year and, in some, a lifetime! In these families SHWAs may never get done. There will be limitations in terms of socioeconomic and educational factors that may make it very difficult for some families to be able to learn or to work on these modules as presently worded. Nonetheless, this limitation could be solved by rewriting modules that even minimally educated families of poor socioeconomic status may understand and follow. Here, we are dealing not only with inability, we are also dealing with motivation and willingness.

If and when applied, limitations will be found on how far families will be willing to go in working on SHWAs. Especially if the level of motivation has not been increased by interaction with the therapist, families may tend to drop out, satisfied with achieving short-term gains. It is doubtful whether all the lessons available in the appendices will be used by most families. Unless the therapist is research-oriented, s/he may have to use these modules selectively and judiciously.

The author may be blind to additional disadvantages that will be gleefully pointed out by inevitable and expected critics of this approach. Eventually, the value (costs, effectiveness, applicability, etc.) of this approach is predicated on whether SHWAs are useful to families or not. Therapists should look out for paradoxical results of SHWAs (Chapter 11); that is, families that are the most displeased with SHWAs are also those that may change the most, whereas very cooperative families sometimes may be those that change the least!

CONCLUSION

There are ways of helping families that can be organized sequentially, in stages of family therapy, eclectically, encompassing a variety of viewpoints, and empirically, evaluating the process and outcome of a particular approach. One can help families and still accumulate records that will improve present methods of helping them even better. Even though the full usefulness of this approach needs to be demonstrated further on empirical grounds (L'Abate, in preparation), its dialectical bases have been made explicit. *Both* the dialectical and the demonstrative need to go hand in hand. Ultimately, the usefulness of any approach has to be judged on how well and how many families it helps. Let us hope that this approach will help many therapists help many families!

Appendices

INSTRUCTIONS FOR ADMINISTERING SYSTEMATIC HOMEWORK ASSIGNMENTS (SHWAs) TO FAMILIES AND COUPLES

SHWAs should be the outcome of a contractual agreement between the therapist and the family from the very outset of therapy ("I would like you to set aside one hour a week to work with each other." "If you cannot follow this assignment and do not do what I ask you to do, I doubt whether I can be of much help to this family"). In other words, from the very beginning of therapy the family needs to agree to match one hour of therapy with one hour of family conferences. With a very resistant family, you may choose to make the next appointment contingent on the family having done whatever homework they have been assigned ("If you find something that works better for you, by all means do it, and then tell me about it so I can use it with other families").

The assignment of SHWAs cannot start until a modicum of stability in the family has been established. You can find out very quickly whether the family is ready to start working with you on these SHWAs by initially prescribing tailor-made assignments. If the family follows your instructions, they may be able to start working with you. Initially you may want to prescribe *defeating patterns*, such as: (1) overuse of blaming (abusive and reactive) YOU rather than congruent I or WE statements, indicating the presence of externalization and projective identification (for lack of better terms!) patterns; (2) overuse or inappropriate use of going back to past events, also in a reactive and abusive fashion; (3) mind-reading and attributions of evil intents to other family members; (4) finding excuses and rationalizations for one's irresponsibilities; and (5) out-and-out defiance and rebellion. You may prescribe all of these and other defeating patterns provided you arrange for: (1) *fixed times* (once a week, once every other day, etc.), with (2) *a predetermined schedule* for a rigid length of time (30 minutes, 1 hour, etc.), (3) at a given and *prearranged time* (7 o'clock, 8 o'clock, etc.). If the family does not do what you tell them, they are defeating you and you need to find out why this happens, perhaps suggesting how they could do the task better.

If and when the family is ready to work with you, and there is an admission of depression in at least one member of the family, you may start assigning the Depression HWAs to *all the members* of the family, so that everybody learns to deal with depression in their lifetime.

If and when these HWAs are completed to the family's satisfaction and to yours, and depression is no longer a problem (i.e., the family is not controlled by the depression or any other symptom), you may start on the Negotiation HWAs.

If and when the previous sequence is completed satisfactorily for the family and for you, you can ask about patterns of crying, i.e., how is crying handled in the family? If you are convinced that the family can cry together whenever there is hurt, you may not need to assign the Intimacy HWAs. If they do not share their hurts together and are not available to each other when any of them hurts, they may need to do so through the Intimacy HWAs.

It is essential to stress the importance of completing the SHWAs. For example, appointments should be made contingent on completion of assignments. In extreme cases, interruption of treatment may be necessary: "I doubt whether I can help this family. Unless you complete your homework, we may need to postpone treatment until you are ready." Make sure that you go over each assignment and show that you care about the assignments by making direct inquiries about their impact on the family. You may need to clarify issues that arise and these issues may in turn be used by you to conduct your own model of therapy.

APPENDIX A
Depression SHWAs

Name _____
Date _____

DEPRESSION PROGRAM
Homework Assignment No. 1

TERRIFIC TRIANGLES: I. THE FAMILY DRAMA

1. To keep the family together and to protect it from change, we often play a triangle in which we, in one way or another, play all three parts at different times. The three parts are the victim, the persecutor, and the rescuer. These basic parts have variations within each part. For instance, we may play the judge of other family members, and on the basis of this part, we may then become jury and executioners. Below you will find three lists that relate to the three basic parts. Read them.

Persecutor	Victim	Rescuer
Judge	Criminal	Therapist
Parent	Defendant	Know-it-all
Juror	Invalid	Expert (teacher, preacher, consultant, etc.)
Policeman	Child	Big daddy
Patriot	Drug addict	Tycoon
Detective	Servant	Peacemaker
Hellfire & brimstone preacher	Martyr	Red Cross nurse or paramedic
Executioner	Sinner	Meddler
Inquisitor	Culprit	Saint
Oppressor	Poor little me	Superman/woman
Inspector general	Oppressed	Wholesaler
Interrogator	Innocent	Advice giver

2. Circle the part and the variations on the part that you recognize in yourself. Then decide which of these you play best (a), second best (b), and third best (c). Describe how you play each part.

a. _____
_____

b. _____
_____

c. _____
_____

(continued)

3. What happens to the rest of your family when you play these parts? Please describe in detail.
_____
_____

4. Do you need to play these parts and what do you get out of playing them? Please answer in detail.
_____
_____

5. Who is responsible for your playing these parts?
_____

6. How do you get yourself set up to play these parts? Please explain in detail.
_____
_____

7. Unless you like playing these parts and you do get something positive out of playing them, how can you avoid setting yourself up to play them? Please explain.
_____
_____

8. Discuss your answers with your partner/family members. Keep notes on the discussion and bring these notes to the next therapy session.

NOTES:
_____
_____
_____
_____
_____
_____
_____
_____

Name _____

Date _____

Homework Assignment No. 2

TERRIFIC TRIANGLES: II. DISTANCE IN THE FAMILY

Another terrific triangle we often play to keep the family together and protect it from change has three parts: the pursuer, the distancer, and the distance regulator. For instance, the distancer may avoid emotional closeness but become a pursuer sexually. An emotional pursuer, by the same token, may become a sexual distancer. The distance regulator may want people to come close, but when they do, they are put off or even rejected.

1. Which of these parts do you play best?

_____

2. How do you play it?

_____

3. Which of these parts do you play second best?

_____

4. How do you play it?

_____

5. Which of these parts do you play third best?

_____

6. How do you play it?

_____

7. What happens to you and to the rest of the family when you play these parts? Please explain in detail.

_____
_____
_____
_____

(continued)

8. How do you set yourself up to play these parts?

_____

9. Unless you like playing them and you get something out of playing them, how can you avoid setting yourself up to play them?

_____
_____

10. Discuss your questions with your partner/family members and keep notes on the discussion. Bring these notes back to the next therapy session.

NOTES:

_____
_____
_____
_____
_____
_____
_____
_____
_____
_____
_____
_____
_____
_____

Name _____

Date _____

Homework Assignment No. 3

DEFINING DEPRESSION

1. What does depression mean to you?

_____
_____
_____

2. Are you willing to consider the following interpretations of depression? (For this step it is sufficient to read the opinions offered.)

Rank

a. Depression is a valuable signal that we could use other people's help and support in our lives. ____

b. Being depressed is a sign of our strength and willingness to recognize what we are feeling. Many people are unwilling or unable to recognize their depression! ____

c. Depression is a feeling that all of us experience to some degree. We cannot live and not be depressed because all of us, as fallible human beings, are vulnerable to hurts. ____

d. Saying that we are depressed indicates that we know how we feel inside and that therefore we can begin to do something about it. If we did not know how we felt or if we did not admit to feeling depressed, we might do something destructive, such as drinking, abusing drugs, gambling, etc. ____

e. Depression can be a useful feeling and one that, used correctly, may eventually lead us to understand and appreciate its importance. ____

f. Instead of being considered an enemy and a foe, depression can be thought of as a friend: something we are able to join, use well, and, eventually, something we learn to live with and enjoy. ____

g. Depression is the royal road to self and selfhood. It allows us to have time to ourselves, to be by ourselves, to listen to ourselves, and thus to learn more about ourselves. ____

h. When we experience our depression fully, we are being honest and real with ourselves. When we deny or reject our depression, we are being phony, essentially withdrawing from our emotional selves. ____

i. Depression is a choice. Up to now, depression has controlled you, your life, and perhaps your marriage and your family. Yet perhaps you can choose to allow it to control you or to learn how to control it. ____

(continued)

3. After you have read these views on depression, rank them from 1 to 9, according to how closely each of them resembles you in your depression: *the most familiar or applicable* (1); *the least familiar to you* (9).

4. If none of the preceding descriptions fit you in any way, please explain why.

_____
_____

5. Even if none of the descriptions seem to fit you, try choosing three that seem as if they might be useful to you as a way of describing depression.

_____
_____

6. If any of the descriptions do fit you, please explain how.

_____
_____

7. **Homework:** Choose three of the most applicable, or useful, of the descriptions of depression and notice carefully how well (or how poorly) these descriptions apply to your depression during the coming week.

Name _____

Date _____

Homework Assignment No. 4
THE POSITIVE ELEMENT

1. We need to check last week's homework. How well did the descriptions you chose apply to your depression during the week?

_____

_____

2. As you may have noticed, depression often contains a positive element that is helpful to the person who is depressed. Write down two of the positive or useful aspects of your depression—however small or insignificant they appear to be.

_____

_____

3. Because depression may contain some useful and valuable ingredients, it would not make sense (nor would it be possible) to try to eliminate depression. We cannot be alive and not be depressed. It may, however, be useful to learn from it and to control it by deciding when to experience depression.

4. **Homework:** This week, allow yourself to be depressed. Now, on three separate occasions, pay attention to the positive and valuable aspects of your depression. Notice the subtle, perhaps small, but real benefits of this experience. Write down the results of this homework assignment. In addition, during the week, decide whether the depression is controlling you or whether you want to control the depression. It will be an interesting week.

_____

_____

_____

_____

_____

_____

_____

_____

_____

Name _____

Date _____

Homework Assignment No. 5
ACHIEVING CONTROL

1. a. We need to check last week's homework. What positive or useful aspects of your depression were you able to identify?

_____

_____

   b. Did you find that you controlled the depression, or was the depression controlling you?

_____

_____

2. Despite the usefulness of depression, most people seem to allow their depression to control and overwhelm them. You will learn that you can choose to allow your depression to control you, or you can learn how to begin to control it. If you are interested in learning how to control your depression, proceed to the next step. If not, stop here and list the many ways that depression is controlling your life.

_____

_____

3. Although depression is a valuable and useful method of learning about ourselves, it is not enough simply to recognize this fact. It is important to achieve some control over when we choose to experience depression.

   To achieve some control over depression, we may begin by learning and practicing how to start depression. Thus, "if you want to stop it, start it!" Most people don't realize that they have the freedom to start a depression on command. We can start a depression by controlling its *content*. For example, we can evoke a depression in the following ways:

   a. by thinking negative thoughts about ourselves

   b. by thinking negatively about the world around us

   c. by thinking negatively about our future

   Which methods can you use to start to make yourself feel depressed?

_____

_____

_____

(continued)

258

Name _____

Date _____

Homework Assignment No. 6
FLEXIBLE CONTROL

1. We need to check on last week's assignment. Describe your two controlled depressive episodes. Review your notes on the main thoughts and feelings you had during these episodes.

_____
_____
_____
_____

2. What did you learn about yourself through these experiences?

_____
_____
_____

3. If you didn't perform this homework assignment, do you feel somewhat depressed about that? If so, write down your thoughts and feelings on this matter. If not, make note of your growing ability not to have to perform perfectly at all times in order to feel OK.

_____
_____
_____

4. Part of learning the art of control is acquiring flexibility and adapting to life's changing conditions. To improve your control of your depression, you may have to arrange to be depressed at different times, for different periods of time, and under varying situations. In this way, you can begin to master your depressive episodes and to learn to observe and study them in all kinds of situations.

   a. At what time do you tend to feel somewhat less depressed?

_____
_____

   b. In what places (home, work, etc.) do you tend to feel less depressed?

_____
_____

(continued)

Which one works best for you? Do you have your own creative and effective ways of becoming depressed?

_____
_____

4. Although depression can often be a valuable and useful experience, it is helpful to learn to control it in order to use it at our leisure. We can control depression by starting it in a specific *place* at a specific *time*.
Where do you most often tend to feel depressed? At home? At work? Outside?

_____

At what times do you tend to feel most depressed? In the morning, the afternoon, the evening, or before going to bed?

_____
_____

5. **Homework:** Begin practicing to control your depression by starting it two times during the following week. Start your depression in the place where you most often feel depressed. However, make sure that you remain alone and isolated during these first depression practice sessions. It is important to be free of distractions so that you can allow yourself to experience your depression fully. In addition, start the depression at the time you most often feel depressed.
Do, however, place a *time limit* on these depressive episodes. Do it for 15 minutes the first time and for 25 to 30 minutes the second time. Remember not to go over the agreed time limit. It may even be useful to set an alarm clock to remind you when the time is up. Finally, in addition to concentrating on being depressed, it is important that you write down the central thoughts and feelings that come to your mind during the controlled depression practice sessions. You can use the experience to learn more about yourself by reviewing your written notes. Good luck in taking this important step.

Name _____

Date _____

Homework Assignment No. 7
LETTING OTHERS HELP

1. Did you do your homework on arranging three depressive episodes this week? What new insights (if any) did you have about your inner depressive processes?

_____
_____
_____

2. As we mentioned in the first lesson, depression can be viewed as an ally, a friend who reminds us that we could use other people's help and support. Who do you most often discuss your depression with?

_____
_____

3. To further increase your control over your depression, it would be useful to enlist the help of these people. Which of the people you listed could you ask to help you to control your depression? If there is no one, try to think of someone who might be willing to help you out (a friend, family member, co-worker).

_____
_____

4. Sometimes it is difficult to find the energy to remember to schedule a depression a specific number of times during the week. A friend can help by reminding you to do so.

5. **Homework:** During this week, find someone who will be willing to remind you to schedule some controlled depressive episodes during the week. That person can even help you to decide which days and how long to be depressed. (Please make sure, however, that you practice at least three times this week. It is important to maintain your skill level.) In addition, your helper can check on your progress during the week to make sure that you are doing your homework correctly. Again, remember to record, in writing, your experience of these controlled depressions.

c. Under what conditions (working, socializing, exercising, etc.) do you tend to feel somewhat less depressed?

_____
_____

5. **Homework:** To acquire further control over your depression, practice getting depressed three times, for 20 minutes each time, during the next week. However, arrange these periods to occur (a) at times you tend to feel most depressed and (b) in places where you often tend to feel less depressed. Write down everything you think and feel. Make sure you keep a written record. Bring your notes with you next time I(we) see you. Remember to recall and write down for later review what you experience during these controlled depressive episodes.

Name _____
Date _____

Homework Assignment No. 8

USING DEPRESSION

1. Did you find someone to help you to schedule your depressions last week? Were you able to follow through and complete your assignment fully?

_____

_____

2. Review your notes on your depressions. Were you able to learn anything more about yourself during your self-initiated depressions?

_____

_____

3. What have you concluded about your growing ability to control your depression at will? Have you noticed any change in your feelings about yourself and that gold mine of potential self-knowledge—your depression?

_____

_____

_____

4. Learning how to schedule, initiate, time, record, and review one's own depressions is clearly a difficult skill to master. Those who are willing and able to practice this skill usually feel more confident and feel better about themselves. They realize that they have truly accomplished something special. They have learned a new skill and have been able to use the depression, at their own leisure, to learn more about themselves. What was your experience of this process?

_____

_____

_____

5. You are entitled to feel proud of yourself for having mastered this new skill. On the other hand, there is no need to feel depressed or to belittle yourself for not having completely mastered this skill. If, after completion of all these lessons, you continue to feel uncomfortable depressed, stop and consider the following step. Pay attention to your depression; remember that it can be a signal reminding us that we need to ask others for help. Are you strong enough to ask for help? Only the strong can give themselves permission to seek help from others.

_____

_____

_____

_____

Name _____
Date _____
Lesson No. _____
Program _____

LESSON FEEDBACK FORM*

Now that you have completed this lesson, please respond to the following questions concerning the assignment itself.

1. How useful did you find this task for understanding the program topic?

_____ very useful
_____ quite useful
_____ somewhat useful
_____ slightly useful
_____ not useful at all

2. How important is the skill or attitude addressed by this task?

_____ very important
_____ quite important
_____ somewhat important
_____ slightly important
_____ not important at all

3. Put into your own words what you got out of doing this task.

_____

_____

_____

_____

4. How could this task be improved or changed?

_____

_____

_____

_____

*This form should accompany every lesson for every program.

6. How could this program be improved?

_____
_____
_____
_____
_____
_____
_____
_____
_____
_____
_____
_____
_____
_____
_____
_____
_____
_____
_____
_____

Name _____
Date _____

DEPRESSION PROGRAM FEEDBACK FORM

Now that you have completed this program, please respond to the following questions concerning the use of these structured depression assignments.

1. Using a scale of 1 to 8, rank the assignments according to their usefulness in coping with depression. Rank the most useful task as "1." Rank the least useful task as "8."

Task	Rank
Drama triangle	____
Distance triangle	____
Defining depression	____
The positive element	____
Achieving control	____
Flexible control	____
Letting others help	____
Using depression	____

2. How useful did you find this program in understanding and coping with depression? Choose one.

____ very useful ____ quite useful ____ somewhat useful ____ slightly useful ____ not useful at all

3. How useful would you rate this program in terms of developing or improving your attitude toward yourself in general? Choose one.

____ very useful ____ quite useful ____ somewhat useful ____ slightly useful ____ not useful at all

4. How likely would you be to recommend this program to other people you know? Choose one.

____ very likely ____ quite likely ____ somewhat likely ____ slightly likely ____ not likely at all

5. Using your own words, what did you find useful about this program?

_____
_____
_____
_____
_____
_____

(continued)

262

Appendix B

Negotiation SHWAs

Name _____

Date _____

NEGOTIATION PROGRAM
Homework Assignment No. 1
THE GOALS OF MARRIAGE

The purpose of this homework assignment is that both of you start thinking about and stating clearly what each of you wants out of this marriage (family).

1. *What?* Write specific constructive results you want to achieve in this marriage (family).

_____

_____

_____

_____

2. *Why?* Write the benefit to each of you from achieving *what*.

_____

_____

_____

3. *How?* Clarify ways you plan to achieve *what*.

_____

_____

_____

4. *When?* State clearly frequencies, times, and extent of the ways of achieving *what*.

_____

_____

_____

(continued)

5. *Set goals for tomorrow.* Write specifically what you will do tomorrow that you have not done today. Note: Discuss your answers with your partner (family members) for at least one hour *before* your next therapy session.

RESULTS
Successful Unsuccessful Canceled

_____

_____

_____

Name _____

Date _____

Homework Assignment No. 2
THE LAW OF GIVE AND TAKE: THE GOLDEN RULE

1. Have you ever heard of the Golden Rule? What does the Golden Rule mean to you?

_____
_____

2. How are the Golden Rule and the Law of Give and Take related to each other?

_____
_____

3. Do you agree that the Golden Rule means dealing with others the way we want them to deal with us? (Please comment.)

_____
_____
_____

4. What happens when we fail to follow this rule in our dealings with others?

_____
_____

5. What happens to your relationship (marriage, family) when you fail to follow this rule?

_____
_____

6. What are the advantages of following the Golden Rule in your relationship?

_____
_____
_____

7. What are the disadvantages?

_____
_____

(continued)

8. What do you think would happen to your relationship if you were to commit yourself to follow the Golden Rule?

_____
_____

9. What do you think would happen to your relationship if both you and your partner (mate, companion, parent, or child) failed to follow it?

_____
_____

10. How committed are you to following this rule, and why?

_____
_____

11. List specific instances of when and where you failed to follow this rule and the outcome of that failure:

_____
_____
_____

12. List specific instances of when and where you followed this rule and the outcome of having followed it:

_____
_____
_____

13. Share your answers with your partner (family members) and discuss similarities and differences in your answers. What did you learn from this discussion?

_____
_____
_____

(continued)

Name _____

Date _____

Homework Assignment No. 3
"I" STATEMENTS

Some people have trouble starting sentences with the pronoun "I"; instead, they most often use the pronoun "you." Using the "you" pronoun can be very hurtful to marriages and to families. The purpose of this task is to give you practice in making "I" statements. Using sentences that begin with "I" can be especially helpful when trying to express feelings or deal with emotional issues in your relationship. The following sentence stems have been found helpful in making "I" statements. One blank has been provided under each heading so that you can make up a stem of your own. Write your completions for each of the sentence stems on the lines provided, and start thinking about other possible completions for these sentences. After completing all the responses, discuss your answers with your partner.

Self

I wish _____
I should _____
I need _____
I feel _____
I _____

Marriage/relationship with partner

It pleases me when _____
I fear _____
I love _____
I hurt _____
I _____

Children

I remember _____
I want _____
It pleases me when _____
It hurts me when _____
I _____

Parents/in-laws

I avoid _____
I understand _____
I must _____
I won't _____
I _____

Siblings or relatives

I feel _____
I ought _____
I avoid _____
I trust _____
I _____

(continued)

14. During the next week, concentrate on writing down four specific instances in which you followed the Golden Rule and the outcome:

Instance 1 _____
_____

Outcome: _____
_____
_____

Instance 2 _____
_____

Outcome: _____
_____
_____

Instance 3 _____
_____

Outcome: _____
_____
_____

Instance 4 _____
_____

Outcome: _____
_____
_____
_____
_____
_____

Name _____

Date _____

Homework Assignment No. 4

STYLES IN INTIMACY

Instructions: The purpose of this task is to identify three styles in relating (*apathetic, reactive,* and *conductive*) used by partners in a relationship and to give you and your partner some practice in telling them apart.

The stimulus sentences listed below attempt to represent typical statements made by one partner to another in a relationship. One partner reads the stimulus sentences, one at a time, while the other partner responds in each of the three styles. Four blanks have been provided for you to supply your own stimulus sentences unique to your relationship. Write your responses to each stimulus sentence in each of the three styles in the spaces provided. After completion, the partners switch roles.

Don't be overly concerned if a particular style or stimulus sentence does not seem to fit your relationship. Do the best you can in responding to each one. We are interested in your learning the styles at this point and in your being able to note differences between them. Don't be afraid to make mistakes or take risks.

By the end of this task see if you can figure out which of these styles of relating you use most often with your partner *and* the specific occasion—setting and context—in which you use it (example—*Reactive:* At the in-laws when my spouse/partner mentions one of my personal faults). Record your answer in the space provided at the end of this task.

Definitions:

Apathetic Response—A response in which you say something not related, ignore your partner, or show other signs/behaviors of inattentiveness. Example—*Partner:* "You're stupid!" *Respondent:* "Guess who's coming over for dinner?"

Reactive Response—An impulsivelike response, often said without thinking, in which you criticize, act defensively, or suggest that you will take care of everything. Example—*Partner:* "You're stupid!" *Respondent:* "What do you think you are?"

Conductive Response—A response in which you request more information from your partner, rephrase what your partner has said to see if you've understood what s/he was trying to say, or otherwise indicate that you are in charge of yourself. Example—*Partner:* "You're stupid!" *Respondent:* "I know that I behave stupidly sometimes. How have I offended you?"

Styles

Stimulus Sentences	Apathetic	Reactive	Conductive
Did your mother/father call today?			
Did you put the garbage out/do the laundry today as you promised?			

(continued)

Work

I sometimes _____

I enjoy _____

I dread _____

I'd like _____

Friends

I sense _____

I fear _____

I wonder _____

I enjoy _____

Leisure time

I like _____

If I could _____

I enjoy _____

I don't want _____

Now spend a few minutes discussing your responses with your partner.

Name _____

Date _____

Homework Assignment No. 5
OPTIONS IN RESPONDING: PART ONE

Instructions: The purpose of this task is to identify the first three of five response options—*Emotional, rational,* and *actional*—in a relationship *and* to give you and your partner some practice telling them apart. Always using emotional, rational, or actional options in responding often does not result in good outcomes for couples when they try to deal with differences or conflicts in their relationship.

The stimulus sentences and situations listed below attempt to represent typical statements made in or typical situations found in relationships. One partner reads the stimulus sentences and situations, one at a time, while the other partner answers in each of the three different response options. Four blanks have been provided for each of you to supply your own stimulus sentences or situations related to your own relationship. Write your responses to each of the stimulus sentences and situations in the spaces provided. After completion, the partners switch roles.

Again, don't be overly concerned if a particular option, stimulus sentence, or stimulus situation does not seem to fit your relationship. Do the best you can in responding to each one. We are interested in your learning the various response options and in your being able to note differences between them. Don't be afraid to make mistakes or take risks.

At the end of this task write down the option(s)—*emotional, rational,* or *actional*—that you think you use most frequently in your relationship *and* the occasion—the setting and the context—in which you use it (example—*Actional:* Friday night when we tried to decide on a movie to see, I stormed out angrily). Record your answer in the space provided at the end of this task.

Definitions:
Emotional Response—A quick or cutting response given without any thought or awareness. Example—*Partner:* "That was sure dumb of you!" *Respondent:* "You're dumb, too!"
Rational Response—A logical or intellectualized response. Example—*Partner:* "That was sure dumb of you!" *Respondent:* "The word 'dumb' needs to be defined."
Actional Response—A response including either a nonverbal behavior or a verbal threat involving action. Example—*Partner:* "That was sure dumb of you!" *Respondent:* (Slams the door as she storms out) or "If you don't take that back, I'm going to slap you!"

Response Options

Stimulus Sentences/ Situations	Emotional	Rational	Actional
I'm very angry at you!			
Why are you so late?			

(continued)

Styles

Stimulus Sentences	Apathetic	Reactive	Conductive
The bank called to tell us the last check you wrote bounced.			
How late did you get in last night?			
How did work/school go today?			
I'm going out with the guys/girls Friday night			
I'm sorry I wasn't there to pick you up.			
What shall we do tonight?			
Make up your own stimulus sentences			

Feedback

Style(s) used most frequently with your partner (*Apathetic, reactive,* and *conductive*): ____/____/____

Occasion—context and setting—with your partner in which this style often occurs (example—*Reactive:* At the breakfast table when I talk about visiting my parents): ____/____/____

Response Options

Stimulus Sentences/ Situations	Emotional	Rational	Actional
You know I love you.			
Did you pay the ——— bill?			
(Your partner comes back from the store. You notice s/he didn't get an item you need very badly and that your partner said s/he'd remember to pick up for you.)			
(You and your partner both want to take a shower. It's agreed s/he can go first. When it's your turn you notice that there is no hot water left.)			
(You've had a hard day. You go home thinking you will be able to relax. You walk in the door and are immediately reminded by your partner that you promised to go somewhere with him/her right after work.)			
(You and your partner have decided to go out this week end. You think it will be just the two of you. On Friday your partner tells you s/he ran into an old acquaintance—that you're not fond of—and has invited him/her to join the two of you.)			

(continued)

Make up your own stimulus sentences:

Response Options

Stimulus Sentences/ Situations	Emotional	Rational	Actional

Feedback

Option(s) used most frequently with my partner (emotional, rational, or actional): —/—/—

Occasion—context and setting—with my partner in which this response option often occurs (Example—*Rational:* At the end of the month when money is tight and my partner buys something I think we don't need, I lecture him/her):

Name _____

Date _____

Homework Assignment No. 6
OPTIONS IN RESPONDING: PART TWO

Instructions: The purpose of this task is to identify two additional response options—*awareness* and *contextual*—in a relationship *and* to give you and your partner practice in telling them apart and in using them. Unlike the first three options covered in Assignment No. 5 (emotional, rational, and actional), both of these response options usually result in good outcomes when partners try to deal with differences or conflicts in their relationship.

The stimulus sentences and situations listed below attempt to represent possible statements made in and situations found in relationships. One partner reads the stimulus sentences and situations one at a time, while the other partner answers using each of the two response options. Four blanks have again been provided for each of you to supply stimulus sentences or situations related specifically to your relationship. Write your stimulus sentences and situations along with responses to them and to each of the supplied stimulus sentences and situations using the different options in responding in the spaces provided. When finished, the partners change roles.

Again, don't be overly concerned if a particular option, stimulus sentence, or stimulus situation does not seem to fit your relationship. Do the best you can in responding to each one. We are interested in your learning these two additional response options and in your being able to use them. Don't be afraid to make mistakes or take risks.

At the end of this task, write down any examples of when you have used either of these options (*awareness* or *contextual*) in your relationship *and* the occasion—setting and context—in which it was used (example—When my partner came home from work last week and criticized me for not being ready to go grocery shopping, I apologized saying that I sometimes take on more than I can finish on time [*awareness*]; I asked if I had done this a lot lately and if something upsetting happened at work or on the way home [*contextual*]). Record your answers in the space provided at the end of this task.

Definitions:

Awareness Response—A response that starts with the "I" pronoun or an "It," a self statement, indicating an awareness of one's own behavior or internal process. Example—*Partner:* "You never listen to me!" *Respondent:* "I know that I sometimes don't pay attention well."

Contextual Response—A response that asks for more information about reasons and background for the other person's statement which is in the form of a self-statement. Example—*Partner:* "I don't want to go back to see them again ever!" *Respondent:* "You seem really upset. Will you tell me what happened? I really need to know more about the situation to understand your response."

Stimulus Sentences/ Situations	Response Options	
	Awareness	**Contextual**
You're just like your father/mother!		

(continued)

Stimulus Sentences/ Situations	Response Options	
	Awareness	**Contextual**
I can't trust you.		
You're really sloppy!		
If only you wouldn't do that 20 times a day!		
(You and your partner have agreed to go to see a movie that starts at 8 p.m. Your partner has to work but promises to be home on time to go. By 8:30 p.m. s/he's not home and hasn't called. At 8:45 p.m. s/he finally walks in the door.)		
(Your partner appears angry and hasn't said anything to you all day.)		
(Your partner tells you s/he feels you aren't affectionate or sexy enough toward him/her.)		
(Your partner teases you about one of your personal or physical characteristics.)		

(continued)

Name _____

Date _____

Homework Assignment No. 7

PRIORITIES

The purpose of this homework is to examine important areas of your life and how they relate to your relationship with your partner (and/or family). Listed below is a series of six stages which attempt to represent the development of a family over time. A category for *married couples* who have decided never to have children is also listed. Please circle *one* stage or category that best fits you currently. If you have been married before, circle the stage or category in which you currently see yourself and your present partner.

Family Life Cycle Stages

1. Unattached young adult
2. Newly married couple
3. Family with young children
4. Family with adolescents
5. Launching children and moving on
6. Family in later life
7. Married couple who has decided not to have children

Keeping your current family life cycle stage or category in mind, please rank-order in terms of importance the following areas in your life. Use a scale from 1 to 7, with your first ranked area being most important to you down to your seventh ranked area being the least important.

Area	Current Ranking of Importance
Selfhood	_____
Marriage/relationship with partner	_____
Children	_____
Parents/in-laws/siblings	_____
Work	_____
Friends	_____
Leisure time	_____

Now rank-order the same areas for both *the stage before and the stage following* the one you have indicated you are currently in. Example: If you see yourself best fitting into Stage 2 now, you would rank-order the areas as you saw them when you were in Stage 1—unattached young adult—*and as you expect them to be in the next stage, Stage 3—family with young children. For those of you currently in Stage 1*—unattached young adult—for your previous stage use your late adolescence. *For those of you in Stage 6*—family in later life—for your next stage use the time when you will be a couple with grandchildren or great-grandchildren. *For those of you who chose Category 7*—married couple who has decided not to have children—for your previous stage use either Stage 1 or 2—unattached young adult or newly married couple—*and* for your next stage, use Stage 6—family in later life.

	Ranking of Importance	
Area	Previous Stage	Next Stage
Selfhood	_____	_____
Marriage/relationship with partner	_____	_____
Children	_____	_____
Parents/in-laws/siblings	_____	_____
Work	_____	_____
Friends	_____	_____
Leisure time	_____	_____

(continued)

Make up your own stimulus sentences:

Response Options

Stimulus Sentences/ Situations	Awareness	Contextual

Feedback

Option(s) used (awareness or contextual): ___/___

Occasion—setting and context—with my partner in which I used it (example —*Awareness*: When I got home late after visiting a friend and my partner was angry at me, I apologized for my tardiness, said this is a pattern we had experienced before, and suggested we attempt to come up with ways to change this):

Now complete the next section on SELFHOOD.

SELFHOOD:

The cornerstone of all these priorities is *selfhood*. How do you define it and what does it mean to you?

_____

SELFISHNESS:

How is selfhood different from selfishness?

_____

How do you express or manifest your selfhood?

_____

RESPONSIBILITY:

What does it mean to you to take responsibility for yourself?

_____

To take responsibility for oneself means to use the personal pronoun "I," instead of the pronoun "YOU." Give instances where your negative use of the pronoun "YOU" instead of the pronoun "I" has resulted in negative consequences for your partner and/or your family.

1. _____

2. _____

3. _____

(continued)

Are you convinced that using sentences with the NEGATIVE YOU produces negative consequences for you and your partner (family)? If you are not yet convinced, go on and use the NEGATIVE YOU. See *what happens* to you and your partner.

PERFECTION:

How would you rate yourself as far as having *high standards* (i.e., perfectionism)? Circle which of these ratings apply to you.

HIGH   MEDIUM   LOW   VERY LOW

If you rate HIGH or MEDIUM discuss what perfectionism does to you and your partner (family).

What are the positive consequences?

_____

What are the negative consequences?

_____

Now briefly describe yourself in four of your major family roles as you were in the past, as you are now in the present, and as you want to be in the future.

ROLE	PAST	PRESENT	FUTURE
As a *Child* (son, daughter) to your parents			
As a *Person* in your own right			
As a *Partner* to your partner			
As a *Parent* to your children			
As a *Parent* to your parents			

(continued)

Name _____

Date _____

Homework Assignment No. 8
THE TRIANGLE OF LIVING

Please answer the following questions to the best of your ability.

Having

1. Money

   a. What does money mean to you (your marriage or family)?

   _____
   _____
   _____

   b. What kinds of conflicts are there about money?

   _____
   _____
   _____

2. Goods

   a. What do goods (possessions, material things) mean to you (your marriage or family)?

   _____
   _____
   _____

   b. What kinds of conflicts are there about goods (gifts, things, purchases)?

   _____
   _____
   _____

Doing

1. Services

   a. Who performs what chores (or services) in this marriage (family)?

   _____
   _____
   _____

   b. How does this arrangement work for this marriage (family)?

   _____
   _____
   _____

(continued)

Now take some time to write down responses to each of the following topics.

Attachments:
Persons who are presently important to you or who were important to you at different times or stages in your life (examples—when you were growing up, getting married, getting your first job).

_____
_____
_____

Beliefs:
In a few words list your most important beliefs or guiding principles of your life.

_____
_____
_____

Commitments:
List areas in your life into which you are now putting most energy or time.

_____
_____
_____

RESOURCES

Finally, rank-order the following relationship and family *resources* for yourself currently. Rank-order them from 1 to 6 with your first ranked resource being most important down to your sixth ranked resource being least important.

Resource	Ranking of Importance
Goods—tangible products, objects, and materials	
Information—advice, opinions, instruction, and enlightenment	
Love—affectionate regard, warmth, and comfort	
Money—income, monetary wealth	
Services—labor for another, work	
Status—self-worth, regard, and esteem	

Now take all the time you need to discuss your rankings and your answers with those of your partner. How helpful or hurtful are these rankings and answers to you, your partner (and/or your family)? Keep a written record of your discussion.

Being

1. LOVE

a. What does love mean to this marriage (family)?

_____
_____

b. How is love shown or demonstrated?

_____
_____

c. Is love used as a commodity to bribe or blackmail family members?

_____
_____

2. IMPORTANCE

a. How important are each of you to yourselves and to others in the family?

_____
_____

b. How is this importance shown or expressed inside the family?

_____
_____

c. How is this importance shown or expressed outside the family?

_____
_____

d. How do you fail to show your individual importance?

_____
_____

(continued)

2. Information

a. What kind of information is allowed in this marriage (family)?
   TV programs (what kind, for how long) and movies

_____
_____

   Newspapers and/or magazines

_____
_____

   Books (who reads what?)

_____
_____

   Relatives (get-togethers, frequency of meetings, feelings about visits, etc.)

_____
_____

   Friends and neighbors

_____
_____

   Others (visitors, drop-ins, entertainments, etc.)

_____
_____

b. Which of the preceding are most important? To whom? How? Why?

_____
_____

(continued)

Name _____

Date _____

Homework Assignment No. 9
GUIDELINES FOR NEGOTIATION

Dear Partners:

The purpose of these guidelines is to help you to learn what most of us do not know how to do, i.e., to negotiate important issues and differences between and among us. These guidelines are based on the assumption that negotiation is the most important factor in most intimate relationships, and especially in marriage. We cannot promise you happiness. However, we can help you learn this process *if each of you is committed to learning*. In our experience with countless couples and families, we have found that the major deficit we have is our inability to negotiate creatively and constructively. We hope these guidelines will be helpful to do so. However, if any one of you is committed to failing and to defeating yourself and the other, there is no question that neither these guidelines nor any other form of service will be helpful to you.

Most of these guidelines are negotiable; that is, if you find that some other approach or deviation from these guidelines is helpful to you, by all means use it. Do let us know what you have found useful so that we can make it part of our experience. There are two guidelines that we feel are *not negotiable* and they are (a) negotiating by appointment, and (b) negotiating in writing.

a. **Negotiating by appointment**: We believe that it is absolutely necessary for a couple or a family to set up *one hour* a week in the home to practice and apply the principles and skills we plan to teach you. If you want to save money and time, there is no substitute for your meeting together at a *prearranged time*, which we consider part of our work. Of course, if you want to defeat us and yourselves, the best way to do it is to avoid setting and keeping these appointments.

b. **Negotiating by writing**: We believe that it is essential for couples to start keeping a record of what they negotiate about. What you negotiate about is *your business*, which you may share with us to the extent that it will help us understand how well you negotiate or fail to negotiate. Each of you should start a notebook where you are going to jot down whenever an issue arises in your relationship that you feel you need to negotiate with your partner. As you progress you may be able to develop *one* notepad for both of you. However, to begin with we would like to see each of you keep separate notes. You may write them before your appointment, during, or after, as you find most comfortable.

Once we have established these two guidelines, we want to let you in on our principle for negotiation, which is at the basis of the next five guidelines to follow:

Principle: On any issue in marriage and family, feelings and emotions must be expressed nonjudgmentally and shared first, followed by a rational discussion of alternative courses of action (if necessary) and an eventual agreement on which course of action would be mutually satisfactory. Once a course of action is implemented, each of you needs to become more aware of how it is or is not working. You need then to get together to reconsider how and why this course of action is working (or not working), what changes are necessary, or other action(s) needed to work for both of you.

We have broken up this principle into five guidelines or steps:

Step 1. **Emotionality**: The function of emotions and feelings in an intimate union is **to be shared** and **to increase intimacy**. If there is no intimacy, there is no negotiation possible, since **most issues found in a marriage and a family are emotional issues**. To deal with emotionality all of us need to practice "I" statements and avoid like the plague making "You" statements. If you want to destroy this marriage and family, of course, you may need to continue using "You" statements followed by "never" or "always." We cannot stop you.

(continued)

Balance of Having-Doing-Being

1. Which of these—having, doing, being—is most important to you?

2. Why? (i.e., What does it get you?)

3. Are you satisfied with the way you rank these resources?

4. If you are satisfied, why?

5. If you are not satisfied, why not?

6. How could each of you do better?

After answering these questions, discuss them with your partner or family.

Name _____

Date _____

NEGOTIATION PROGRAM FEEDBACK FORM

Now that you have completed this program, please respond to the following questions concerning the use of these homework assignments.

1. Using a scale of 1 to 9, rank the homework assignments according to their usefulness in developing effective communications for your family. Rank the *most useful assignment* as "1." Rank the *least useful* as "9."

Assignments	Rank
The goals of marriage	___
The Golden Rule	___
"I" statements	___
Apathetic, reactive, and conductive styles	___
Emotional, rational, and action options	___
Awareness and contextual options	___
Priorities	___
The triangle of living	___
Negotiation guidelines	___

2. How useful did you find this program for facilitating/developing more effective negotiation skills in your family? Choose one.

— very useful —quite useful — somewhat useful — slightly useful —not useful at all

3. How helpful would you rate this program for teaching/developing negotiation skills to other families? Choose one.

— very helpful — quite helpful — somewhat helpful — slightly helpful — not helpful at all

4. How useful would you rate this program in terms of developing or improving your relationships in general? Choose one.

— very useful — quite useful — somewhat useful — slightly useful — not useful at all

5. How likely would you be to recommend this program to other couples you know? Choose one.

— very likely — quite likely — somewhat likely — slightly likely — not at all likely

6. Using your own words, what did you find useful about this program?

_____

_____

_____

7. How could this program be improved?

_____

_____

_____

Once feelings have been expressed and shared by both of you (i.e., by using "I" statements) you may be ready to enter the next step. In any of these steps and especially the first step, you may need more than one meeting to conclude matters. The longer it takes to finish each step, the more stressed and troubled the relationship is. If you cannot share your feelings properly, STOP! There is no need to go any further.

Step 2. **Rationality**: At this point, each of you may need to generate as many alternative actions (solutions, possibilities, etc.) that may seem to alleviate or to solve whatever problem you are negotiating. Generate as many alternatives as you can freely, no matter how outlandish they may be. Once each of you has done it, come up with whatever patterns (actions or solutions) that may be helpful and satisfactory to you. If you can't and have reached a stalemate or you are becoming emotional, STOP and agree to continue next week at an appointed time to see whether you can come up with a solution to help (re)solve this impasse.

Step 3. **Activity**: Implement whatever course of action you have agreed upon. However, keep in mind that whatever you have agreed to do or not to do is *preliminary and tentative*. It does not become set until each of you is able to evaluate its usefulness and you have shared with the other whatever misgivings (or lack of them) you may have. Give yourself time for this pattern to take place before evaluating its success or failure (up to three months if appropriate).

Step 4. **Evaluation** *(Awareness and Feedback)*: Is the agreed-upon solution working? How well and at what costs? What rewards? Should you (a) persist with it, (b) change parts of it and improve it, or (c) start using an altogether different solution?

At this point (as in Step 1), you need to share whatever feelings you may have about what is going on before considering alternatives or changes.

Step 5. **Context**: It is important that throughout this process (Steps 1 through 4) you become aware of whatever physical and time contexts and constraints you may be negotiating about. Are you negotiating only within your relationship? Or are you negotiating issues or conflicts that include others outside your relationship, such as: your children, in-laws, neighbors, or agencies (schools, health care)? Are you dealing with the past, present, or future? You may need to clarify the limits of your negotiation in terms of how and what you control (usually the past and the future are not negotiable).

In spite of these guidelines, we know that you will experience defeats, failures, false starts, wrong turns, detours, and blind alleys. They are all part of the process of trial and error that is necessary to learn to negotiate.

To gain some experience in applying these guidelines for negotiation, we have constructed an exercise for you and your partner to do. Please list below five issues, differences, or troublesome aspects of your relationship that you feel you would like to negotiate. Rank-order them from 1 to 5 with your first ranked item being a small difference or issue in your relationship down to your fifth ranked item being one of large conflictual size or difficulty. Use all numbers from 1 to 5 only once. Each of you is to make up a list of your own.

After you've made up your list, pick either your number 1 or 2 ranked issue and apply the guidelines for negotiation of this issue with your partner. At this point we want you to tackle only an issue or conflict of low intensity. We suggest you pick an easy issue at first because we want you to (a) learn the process of negotiation with a minimum of trouble and (b) experience some initial success with this new approach. Once you have learned the process, you can use it as an approach to larger and more difficult issues requiring future negotiations in your relationship. Good Luck!

Issue/Difference/Conflict: Rankings

1. _____   ___

2. _____   ___

3. _____   ___

4. _____   ___

5. _____   ___

Appendix C

Intimacy SHWAs

Name _____

Date _____

INTIMACY PROGRAM

Homework Assignment No. 1

LOVE-CARING

1. What is love? Please write your definition.

_____

Please think for a moment about the following definition of love. Love includes at least four separate and distinct processes: (a) caring, (b) seeing the good, (c) forgiveness, and (d) intimacy. Can you improve on these four?

_____
_____
_____
_____

2. For you, what is caring?

_____
_____

a. What is showing care?

_____
_____

b. How do you show caring emotionally?

_____
_____

c. Physically?

_____
_____

d. Mentally?

_____
_____

(continued)

3. How do you take care of yourself?

a. Emotionally _____
b. Physically _____
c. Mentally _____

4. How do you express your care for the people you love and who love you? Please describe in detail.

a. Partner

_____
_____
_____
_____

b. Children

_____
_____

c. Parents (and in-laws)

_____
_____

5. How could you improve the way you care for yourself? By what means?

_____
_____

a. What would you do?

_____
_____

(continued)

6. How can you improve caring for those you love and who love you? (What exactly would you do?)

a. Partner

_____
_____
_____

b. Children

_____
_____
_____

c. Parents

_____
_____
_____

d. In-laws

_____
_____
_____

e. Others (who are they?)

_____
_____
_____

7. How does your caring compare and how is it different from the ways your partner cares for you?

_____
_____
_____

(continued)

8. Families differ in the way caring is expressed. For example, different cultures can vary markedly in how they express caring. Does it seem to you that some families you have known are better at showing care than others? _____ Who are they and what did they do?

_____
_____
_____

9. Compare and contrast your answers with your partner and see if you can come up with an agreement of how you *both* care for yourselves and each other.

_____
_____
_____

Name _____

Date _____

Homework Assignment No. 2
SEEING THE GOOD

1. Check on the outcome of previous homework.

_____
_____

2. What does "seeing the good" mean to you?

_____
_____

3. What do you see that is good in yourself (explain)? Is it hard to see the good in yourself? Write down your positive points or characteristics. How do you feel when you think of the good in yourself?

_____
_____
_____

4. Why do you think you may have a hard time seeing the good in yourself?

_____
_____
_____

5. Now write down possibly negative points or characteristics about yourself. How does this make you feel?

_____
_____
_____

6. Is it easier/harder to see the bad? Why?

_____
_____
_____

(continued)

7. How would we benefit by seeing the good in ourselves and in others? Do you see the good in others? Is it easy?

_____
_____

8. Is it easier to see their faults? Do you have a reason why? What is your reason?

_____
_____

9. Why should we seek the good?

_____
_____

Would you accept as an answer a reduction of tension within ourselves and others?

_____
_____

10. If you cannot see the good in yourself, how can you see it in others?

_____
_____

11. Please list your significant others; rate your ability to see the good in each one. Who is the easiest/hardest?

	Easy	Moderate	Difficult	Impossible	Why?
Partner					
Mother					
Father					
Sister (1)					

(continued)

	Easy	Moderate	Difficult	Impossible	Why?
Sister (2)					
Other sisters					
Brother (1)					
Brother (2)					
Other brothers					
Best friend (1)					
Best friend (2)					

12. **Homework:** During the next week discuss these questions with your partner and write down below all instances in which you exercised SEEING THE GOOD in yourself and others.

Yourself	Your Partner

(continued)

At the end of the week,

13. Compare this list with your partner:

   a. What similarities and differences did you find?

_____
_____
_____

   b. Can you find a substitute for seeing the good?

_____
_____
_____

14. How will you and your partner continue to see the good in yourselves and each other?

_____
_____
_____

Name _____

Date _____

Homework Assignment No. 3

LOVE-FORGIVENESS

1. How did you feel about last week's homework? What were the results?

_____
_____

2. If you failed to perform this homework assignment, can you forgive yourself? If YES, explain; if NO, explain.

_____
_____

3. Is it easy or hard for you to forgive?

_____
_____
_____

4. Please think for a moment about the following concept of forgiveness: Forgiveness is canceling our expectation of perfection in ourselves and others. Could you accept this definition? Why/why not?

_____
_____
_____

5. Do you think it is possible to love yourself and others without forgiveness? Explain.

_____
_____
_____

6. What kinds of feelings do you have when you forgive or are forgiven?

_____
_____

a. Is it the same as forgiving yourself?

_____
_____

(continued)

b. How do you feel when you forgive yourself?

_____
_____

7. Who has been the most forgiving person in your life? What did you learn from him/her?

_____
_____

8. Who has been the least forgiving person in your life? What did you learn from that experience?

_____
_____

9. Often we equate perfection with goodness and imperfection with badness. This is a very destructive match. To be perfect means to be heavenly and to be imperfect means to be human. To be human means to make mistakes. How do you feel about forgiving yourself for being human and having made mistakes?

_____
_____
_____

10. Why do you not forgive yourself?

_____
_____

a. Are some things easier to forgive?

_____
_____

b. Why?

_____
_____

11. Why do you find it hard to forgive others?

_____
_____

(continued)

12. If you were to forgive yourself or your partner, would you hesitate and resist?

13. What would you have to give up in order to forgive?

14. Do you think you could use forgiveness to restore love in your life? In what way?

15. Please list several ways you could use forgiveness to restore a damaged relationship or hurt feelings.

16. What would you give up in the process?

17. **Homework**: Discuss these questions with your mate and during the next week list all the instances in which you use forgiveness. Use the rest of this sheet to list all the instances of forgiveness for the next week.

(continued)

Name _____
Date _____

Homework Assignment No. 4

LOVE-INTIMACY (I)

1. Did you do your homework on forgiving? What improvements (if any) have you made in forgiving?

   a. Forgiving yourself?

   b. Forgiving others?

2. What does intimacy mean to you?

3. Please think for a moment about the following definition of intimacy: Intimacy is sharing hurts and the sharing of our hurts and fears of being hurt with those we love and who love us. Does this have meaning for you? Yes _____ No _____ What meaning does this have for you?

4. This definition stresses that love and hurt are intertwined to the extent that we hurt when those we love also hurt. (Comment)

5. If this definition is acceptable to you, we need to define HURT as any action, situation, or event that saddens us, like frustrations, losses, rejections, and humiliations. Facing up to our errors, mistakes, and neediness can also be hurtful. Can you think of other hurts?

(continued)

6. When is the last time you shared your hurts with your partner?

What happened?

7. Sharing our hurts and our fears of being hurt with those we love and who love us is very hard because:

   a. We need to have a sense of self to share it with others. How does this point apply to you?

   b. We only hurt the ones we love. How does this point apply to you?

   c. We need to seek comfort from the very ones we have hurt or who have hurt us. How does this point apply to you?

8. **Homework**: Discuss these issues with your partner and think of instances where you were able (or failed) to share your hurts with those you love and who love you; take the risk and discuss a recent failure on your part to share your hurts with your partner.

Name _____

Date _____

Homework Assignment No. 5
LOVE-INTIMACY (II)

1. What are some recent instances where you were able to or failed to share your hurts with someone you love?

_____
_____
_____

What happened?

_____
_____
_____

2. Up till now, how have you dealt with your hurts and fears of being hurt? List the ways and describe how you may have avoided sharing these hurts with someone you love.

_____
_____
_____

3. How did your approach work for you in the past? Did you get what you wanted?

_____
_____
_____

4. How did it work for those who love you?

_____
_____
_____

5. Are you now ready to share your hurts with the one you love? If YES, why? If NO, why?

_____
_____
_____

(continued)

6. What are you afraid might happen if you did share your hurts?

_____
_____

7. Sharing of hurts is very scary because we are afraid of losing our sense of self, losing our mind, losing control, breaking down, or even losing our lives. What does sharing of your hurts mean to you?

_____
_____

8. If you are not ready to share your hurts with your partner, would you be willing to share his/her hurts? If YES, why? If NO, why?

_____
_____

9. **Homework:** Discuss these issues with your partner and think more about possible reasons why you may not be ready to share your hurts with him/her. Write here any added comments you could not write above.

_____
_____
_____
_____
_____
_____
_____

Name _____

Date _____

Homework Assignment No. 6

LOVE-INTIMACY (III)

1. a. What have you concluded about your inability to share your hurts with your partner?

   _____

   _____

   _____

   b. Is your nonsharing of hurts due to unwillingness or to inability?

   _____

   _____

   c. Do you think that you could develop this skill—sharing hurt—with time? _____

   _____

2. Are you willing to work on sharing your hurts? If you are not ready, stop here. If you are ready, go on.

3. The two hardest words in the English language are "I hurt." The three hardest words are "It hurts me." Before sharing with your partner, allow yourself to get in touch with whatever hurts you. Close your eyes if necessary and concentrate on getting in touch with your hurts. When you are ready, complete the following:

   a. I hurt when _____

   b. It hurts me when _____

4. We do not need to find excuses or reasons for our hurts. We hurt because we are human beings, not robots. Do not allow anyone, especially you yourself, to belittle your hurts or "reason" you out of your hurts. We are entitled to feel hurt. However, we are not entitled to use our hurts to clobber our partners with them. Please comment.

   _____

   _____

   (continued)

5. How we share our hurts is one thing; how we express them is another. Please comment.

   _____

   _____

6. Take the risk of sharing your hurts with your partner. Then write in the space below what happened.

   _____

   _____

7. Now that this sharing has taken place, did you find it helpful to you? If not, why not? If yes, why?

   _____

   _____

8. Review the whole process from the beginning. Write down any comment or reaction that would be useful in improving this approach.

   _____

   _____

   _____

Name _____

Date _____

INTIMACY PROGRAM FEEDBACK FORM

Now that you have completed this program, please respond to the following questions concerning the usefulness of these intimacy tasks.

1. Using a scale of 1 to 6, rank the six intimacy assignments according to their usefulness in improving/developing closeness with your partner. Rank the most useful task as "1." Rank the least useful task at "6."

Task	Rank
Love-caring	____
Seeing the good	____
Love-forgiveness	____
Love-intimacy (I)	____
Love-intimacy (II)	____
Love-intimacy (III)	____

2. How useful did you find the entire program for improving/developing greater intimacy between you and your partner and between you and your family? Choose one of the following:

____ very useful ____ quite useful ____ somewhat useful ____ slightly useful ____ not useful at all

3. How would you rate this program's helpfulness for teaching couples and families to develop intimacy? Choose one of the following:

____ very helpful ____ quite helpful ____ somewhat helpful ____ slightly helpful ____ not helpful at all

4. How would you rate this program's usefulness in developing or improving your relationship in general? Choose one of the following:

____ very useful ____ quite useful ____ somewhat useful ____ slightly useful ____ not useful at all

5. How likely would you be to recommend this program to other couples of families you know? Choose one of the following:

____ very likely ____ quite likely ____ somewhat likely ____ slightly likely ____ not likely at all

6. Using your own words, what did you find useful about this program?

_____
_____
_____

(continued)

7. How could this program be improved?

_____
_____
_____
_____
_____
_____
_____
_____
_____
_____
_____
_____
_____
_____

Appendix D

Follow-Up Questionnaire

FOLLOW-UP QUESTIONNAIRE

Name _____
Date _____
Services rendered from (date) _____
to _____

1. Current status:
_____ married
_____ divorced
_____ remarried
_____ widowed

2. Current job or position:
_____

3. Family composition:
a. Spouse: Education _____ Occupation _____
b. Children (list age, sex, and current occupation if applicable)
_____
_____
_____
_____

c. State age, sex, and occupation of anyone else living in your household:
_____
_____
_____

d. If you have children in school, how are they doing?
_____ very well
_____ well
_____ not well

4. Work history:
Since the termination of family therapy, you have worked steadily at the same job for how many years? _____
changed jobs _____ times.
been unemployed for _____ (length of time).
Other: _____

5. Current work:
a. How satisfied are you with your current job?
_____ very satisfied
_____ satisfied
_____ not satisfied

(continued)

b. How well did family therapy help you in coping with your current job?
_____ very well
_____ OK
_____ not very well

c. What might family therapy have done to prepare you better for your current job?
_____
_____
_____
_____

6. Medical history:
a. How healthy are you?
_____ very healthy
_____ somewhat healthy
_____ not so healthy
Comments or exceptions: _____

b. How healthy is your family as a whole?
_____ very healthy
_____ somewhat healthy
_____ not so healthy
Comments or exceptions: _____

7. Mental health:
a. How satisfied are you with your life?
_____ very satisfied
_____ somewhat satisfied
_____ not very satisfied

b. Please give us any information that will help us understand your current status and level of satisfaction.
_____
_____
_____

8. Family therapy:
a. On a scale from 1 to 5 (1 = completely satisfied; 5 = completely dissatisfied), how satisfied were you with the family therapy services?
Circle one: 1   2   3   4   5

(continued)

b. Have there been significant life changes (births, deaths, weddings, moves, job changes) in your immediate family since family therapy ended? If yes, please explain.

_____

_____

_____

c. Have you or members of your family received further professional help or therapy since the termination of family therapy here?

_____

_____

d. If you and your family are having problems, what do you think we should do or should have done to prevent those problems?

_____

_____

_____

_____

e. All things considered, which of the following best describes your life and the lives of your immediate family since you began family therapy?

_____ better
_____ same
_____ worse

f. Which of the following best describes your initial problem after family therapy?

_____ much better
_____ no change
_____ worse
_____ much worse

g. During therapy, did you notice changes in you and in members of your family? Please explain your answer.

_____

_____

_____

h. Since you finished therapy, have there been improvements in old problems that were not directly dealt with in therapy? Please explain.

_____

_____

_____

(continued)

After completing the questionnaire, please return it to us. Thank you for your help. We will appreciate any suggestions that will help us to improve our services to families. Feel free to add other comments on the remainder of this page.

_____

_____

_____

_____

_____

_____

_____

_____

_____

_____

_____

_____

_____

_____

References

Adams, L. (1971). Multiple family set therapy. In J. O. Bradt & C. J. Moynihan (Eds.), *Systems therapy: Selected papers, theory, technique, research*. Washington, DC, 5225 Longhboro Rd, NW, pp. 343–348.

Adler, G., & Myerson, P. G. (Eds.). (1973). *Confrontation in psychotherapy*. New York: Science House.

Ainsworth, M. D. S. (1979). Object relations, dependency, and attachment: A theoretical review of the infant-mother relationship. *Child Development, 50*, 969–1025.

Alexander, J., & Barton, C. (1976). Behavioral systems therapy with delinquent families. In D. H. L. Olson (Ed.), *Treating relationships*. Lake Mills, IA: Graphic.

Alexander, J., & Parsons, B. V. (1982). *Functional family therapy*. Monterey, CA: Brooks/Cole Publishing.

Alkire, A. A. (1972). Enactment of social power and role behavior in families of disturbed and nondisturbed preadolescents. *Developmental Psychology, 7*, 270–276.

Allman, L. R. (1982a). The aesthetic preference: Overcoming the pragmatic error. *Family Process, 21*, 43–45.

Allman, L. R. (1982b). The poetic-mind: Further thoughts on an "aesthetic preference." *Family Process, 21*, 415–428.

Allport, G. W. (1968). The fruits of eclecticism: Bitter or sweet? *Acta Psychologica, 23*, 27–44.

Anderson, C. D. (1981). Expression of affect and physiological response in psychosomatic patients. *Journal of Psychosomatic Research, 25*, 143–149.

Anderson, C. W. (1980). Attachment in daily separations: Reconceptualizing day care and maternal employment issues. *Child Development, 51*, 242–245.

Andolfi, M. (1979). *Family therapy: An interactional approach*. New York: Plenum Press.

Annet, J. (1969). *Feedback and human behavior*. Baltimore: Penguin Books.

Anonymous. (1972). Toward the differentiation of self in one's own family. In J. L. Framo (Ed.), *Family interaction: A dialogue between family researchers and family therapists*. New York: Springer.

Antonucci, T. (1976). Attachment: A life-span concept. *Human Development, 19*, 135–142.

Applebaum, S. Q. (1977). *The anatomy of change: A Menninger Foundation report on testing the effects of psychotherapy*. New York: Plenum Press.

Argyle, M. (1980). The analysis of social interactions. In M. Brenner (Ed.), *The structure of action*. New York: St. Martin's Press, p. 362.

Armstead, R. W. (1977). The relationship of body awareness and physical attractiveness to emotional adjustment. Unpublished dissertation, California School of Professional Psychology, San Francisco, *Dissertation Abstracts International*, pp. 4661–4662.

Aronfreed, J. (1968). *Conduct and conscience: The socialization of internalized control over behavior*. New York: Academic Press.

Ashby, W. R. (1970). Analysis of the system to be modeled. In R. M. Stogdill (Ed.), *The process of model building in the behavioral sciences*. Columbus, OH: Ohio State University Press.

Aubrey, R. F. (1980). Technology of counseling and the science of behavior: A rapprochement. *The Personnel and Guidance Journal, 58*, 318–327.

Ausne, B. (1977). *Reason and action*. Boston: D. Reidel.

Averill, J. R. (1979). The emotions. In E. Staub (Ed.), *Personality: Basic aspects and current research*. Englewood Cliffs, NJ: Prentice-Hall, pp. 133–199.

Averill, J. R. (1980). Anger. In R. A. Dienstbier (Ed.), *Nebraska symposium on motivation 1978: Human emotion*. Lincoln, NE: University of Nebraska Press, 1978, pp. 1–80.

Bach, G. R., & Wyden, P. (1968). *The intimate enemy: How to fight fair in love and marriage*. New York: William Morrow & Co.

Baggozzi, R. P. (1978). The construct validity of the affective behavioral and cognitive components of attitude by analysis of covariance structures. *Multivariate Behavioral Research, 13*, 9–31.

Bahr, S. J., Bowerman, D. E., & Gecas, V. (1974). Adolescent perceptions of conjugal power. *Social Forces, 52*, 357–367.

Bales, R. F. (1951). *Interaction process analysis*. Cambridge, MA: Addison–Wesley.

Balswick, J. (1979). The inexpressive male: Functional conflict and role theory as contrasting explanations. *Family Coordinator, 28*, 330–336.

Bandura, A. (1982). Self-efficacy mechanism in human agency. *American Psychologist, 37*, 122–147.

Barrilleaux, S. P., & Bauer, R. H. (1976). The effects of Gestalt awareness training on experiencing levels. *International Journal of Group Psychotherapy, 26*, 431–440.

Barron, J. (1971). *Psychotherapy: A psychological perspective*. New York: Simon & Schuster.

Barry, W. H. (1970). Marriage research and conflict: An interpretative review. *Psychological Bulletin, 73*, 41–54.

Barton, C., & Alexander, J. F. (1981). Functional family therapy. In A. S. Gurman & D. P. Kniskern (Eds.), *Handbook of family therapy*. New York: Brunner/Mazel.

Bateson, G. (1972). *Steps to an ecology of mind*. San Francisco: Chandler Publishing.

Bateson, G. (1977). Epilogue: The growth of paradigms for psychiatry. In P. F. Ostwald (Ed.), *Communication and social behavior: Clinical and therapeutic aspects of human behavior*. New York: Grune & Stratton, pp. 331–337.

Battle, J. (1978). Relationship between self-esteem and depression. *Psychological Reports, 42*, 745–746.

Baumrind, D. (1971). Current patterns of parental authority. *Developmental Psychology Monographs, 1*, 1–103.

Beattle, S., & Viney, L. L. (1981). Appraisal of lone parenthood after marital breakdown. *Journal of Personality Assessment, 45*, 415–423.

Beavers, W. R., & Voeller, M. N. (1983). Family models: Comparing and contrasting the Olson circumplex model with the Beavers systems model. *Family Process, 22*, 85–98.

Beels, C. C., & Ferber, A. (1969). Family therapy: A view. *Family Process, 8*, 28–31.

Bell, J. E. (1975). *Family therapy*. New York: Jason Aronson.

Bentley, A. F. (1950). Kinetic inquiry. *Science, 112*, 725–783.

Bergin, A. E., & Garfield, S. L. (Eds.). (1971). *Handbook of psychotherapy and behavior change: An empirical analysis*. New York: John Wiley & Sons.

Bergin, A. E., & Lambert, M. J. (1978). The evaluation of therapeutic outcome. In S. L. Garfield & A. E. Bergin (Eds.), *Handbook of psychotherapy and behavior change*. New York: John Wiley & Sons.

Bernal, G., & Baker, J. (1979). Toward a metacommunicational framework of couple interaction. *Family Process, 18*, 298–302.

Berne, E. (1971). *What do you say after you say hello?* New York: Grove Press.

Beutler, L. E., & Mitchell, R. (1981). Differential psychological outcome among depressed and impulsive patients as a function of analytic and experiential treatment procedures. *Psychology, 44*, 297–306.

Bird, B. (1955). *Talking with patients*. Philadelphia: J. B. Lippincott.

Bochner, A. (1978). On taking ourselves seriously: An analysis of some persistent problems and promising directions in interpersonal research. *Human Communication Research, 4*, 179–191.

Bockus, F. (1980). *Couple therapy*. New York: Jason Aronson, Inc.

Bohen, H. H., & Viveros-Long, A. (1981). *Balancing jobs and family life: Do flexible work schedules help?* Philadelphia: Temple University Press.

Boring, E. G. (1930). Psychology for eclectics. In C. C. Murchison (Ed.), *Psychology of 1930*. Worcester, MA: Clark University Press.

Boszormenyi-Nagy, I, & Spark, G. (1973). *Invisible loyalties*. New York: Harper and Row.

Boszormenyi-Nagy, I., & Ulrich, D. N. (1981). Contextual family therapy. In A. S. Gurman & D. P. Kniskern (Eds.), *Handbook of family therapy*. New York: Brunner/Mazel.

Bowen, M. (1978). *Family therapy in clinical practice*. New York: Jason Aronson.

Bowen, M. (1985). Foreword. In S. R. Sauber, L. L'Abate, & G. R. Weeks, *Family therapy: Basic concepts and terms*. Rockville, MD: Aspen Systems Corp.

Bower, G. H. (1981). Mood and memory. *American Psychologist, 36*, 129–148.

Bowerman, C. D., & Bahr, S. J. (1973). Conjugal power and adolescent identification with parents. *Sociometry, 36*, 366–377.

Bowlby, J. (1982). Attachment and loss: Retrospect and prospect. *American Journal of Orthopsychiatry, 52*, 664–678.

Bradbard, M. B., & Endsley, R. C. (September 1978). *Developing young children's curiosity: A review of research with implications for teachers.* ERIC Clearinghouse on Early Childhood Education, Urbana, IL: Document 162–721.

Bradt, J. O. (1971). Some traditional concepts: Roadblocks of change. In J. O. Bradt & C. J. Moynihan (Eds.), *Systems therapy: Selected papers. theory. technique. research.* Washington, DC, 5225 Longhboro Road, NW.

Braithwaite, R. B. (1953). *Scientific explanation.* Cambridge, England: Cambridge University Press.

Brandsma, J. M. (1975). Self-concept, science, and the concept of a fallible human being. *Rational Living, 10*, 15–18.

Brodkin, A. M. (1980). Family therapy: The making of a mental health movement. *American Journal of Orthopsychiatry, 50*, 4–17.

Brody, S. (1964). *Passivity: A study of its development and expression in boys.* New York: International Universities Press.

Broffenbrenner, U. (1976). Who cares for America's children? Testimony before a joint House-Senate hearing on the *Child and Family Services Act, 1975.* Washington, DC: U.S. Government Printing Office, pp. 1798–1916.

Broffenbrenner, U. (1977). Toward an experimental ecology of human behavior. *American Psychologist, 32*, 513–531.

Brown, G. W., Birley, J. L. T., & Wing, J. K. (1972). Influence of family life on the course of schizophrenic disorders: A replication. *British Journal of Psychiatry, 121*, 241–258.

Buchler, J. (1961). *The concept of method.* New York: Columbia University Press.

Buie, D. H., & Adler, G. (1973). The uses of confrontation in the psychotherapy of borderline patients. In G. Adler and P. G. Myerson (Eds.), *Confrontation in psychotherapy.* New York: Science House.

Bunge, M. (1959). *Metascientific queries.* Springfield, IL: Charles C Thomas.

Burgess, R. L., & Conger, R. D. (1978). Family interaction in abusive, neglectful, and normal families. *Child Development, 49*, 1163–1173.

Campbell, D. T. (1975). On the conflicts between biological and social evolution and between psychology and moral tradition. *American Psychologist, 30*, 1103–1126.

Carkhuff, R. R. (1972). *The art of helping.* Amherst, MA: Human Resource Development Press.

Carlozzi, A. F., Gaa, J. P., & Liberman, D. B. (1983). Empathy and ego development. *Journal of Counseling Psychology, 30*, 113–116.

Case, N. S., & Landesman, C. (Eds.). (1968). *Readings in the theory of action.* Bloomington, IN: Indiana University Press.

Christensen, B., & Scoresby, A. L. (1975). *The measurement of complementary, symmetrical and/or parallel relationships in family dyads.* Unpublished manuscript, Brigham Young University.

Christensen, B., & Scoresby, A. L. (1976). *Factorial validity of the relationship styles inventory.* Unpublished manuscript, Brigham Young University.

Cohen, A. I. (1981). Confrontation analysis in groups: Goals of treatment. *Psychotherapy: Theory, Research and Practice, 18*, 441–456.

Coleman, K. H. (1980). Conjugal violence: What 33 men report. *Journal of Marital and Family Therapy, 6*, 207–213.

Coleman, S. B. (1985). *Failures in family therapy.* New York: Guilford Press.

Coombs, R. H. (1966). Value consensus and partner satisfaction among dating couples. *Journal of Marriage and the Family, 28*, 166–173.

Cooney, R. W., & Selman, R. L. (1980). Children's use of social conceptions: Toward a dynamic model of social cognition. *The Personnel and Guidance Journal, 58*, 344–352.

Corwin, H. A. (1973). Therapeutic confrontation: From routine to heroic. In G. Adler & P. G. Myerson (Eds.), *Confrontation in psychotherapy.* New York: Science House.

Coyne, J. C., Denner, B., & Ransom, D. C. (1982). Undressing the fashionable mind. *Family Process, 21*, 391–396.

Cox, F. D. (1967). *Youth, marriage and the seductive society.* Dubuque, IA: W. C. Brown Co.

Cramer, S. H. (Ed.). (1985). *Perspectives on work and the family.* Rockville, MD: Aspen Publications.

Cromwell, R. E., & Olson, D. H. (Eds.). (1975). *Power in families*. New York: John Wiley & Sons.

Curle, A. (1972). *Mystics and militants: A study of awareness, identity and social acceptance*. New York: Harper & Row.

Davis, M. H. (1983). Measuring individual differences in empathy: Evidence for a multi-dimensional approach. *Journal of Personality and Social Psychotherapy, 44*, 113–126.

Davitz, J. R. (1969). *The language of emotion*. New York: Academic Press.

Dell, P. F. (1982a). In search of truth: On the way to clinical epistemology. *Family Process, 21*, 407–414.

Dell, P. F. (1982b). Family theory and the epistemology of Humberto Maturana. In F. W. Kaslow (Ed.), *The international book of family therapy*. New York: Brunner/Mazel.

Derlega, V. J. (1984). Self-disclosure and intimate relationships. In V. J. Derlega (Ed.), *Communication, intimacy, and close relationships*. Orlando, FL: Academic Press.

Derlega, V. J., Wilson, M., & Chalkin, A. L. (1976). Friendship and disclosure reciprocity. *Journal of Personality and Social Psychology, 34*, 578–582.

Deutsch, M. (1973). *The resolution of conflict*. New Haven, CT: Yale University Press.

Dewey, J., & Bentley, A. F. (1949). *Knowing and the known*. Boston: Beacon Press.

Dienstbier, R. A. (1978). Emotional inhibition theory: Establishing roots and exploring future perspectives. In R. A. Dienstbier (Ed.), *Nebraska symposium on motivation—1978: Human emotion*. Lincoln, NE: University of Nebraska Press.

Doane, J. A., Golstein, M. J., & Rodnick, E. H. (1981). Parental patterns of affective style and the development of schizophrenia spectrum disorders. *Family Process, 20*, 337–349.

Doane, J. A., Jones, J. E., Fisher, L., Kitzler, B., Singer, M. T., and Wynne, L. C. (1982). Parental communication deviance as a predictor of competence in children at risk for adult psychiatric disorder. *Family Process, 21*, 211–223.

Douds, J. (1967). The search for an honest experience: Confrontation in counseling and life. In R. R. Carkhuff & B. G. Berensen, *Beyond counseling and psychotherapy*. New York: Holt, Rinehart, & Winston.

Druckman, D. (Ed.). (1977). *Negotiation: Social-psychological perspectives*. Beverly Hills, CA: Sage Publications.

Duval, S. S., & Wicklund, R. A. (1972). *A theory of objective self-awareness*. New York: Academic Press.

Egan, G. (1976). Confrontation. *Group and Organization Studies, 1*(2), 223–243.

Ellis, A. (1982). Feedback: Major systems. *The Personnel and Guidance Journal, 61*, 6–7.

Epstein, N. B., & Bishop, D. S. (1981). Problem-centered systems therapy of the family. In A. S. Gurman & D. P. Kniskern (Eds.), *Handbook of family therapy*. New York: Brunner/Mazel.

Evans, N. S. (1976). Mourning as a family secret. *Journal of the American Academy of Child Psychiatry, 15*, 502–509.

Fagan, J. (1970). The tasks of the therapist. In J. Fagan & I. L. Shepherd (Eds.), *Gestalt therapy now: Theory, techniques, applications*. Palo Alto, CA: Science and Behavior Books.

Farley, J. E. (1979). Separation and individuation tolerance: A developmental conceptualization of the nuclear family. *Journal of Marital and Family Therapy, 5*, 61–67.

Feuerlicht, I. (1978). *Alienation: From the past to the future*. Westport, CT: Greenwood.

Fisch, R., Weakland, J. H., & Segal, L. (1982). *The teaching of change: Doing therapy briefly*. San Francisco: Jossey-Bass.

Fisher, S. (1976). Conditions affecting boundary responses to messages out of awareness. *Journal of Nervous & Mental Disease, 162*, 313–322.

Fitzpatrick, M. A., & Best, P. G. (1979). Dyadic adjustment in traditional, independent and separate relationships: A validation study. *Communication Monographs, 46*, 167–178.

Fitzpatrick, M. A., Fallis, S., & Vance, L. (1982). Multifunctional coding of conflict resolution strategies in marital subjects. *Family Relations, 31*, 61–70.

Foá, U., & Foá, E. (1974). *Societal structures of the mind*. Springfield, IL: Charles C Thomas.

Fogarty, T. F. (1971). Family structure in terms of triangles. In J. O. Bradt & C. J. Moynihan (Eds.), *Systems therapy: Selected papers, theory, technique, research*. Washington, DC, 5225 Longhboro Road, NW.

Fogarty, T. F. (1979). Triangles. *The Best of the Family 1973–1978*. Special Issue, pp. 41–49.

Fogarty, T. F. (1980). Operative principles—Part III: Facts and feelings. *The Family, 8*, 56–61.

Framo, J. L. (1982). *Explorations in marital and family therapy*. New York: Springer Publishing Co.

Frantz, T. T. (Ed.). (1984). *Death and grief in the family*. Rockville, MD: Aspen Publications.

Freeman, D. (1976). Phases of family treatment. *The Family Coordinator, 21*, 265–270.

French, J. R. P., Jr., & Raven, B. (1959). The bases of social power. In D. Cartwright (Ed.), *Studies in social power*. Ann Arbor: University of Michigan, Institute for Social Research.

Fried, E. (1970). *Active/passive: The crucial psychological dimension.* New York: Grune & Stratton.

Frey, J., III. (1984). A family/systems approach to illness-maintaining behaviors in chronically ill adolescents. *Family Process, 23,* 251–260.

Gardner, A., & Pritchard, M. (1977). Mourning, mummification and living with the dead. *British Journal of Psychiatry, 130,* 23–28.

Gardner, H. (1983). *Frames of mind: The theory of multiple intelligences.* New York: Basic Books.

Gardner, P., & Loei, T. P. (1981). Depression and self-esteem: An investigation that used behavioral and cognitive approaches to the treatment of clinically depressed clients. *Journal of Clinical Psychology, 37,* 128–135.

Garfield, S. L. (1981). Psychotherapy: An 80-year appraisal. *American Psychologist, 36,* 174–183.

Garfield, S. L., & Bergin, A. E. (Eds.). (1978). *Handbook of psychotherapy and behavior change: An empirical analysis.* New York: John Wiley & Sons.

Garfield, S. L., & Kurtz, M. (1976). Clinical psychologists in the 1970's. *American Psychologist, 31,* 1–9.

Gaylin, W. (1979). *Caring.* New York: Avon Publications.

Geerken, M., & Gove, W. R. (1983). *At home and at work: The family's allocation of labor.* Beverly Hills, CA: Sage Publications.

Gendlin, E. (1978). *Focusing.* New York: Everest House.

Gibb, J. R., & Gibb, L. (1969). Leaderless groups: Growth-centered values and potentialities. In H. A. Ott & J. Mann (Eds.), *Ways of growth: Approaches to expanding awareness.* New York: Viking Press, pp. 101–114.

Gibbs, I. P. (1982). *Social control: Views from the social sciences.* Beverly Hills, CA: Sage Publications.

Ginsburg, G. P. (1980). A conception of situated action. In M. Brenner (Ed.), *The structure of action.* New York: St. Martin's Press.

Goethals, G. R. (1984). Review of psychology's sanction for selfishness. *Contemporary Psychology, 29,* 296.

Goev, D. M. (1976). *The psychology of loneliness.* Chicago: Adams.

Gordon, T. (1970). *Parent effectiveness training.* New York: McKay.

Gottman, J. M. (1979). *Marital interaction: Experimental investigations.* New York: Academic Press.

Gottsegen, G. B., & Gottsegen, M. G. (1979). Countertransference: The professional identity defense. *Psychotherapy: Theory, Research and Practice, 16,* 57–60.

Guerney, B. G., Jr. (1977). *Relationship enhancement: Skill training programs for therapy, problem prevention and enrichment.* San Francisco: Jossey-Bass.

Gurman, A. S. (1979). Dimensions of marital therapy: A comparative analysis. *Journal of Marriage and Family Therapy, 5,* 5–16.

Gurman, A. S. (1983). Family therapy research and the "new epistemology." *Journal of Marital and Family Therapy, 9,* 227–234.

Gurman, A. S., & Kniskern, D. P. (1981). *Handbook of family therapy.* New York: Brunner/Mazel.

Haley, J. (1963). *Strategies of psychotherapy.* New York: Grune & Stratton.

Haley, J. (1976). *Problem-solving therapy.* San Francisco: Jossey-Bass.

Hall, E. T. (1976). *Beyond culture.* New York: Anchor Press/Doubleday & Co.

Hampshire, J. (1967). *Thought and action.* New York: The Viking Press.

Hansen, J. C., & L'Abate, L. (1982). *Approaches to family therapy.* New York: Macmillan.

Harper, J. M., Scoresby, A. L., & Boyce, W. D. (1977). The logical levels of complementary, symmetrical, and parallel interaction classes in family dyads. *Family Process, 16,* 199–209.

Hart, J. T., & Tomlinson, T. M. (1970). *New directions in client-centered therapy.* Boston: Houghton Mifflin Co.

Hawkins, J. L. (1976). Counselor involvement in marriage and family counseling. *Journal of Marriage and Family Counseling, 2,* 37–47.

Heath, D. H. (1980). Wanted: A comprehensive model of healthy development. *The Personnel and Guidance Journal, 58,* 391–399.

Heider, F. (1958). *The psychology of interpersonal relations.* New York: John Wiley & Sons.

Henderson, S. (1977). The social network, support and neurosis: The function of attachment in adult life. *British Journal of Psychiatry, 131,* 185–191.

Hermann, M. G., & Kogan, N. (1977). Effects of negotiators' personalities on negotiating behavior. In D. Druckman (Ed.), *Negotiation: Social-psychological perspectives.* Beverly Hills, CA: Sage Publications.

Hershenson, D. B. (1982). A formulation of counseling based on the healthy personality. *Personnel and Guidance Journal, 60,* 406–409.

Herzberg, A. (1946). *Active psychotherapy*. New York: Grune & Stratton.

Hill, D. (1981). Mechanisms of the mind: A psychiatrist's perspective. *British Journal of Medical Psychology, 54*, 1–13.

Hoffman, M. L. (1979). Development of moral thought, feeling, and behavior. *American Psychologist, 34*, 958–966.

Hughes, P., and Brecht, G. (1975). *Vicious circles and infinity: A panoply of paradoxes*. Garden City, NY: Doubleday & Co.

Hunt, W. (Ed.). (1971). *Human behavior and its control*. Cambridge: Schenkman.

Hunter, R. C. A. (1978). Forgiveness, retaliation and paranoid reactions. *Canadian Psychiatric Association Journal, 23*, 167–173.

Hutchins, D. E. (1979). Systematic counseling: The T-F–A model for counselor intervention. *Personnel and Guidance Journal, 57*, 529–531.

Hutchins, D. E. (1982). Ranking major counseling strategies with the TFA/Matrix system. *Personnel and Guidance Journal, 60*, 427–430.

Izard, C. E. (1977). *Human emotions*. New York: Plenum Press.

Izard, C. E. (1978). Emotions as motivations: An evolutionary-developmental perspective. In R. A. Dienstbier (Ed.), *Nebraska symposium on motivation: Human emotions*. Lincoln, NE: University of Nebraska Press, pp. 163–200.

Jaccard, J., & Crawford, R. (1983). *Psychological foundations of attitude and behavior*. New York: Free Press.

Jacobs, A., & Willens, J. G. (1970). Training role behaviors in schizophrenics. *Proceedings of the Annual Convention of American Psychologists Association, 5*, 501–502.

Jacobs, S., & Ostfeld, A. (1977). An epidemiological review of the modality of bereavement. *Psychosomatic Medicine, 39*, 344–357.

Jaffe, J., Peterson, R., & Hodgson, R. (1980). *Addictions: Issues and answers*. New York: Harper & Row.

Janis, I. L., Mahl, G. F., Kagan, J., & Holt, R. R. (1969). *Personality: Dynamics, development, and assessment*. New York: Harcourt, Brace & World.

Jenkin, N. (1957). Affective processes in perception. *Psychological Bulletin, 54*, 100–127.

Jessee, E., & L'Abate, L. (1985). Paradoxical treatment of depression in married couples. In L. L'Abate (Ed.), *Handbook of family psychology and therapy*. Homewood, IL: Dorsey Press.

Johnson, M. P. (1973). Commitment: A conceptual structure and empirical application. *Sociological Quarterly, 14*, 395–406.

Johnson, P. A., & Rosenblatt, P. C. (1981). Grief following childhood loss of a parent. *American Journal of Psychotherapy, 35*, 419–425.

Jourard, S. M. (1958). *Personal adjustment: An approach through the study of healthy personality*. New York: Macmillan.

Jurkovic, C. G., & Selman, R. L. (1980). A developmental analysis of intrapsychic understanding: Treating emotional difficulties. In R. L. Selman and C. G. Jurkovic (Eds.), *New directions for child development: Clinical child development*. San Francisco: Jossey-Bass, pp. 91–112.

Kaffman, M., & Elizur, E. (1979). Children's bereavement reactions following death of the father. *International Journal of Family Therapy, 1*, 203–229.

Kagan, J. (1965). Reflection-impulsivity: Significance of conceptual tempo. In J. D. Krumholtz (Ed.), *Learning and the educational process*. Chicago: Rand McNally.

Kandel, D. B. (1978). Similarity in real-life adolescent friendship pairs. *Journal of Personality and Social Psychology, 36*, 306–312.

Kanouse, D. E., & Hanson, L. R., Jr. (1971). Negativity in evaluation. In E. E. Jones et al., *Attribution: Perceiving the causes of behavior*. Morristown, NY: General Learning Series.

Karpman, S. (1968). Fairy tales and script drama analysis. *Transactional Analysis Bulletin, 7*, 39–43.

Keeney, B. P. (1983). *Aesthetics of change*. New York: Guilford Press.

Keeney, B. P., & Sprenkle, D. H. (1982). Ecosystemic epistemology: Critical implications for the aesthetics and pragmatics of family therapy. *Family Process, 21*, 1–10.

Kegan, R. (1980). Making meaning: The constructive developmental approach to persons and practice. *The Personnel and Guidance Journal, 58*, 373–380.

Kelly, G. A. (1955). *The psychology of personal constructs* (Vols. 1 & 2). New York: Norton.

Kempler, W. (1981). *Experiential psychotherapy within families*. New York: Brunner/Mazel.

Kessell, K., Jaffee, N., Tuchman, B., Watson, C., & Deutsch, A. (1980). A typology of divorcing couples: Implications for mediation and the divorce process. *Family Process, 19*, 101–116.

Kezur, D. (1978). The development of maternal attachment. *Smith College Studies in Social Work, 48*, 183–208.

Kimberlin, C. L., & Friesen, D. D. (1980). Sex and conceptual level: Empathetic responses to ambivalent affect. *Counselor Education and Supervision, 19*, 253–258.

Kimble, G. A. (1984). Psychology's two cultures. *American Psychologist, 39*, 833–839.

Klinger, E. (1977). The nature of fantasy and its clinical uses. *Psychotherapy: Theory, Research, and Practice, 14*, 223–231.

Kniskern, D. P. (1983). The new wave is all wet . . . *The Family Therapy Networker, 7*, 38, 60–62.

Korchin, S. (1976). *Clinical psychology.* New York: Basic Books.

Kreilkamp, T. (1976). *The corrosion of the self: Society's effects on people.* New York: New York University Press.

Kubistant, T. M. (1981). Resolutions of loneliness. *Personnel and Guidance Journal, 59*, 461–465.

Kuhn, T. S. (1962). *The structure of scientific revolutions.* Chicago: University of Chicago Press.

L'Abate, L. (1957). Sanford's uncertainty hypothesis in children. *ETC: Review of General Semantics, 11*, 210–213.

L'Abate, L. (1960). Personality correlates of manifest anxiety in children. *Journal of Consulting Psychology, 24*, 242–248.

L'Abate, L. (1964). *Principles of clinical psychology.* New York: Grune & Stratton.

L'Abate, L. (1968). The laboratory method as an alternative to existing mental health models. *American Journal of Orthopsychiatry, 38*, 296–297.

L'Abate, L. (1969). A communication-information model. In L. L'Abate (Ed.), *Models of clinical psychology.* Atlanta, GA: Georgia State University, pp. 65–71.

L'Abate, L. (1972). An empiricist's rebuttal to humanistic ideology. *World Journal of Psychosynthesis, 4*, 19–24.

L'Abate, L. (1973a). Psychodynamic interventions: A personal statement. In R. H. Woody & Jane D. Woody (Eds.), *Sexual, marital and familial relations: Therapeutic interventions for professional helping.* Springfield, IL: Charles C Thomas, pp. 122–180.

L'Abate, L. (1973b). The laboratory method in clinical child psychology: Three applications. *Journal of Clinical Child Psychology, 2*, 8–10.

L'Abate, L. (1975a). A positive approach to marital and family intervention. In L. R. Wolbert & M. L. Aronson (Eds.), *Group therapy 1975: An overview.* New York: Stratton Intercontinental Medical Book Corp. Reprinted also in L'Abate, L. (1983). *Family therapy: Theory, therapy, and training.* Washington, DC: University Press of America.

L'Abate, L. (1975b). Pathogenic role rigidity in fathers: Some observations. *Journal of Marriage and Family Counseling, 1*, 69–79.

L'Abate, L. (1976). *Understanding and helping the individual in the family.* New York: Grune & Stratton.

L'Abate, L. (1977). Intimacy is sharing hurt feelings: A reply to David Mace. *Journal of Marriage and Family Counseling, 3*, 13–16.

L'Abate, L. (1979). Aggression and construction in children's monitored play therapy. *Journal of Counseling and Psychotherapy, 2*, 137–158.

L'Abate, L. (1980). Inexpressive males or overexpressive females? A reply to Balswick. *Family Relations, 29*, 229–230.

L'Abate, L. (1981a). The role of family conferences in family therapy. *Family Therapy, 8*, 33–38.

L'Abate, L. (1981b). Toward a systematic classification of counseling and therapy, theories, methods, processes, and goals: The E-R-A model. *The Personnel and Guidance Journal, 59*, 263–265.

L'Abate, L. (1983a). Issues of reductionism: Can circular models be reduced to linearity? *Zeitschrift fur Systemische Therapie, 2*, 39–43.

L'Abate, L. (1983b). The answer is no! Reply to Coyne's comments. *Zeitschrift fur Systemische Therapie, 2*, 61–62.

L'Abate, L. (1983c). Styles in intimate relationships: The A-R-C model. *The Personnel and Guidance Journal, 61*, 277–283.

L'Abate, L. (1983d). *Family psychology: Theory, therapy, and training.* Washington, DC: University Press of America.

L'Abate, L. (1985). Paradoxical techniques: One level of abstraction in family therapy. In G. R. Weeks (Ed.), *Promoting change through paradoxical therapy.* Homewood, IL: Dorsey, pp. 111–133.

L'Abate, L. (1985a). Descriptive and explanatory levels in family therapy: Dependency, distance, and defeats. In L. L'Abate (Ed.), *Handbook of family psychology and therapy.* Homewood, IL: Dorsey Press.

L'Abate, L. (in preparation). The laboratory method in clinical psychology.

L'Abate, L., Berger, M., Wright, L., & O'Shea, M. (1979). Training family psychologists: The Family Studies Program at Georgia State University. *Professional Psychology, 10*, 58–64.

L'Abate, L., & Curtis, L. (1975). *Teaching exceptional children.* Philadelphia: W. B. Saunders.

L'Abate, L., & Frey, J., III. (1981). The E-R-A model: The role of feelings in family therapy reconsidered: Implications for a classification of theories of family therapy. *Journal of Marital and Family Therapy, 7,* 143–150.

L'Abate, L., Frey, J., III, & Wagner, V. (1982). Toward a classification of family therapy theories: Further elaborations and implications of the E-R-A-Aw-C model. *Family Therapy, 9,* 251–262.

L'Abate, L., & Gale, E. (1969). Neurological status and psychological functioning. *Perceptual and Motor Skills, 29,* 999–1007.

L'Abate, L., Ganahl, G., & Hansen, J. C. (1986). *Methods in family therapy.* Englewood Cliffs, NJ: Prentice-Hall.

L'Abate, L., Hastrup, J., & Frey, J., III. (submitted for publication). Crying: The last taboo?

L'Abate, L., & L'Abate, B. L. (1979). The paradoxes of intimacy. *Family Therapy, 8,* 175–184.

L'Abate, L., & McHenry, S. (1983). *Handbook of marital interventions.* New York: Grune & Stratton.

L'Abate, L., & Samples, G. T. (1983). Intimacy letters: Invariable prescription for closeness-avoidant couples. *Family Therapy, 10,* 37–45.

L'Abate, L., & Sloan, S. Z. (1984). A workshop format to facilitate intimacy in married couples. *Family Process, 33,* 245–250.

L'Abate, L., Sloan, S., Wagner, V., & Malone, K. (1980). The differentiation of resources. *Family Therapy, 7,* 237–246.

L'Abate, L., & Wagner, V. (1985). Theory-derived, family-oriented test batteries. In L. L'Abate (Ed.), *Handbook of family psychology.* Homewood, IL: Dorsey Press.

L'Abate, L., Weeks, G. R., & Weeks, K. (1977). Protectiveness, persecution, and powerlessness. *International Journal of Family Counseling, 5,* 72–76.

L'Abate, L., Weeks, G. R., & Weeks, K. (1979). Of scapegoats, strawmen and scarecrows. *International Journal of Family Therapy, 1,* 86–96.

Lang, P. G. (1971). The application of psychophysiological methods. In A. E. Bergin and S. L. Garfield (Eds.), *Handbook of psychotherapy and behavior change: An empirical analysis.* New York: John Wiley & Sons, pp. 75–125.

Langer, E. J. (1983). *The psychology of control.* Beverly Hills, CA: Sage Publications.

Lazarus, A. A. (1976). Multimodal behavior therapy: Treating the basic ID. In A. A. Lazarus (Ed.), *Multimodal behavior therapy.* New York: Springer.

Lazarus, R. S. (1976). *Patterns of adjustment.* New York: McGraw-Hill.

Lazarus, R. S. (1982). Thoughts on the relations between emotion and cognition. *American Psychologist, 37,* 1019–1024.

Lazarus, R. S., & Monat, A. (1979). *Personality.* Englewood Cliffs, NJ: Prentice-Hall.

Lederer, W. J., & Jackson, D. D. (1968). *The mirages of marriage.* New York: W. W. Norton.

Leeper, R. W. (1970). The motivational and perceptual properties of emotions as indicating their fundamental character and role. In M. B. Arnold (Ed.), *Feelings and emotions.* New York: Academic Press.

Lefkowitz, M. M., Huesmann, L. R., & Eron, L. D. (1978). Parental punishment: A longitudinal analysis of effects. *Archives of General Psychiatry, 35,* 186–191.

Lefkowitz, M. M., & Tesiny, E. P. (1984). Rejection and depression: Prospective and contemporaneous analyses. *Developmental Psychology, 20,* 776–785.

Lerner, J. W., & Egan, R. W. (1979). Clinical teaching update. *Journal of Clinical Child Psychology, 8,* 219–222.

Levant, R. F. (1984). *Family therapy: A comprehensive overview.* Englewood Cliffs, NJ: Prentice-Hall.

Levenson, E. A. (1972). *The fallacy of understanding: An inquiry into the changing structure of psychoanalysis.* New York: Basic Books.

Levin, E. L. (1976). *The marital power structure.* Unpublished doctoral dissertation, Georgia State University.

Levinger, G. (1965). Marital cohesiveness and dissolution: An integrative review. *Journal of Marriage and the Family, 27,* 19–28.

Levinger, G., & Senn, D. (1967). Disclosure of feeling in marriage. *Merrill-Palmer Quarterly, 13,* 237–249.

Lewis, H. (1971). *Shame and guilt in neurosis.* New York: International Universities Press.

Lewis, J. M., Beavers, W. R., Gossett, J. T., & Phillips, V. A. (1976). *No single thread: Psychological health in family systems.* New York: Brunner/Mazel.

Lewis, R. A. (1978). Emotional intimacy among men. *Journal of Social Issues, 34,* 108–121.

Lewis, W. (1984). In search of outcome. *The Underground Railroad, 5,* 8–9.

Liddle, H. A. (1979). Family therapy training in the 1980s: Some critical points and issues. *AAMFT Newsletter, 2*, 10–13.

Liddle, H. A. (1982). On the problems of eclecticism: A call for epistemologic clarification and human-scale theories. *Family Process, 21*, 243–250.

Lieberman, D. A. (1979). Behaviorism and the mind: A (limited) call for a return to introspection. *American Psychologist, 34*, 319–333.

Lieberman, M. A., Yalom, I. D., & Miles, M. B. (1973). *Encounter groups: First facts*. New York: Basic Books.

Lindsay, M. (1978). Self-constructs and social education. *Theory and Research in Social Education, 6*, 26047.

Lineham, M. M., & Egan, J. (1979). Assertion training for women. In A. S. Bellack & M. Hersen (Eds.), *Research and practice in social skills training*. New York: Plenum.

Loevinger, J. (1976). *Ego development*. San Francisco: Jossey-Bass.

Looft, W. R. (1973). Socialization and personality throughout the life span: An examination of contemporary psychological approaches. In P. Baltes & K. W. Schaie (Eds.), *Life span developmental psychology: Personality and socialization*. New York: Academic Press, pp. 25–52.

Luft, T. (1969). *Of human interacting*. Palo Alto, CA: National River Books.

Lunde, D. T. (1974). Eclectic and integrated theory: Gordon Allport and others. In A. Burton (Ed.), *Operational theories of personality*. New York: Brunner/Mazel.

Maccoby, E. E., & Jacklin, C. N. (1974). *The psychology of sex differences*. Stanford, CA: Stanford University Press.

Madanes, C. (1981). *Strategic family therapy*. San Francisco: Jossey-Bass.

Mandler, G. (1975). *Mind and emotion*. New York: John Wiley & Sons.

Margolis, S. T., & Derlega, V. J. (1982). Why loneliness occurs: The interrelationship of social-psychological and privacy concepts. In L. A. Peplau and D. Perlman (Eds.), *Loneliness: A source book of current theory, research and theory*. New York: John Wiley Interscience.

Martin, B. (1975). Parent-child relations. In F. P. Horowitz (Ed.), *Review of child development* (Vol. 4). Chicago: University of Chicago Press.

Maslow, A. H. (1968). *Toward a psychology of being*. New York: Van Nostrand Reinhold.

May, R. (1969). *Love and will*. New York: W. W. Norton.

McCall, G. O., & Simmons, J. L. (1966). *Identities and interactions*. New York: The Free Press.

McCubbin, H. I., & Patterson, J. (1983). The family stress process: The double ABCX model of adjustment and adaptation. In H. I. McCubbin, M. B. Sussman, & J. M. Patterson (Eds.), *Social stress and the family: Advances and developments in family stress, theory, and research*. New York: Haworth Press.

McDonald, G. W. (1980). Family power: The assessment of a decade of theory and research, 1970–1979. *Journal of Marriage and the Family, 42*, 841–854.

Mehrabian, A. (1977). Individual differences in stimulus screening and arousability. *Journal of Personality, 45*, 237–250.

Mellinger, G. D. (1956). Interpersonal trust as a factor in communication. *Journal of Abnormal and Social Psychology, 52*, 304–309.

Mettetal, G., & Gottman, J. M. (1980). Reciprocity and dominance in marital interaction. In J. P. Vincent (Ed.), *Advances in family intervention, assessment, and theory: A research annual*. Greenwich, CT: JAI Press.

Meyerson, R. (1974). What is apathy? *Counterpoint, 1*, 90–92.

Middleberg, C. V., & Gross, S. J. (1979). Families' affective rules and their relationship to the families' adjustment. *The American Journal of Family Therapy, 7*, 137–145.

Mijuskovic, B. (1977). Loneliness and a theory of consciousness. *Review of Existential Psychology and Psychiatry, 15*, 19–31.

Miller, S., Nunnally, E. W., & Wackman, D. B. (1975). *Alive and aware: Improving communication in relationships*. Minneapolis: Interpersonal Communications Program.

Mintz, J., & Luborsky, L. (1971). Segments versus whole sessions: Which is better unit for psychotherapy process research? *Journal of Abnormal Psychology, 78*, 180–191.

Mintz, J., Luborsky, L., & Auerbach, A. H. (1971). Dimensions of psychotherapy: A factor analytic study of psychotherapy sessions. *Journal of Consulting and Clinical Psychology, 36*, 106–120.

Minuchin, S. (1974). *Families and family therapy*. Cambridge, MA: Harvard University Press.

Minuchin, S., Rosman, R., & Baker, L. (1978). *Psychosomatic families: Anorexia nervosa in context*. Cambridge, MA: Harvard University Press.

Mitroff, I. (1974). On the norms of science: A report of a study of the Apollo moon scientists. *Communication and Cognition, 7,* 125–151.

Moriarty, D. M. (1967). *The loss of loved ones: The effects of a death in the family on personality development.* Springfield, IL: Charles C Thomas.

Murphy, G., & Leeds, M. (1975). *Outgrowing self-deception.* New York: Basic Books.

Murray, E. J., & Jacobson, L. I. (1971). The nature of learning in traditional and behavioral psychotherapy. In A. E. Bergin & S. L. Garfield (Eds.), *Handbook of psychotherapy and behavior change: An empirical analysis.* New York: John Wiley & Sons, pp. 709–747.

Myerson, P. G. (1973). The meanings of confrontation. In G. Adler & P. G. Myerson (Eds.), *Confrontation in psychotherapy.* New York: Science House.

Naar, R. (1979). What, when and for what: Suggested multi-model approach to therapy. *Psychotherapy: Theory, Research, and Practice, 16,* 9–17.

Naylor, A. (1982). Premature mourning and failure to mourn: Their relationships to conflict between mothers and intellectually normal children. *American Journal of Orthopsychiatry, 52,* 679–687.

Neill, J. R., & Kniskern, D. P. (Eds.). (1982). *From psyche to system: The evolving therapy of Carl Whitaker.* New York: Guilford Press.

Netzer, C. (1980). Hubris in the family. *International Journal of Family Therapy, 2,* 18–22.

Nichols, M. (1984). *Family therapy: Concepts and methods.* New York: Gardner Press.

Nicholson, R. A., & Berman, J. S. (1983). Is follow-up necessary in evaluating psychotherapy? *Psychological Bulletin, 93,* 261–278.

Nock, S. L., & Kingston, P. W. (1984). The family work day. *Journal of Marriage and the Family, 46,* 333–343.

Norcross, J. C., & Prochaska, J. O. (1982). A national survey of clinical psychologists: Affiliations and orientations. *The Clinical Psychologist, 35*(1), 4–6.

Olmstead, P. (February 1977). *Parental teaching strategies. A review of selected observational studies.* Urbana, IL: ERIC, Document 140–146.

Olmstead, P. (April 1979). *An observational study of parental behavior and its relationship to child achievement.* Urbana, IL: ERIC, Document 168–721.

Olson, D. H., Sprenkle, D. H., & Russell, C. S. (1979). Circumplex model of marital and family systems: Cohesion and adaptability dimensions, family types, and clinical applications. *Family Process, 21,* 3–28.

Orlinsky, D. E., & Howard, K. I. (1978). The relation of form to outcome in psychotherapy. In S. L. Garfield & A. E. Bergin (Eds.), *Handbook of psychotherapy and behavior change.* New York: John Wiley & Sons.

Osofsky, J. P. (Ed.). (1979). *Handbook of infant development.* New York: John Wiley & Sons.

Otto, H. A., & Mann, J. (Eds.). (1969). *Ways of growth: Approaches to expanding awareness.* New York: Viking Press.

Palmer, J. O. (1980). *A primer of eclectic psychotherapy.* Monterey, CA: Brooks/Cole.

Parkes, C. M., & Stevenson-Hinde, J. (Eds.). (1982). *The place of attachment in human behavior.* New York: Basic Books.

Parloff, M. B., Waskow, I. E., & Wolfe, B. E. (1978). Research on therapist variables in relation to process and outcome. In S. L. Garfield & A. E. Bergin (Eds.), *Handbook of psychotherapy and behavior change: An empirical analysis.* New York: John Wiley & Sons.

Patterson, G. (1985). Beyond technology: The next stage in developing an empirical base for training. In L. L'Abate (Ed.), *Handbook of family psychology and therapy.* Homewood, IL: Dorsey Press.

Patton, D., & Waring, E. M. (1984). The quality and quantity of intimacy in the marriages of psychiatric patients. *Journal of Sex & Marital Therapy, 10,* 201–206.

Peele, S., & Brodsky, A. (1975). *Love and addiction.* New York: New American Library.

Phillips, C. E., & Corsini, R. J. (1982). *Give in or give up: A step-by-step marriage improvement manual.* Chicago, IL: Nelson-Hall.

Phillips, E. L. (1978). *The social skills basis of psychopathology: Alternatives to abnormal psychology.* New York: Grune & Stratton.

Phillips, L. (1968). *Human adaptation and its failures.* New York: Academic Press.

Pittman, F. (1983). Of cults and superstars. *The Family Therapy Networker, 7,* 28–29.

Plutchik, R. (1980). A general psychoevaluationary theory of emotion. In R. Plutchik & H. Kellerman (Eds.), *Emotion: Theory, research and experience.* New York: Academic Press.

Poe, C. A., & Mills, D. H. (1972). Interpersonal attraction, popularity, similarity of personal needs, and psychological awareness. *Journal of Psychology, 8*(1), 139–149.

Polanski, N. A., Chalmers, M. A., Butterwieser, E., & Williams, D. P. (1981). *Damaged parents: An anatomy of neglect*. Chicago: University of Illinois Press.

Pontalti, C., Arnetoli, C., Dastoli, C., Martini, A., Stoppa, G., & Colamonico, P. (1979). Dalle structure di comunicaziome alla organizzazione, fantasmatica del mondo psicologico della coppia. *Archivio di Psicologica Neurologia e Psichiatria, 40*, 251–272.

Popper, K. R. (1959). *The logic of scientific discovery.* New York: Basic Books.

Porter, E. H., Jr. (1950). *An introduction to therapeutic counseling.* Boston: Houghton Mifflin Co.

Powell, J. (1969). *Why am I afraid to tell you who I am?* Allen, TX: Fergus Communication.

Prichard, H. A. (1968). Acting, willing, desiring. In A. R. White (Ed.), *The philosophy of action.* London: Oxford University Press.

Prichard, M. S. (1976). On taking emotions seriously: A critique of B. F. Skinner. *Journal for the Theory of Social Behavior, 21*, 41–48.

Pronko, N. H. (1951). *Empirical foundations of psychology.* New York: Reinhart.

Rapaport, A. (1950). *Science and the goals of man: A study in semantic orientation.* New York: Harper & Brothers.

Rapaport, A. (1954). *Operational philosophy: Integrating knowledge and action.* New York: Harper & Brothers.

Rausch, H. L., Barry, W. A., Hertel, R. K., & Swain, M. A. (1974). *Communication, conflict, and marriage.* San Francisco: Jossey-Bass.

Readance, J. E., & Bleau, T. W. (1978). Modification of impulsive cognitive styles: A survey of the literature. *Psychological Reports, 43*, 327–337.

Reichenbach, H. (1969). *The rise of scientific philosophy.* Berkeley: The University of California Press.

Reusch, J. (1977). Prologue: Communication. A program of studies in human relations. In P. F. Ostwald (Ed.), *Communication and social interaction: Clinical and therapeutic aspects of human behavior.* New York: Grune & Stratton, pp. 1–13.

Rickert, H. (1962). *Science and history: A critique of positivistic epistemology.* Princeton, NJ: N. Van Nostrand.

Riegel, K. F. (Ed.). (1975a). *The development of dialectic operations.* Basel, Switzerland: Karger.

Riegel, K. F. (1975b). Adult life crises: A dialectic interpretation of development. In N. Datan & L. H. Ginsberg (Eds.), *Life-span developmental psychology: Normative life crises.* New York: Academic Press, pp. 99–128.

Riegel, K. F. (1975c). Structure and transformation in modern intellectual history. In K. F. Riegel & G. D. Rosenwald (Eds.), *Structure and transformation: Developmental and historical aspects.* New York: John Wiley & Sons.

Robertson, M. (1979). Some observations from an eclectic therapist. *Psychotherapy: Theory, Research, and Practice, 16*, 18–21.

Rogers, C. R. (1961). *On becoming a person.* Boston: Houghton-Mifflin.

Rogers, C. R. (Ed.). (1967). *The therapeutic relationship and its impact: A study of psychotherapy with schizophrenics.* Madison: The University of Wisconsin Press.

Rohrbaugh, M. (1983). Family therapy schizophrenic research: Swimming against the mainstream. *The Family Therapy Networker, 7*, 29–31, 62.

Rosenblatt, P. C., Titus, S., Nevaldine, A., & Cunningham, M. (1979). Marital system differences and summer-long vacations: Togetherness, apartness, tensions. *American Journal of Family Therapy, 7*, 77–84.

Rotter, J. B., Chance, J. E., & Phares, E. J. (1972). *Applications of a social learning theory of personality.* New York: Holt, Rinehart, & Winston.

Roy, A. (1981). Vulnerability factors and depression in men. *British Journal of Psychiatry, 138*, 75–77.

Royce, R. (1982). Philosophic issues, division 24, and the future. *American Psychologist, 37*, 258–266.

Rubin, S. (1981). A two-track model of bereavement: Theory and application in research. *American Journal of Orthopsychiatry, 51*, 101–109.

Rubinstein, D. (1977). The concept of action in the social sciences. *Journal for the Theory of Social Behavior, 2*, 209–236.

Ruesch, J. (1977). Prologue: Communication. A program of studies in human relations, In P. F. Ostwald (Ed.), *Communication and social interaction: Clinical and therapeutic aspects of human behavior.* New York: Grune & Stratton.

Rupert, P. A., & Baird, R. (1979). Modification of cognitive tempo on an optic-visual matching task. *Journal of Genetic Psychology, 135*, 165–174.

Rybzynski, W. (1983). *Taming the tiger.* New York: Viking Press.

Rychlak, J. F. (1968). *A philosophy of science for personality theory.* Boston: Houghton-Mifflin.

Safir, M. A. (1981). Sex and hemisphere differences in access to codes for processing emotional expressions and faces. *Journal of Experimental Psychology: General, 110*, 86–100.

Sampson, E. E. (1981). Cognitive psychology as ideology. *American Psychologist, 36*, 730–743.

Sanders, C. M. (1979–80). A comparison of adult bereavement in the death of a spouse, child and parent. *Omega: Journal of Death and Dying, 10,* 303–322.

Sarason, S. B. (1984). If it can be studied or developed, should it be? *American Psychologist, 39,* 477–485.

Sartre, J. P. (1977). *Existentialism and humanism.* Brooklyn, NY: Haskell House Publishers.

Satir, V. (1972). *Peoplemaking.* Palo Alto, CA: Science and Behavior Books.

Satir, V., Stachowiak, J., & Taschman, H. A. (1975). *Helping families to change.* New York: Jason Aronson.

Scanzoni, T., & Szinovac, M. (1980). *Family decision making: A developmental sex role model.* Beverly Hills, CA: Sage Publication.

Schachtel, E. G. (1959). *Metamorphosis: On the development of affect, perception, attention, and memory.* New York: Basic Books.

Schaefer, E. S. (1976). The scope and focus of research relevant to intervention: A socio-ecological perspective. *Child and Family Services Act, 1975.* Washington, DC, U.S. Government Printing Office, pp. 1525–1543.

Schafer, R. (1976a). *Action: A new language for psychoanalysis.* New Haven: Yale University Press.

Schafer, R. (1976b). Emotion in the language of action. *Psychological Issues, 9,* 106–133.

Schaffer, H. R., & Crook, C. K. (1980). Child compliance and maternal control techniques. *Developmental Psychology, 16,* 54–61.

Schaffer, N. D. (1982). Multidimensional measures of therapist behavior as predictors of outcome. *Psychological Bulletin, 92,* 670–681.

Scheflen, A. E. (1981). Levels of schizophrenia. New York: Brunner/Mazel.

Schlenker, B. R. (1980). *Impression management: The self-concept, social identity, and interpersonal relations.* Monterey, CA: Brooks/Cole.

Schneider, J. (1984). *Stress, loss, and grief.* Baltimore: University Park Press.

Schoenberg, B., et al. (1970). *Loss and grief.* New York: Columbia University Press.

Schofield, L. J., & Abbuhl, S. (1975). The stimulation of insight and self-awareness through body-movement exercise. *Journal of Clinical Psychology 31*(4), 745–746.

Schopler, J. (1965). Social power. In L. Berkowitz (Ed.), *Advances in experimental social psychology* (Vol. 2). New York: Academic Press.

Schwartz, F. (Ed.). (1974). *Scientific thought and social reality: Essays by Michael Polanyi.* New York: International Universities Press.

Schwartz, R. C., & Breunlin, D. (1983). Research: Why clinicians should bother with it. *The Family Therapy Networker, 7,* 23–27, 57–59.

Sears, R. R., Maccoby, E. E., & Levin, H. (1957). *Patterns of childrearing.* Evanston, IL: Row, Peterson.

Selman, R. L. (1980). *Growth of interpersonal understanding: A developmental and clinical analysis.* New York: Academic Press.

Selman, R. L., Jaquette, D., & Lavin, D. R. (1977). Interpersonal awareness in children: Toward an interpretation of developmental and clinical child psychology. *American Journal of Orthopsychiatry, 47,* 264–274.

Selvini-Palazzoli, M., Boscolo, L., Cecchin, G., & Prata, G. (1978). *Paradox and counterparadox.* New York: Jason Aronson.

Selvini-Palazzoli, M., Boscolo, L., Cecchin, G., & Prata, G. (1980). Hypothesizing-circularity-neutrality: Three guidelines for the conductor of the session. *Family Process, 19,* 3–12.

Serafica, F. C. (1978). The development of attachment behaviors: An organismic-developmental perspective. *Human Development, 21*(2), 119–140.

Shapiro, E. K., & Weber, E. (1981). *Cognitive and affective growth: Developmental interaction.* Hillsdale, NJ: Lawrence Erlbaum Associates.

Shotter, J. (1975). *Images of man in psychological research.* London: Methuen.

Shulman, B. H. (1972). Confrontation techniques. *Psychotherapy: Theory, research, and practice, 1,* 177–183.

Shur, E. (1976). *The awareness trap: Self-absorption instead of social change.* New York: Quadrangle/New York Times Books.

Sidman, M. (1960). *Tactics of scientific research: Evaluating experimental data in psychology.* New York: Basic Books.

Sifneos, P. E., Apfel-Savitc, R., & Frankel, F. H. (1977). The phenomenon of alexithymia: Observations in neurotic and psychosomatic patients. *Psychotherapy and Psychosomatics, 28,* 47–57.

Sillars, A. (1980). *Conflict resolution strategies.* Doctoral dissertation, University of Wisconsin.

Skinner, A. C. R. (1976). *Systems of family and marital therapy.* New York: Brunner/Mazel.

Slack, C. W. (1972). The theory of triads. *Educational Technology, 12,* 23–29.

Slipp, S., & Kressel, K. (1978). Difficulties in family therapy evaluation: I.Q. comparison of insight vs. problem-solving approaches. II. Design critique and recommendations. *Family Process, 17*, 409–422.

Sloan, S. Z., & L'Abate, L. (1985). Intimacy. In L. L'Abate (Ed.), *Handbook of family psychology and therapy.* Homewood, IL: Dorsey Press.

Smith, D. (1982). Trends in counseling and psychotherapy. *American Psychologist, 37*, 802–809.

Smither, S. (1977). Reconsideration of the developmental study of empathy. *Human Development, 20*, 253–276.

Snygg, D., & Combs, A. W. (1949). *Individual behavior.* New York: Harper.

Solley, C. M., & Murphy, G. (1960). *Development of the perceptual world.* New York: Basic Books.

Spiegel, J. (1971). *Transactions: The interplay between the individual. family, and society.* New York: Science House.

Sroufe, L. A. (1979). Socioemotional development. In J. D. Osofsky (Ed.), *Handbook of infant development.* New York: John Wiley & Sons.

Stahmann, R. F., & Harper, J. M. (1982). Therapist-patient relationships in marital and family therapy. In M. J. Lambert (Ed.). *Psychotherapy and patient relationships.* Homewood, IL: Dorsey Press.

Stanton, M. D. (1979). Drugs and the family: A review of recent literature. *Marriage and Family Review, 2*, 1–10.

Stanton, M. D., Todd, T. C., et al. (1982). *The family therapy of drug abuse and addiction.* New York: The Guilford Press.

Steiner, C. M. (1974). *Scripts people live: Transactional analysis of life scripts.* New York: Groves Press.

Stierlin, H. (1983). Family therapy: A science or an art? *Family Process, 22*, 413–423.

Stogdill, R. M. (Ed.). (1970). *The process of model building in the behavioral sciences.* Columbus, OH: Ohio State University Press.

Strong, S. & Claiborn, C. D. (1982). *Change through interaction: Social psychological processes of counseling and psychotherapy.* New York: Wiley Interscience.

Strongman, K. T. (1978). *The psychology of emotion.* New York: John Wiley & Sons.

Strupp, H. H. (1973). *Psychotherapy: Clinical research and theoretical issues.* New York: Jason Aronson.

Strupp, H. H. (1982). On the technology of psychotherapy. *Archives of General Psychiatry, 24*, 270–279.

Sullivan, H. S. (1953). *The interpersonal theory of psychiatry.* New York: W. W. Norton.

Sullivan, H. S. (1954). *The psychiatric interview.* New York: W. W. Norton.

Swingle, P. G. (1976). *The management of power.* Hillsdale, NJ: Lawrence Erlbaum & Associates.

Tamashiro, R. T. (1978). Developmental stages in the conceptualization of marriage. *The Family Coordinator, 27*, 237–244.

Tamminen, A. W., & Sumaby, M. H. (1981). Helping counselors learn to confront. *Personnel and Guidance Journal, 60*, 41–45.

Thompson, L., & Walker, A. J. (1984). Mothers and daughters: Aid patterns and attachment. *Journal of Marriage and the Faculty, 46*, 313–322.

Thorne, F. C. (1946). Directive psychotherapy: IV. The techniques of psychological palliation. *Journal of Clinical Psychology, 2*, 68–79.

Tiedeman, D. V. (1978). Discerning "I" power in the developmental paradigm at mid-life. *Character Potential: A Record of Research, 8*(3), 148–151.

Tolstedt, B. E., & Stokes, J. P. (1984). Self-disclosure, intimacy, and the depenetration process. *Journal of Personality and Social Psychology, 46*, 84–90.

Tomkins, S. S. (1978). Script theory: Differential magnification of affects. In R. A. Dienstbier (Ed.), *Nebraska symposium on motivation: Human emotion.* Lincoln, NE: University of Nebraska Press.

Tomkins, S. S., & Izard, E. C. (Eds.). (1965). *Affection, cognition, and personality.* New York: Springer.

Tomm, K. (1983). The old hat doesn't fit. *The Family Therapy Networker, 7*, 39–41.

Toulmin, S. (1961). *Foresight and understanding: An inquiry into the aims of science.* Bloomington, IN: Indiana University Press.

Trollope, A. (1959). *The Claverings.* London: Oxford University Press.

Turner, M. B., & Gross, S. J. (1976). An approach to family therapy: An affective rule-altering model. *Journal of Family Counseling, 4*, 50–56.

Ulrici, D., & L'Abate, L., Wagner, V. (1981). The E-R-A model: A heuristic framework for classification of skill training programs for couples and families. *Family Relations, 30*, 307–315.

Urmson, J. W. (1968). Motives and causes. In A. R. White (Ed.), *The philosophy of action.* London: Oxford University Press.

Vachon, R., et al. (1976). Stress reaction to bereavement. *Essence, 1*, 23–33.

Vaughn, L. E., & Leff, J. P. (1976). The influence of family and social factors on the cause of psychiatric illness. *British Journal of Psychiatry, 129*, 125–137.

Vincent, J. P. (Ed.). (1980). *Advances in family intervention, assessment, and theory: A research annual.* Greenwich, CT: JAI Press.

von Bertalanffy, L. (1968). *General systems theory.* New York: Braziller.

Wahler, R. G. (1980). The multiply entrapped parent: Obstacles to change to parent-child problems. In J. P. Vincent (Ed.), *Advances in family intervention, assessment, and theory: A research annual.* Greenwich, CT: JAI Press.

Wallach, M. A., & Wallach, L. (1983). *Sanction for selfishness: The error of egoism in theory and therapy.* San Francisco: W. H. Freeman & Co.

Warburton, J. R., & Alexander, J. F. (1985). The family therapist: What does one do? In L. L'Abate (Ed.), *Handbook of family psychology and therapy.* Homewood, IL: Dorsey Press.

Waring, E. M. (1980a). Marital intimacy, psychosomatic symptoms, and cognitive therapy. *Psychosomatics, 21*, 595–601.

Waring, E. M. (1980b). Marital intimacy and nonpsychotic emotional illness. *Psychiatric Forum, 9*, 13–19.

Waring, E. M. (1980c). Marital intimacy, psychosomatic symptoms and cognitive therapy. *Psychosomatics, 21*, 595–601.

Waring, E. M. (1981). Facilitating marital intimacy through self-disclosure. *American Journal of Family Therapy, 9*, 33–42.

Waters, E., Wippman, J., & Sroufe, L. (1979). Attachment, positive affect, and competence in the peer group: Two studies in construct validation. *Child Development, 50*(3), 821–829.

Wathney, S., & Balbridge, B. (1980). Strategic interventions with involuntary patients. *Hospital and Community Psychiatry, 31*, 696–701.

Watzlawick, P. (1977). The pathologies of perfectionism. *Etc., 34*, 12–18.

Watzlawick, P. (1978). *The language of change: Elements of therapeutic communication.* New York: Basic Books.

Watzlawick, P. (1982). Hermetic pragmesthetics or unkempt thoughts about an issue of family process. *Family Process, 21*, 401–403.

Watzlawick, P., Weakland, J., & Fisch, R. (1974). *Change: Principles of problem formation and problem resolution.* New York: W. W. Norton.

Weakland, J., Fisch, R., Watzlawick, P., & Bodin, A. (1974). Brief therapy: Focused problem resolution. *Family Process, 13*, 141–168.

Weeks, G., & L'Abate, L. (1982). *Paradoxical psychotherapy: Theory and practice with individuals, couples, and families.* New York: Brunner/Mazel.

Weinraub, M., Brooks, J., & Lewis, M. (1977). The social network: A reconsideration of the concept of attachment. *Human Development, 20*(1), 31–47.

Weisman, A. (1973). Confrontation, countertransference, and context. In G. Adler & P. G. Myerson (Eds.), *Confrontation in psychotherapy.* New York: Science House.

Weiss, L., & Lowenthal, M. F. (1975). Life course perspectives on friendship. In M. F. Lowenthal, M. Thurnher, & D. Chiviboga (Eds.), *Four stages of life.* San Francisco: Jossey-Bass.

Weiss, R. L. (1980). Strategic behavioral marital therapy: Toward a model for assessment and intervention. In J. P. Vincent (Ed.), *Advances in family intervention, assessment and theory.* Greenwich, CT: JAI Press, pp. 229–271.

Weissman, M. M. (1979). The psychological treatment of depression: Evidence for the efficacy of psychotherapy alone, in comparison with, and in combination with pharmacotherapy. *Archives of General Psychiatry, 36*, 1261–1269.

Whitaker, C. A. (1982). Comments on Keeney and Sprenkle's paper. *Family Process, 21*, 405–406.

White, A. R. (Ed.). (1968). *The philosophy of action.* London: Oxford University Press.

Whitehead, A. N., & Russell, B. (1950). *Principia mathematica.* London: Cambridge University Press.

Wilbur, M. P., & Wilbur, J. R. (1980). Categories of nonverbal behavior: Implications for supervision. *Counselor Education and Supervision, 19*, 197–209.

Wilder, C. (1982). Muddles and metaphors: A response to Keeney and Sprenkle. *Family Process, 21*, 397–400.

Willems, E. P., & Stuart, D. G. (1980). Behavioral ecology as a perspective on marriages and families. In J. P. Vincent (Ed.), *Advances in family intervention, assessment, and theory: A research annual.* Greenwich, CT: JAI Press.

Woodward, C. A., Santa-Barbara, J., Levin, S., & Epstein, N. B. (1978). Outcome of counselor satisfaction with brief family therapy. *Family Process, 17*, 399–407.

Woolfolk, R. L. (1976). A multimodel perspective on emotion. In A. A. Lazarus (Ed.), *Multimodel behavior therapy*. New York: Springer.

Worden, J. W. (1982). *Grief counseling and grief therapy: A handbook for the mental health practitioner*. New York: Springer.

Worthy, M. (1974). *Eye color, sex, and race*. Anderson, SC: Broke-Hallux.

Wozniak, R. H. (1975). Dialecticism and structuralism: The philosophical foundation of Soviet psychology and Piagetian cognitive developmental theory. In K. F. Riegel & G. C. Rosenwald (Eds.), *Structure and transformation: Developmental and historical aspects*. New York: John Wiley & Sons, pp. 25–45.

Wynne, L. C. (1983). Family research and family therapy: A reunion? *Journal of Marital and Family Therapy, 9*, 113–117.

Yarrow, L. (1979). Emotional development. *American Psychologist, 34*, 951–957.

Young, M., & Willmott, P. (1975). *The symmetrical family: A study of work and leisure in the London region*. London: Penguin Press.

Yudlin, E. G. (1976). Activity as an explanatory principle and as a subject-matter of scientific study. *Voprosy Filosofi, 5*, 65–78.

Zajonc, R. B. (1980). Feeling and thinking: References need no inferences. *American Psychologist, 35*, 151–175.

Zajonc, R. B. (1984). On the primacy of affect. *American Psychologist, 39*, 117–123.

Zantman, I. W. (Ed.). (1976). *The 50% solution*. Garden City, NY: Doubleday Anchor.

Zisook, S., Devaul, R. A., & Click, M. A. (1982). Measuring symptoms of grief and bereavement. *American Journal of Psychiatry, 139*, 1590–1593.

Author Index

Subject Index

317